Innocents on the Ice

Innocents on the Ice

A Memoir of Antarctic Exploration, 1957

by
John C. Behrendt

University Press of Colorado

Copyright © 1998 by the University Press of Colorado
International Standard Book Number 0-87081-551-2

Published by the University Press of Colorado
P.O. Box 849
Niwot, Colorado 80544

The University Press of Colorado is a cooperative publishing enterprise supported, in
part, by Adams State College, Colorado State University, Fort Lewis College, Mesa State
College, Metropolitan State College of Denver, University of Colorado, University of
Northern Colorado, University of Southern Colorado, and Western State College of
Colorado.

The paper used in this publication meets the minimum requirements of the American
National Standard for Information Sciences – Permanence of Paper for Printed Library
Materials. ANSI Z39.48-1984

LIBRARY OF CONGRESS CATALOGING-IN-PUBLICATION DATA

Behrendt, John C., 1932–
    Innocents on the ice : a memoir of Antarctic exploration, 1957 /
by John C. Behrendt.
        p. cm.
    Includes bibliographical references and index.
    ISBN 0-87081-493-1 (cloth : alk. paper) – ISBN 0-87081-551-2 (pbk.: alk. paper)
    1. Behrendt, John C., 1932–Diaries. 2. Antarctica–Discovery
and exploration–History. 3. Antarctica–Discovery and exploration–
United States History. I. Title.
G850.B44 1998
919.8'904–dc21   98-26379
                                                                      CIP

To Kurt and Marc, innocents abroad, each in his own time and place

Contents

Preface

I was a 24-year-old graduate student when I sailed from the U.S. Navy base at Davisville, Rhode Island, to participate in the International Geophysical Year (IGY) expedition. IGY was the 18-month period 1 July 1957 to 31 December 1958, during which a worldwide program of geophysical research was conducted by 70 countries and about 30,000 scientists. A large part of this effort was concentrated in Antarctica.

I had romanticized Antarctic exploration since childhood, and although the pursuit of science and a Ph.D. degree was my ostensible purpose, the romance/adventure part was what really drew me south to the seventh continent. What I didn't know then was that adventures in Antarctica only happen when someone makes a mistake.

In 1956 I had just finished my master's degree in geophysics and had obtained a position as assistant seismologist to work on the IGY glaciological program. The main purpose of the IGY oversnow traverse program was to measure the ice-sheet thickness and its physical properties including snow accumulation. We now know that the average thickness of the Antarctic ice sheet is about two miles (3 km), with much of it below sea level. But in 1956 the only direct clue to this great mass was a short seismic reflection traverse by the Norwegian-British-Swedish Expedition a few years earlier.

Specifically not included in the IGY program in Antarctica were geological research and topographic mapping because of the possible political problems related to potential mineral resources and competing territorial claims. The cold war was at its height, and negotiation of the Antarctic Treaty was still three years in the future.

"You can only go to Antarctica for the first time once." Thus I was told, so I recorded events conscientiously in a daily journal from our departure in November 1956 until our return in January 1958 to Buenos Aires, Argentina. My IGY trip became a turning point in my life and led to a career in which Antarctic science has been prominent. I have made 12 Antarctic trips over the past 40 years (scattered throughout every decade since the IGY), most recently in 1995.

Since the 1950s much has changed in the way Antarctic science and U.S. Antarctic expeditions operate. Most notable are the presence of women, greater safety, mail delivery more than once a year, improved radio communication, better transportation (in the IGY we spent 15 months to get a three-month field season), and fresh food during the summer. When we headed to the Weddell Sea and the Filchner Ice Shelf to set up the Ellsworth research station and carry out a 1,200-mile oversnow traverse in motorized Sno-Cats, not only were there no maps of the area, no one had ever been there or even seen 90 percent of it from the air.

I use the word "Innocents" in the title partly because most of our nine-man scientific party were quite young and totally inexperienced in Antarctica and the "Navy way" of doing things there. "Innocent" is also appropriate because the senior Navy people and the scientists who conceived the IGY program had little comprehension of how each other functioned, both in the U.S. and in Antarctica. We planned to use state-of-the-art equipment (untried in Antarctica) to carry out our research, but Americans had never operated motor vehicles in fieldwork on the Antarctic snow surface away from bases before. "The Ice" is originally a common New Zealand expression for Antarctica.

Although the IGY was a purely scientific program, the U.S. Antarctic Program was strictly U.S. Navy (Operation Deep Freeze) because of historic considerations dating back to the Wilkes Expedition in 1840, the (private) Byrd Expeditions of 1928–30 and 1933–35, and the Navy Operations Highjump in 1946–47 and Windmill in 1948–49. At all of the American Antarctic scientific stations except Ellsworth, there was a joint station leadership, comprising a naval officer (usually a lieutenant) in charge of operations, and a civilian leader responsible for the scientific research.

Ellsworth Station was the most isolated of the seven American stations, or bases, because the southern Weddell Sea is permanently covered with heavy pack ice and there was essentially no air transportation. One person, Capt. Finn Ronne, filled both the role of civilian station scientific leader and naval officer in charge. He was the only member of our 39-man party who had ever been to Antarctica. On the basis of his three previous winters there, he assumed he could tell scientists how to do their work. But it never occurred to our scientific party to look at it this way. Therein lay the root of all of our problems during our difficult 1957 Antarctic winter.

Acknowledgments

Without the help and encouragement of many people over 40 years, I never would have been able to turn a handwritten journal (originally transcribed by Donna Ebben in 1960) into a book. David and Mary Behrendt, Art Ford, Mildred Crary, Faith Rogers, Barb Mieras, Sharon Harbison, and Laura Backus read the journal and encouraged me to pursue the project. Kim Malville, Nolan Aughenbaugh, Conrad Jaburg, and Jack Brown each made significant contributions. Susan Baur, Colin Bull, Bob Tingey, and Michael Parfit provided professional advice at several times. I thank my editor, Jody Berman, for the many hours she put in, making the manuscript more readable. Finally I owe a debt of gratitude to the scientists and Navy men of Ellsworth Station, Antarctica, during the long winter of 1957. I only hope they realize that this is just my side of the story and any errors or misunderstandings will be forgiven. We were all *innocents on the ice.*

Editorial Note

Journal entries are indented from the main text. Journal entries and other quoted material have been edited for punctuation and clarity. A journal entry without a date preceding it is a continuation from the prior entry above it. For ease of reading some material has either been shortened, incorporated into the main text, paraphrased, or omitted entirely. Brackets are used to clarify syntax, provide brief definitions, or to give currently accepted names for geographic features (from *Geographic Names of Antarctica*, second edition, 1995). Radio messages originally had no punctuation and were all capital letters; punctuation has been added here.

The photographs (most taken by me) are from my personal collection unless noted otherwise.

Roster of Men at Ellsworth Station 1957

Scientific Staff

Nolan P. Aughenbaugh ("Augie," "Aug"), assistant seismologist (geologist)
John C. Behrendt, assistant seismologist
John B. Brown ("Jack"), ionospheric physicist
Gerrard R. Fierle ("Jerry"), chief meteorologist
J. McKim Malville ("Kim"), chief Aurora Program
Hugo A.C. Neuburg, chief glaciologist
Donald D. Skidmore, ionosphere assistant
Edward C. Thiel ("Ed"), chief seismologist
Paul T. Walker, assistant glaciologist

Naval Staff

Officers

Finn Ronne, captain, USNR, OINC Ellsworth Station and station scientific
    leader
Conrad J. Jaburg ("Con"), lieutenant, USN (pilot), VX-6
Charles McCarthy ("Mac"), lieutenant commander (pilot), OINC VX-6
Clinton R. Smith ("Clint"), lieutenant, USNR (Medical Corps) (physician),
    OINC Det. Bravo
William H. Sumrall, lieutenant junior grade (pilot), USNR, VX-6
VX-6 refers to airdales
Det. (Detachment) Bravo refers to Seabees

Enlisted Men

Thomas Ackerman, AG3, USN, Det. Bravo
John E. Beiszer, AD1, USN, VX-6
Ronald D. Brown ("Brownie"), AD3, USN, VX-6
William A. Butler, AG3, USN, Det. Bravo
Gary C. Camp, AG2, USN, Det. Bravo
Walter M. Cox ("Wally"), PH1 (photographer), USN, Det. Bravo
Carl L. Crouse, CDCN, USN, Det. Bravo
Edward H. Davis ("Ed"), CSCA (cook), USN, Det. Bravo
Walter L. Davis ("Walt"), CMCA (mechanic), USN, Det. Bravo

Frederick F. Drydal, AM1, USN, VX-6

Charles W. Forlidas ("Chuck"), RM2 (radio man), USN, Det. Bravo

David B. Greaney, Jr., AE1, USN, VX-6

Richard W. Grob ("Dick"), CS2 (baker), USN, Det. Bravo

James L. Hannah ("Jim"), CE1 (electrician), USN, Det. Bravo

Robert E. Haskill ("Bob"), RM1 (radio man), USN, Det. Bravo

Earl F. Herring, AK1, USN, VX-6

Allen M. Jackson, AT1, USN, VX-6

Kenneth K. Kent, ETCA (electronics technician), USN, Det. Bravo

Larry R. Larson, AT2, USN, VX-6

Atles F. Lewis ("Lewie"), ADCA, USN, VX-6

Melvin Mathis ("Doc"), HM1, USN, Det. Bravo

Walter H. May ("Walt"), AGC, USN, Det. Bravo

Clyde J. McCauley, BM3, USN, Det. Bravo

James A. Ray ("Jim"), UT2, USN, Det. Bravo

Albert Spear ("Al"), BUC, USN, Det. Bravo

When we are young we do not look in mirrors. It is when we are old, concerned with our name, our legend, what our lives will mean in the future. We become vain with the names we own, our claims to have been the first eyes, the strongest army, the cleverest merchant. It is when he is old that Narcissus wants a graven image of himself.

—Michael Ondaatje, *The English Patient,* 1992

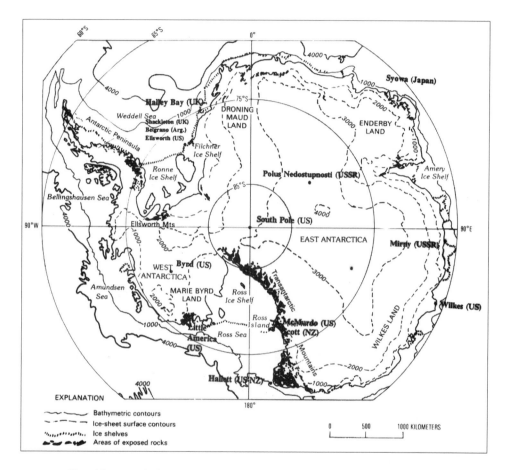

1. United States and selected other 1957 stations and bases on modern map of Antarctica. All place names are accepted by U.S. Board of Geographic Names. Elevations in meters. (From USGS.)

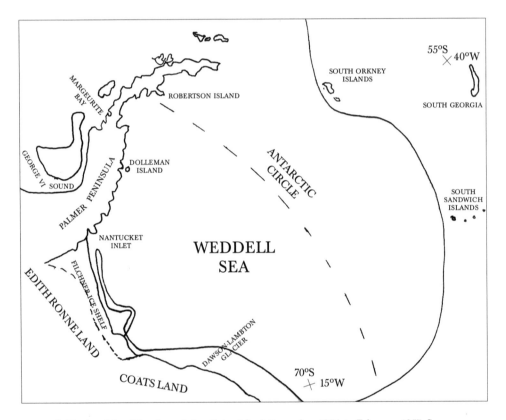

2. Tracks of the *Wyandot* and the *Staten Island,* December 1956 to February 1957. Some names have changed (see Maps 1 and 4), but those appearing here were used at the time. (From the U.S. Hydrographic Office, Chart 2562, available in 1956.)

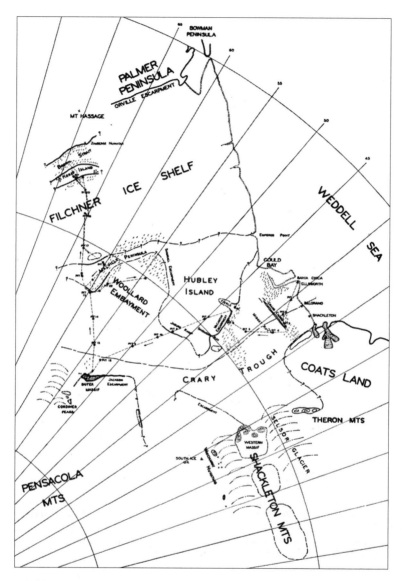

3. Filchner Ice Shelf Traverse track and features discovered. Most names proposed were not accepted by U.S. Board of Geographic Names. (See Map 4 for correct names.) The feature named Malville Peninsula had disappeared due to ice thinning (global warming?) by 1969. (From H.A.C. Neuburg, E. Thiel, P. T. Walker, J. C. Behrendt, and N. B. Aughenbaugh, "The Filchner Ice Shelf," *Annals of American Geographers* 49, no. 2 [1959]: 110–19.)

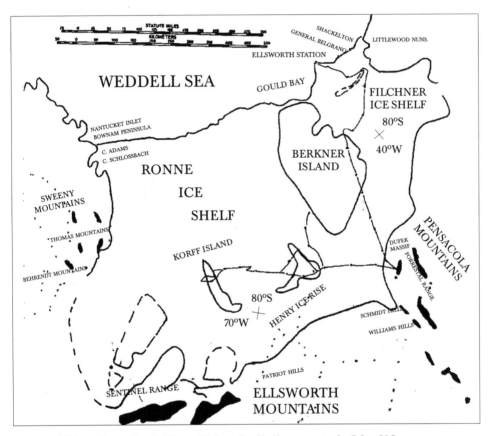

4. Filchner-Ronne Ice Shelf area. Filchner Ice Shelf traverse track. Other U.S. oversnow geophysical traverses (1959–1964) indicated by points. Only selected mountain ranges and other geographic features indicated. All names on this map are accepted by U.S. Board of Geographic Names. (From compilation by American Geographical Society, from various sources, including some U.S. Geological Survey satellite images, up to 1969.)

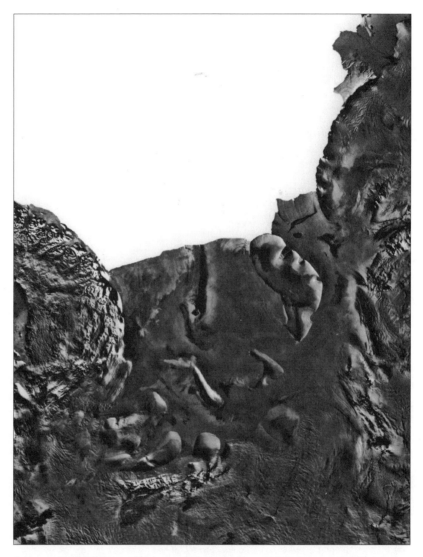

5. Composite HVHRR satellite image of Antarctica from 1980s coverage. Compare map 4. Clouds partly obscure image. Note the size of Grand Chasm; it had increased since 1957. In 1986 Grand Chasm broke completely away, and the part of the ice shelf to its north broke into several icebergs. (From J. G. Ferrigno, J. L. Mullins, J. A. Stapleton, P. S. Chavez Jr., M. G. Velasco, R. S. Williams Jr., G. F. Delinski Jr., and D. Lear, Satellite Image Map of Antarctica, USGS Map I-2560, 1996.)

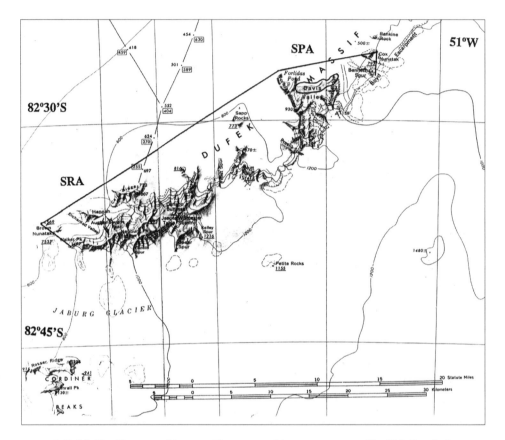

6. Dufek Massif, topographic map. All names on this map are accepted by U.S. Board of Geographic Names. The area marked SRA is the Special Reserved Area 1 approved by the Antarctic Treaty Consultative Meeting in Bonn in 1991. SPA refers to the small marked area within the SRA-designated Forlidas Ponds Special Protected Area and also includes the immediate area surrounding Forlidas Pond, also approved at the 1991 Bonn Antarctic Treaty Consultative Meeting. Elevations in meters. (From USGS.)

Innocents on the Ice

1
Introduction

On 6 December 1957, when we awoke about 1700 we could see the range of mountains for which we have aimed so long, directly on course to the south. The highest peaks of the Dufek Massif are a little over 6700 ft (2200 m), but we are on the Filchner Ice Shelf, near sea level. As we slowly drove in our Sno-Cat, at about four miles/hour towards the base of the peaks, we climbed to a level of 1500–2000 ft. It was clear and sunny and the mountains unfolded an ever-changing panoramic view as we approached. Beautiful glaciers, cirques, ridges covered with spectacular spires, and very rugged peaks and pinnacles abounded everywhere. I stopped 10 ft from the rock and upon descending from the vehicle proceeded with rock hammer in hand towards the spur. It was a wonderful feeling to stand on solid ground again after more than a year.

With the exception of ice-covered Berkner Island, which we had crossed a few days before, we had been on a ship or on the 700–4000-ft-thick floating Filchner Ice Shelf since we left Punta Arenas, Chile, one year earlier.

[Several days later . . .] No one else was up yet, so I climbed the ridge where we were parked, to get some pictures of the peaks in back. I found a nice warm slab of rock upon which I rested and enjoyed the scenery. There was a small circular depression in the rock that was filled with meltwater. After I had drunk all I wanted, I made use of it as a washbasin.

This was probably the first time I had washed since leaving Ellsworth Station. Cleanliness was not a high priority on the over-snow traverses, as normally our only water came from melting the snow. This process took fuel; and besides, we usually didn't feel like making the effort.

1

We were about 350 miles south of Ellsworth Station, situated at the south coast of the ice-covered Weddell Sea. After a three-month voyage through the pack ice the previous austral summer and the dark, cold Antarctic winter, we were approaching one of the high points of our scientific oversnow traverse on the unexplored Filchner Ice Shelf.

We still had more than 700 miles ahead of us, into the unknown ice sheet to the northwest. The five of us, glaciologists and geophysicists, had already driven our two Sno-Cats nearly 500 miles across the ice shelf, confronting harrowing crevasse accidents, and crossing previously unknown Berkner Island. We had measured ice thickness, the depth to the underlying bedrock, snow accumulation, average yearly temperature, the gravity and magnetic fields, and were now about to make our first geologic observations.

As we camped after our arrival at the mountains, we were roused by the noise of Maj. Jim Lassiter's United States Air Force (USAF) C-47 [part of a CIA aerial photography operation] taxiing up right next to us on skis.

This resupply flight brought fuel, food, and other supplies.

They brought a 100-watt radio transmitter for us but just before leaving Ellsworth Station, Capt. Finn Ronne, the Navy Commanding Officer and IGY station scientific leader there decided that we couldn't have it until Admiral Dufek [Commanding Officer of Navy Operation Deep Freeze] gave the OK, so they sent a dispatch to him requesting same. They didn't receive an answer and took it back. We have managed to get only one radio contact with Ellsworth Station in the past three weeks and in all probability this condition will continue or get worse if we have to rely on the small, low power "Angry 9" radio. Jim Lassiter told Ed and Hugo [co-leaders of our oversnow traverse party] that he would have given it to them if it hadn't been for this latest stunt of Ronne's (My words not his). Ed argued the point that we couldn't even notify the station in a medical emergency or in case of vehicle breakdown. Ronne, who had flown out with Lassiter, only answered that Dufek might not like it if we took the USAF radio without his approval. The C-47 will look for us somewhere along our proposed course in 10 or 12 days. No one has even flown over this area, so we have no idea of what we may run into, to delay or stop us. Oh well, *c'est la vie*. We can't find

2

a good reason for Finn Ronne's not wanting us to have a radio that we can communicate to base with.

I realized later that Ronne did not want us to communicate with other Antarctic bases and field parties. This had been the situation throughout the long Antarctic winter, completed two months earlier at Ellsworth Station. Ronne's refusal to let us take the radio from Lassiter was probably the most serious thing he did all year, and potentially disastrous for us on the traverse. We had no radio contact with anyone until we arrived at the rendezvous point about 250 miles across crevassed unexplored ice shelf, three weeks later. In the following chapters I attempt to explain how we had arrived at this peak experience of our traverse, as well as the impasse with Ronne, at this time and place 40 years ago. Although Antarctica has changed very little, there are fortunately so many changes in the way we do things there that the events at Ellsworth Station and on the Filchner Ice Shelf Traverse seem almost incredible, contrasted with the United States Antarctic Program in the late 1990s.

I first traveled to Antarctica in 1956, at the beginning of the "scientific era" ushered in by the International Geophysical Year (IGY). The only ostensible purpose of the expeditions of 12 countries was the peaceful, coordinated, scientific study of the ice-covered continent. There were, of course, the hidden agendas of the cold war, the existing claims of seven countries, and the territorial interests of the U.S. and the Soviet Union (and now Russia), who both still maintain they have a "basis" for a claim.

U.S. Navy Operations Highjump in 1946–47 and Windmill in 1948–49 were two earlier expeditions under a directive from Adm. Chester W. Nimitz, chief of naval operations, and were assigned the political task "of consolidating and extending United States sovereignty over the largest practicable area of the Antarctic continent."[1] I assume the same directive or a similar one directed Navy Operation Deep Freeze during the IGY.

The National Science Foundation (NSF) was not part of the U.S. Antarctic Program during the IGY or post-IGY period. The entire scientific program then was managed by the U.S. National Committee for the IGY at the National Academy of Sciences (NAS). As the NAS does not normally employ scientists in operational scientific programs, the money appropriated by Congress was passed to the Arctic Institute of North America and several federal agencies that employed many of us scientists directly, and provided scientific equipment and supplies. The big budget was that of the Navy and was funded through the Department of Defense. IGY was originally planned to be a one-time-only expedition (Navy Operation Deep Freeze I, II, III, and IV) from 1955 to 1959. However, Navy Operation Deep Freeze operated eventually under NSF funds until it was phased out in 1997.

The Antarctic Treaty was negotiated by 12 nations in 1959, largely as the result of the peaceful cooperation and scientific success of the IGY and the continuation of the research programs on Antarctica in the following years. Ratified in 1961, the treaty prohibited military operations on the continent and provided for the interchange of scientific data. This book is an account of my personal experiences, as a small part of this ambitious undertaking.

In 1956, I was tall (over 6 ft, 3 in.), skinny, and very nearsighted with thick glasses. I had a lot of outdoor experience, including much rock climbing, rapids canoeing, backpacking, mountaineering, and a summer of glacier fieldwork. I was used to spending my free time taking photographs, reading, listening to music, and playing bridge. I had little dating experience with women (whom we called "girls" in 1956) other than as close climbing and camping friends, although I was romantically interested in a nursing student named Ruth, as I headed for Antarctica.

I was born and raised in Stevens Point, in central Wisconsin. My parents were also Wisconsin natives, son and daughter of immigrants from Germany and Norway, respectively. My father, Allen Behrendt, was born in 1888, also in Stevens Point, and had a younger sister. He quit high school in about 1903 to help in his parents' grocery store, and continued in small business and sales jobs almost to the end of his 82-year life. Although reasonably successful until the depression, our family never had much money after I was born in 1932 and my brother, David, in 1935. My father had a great love of reading and was a "news junkie." From my earliest recollections I can see him with a book, newspaper, or listening to news on the radio. He was an avid trout fisherman and introduced Dave and me to the sport of fishing when we were very young.

My mother, Vivian Frogner, was born in 1903 and lived until 1992. She was the youngest of 10 children and grew up in various small Wisconsin towns. She went to a normal school in Stevens Point (now a campus of the University of Wisconsin), and after two years became an elementary teacher. She was forced to quit her job after she and Allen were married in 1931, because married women were not allowed to work during the depression. She returned to teaching when I was 21.

Mom spent part of her childhood on a farm; my love of the outdoors came as much from her and two of her brothers as from my father. One of my earliest recollections, when I was two years old, is of the family picnicking next to a stream as she and I watched my dad trout fishing nearby.

Even more than my passion for nature, my parents instilled in me a lifelong devotion to learning, an obvious advantage for a research scientist. It was always assumed that my brother and I would go to college, although when I showed an interest in the University of Wisconsin at Madison, I know now that my parents could not imagine how to pay for it.

I received a "tuition only" ($43/year) scholarship to Central State College in Stevens Point, as the old teachers college was known in 1950. I lived at home and worked for my spending money. I guess the cold Wisconsin winters prepared me for Antarctica; I recall walking a mile to take a final exam as a freshman at −44°F. After two years, I left for Madison to major in physics because I was interested in the atomic bomb.

Madison opened a new and formative period of my life. My parents paid my room rent of $15 a month for two years and I earned the rest. One summer I punched a time card in the Allis Chalmers factory in Milwaukee and became a member of the United Auto Workers Local 243. In Madison I had a 20-hour-per-week job in the physics department, scanning photographic plates exposed to particle accelerators for traces of pions, muons, and hyperfragments. Although I only made $0.85 an hour, and tuition was $175 a semester, I still saved enough money to buy a $200 Kodak Retina IIa 35-mm camera, which I used not only through four years at the university, but took to Antarctica in 1956.

I graduated in physics in 1954, but by that time the thought of spending my life in a laboratory had lost its appeal. I met Prof.

George Woollard who offered me a summer job as a geophysical field assistant and convinced me to enroll in graduate school as his student at Madison. I recall hearing from my dad that the draft board in Stevens Point was irritated about this summer job because I had already been on their list for induction but had been deferred as a student through the Korean war (1950–53). My summer deferment would continue as a graduate student and during my trip to Antarctica, which was considered a "critical occupation" of national security.

I had never left the state of Wisconsin until I was 18. However, during the summer of 1954 I worked in every state but three west of the Mississippi River, collecting gravity data (on Air Force funds) for George Woollard's gravity map on the U.S. The following summer I was Ed Thiel's assistant collecting gravity and magnetic data in the Uinta Mountains, Utah. At the end of that summer, I made my first airplane flight to Alaska, hitchhiking with Ed on U.S. Air Force planes. Woollard arranged Air Force travel orders for us. Ed and I made a gravity and magnetic survey of the Yukon River from Whitehorse, Yukon County, to Circle City, Alaska, with Ned Ostenso, who was also heading for Antarctica in 1956.

I continued working part-time in the physics department through my master's degree, until Woollard (actually his wife, Eleanor, although I did not realize it at the time) loaned me $700, which covered my room, board, and tuition for my last semester, when I wrote my thesis using the magnetic data that I had collected with Ed in Utah.

By the time I completed my doctoral thesis at Madison in 1961, I had worked in every state, every province of Canada, every continent, and sailed on every ocean, mainly through George Woollard's direction. I never recovered from this travel addiction.

After my parents, Woollard was the most influential person in shaping my life. Through his influence in the old boys' network (with Maurice Ewing and Bert Crary, in particular), I obtained the IGY job in Antarctica (along with Ed Thiel, Ned Ostenso, and Hugh Bennett–Woollard's students–as well as Charlie Bentley, Ewing's student). I learned to do research from Woollard by osmosis and example rather than by close direction. He provided me the opportunity and let me sink or swim. Although I floundered a bit at first, I learned to swim effectively enough for an exciting geophysical career that began that summer of 1954 and still continues.

Note

1.   Sullivan, *Quest for a Continent* (London: Secker and Warburg, 1957).

2
Voyage to the Weddell Sea

On a cold rainy Wednesday, 7 November 1956, I joined the 8 others of our scientific party, and 29 U.S. Navy men with whom we would "winter over" on our ship, the *Wyandot,* at the Navy base at Davisville, Rhode Island. Our station scientific leader and Navy officer in charge, Capt. Finn Ronne (USNR), would board later in South America. There were 450 men aboard including 9 scientists, 15 ship's officers, and other officers. The ship's company was about 240. The rest included the men who would construct Ellsworth Station, aircrews, observers, and a few reporters.

The *Wyandot* (AKA 92) was an attack cargo ship hit by bombs while participating in the Okinawa landings in World War II. She was 459 ft long and 63 ft wide, with a gross tonnage of 13,860 and a speed of about 16 knots. The ship, which was headed for the Weddell Sea, was part of Operation Deep Freeze II, U.S. Navy Task Force 43 (TF 43), the Navy designation of the IGY Antarctic support effort in the 1956–57 austral summer. Rear Adm. George Dufek was Commander Task Force 43 (CTF 43), which comprised 3,525 men, 12 ships, including 4 icebreakers, and 2 air squadrons. The *Wyandot* would be joined in Panama by the Navy icebreaker *Staten Island.* These two ships would proceed to Antarctica, commanded by Navy Capt. Edwin A. McDonald (USN) as commodore of Task Group 43.7 (CTG 43.7).

The Navy mission was to establish Ellsworth Station at the western end of the Ronne Ice Shelf (then called Filchner Ice Shelf) at the base of the Antarctic Peninsula (still called Palmer Peninsula on American maps in 1956). We nine civilian scientists were to carry out research there. Five of us planned to make an oversnow geophysical-glaciological traverse in two tracked Sno-Cat tractors into unexplored area to the south. IGY was scheduled to start on 1 July 1957 and last for 18 months to cover a complete year in both

9

the Northern and Southern Hemispheres. Our team would be replaced in early 1958 by a similar scientific and Navy support group to carry on through the IGY with the work we started.

8 Nov., Thurs. We learned the names of the other U.S. IGY stations which are all being constructed this season:

Ellsworth Station [on the Filchner Ice Shelf];
South Pole Station [officially Amundsen-Scott Station], 90°S;
Wilkes Station, 66°15'S, 110°31'E;
Byrd Station, on the West Antarctic ice sheet in Marie Byrd Land, 80°S, 120°W;
Little America V [on the edge of the Ross Ice Shelf, the primary U.S. scientific station], 78°11'S, 162°10'W; and
Hallett Station, on the Ross Sea Coast, 72°18'S, 170°18'E, to be jointly operated with New Zealand.

McMurdo Naval Air Facility, at 77°15'S, 166°36'E, was not mentioned because it was strictly a U.S. Navy support base and no scientific personnel were stationed there during the 1957 IGY winter. Today McMurdo Station is the main U.S. Antarctic facility.

We sailed at 1430 on 9 November 1956 amidst stirring (recorded) martial music. A number of families of the crew saw us depart. As we slowly moved away, a small group of the IGY secretaries stood on the pier, holding a sign asking, "Is this trip really necessary?" This was an expression common during World War II, as a gasoline conservation slogan seen on billboards throughout America. By 1956 it was a cliché but by 1998 was totally unfamiliar to anyone under 50.

We were all quite excited after months of anticipation. The sun was shining and there was a brisk wind as the *Wyandot* moved out among the islands of Narragansett Bay, our last view of the U.S. for nearly a year and a half.

It was my first time at sea, so everything was new. I recall to this day my first encounter with the slight smell of diesel fuel, the throb of the engines, and vibration always present onboard a ship. Every vessel I have boarded since evokes this comfortable, familiar feeling, which I first experienced on the *Wyandot*.

I was assigned to a stateroom on the main deck with five other men; one a Navy lieutenant and the rest GS 9s like me. Although only one of us actually worked for the U.S. government and had a civil service grade, we were assigned apparent grades of GS 9 and GS 11 corresponding to Navy ranks of lieutenant and lieutenant commander, respectively.

We GS 9s were earning $5700 per year (in 1997 a GS 9 salary in Denver was $31,665), and we also received a bonus of $1800 per year to be paid on our return to the States if we worked satisfactorily. We all signed contracts with the Arctic Institute of North America, our employer, to this effect. I was very pleased at the high pay, but station scientific leader Finn Ronne later complained that we received far too much.

Our stateroom was on the starboard side of the ship, and we had a single porthole that provided the only ventilation. We slept in three two-decker bunk beds oriented along the axis of the ship. We each had a tall locker in which to hang clothes, and a drawer beneath the bunks, at deck level. There was no air-conditioning on the *Wyandot,* and the temperatures were extremely hot inside, in the tropics. The best ventilation in our cabin was an air scoop in the single porthole. My top bunk was on the inboard side of the room directly beneath a heating duct, so it was also quite hot there when we arrived at the ice and the heating was turned on.

I had never been in the service, and this was my introduction to the military's way of life. We civilian "scientists" lived in officers' quarters, wore starched khakis, and were expected to "muster" at 8 A.M. with the rest of the ship's crew. We also were expected to snap to attention in the wardroom (the officers' dining room and lounge) when the ship's captain (Capt. Francis M. Gambacorta, USN) entered for the evening movie. Not surprisingly, we slightly resented it but went along because after all we were "guests" in their home. Captain Gambacorta (and later two other captains, when they were onboard) ate in a private mess, adjacent to his cabin.

The wardroom symbolized everything "Navy" about our new way of life at sea. We were served our meals on white linen table cloths instead of the green felt covers present for the rest of the 24-hour day. We ate off white china and used silver utensils and silver sugar and cream sets. Filipino and black stewards served us individually and made up our beds each day. The wardroom was usually open for coffee and lounging at all other times. As we civilians and many of the Seabee (CB, from Construction Battalion) officers and flying officers had no particular duties aboard ship, we spent many hours a day there. The wardroom and our staterooms were "officers' country" and off-limits to the enlisted men onboard, except as official duties required. All of this "class" distinction was foreign to me and made me slightly uncomfortable. We scientists came to accept the distinction between "officers" and "men" onboard the *Wyandot,* but it was to cause much aggravation when we arrived in Antarctica.

There was a large chart (map) of Antarctica and its surrounding sea prominently displayed in the wardroom on the inboard bulkhead wall. Our progress towards Antarctica and the Ellsworth Station site was plotted daily on this chart as we approached the continent. Because of the large number of officers onboard, the meals were served in two sittings, with the scientists and other passengers usually in the second sitting.

9 Nov., Fri. On the first day, towards evening we hit some dirty weather which caused the ship to roll. We had lobster for dinner and it was a humorously painful sight to see Hugo Neuburg, who likes it, trying to force it down despite the onset of seasickness. The night was pretty violent for us land folk, with junk flying all over the room.

We soon learned to tie down everything securely. No one in our stateroom suffered from seasickness except our only officer roommate, Lt. (jg) John Dorn, who took about a week to recover, as I recall. After two weeks at sea with the men I would be living with for the next year, I wrote a brief description of each of them.

Kim (John McKim) Malville, 22, single, from San Francisco. B.S. physics from Cal. Tech. in '56. He is the aurora and air-glow man of our contingent. Seems pleasant, quite intelligent, with a fine sense of humor. He is a rock climber with the Sierra Club.

Nolan Aughenbaugh, Augie, 28, single, Akron, Ohio, B.S. geology, Purdue '54, nearly completed M.S. at University of Michigan. Marine Corps, was a drill instructor. He will be surveying and doing geologic fieldwork on traverse. Easy going, jovial sort of character. Pointed sense of humor at times.

Jerry Fierle, 36, no home, meteorologist, wife deceased, served on a destroyer in WW II; works in Alaska. Short, smokes cigars, agreeable personality with certain prejudices towards all officers.

Paul Walker, 22, Pasadena, B.S. geology, Occidental College '56; assistant glaciologist on traverse. Skier and some mountaineering experience. Engaged to girl in Pasadena. Has traveled on summer jobs quite a bit in Alaska and Greenland. A fair amount of glaciological experience. He is the only traverse person who smokes.

Don Skidmore, 27, Boston area, B.A. business, married, four children. Enjoys games and is quite proficient in most; clowns a lot. Several years in Merchant Marine. Assistant in the ionosphere physics program.

Ed Thiel, 28, Wausau, Wisconsin, single, Ph.D. geology, Wisconsin '55, chief seismologist and traverse co-leader.

Hugo Neuburg, 36, Yonkers, N.Y., B.S. physics, single, much arctic and outdoor experience, physicist with cosmic rays as his specialty. A very strong person physically and otherwise. Always jovial and has become quite popular with everyone onboard. Doesn't smoke or drink. Chief glaciologist and co-leader of traverse party. Strikes one as being a good man to have around and is probably the most interesting person in our company.

Jack (John) Brown, Bethany Beach, Del., B.S. physics, chief of ionosphere program. Reads *Pogo,* not too much outdoor experience which reflects itself in his consternation when things don't go as planned or stated. Enjoyable company and quite well educated.

Jim Weinman, B.S. at Illinois Tech, just completing Ph.D. in physics at Wisconsin. Single, hired by Woollard to make gravity tie from Weddell Station to South America. Doesn't plan on wintering over. A cheerful soul who can appreciate or perpetrate a practical joke.

Ed Thiel was my direct boss and mentor. He was directly responsible, along with George Woollard, for my being selected to go to Antarctica on this IGY expedition. I was Ed's field assistant in the Uinta Mountains in 1955 and in Alaska on the Lemon Creek Glacier during the summer of 1956.

10–15 Nov., Sat.–Thurs. At General Quarters we civilians go to the wardroom and play bridge. In Abandon Ship drill I go to the fantail. Every so often a bosun's whistle would shrill out and a voice shout something incoherently over the P.A. system. We asked each other what was said, shrugged shoulders, and went back to our game. We missed a life raft demonstration as a result. Whistling is *verboten* on board, as is discussions of politics, religion, and sex in the wardroom.

11 Nov., Sun. Brunch consisting of steak, potatoes, scrambled eggs, pastry, toast, fruit, milk, and coffee. They are really feeding us pretty good. Augie beat me at chess and we went to lunch.

Only two weeks before this, I had been a starving grad student who could never afford steak and eggs for breakfast.

As we headed south, it was so nice and warm outdoors that the evening movies were held on the #4 hatch. We saw part of Richard Byrd's 1928 Antarctic expedition and *War Arrow*, with Jeff Chandler. The moon was half full and the night was beautiful. We proceeded through the Windward and Leeward, and Crooked Island Passages in the Caribbean Sea to the entrance of the Panama Canal passing between islands and meeting numerous ships.

As the weather became increasingly hotter, particularly down in our stateroom, Jack Brown, Don, and I went up on the signal bridge to sleep several nights but occasionally were forced in when it began to rain.

I had a discussion with Ike Schlossbach, an old Antarctic veteran and retired Navy commander just going for the ride. He plans on building a hotel on the Palmer Peninsula for tourists. Combination gambling casino, brothel, etc. No taxes; all gravy.

Ike Schlossbach was also on the U.S. Antarctic Service Expedition in 1939–41 and the Ronne Antarctic Research Expedition in 1946–48. He was on the Deep Freeze Expedition as an observer.

16 Nov., Fri. We reached the Panama Canal at dawn, started up the channel about 1100, and entered the first of the three Gatum locks at noon. We reached the other side and docked about 1900. We had gone along heavily jungled banks. At night we went into Panama City.

I didn't write about the *exibiciones* in the whorehouse called the Teenagers Club. It was, after all, the 1950s, and we were all quite naive (and shocked).

17 Nov., Sat. The icebreaker *Staten Island* (Cmdr. James B. Elliott, USN, captain), which will accompany us south has docked at the other side of our pier. Paul had bought a uke and it was very amusing to see Ike Schlossbach playing and singing *On the Beach at Waikiki* in the middle of a street in Panama City.

19 Nov., Mon. We sailed at 0800. We are in the Humbolt Current and the weather is much cooler. For the first time since we left Davisville it was comfortable sleeping indoors. I even pulled the sheet over me. In the afternoon a few of us stood watching the flying fish; some would remain in the air for five seconds.

21 Nov., Wed. Today we crossed the equator at 80°W. Neptune Rex came aboard about 0800 and the ceremonies began shortly. I was one of the first 15 or so. We polliwogs [those who had not crossed the equator on a ship] all stood around in our underwear on the quarterdeck waiting. There was a cold wind, and I was glad to get started. They took us individually.

For weapons the shellbacks [those who had crossed "the line" previously] had clubs made of rolled canvas and rubber. These sufficed. The usual college rah-rah spirit with eggs, grease, hair cutting, eating oil and dried grasshoppers, and a garbage chute to crawl through. The Royal Court was colorfully costumed, and the Royal Baby's belly (which we all kissed) was coated with worm gear grease. Fortunately my hair was too short to cut with a tin snips, and I escaped with a scraped knee. Don lost a shock of hair and vows revenge. Most of the officers and civilians took it in the right spirit, but a few were rather bitter (some had been hit in the balls). I can't say I blame them particularly. Our lone marine officer, a pilot, was given an especially rough time. A number of people were paddled so hard they bled (including Augie and me). There was a fire hose (saltwater) to take the first layer off. I cleaned up and went back to get some pictures.

The somewhat sadistic custom of hazing ceremonies on ships crossing the equator dates back to northern Europeans in the sixteenth century. Samuel Eliot Morrison searched for references to this tradition and reported the earliest he could find was on a French ship on a voyage to Brazil in 1557. He reported that "the sailors went through their accustomed ceremonies . . . namely, bind a man with ropes and plunge him into the sea, or blacken his face well with an old rag rubbed on the bottom of the kettle and then shave it off, so as to give those who had never before passed the equator something to remember. But one can buy oneself off and be exempt from all that by paying for wine for all hands, as I did."[1] So, I guess we got off lightly in 1956!

Tonight, the day we crossed the equator, I wore my windbreaker parka to the movie out on deck.

We proceeded uneventfully south, celebrating Thanksgiving with turkey and all of the trimmings. We saw whales spouting, and porpoises and a shark following us. We exercised on deck and passed the time getting to know each other, reading and playing bridge.

23 Nov., Fri. Hugo and Ed gave lectures yesterday in the wardroom on the seismic, gravity, and magnetic program and the glaciology program. We had a lecture today on base building. The base is scheduled to be built in 40 days. First, a site has to be found and a safe trail from the ship established. A temporary camp for the construction crew consisting of Jamesway huts follows. Finally, the main construction of camp, air strip, and two towers for scientific observations.

26 Nov., Mon. Our ships arrived at the Chilean port of Valparaiso. To our left we could see Vina del Mar, a small suburb with many nice homes and the gambling casino.

In November 1990 I was to spend two weeks in Vina del Mar as part of the U.S. delegation negotiating the Environmental Protocol to the Antarctic Treaty. What goes around, comes around. We civilians took the opportunity to spend a few days in Santiago, several hours away by train.

29 Nov., Thurs. The last night in port I ate two fillets at the Casino and picked up a violent case of stomach flu. Spent all day in bed. We sailed at 1500 on Friday, 30 November and everything was secured for heavy weather. It is staying light quite late now (until 2100) as it is summer, and we are getting farther south. It was quite cool.

The seas were a little rougher the next day with foggy, rainy, and windy weather. The icebreaker, because of its round hull, is really rolling and pitching. She is so low in the water that on some rolls the decks go under.

Two years later I spent three months in Antarctica on *Staten Island*'s sister icebreaker, the *Edisto,* and had the direct experience of this rolling in 50-foot seas. In a much smaller ship, the geophysical research vessel *S. P. Lee,* I had the opportunity to experience similar waves in the Ross Sea (Antarctica) in March 1984. By contrast, the 13,000-ton *Wyandot* was an easy-riding ship.

> *3 Dec., Mon.* Lieutenant Commander Botto [onboard as an observer] of the Chilean Navy piloted us through the Chilean inland passage. We entered this at 1400 from the Bay of Penas and immediately were in calm water. We are now sailing between low mountains poking up 1000–3000 ft out of the water. Many steep cliffs and waterfalls can be observed. As the afternoon progressed the sun came out and we saw some blue sky. The higher peaks are snow covered, and we have seen several small mountain glaciers. There were lots of birds and some dolphins.
>
> About 1930 we went through the tight part of English Narrows with no more than a ship-length clearance on either side, and less in some places, in the tricky S-shaped curve. There are no signs of habitation along the heavily forested banks. This country, in spite of the well-charted channel, is quite unexplored by land. Finn Ronne said they saw some rather primitive-looking Indians when they went through on his expedition in 1946. It is now quite cool, and we wear coats when outside for any length of time.

That brief comment was my first journal mention of Ronne, who had come aboard in Valpariso. In writing this book, I find it interesting that I had never described Finn Ronne in my journal.

Ronne was a short man, 57 years old (by far the oldest of our wintering group), very physically vigorous, and balding. At first acquaintance he was quite charming, with a pleasant Norwegian accent and an engaging personality. He did not wear a beard and was quite fastidious about his personal appearance, unlike many of us.

According to his autobiography, *Antarctica, My Destiny,* Ronne had graduated with a degree in Norway in mechanical and marine engineering and later took postgraduate courses in naval architecture and boiler construction. Ronne was smart, ambitious–a self-made man. He emigrated to the U.S. in 1923 and first went to Antarctica in 1933 as a member of the Second Byrd Expedition, where he wintered over at Little America II. He participated in dogsled field parties on that expedition and later on the United States–Antarctic Service Expedition (1939–41), where he wintered over at East Base. There he led a field exploration party on George

VI Sound. Ronne served as a desk officer in the Navy in World War II, reaching the rank of commander.

In 1946–48 Ronne led a private expedition to East Base. His wife, Edith (Jackie), and another woman, Jennie Darlington, a pilot's wife, were the first women to winter over in Antarctica. The Ronne Antarctic Research Expedition made significant geographic explorations in the southern Antarctic Peninsula (then Palmer Peninsula) and a flight along the Ronne Ice Shelf (then, and at the time of IGY known as Filchner Ice Shelf). In 1957 Ronne was a Navy captain, USNR. In my journal, when not using his name, I normally referred to Ronne as "the Captain," which was common usage at Ellsworth.

> *4 Dec., Tues.* We continued through the inland passage and entered the Straits of Magellan. More mountains and more rugged scenery.
>
> We dropped anchor in Punta Arenas Harbor this morning. [In 1956 the docks were not capable of handling ships the size of our two.] We are about a mile offshore, and *Staten Island* is in a little from us. The land looks pretty bleak and flat around here, with not many trees. Somewhat rainy weather most of the day. We received some mail, which was the last we will get until 1958.
>
> We went ashore in the afternoon, ferried by the *Wyandot*'s landing craft, and looked around Punta Arenas. This town of 30,000 is the southernmost city in the world. It is quite quiet and respectable by comparison with the other ports I've been in this trip. I had no money so I went back to the ship for evening chow. About 1900 a windstorm came up; Beaufort 9 was recorded and it was blowing hard all night. We were fueling from a Chilean Navy tanker at the time. Spray was flying all over, and as it was sunny the effect was quite beautiful. About 400 of our people were stranded on the beach.

We sailed out of Punta Arenas after dark on that evening of 7 December and proceeded through the Straits of Magellan into the Southern Ocean. We set our course to the southeast towards the Weddell Sea. The plan was to avoid as much of the ice pack as possible and eventually head due south about 15°W. We didn't see civilization again until 31 January 1958.

> *9 Dec., Sun.* 0000 Z (Universal time) 53.7°S, 65.6°W. By now it never gets totally dark anymore. We are supposedly sailing in the most

stormy seas on earth (Drake Passage), but excepting a fairly heavy swell, it is quite calm with overcast skies and light rain.

10 Dec., Mon. 0000 Z, 55.6°S, 60.0°W. Captain McDonald, who has a number of years experience of navigating ships in Antarctic seas, gave a lecture on managing ships in ice. He mentioned that we would probably be seeing bergs soon. Charles J. "Mac" McCarthy (officer-in-charge of the Navy VX-6 detachment and who will be executive officer, under Ronne, at Ellsworth Station) gave a lecture on air operations. He explained Navy Squadron VX-6 and their Antarctic record so far in Deep Freeze I and II.

Last year most of their aircraft were destroyed or rendered inoperable. This year one P2V [Navy Neptune aircraft] has crashed at McMurdo, killing four. We will have three UCs [single-engine Otters] and one HO4S [helicopter]. The former Otters have an operational range of 250 miles while the helicopter has approximately 175 miles. Maximum cargo load for each is 1000 lbs. Conrad J. Jaburg, Lt., USN, is the helicopter pilot. McCarthy and William H. Sumrall, Lt. (jg), USNR, are the other two pilots.

Ronne told us he had been refused dogs. He said "they" were paying $45,000 for 30 dogs to be used at the other stations. Ronne complained that "they" hadn't asked him or considered any of his recommendations regarding selection of equipment and personnel. He intimated severe personality problems among the wintering-over personnel last winter during Deep Freeze I. He told us that on the Second Byrd Expedition, which Ronne was on, the camp was split 27–26. Byrd was "Alone" (title of Byrd's book) a distance south of Little America. On Ronne's own expedition, he selected 20 from 1100 applicants and still had "two bad eggs." The fact that he is the only one of us who has wintered over is somewhat disconcerting to him.

Dogs are now illegal in Antarctica under the Environmental Protocol to the Antarctic Treaty, signed in Madrid in 1991. Biologists, fearing that canine distemper might devastate the Antarctic seal population, convinced their governments of the wisdom of this action. Feelings against the prohibition of dogs ran high among some old Antarctic explorers, but Argentina and Australia, the last holdouts in this negotiation, eventually gave in.

The U.S. delegation, which led the effort to eliminate dogs from Antarctica, found itself in the embarrassing position at the 1992 Antarctic Treaty meeting in Venice of requesting a special consideration so that Norman Vaughan (of the First Byrd Expedition) could take dog teams to Mt. Vaughan in Antarctica. Senator Stevens of Alaska had blocked ratification of the Environmental Protocol in the Senate unless the Bush administration would agree to this special pleading, which it ultimately did. However, a plane attempting to fly in with the dogs in the summer of 1993 crash-landed in the middle of West Antarctica (at Patriot Hills blue-ice landing site), and three dogs ran away and disappeared. No doubt they died in a few weeks of cold and starvation. The others were flown out of Antarctica. Thus ended the story of U.S. dogs in Antarctica.

> From [radio] messages, we heard that a P2V has landed at the Pole and can't take off.

The first flight to ever land at the South Pole took place on 31 October 1956, when Admiral Dufek flew in on an R4D (a DC-3) on skis. By December, ski planes had been landing more or less routinely, and parachute drops of supplies and fuel from Air Force C-124 Globemasters were under way there. Construction was proceeding on the South Pole Station, and a number of heavy tractors left Little America Station to construct and supply Byrd Station. Although the tractors had trouble with crevasses (cracks in a moving glacier), they pushed through all right. The previous March, a Navy man had been killed when his tractor went into a crevasse at the beginning of the route.

> *11 Dec., Tues.* 0000 Z, 57.3°S, 53.5°W. The first ice was spotted about 2200, a small bergy bit [a remnant of an iceberg]. It snowed off and on.

> *12 Dec., Wed.* 0000 Z, 59.1°S, 47.8°W. We saw ice- and snow-covered mountains of the South Orkney Islands from about 40 miles to the north as we passed. These islands are part of the Falkland Islands Dependency of U.K. Argentina also claims them and has a weather station there. We have an Argentine observer onboard also. I saw a good-sized bergy bit. There were flocks of cape pigeons all around the ship.

Birds followed ships because all of our garbage was tossed off the fantail. At present, because trash is no longer allowed to be dumped overboard, the birds no longer follow the ships.

It began to snow about 0900 and decks soon became covered. All weather decks are restricted. Visibility was very poor all day, and they have been blowing the fog horn. I finally beat Augie at chess, after three defeats and one tie.

13 Dec., Thurs. 0000 Z, 60.4°S, 42.2°W. We saw icebergs all through the day. Most were of the tabular type; some are miles long.

The icebergs had broken off the ice shelves far to the south of us and were drifting north; they would melt shortly after crossing the Antarctic convergence, where the cold Antarctic water coming from the south slips beneath the less dense, warmer water to the north. There the sea surface temperature increases markedly.

The great ice shelves (e.g., Filchner and Ross) are floating sheets over 4000 ft thick (1300 m), as we later measured, which have flowed from the grounded Antarctic ice sheet in the continental interior. These ice shelves thin by spreading and melting and are commonly 600 ft (200 m) or thinner at the ice front, or "barrier." The steep cliff that marks an ice front results from the breaking off of one of these tabular icebergs.

I spent the better part of the morning trying to get pictures of albatross. These are beautiful birds to watch as they follow the ship.

The albatrosses' wingspan is about seven feet, and they soar in the wind without apparently moving a wing. It was fascinating to see one skim the sea surface and then with a slight movement avoid a wave as it broke into a foamy crest.

The weather closed in towards late afternoon. The pack ice is a few miles to starboard. *Staten Island* tried to get into the pack but went from 3/10ths to 10/10ths cover in two miles. The temperature is quite cold, so people topside are wearing winter clothing.

14 Dec., Fri. 0000 Z, 60.3°S, 34.6°W. By now many icebergs are visible everywhere. Our course has been approximately due east in our attempt to sail around the pack. This afternoon we met six Norwegian whalers [killer boats]. These were quite small and were pitching violently. The bows would go completely under. Ronne [who immigrated from Norway in 1923] talked with them.

15 Dec., Sat. 0000 Z, 59.0S, 29.3W. Don came down at 0600 to tell us we are passing Bristol Island, one of the South Sandwich Islands. It was quite close and consisted of three peaks several thousand feet high. There were several smaller islands in line to the west. The sun was out, and it was quite warm out of the wind. One of the helicopters flew about 20 miles into the pack and found it pretty solid. McDonald, Ronne, and the Chilean and Argentine observers transferred to *Staten Island* by landing craft.

Captain McDonald, USN, commanded Task Group 43.7 from whichever ship he was on.

We have been going through bergs all day, and when the sun was out it was quite beautiful. On some bergy bits we observed a number of penguins.

16 Dec., Sun. 0000 Z, 60.5°S, 23.2°W. We are still zigzagging in our attempt to find a lead [a linear path of open water] through the pack but are still outside. We saw many icebergs, bergy bits, growlers [small pieces of icebergs], and brash [loose pieces of sea ice]. Also thick pans of sea ice. The weather continues bad—snow and fog.

Although the modern icebreakers of the 1990s can more or less easily cruise directly through 10/10ths (100%) coverage of thick pack ice, the *Staten Island,* a Wind Class icebreaker of 1940s design and construction, was quite limited in ice-breaking capability. But the *Wyandot* had no ice-breaking capability at all and was utterly dependent on leads and occasional ice breaking by the *Staten Island.*

It was quite bitter outside although the temperature was only near freezing. In the afternoon we passed through brash and milky-looking water (due to ice crystal formation). One could observe the increase in viscosity in the near-freezing water as the surface had an oily, or syrupy, appearance. We saw more penguins and snow petrels, and someone reported a seal.

17 Dec., Mon. 0000 Z, 61.1°S, 16.4°W. This morning we entered the pack ice in earnest at about 62°S, 14°W. I estimated about 7/10ths coverage of medium-sized floes. *Staten Island* is approximately 500 ft ahead although this distance closes rapidly when she stops. Even these small floes shake the ship quite noticeably when we hit one squarely. Most, of course, are cleared away by the icebreaker. A sharp turn leaves us to plow our own path, however.

When we entered the pack it seemed much warmer, due largely to the reflection of so much light. Sunglasses were essential all day even though the sky was overcast.

Unfortunately, the prescription sunglasses I was issued were unusable, so I wore plain dark-glass sunglasses or plastic dark goggles over my regular glasses for the next year. Neither I nor anybody else in our group became snow-blind, but by 1994 I needed surgery for cataracts.

As we entered the pack, we saw good examples of "sea and ice sky" (ice blink). This is a phenomenon whereby the overcast reflects the snow-covered pack ice beyond the horizon and provides a "sky map." In a complementary fashion, leads in the pack ice or large open-water areas do not reflect. Although radar also showed the ice pack more or less clearly, the sky map was quite useful in following leads. Of course, in 1956 we had no satellite receiver to directly "see" the pack ice cover over a large area as we did in the Ross Sea in 1988.

18 Dec., Tues. 0000 Z, 62.48°S, 14.4°W. We continued through the pack all day. Around midnight we came into a large polynya [a lakelike clear area in the ice pack] where *Staten Island* put in an oceanographic station. Snow petrels are the only flying birds left, but we see penguins all the time, including the first emperor penguin. Seals are becoming frequent also and we saw a whale.

19 Dec., Wed. 0000 Z, 64.2°S, 13.4°W. We proceeded at 5–7 knots through the pack. A seam somewhere forward has been strained, and water comes in when the ship is turned more than 10.

As this was my first time at sea, I didn't realize how little ship captains (and crews) appreciate damage and flooding. The captains of the *Wyandot* and *Staten Island* showed an amazing degree of patience in the next two months.

I like to stand up at the bow and just watch the ice go by. Occasionally a big pan would drift into the channel cut by the icebreaker and we would plow through it. It is now never night and men going on watch at midnight wear sunglasses.

20 Dec., Thurs. 0000 Z, 65.5S, 11.9W. We crossed the Antarctic Circle today. There was a very strong cold wind (up to 60 mph). We had a few sunny moments, which is a great improvement over the blinding white overcast.

21 Dec., Fri. 0000 Z, 67.6S, 11.9W. We still have about 1000 miles to go, and the tentative arrival date has been pushed back to the first of the year. This endless monotony of nothing to do and no place to go is tiring. All day we continued slowly and with difficulty through 10/10ths pack ice. *Staten Island* kept getting stuck, and we would have to run our bow into the ice to one side to prevent collision. The continual beating our hull is taking isn't doing it much good. We must have sprung something else, as an oil slick can be seen in the open water around the bow when we are stopped.

Staten Island breaking ice in Weddell Sea, followed by *Wyandot* (Official U.S. Navy Photo).

I started reading *Antarctic Conquest* by Ronne, tonight. This is his account of the Ronne Antarctic Research Expedition in 1946–48. Jennie Darlington has written a book entitled *My Antarctic Honeymoon* which I will read next. The second book really blasts Ronne, I understand. I will reserve judgment for a few months. These two books have stimulated discussion. There are some in the group who consider Ronne's attitude in preserving the Navy way of life (the men will do the cooking, etc., and we will all be served—at separate tables, etc.) going a little too far. Both Ronne and Darlington speak highly of Ike Schlossbach; he skippered their ship.

This boring ship life is getting on people's nerves and already I can see the makings of some discontent. Ronne makes the statement in his book: "My experience is that in general the members of expeditions do not get along very well with each other."[2]

22 Dec., Sat. 0000 Z, 69.6S, 11.4W. We are lying to in the pack until the ice loosens up.

One of the advantages of living as an officer and lounging in the wardroom was the opportunity to read the messages that the ship sent and received each day. There was a binder containing the ship message traffic, which was updated regularly and which we scientists read avidly. In addition to usually boring material, the messages included information copies to the *Wyandot* from the other Navy ships and "bases," or IGY stations, as the case might be, all of which were part of Task Force 43 (Operation Deep Freeze). I took the opportunity to copy those of interest, somewhat to the annoyance of the ships' officers, I suppose, who didn't do that sort of thing. These messages are the source of information about other parts of Operation Deep Freeze, included here from time to time. I am sure that the Navy did not bother to keep these documents in archives, so any copies we civilians made are the only ones preserved. This one was sent from Captain McDonald on the *Staten Island* to his commanding officer, Rear Admiral Dufek, in the Ross Sea area:

SITREP [SITUATION REPORT] RAN OUT OF PUSH 50 MILES SHORT OF CAPE NORVEGIA. MASSIVE 1- TO 5-MILE FLOES 10–25 FT THICK. PROGRESS IMPOSSIBLE UN-TIL PRESSURE SUBSIDES. WAITING FOR IMPROVE-MENT. OPEN LEAD SIGHTED ALONG SHELF.

The situation is somewhat exaggerated in this message. The only ice around us is only a foot or two thick.

I later realized how little I knew about estimating ice thickness from the height of the decks above the water. The thickness stated in the message was correct. Besides, McDonald was reporting to his commanding officer, not writing a press release. This was a distinction I appreciated only after some time.

The sun came out and the weather was quite warm. The beautiful hummocky ice lay solid around us in all directions with shadows showing the surface relief. Here and there icebergs could be seen poking up through the pack. Up on the flying bridge, I sat on an ammunition container and enjoyed the warm radiation. Two seamen were ascending the main mast to the very top; another fellow a few yards away was playing "Yellow Rose of Texas" on a harmonica while overhead *Staten Island*'s H04S presented a striking contrast of fuchsine red against the blue sky. Some of the men were fishing in a hole in the ice near our stern.

The ammunition container on which I sat was for the twin machine guns mounted on the starboard and port wings of the bridge of the *Wyandot. Staten Island* had a five-inch gun on the foredeck. This was before the Antarctic Treaty, including its disarmament article, signed in 1961. The U.S. Coast Guard icebreakers now operating in the Antarctic, instead of the Navy, do not carry mounted guns.

We lost 9000 gallons of fuel when our seam was ruptured the other day. All around the ship now the black sludge contaminated by seawater can be seen on the ice. Trash, sweepings, and garbage add their beauty to the somewhat messy sight. I hate to think what the ice would look like if we were stuck here a month.

This afternoon Lieutenant Clark, Augie, and I trimmed the Christmas tree in the wardroom. It and several others were picked up at Valparaiso. It was somewhat lopsided, and there weren't many branches near the bottom, but we all agreed that it was one of the top ten trees in the Weddell Sea.

The evening movie, *Hell Below Zero,* starring Alan Ladd, was greatly appreciated. It concerned a whaling ship marooned in the pack ice of the Weddell Sea not many miles from our present location. The Norwegian ship *Kista Dan,* which the Australians used at Mawson in 1955–56 was the central ship in the movie. It caused quite a few laughs. There was only one thing wrong with it–I haven't seen any beautiful women like that down here. I finished reading Ronne's book and started Jennie Darlington's book.

23 Dec., Sun. 0000 Z, 70.7S, 11.9W. Another beautiful sunny day. At 1400 we started on, but soon were stuck in the thick (15-ft) floes. It took an hour for the breaker to clear us and get under way again. I began to appreciate the true ice thickness when I saw the bow of the breaker slide up on the ice and the ice just sagged. A little fur-

Oil spill from ruptured hold of *Wyandot* with Adélie penguin and pack ice.

ther and it finally broke. The captain of *Staten Island* himself had the con, and we could hear him shouting orders all over the ship. About 1800 we could see the coast of Antarctica very faintly on the horizon about 40 miles away.

It is hard to get used to the sun; not only is it above the horizon 24 hours a day but sometimes it moves from west to east and sometimes east to west. Half the time it is to the north and half to the south. About 2200 some very fine examples of mirages appeared, icebergs inverted. These icebergs were actually over the horizon. *24 Dec., Mon.* 70.8°S, 12.1°W. We have come eight miles since we started yesterday. Overcast day with some snow falling. The following dispatch was sent [by Gambacorta] from *Wyandot:*

CASREP [CASUALTY REPORT] TIPS OF ALL BLADES PROP SHEARED OFF BY CONTACT WITH ICE. TWO BLADES LOST ABOUT ONE THIRD, ONE ABOUT ONE QUARTER, AND FOURTH ABOUT ONE HALF. DAMAGE OCCURRED DURING TRANSIT WEDDELL SEA CONSOLIDATED ICE PACK HAVING 15–25 FT THICKNESS WITH HUMMOCKS AND PRESSURE RIDGES UP TO 12 FT IN HEIGHT.

NEGOTIATION OF NUMEROUS SHARP TURNS TO FIND MOST FAVORABLE PATH WITH NECESSARY

27

Mirages (inverted icebergs) caused by refraction due to temperature inversion over pack ice in foreground.

BACKING AND TWISTING CONSIDERED CAUSE–CAN CONTINUE PRESENT ASSIGNMENT AT REDUCED SPEED. OPERATIONAL READINESS SERIOUSLY IMPAIRED. WILL ADVISE STATUS WHEN OPERATIVE CONDITIONS PERMIT FURTHER INVESTIGATION.

Another dispatch from Captain McDonald on our operational status followed:

FINALLY ARRIVED WITHIN 32 MILES OF CAPE NORVEGIA BUT AT EXPENSE PROPELLER DAMAGE TO WYANDOT–ONLY RECOURSE IS TO WAIT UNTIL ICE CONDITIONS IMPROVE. ICE COVERAGE 9–10 TENTHS MASSIVE THICK FLOES WITH MANY PRESSURE RIDGES. BELIEVE DETERMINATION IGY SITE SHOULD BE MADE LATER AND DEPENDENT UPON DEVELOPMENTS IN ICE CONDITIONS AND OPERATING CAPABILITIES OF SHIP.

On Christmas Eve, we received the following dispatch from Admiral Dufek:

MERRY CHRISTMAS. WE KNOW YOU ARE HAVING

TOUGH GOING. REMEMBER THAT OLD POLAR SAY-
ING: "PATIENCE."

Dec. 24, Mon. Thus it is that on this Christmas Eve we are lying to in
the ice again. *Wyandot*'s bow is tied to *Staten Island*'s stern. A rope
ladder at a 60 angle is the method of communication between the
vessels. The first man up was Captain McDonald; in the process
the ladder flipped over and left the CTG 43.7 dangling over the ice-
covered water. He climbed up OK and although the ladder flipped
on about 10% of the people, no one fell off.

Our choral group sang on #4 hatch after evening chow, accompanied by a piano. . . . After we finished we went up on the bow
and sang to *Staten Island.* They had a crowd out with their electric
piano and invited us over. About 20 of us negotiated the tricky ladder, and we had a good sing on their flight deck despite the cold.
The ladder didn't improve with so much usage and was even more
unstable on the way up; our bow is about 20 ft above their fantail.

25 Dec., Tues. Christmas. We are still lying to in the ice pack. The
weather was overcast. After church the annual Christmas custom of
"splicing the main brace" was followed. This is one of the few times
that liquor is allowed on board a Navy ship. Everybody received a
drink (a two-ounce bottle of medicinal brandy). We had a big turkey and ham dinner.[3]

26 Dec., Wed. 0000 Z, 70.8°S, 12.3°W. [We had drifted with the pack
ice.] A beautiful, clear, warm sunny day. We started moving with
great difficulty again after having been essentially beset (stuck) in
the ice with little or no progress for five days.

27 Dec., Thurs. 0000 Z, 71°06'S, 12°57'W. All day we continued in a
southwesterly direction intermittently through open water and pack
ice. The air seemed much colder over the water. Ronne sent a message requesting that the steward Morrison winter over. The answer
received today was "Negative."

Morrison would have been the only black person to winter
over with us had he stayed, or the only steward at an IGY station.
The only black, to my knowledge, to winter over in Antarctica
during the IGY was meteorologist Robert Johns, at Byrd Station.
By the early 1990s there were a sizable number of African Americans and other racial and ethnic minorities in the military and National Science Foundation (NSF) groups in Antarctica, but few in
the scientific parties and almost none in the Antarctic Support

Associates personnel. Women are fairly well represented (20–40%) in all groups today.

> *28 Dec., Fri.* 0000 Z, 72°02'S, 15°23'W. We entered a lead a number of miles wide and sailed down this channel all day. We are travelling along the barrier (the 100-ft or less high ice front of the floating ice shelf) a few miles away. We have been making 10–12 knots with no trouble from the prop. There was salt in the freshwater system.

Two days later the trouble with the water system recurred. All of the water for drinking and washing was distilled from seawater, and on a ship like the *Wyandot,* with 450 men aboard, it seems always to be in short supply.

> *29 Dec., Sat.* 0000 Z, 73°25'S, 20°13'W. We cruised at 11 knots. The lead was so wide that we couldn't see the pack edge. About 1800 we passed the Halley Bay Base (U.K.), at 77°31'S, 26°36'W. All day we have been fairly close to the barrier. The sheer wall was marked by vertical striae where icebergs had calved off. I saw lots of icicles on the face.

> *30 Dec., Sun.* 0000 Z, 75°42'S, 26°57'W. We continued southwest through an open lead obstructed occasionally by loose pack. There were many more icebergs. During one maneuver in the morning we had to come quite close to a berg and hit it bow on. Fortunately we were travelling very slowly and no damage was done. It was an impressive sight to see the berg that close. Later in the morning a chunk of ice punched a hole in #94 frame bulkhead and we took in water. This was patched, although there is a large dent.
> The weather is getting colder; the low was 20°F.

> *31 Dec., Mon.* 0000 Z, 77°S, 34°15'W. It was quite cold (17°F at 0700) and overcast. All day we have been crossing a short distance north of the Filchner Ice Shelf in the same area where the German Filchner Expedition in the ship *Deutschland* was beset in early 1912, and Shackleton's ship, *Endurance,* was frozen in for the winter in 1915.

Endurance drifted north for the winter and was eventually crushed and sunk. Fortunately for me water-depth measurements were made throughout this drift, which I used in my 1961 doctoral thesis.

The Filchner party (1911–13) built a small base on the ice shelf that bears his name, near the site of Shackleton base. This portion of the shelf became an iceberg when it calved off the ice shelf and drifted north. The nearby *Deutschland* evacuated its people and was later beset in the pack ice for the 1912 winter.

We passed Shackleton base at 0400 and General Belgrano Station (Argentina) at about 0900. Ronne and McDonald flew in. A helicopter cracked up on the flight deck of *Staten Island* in take-off, but no one was hurt. The machine was a total loss, however.

There were seven civilian men at Shackleton waiting for their ship to arrive. This base, named just "Shackleton" as far as I can determine, was the starting point for the British Commonwealth Transantarctic Expedition (TAE), which planned to cross the continent in the 1957–58 summer.

The water depth as we headed west increased to about 4000 ft (1300 m) and then decreased again as we approached Gould Bay. This was the first measured transect of what is now known as the Thiel Trough, although the *Deutschland* made a few soundings in the Thiel Trough in 1912. We had been hitting nine-tenths pack now and then. The cold weather froze the surface, and there was a skin of ice covering all of the open water.

1 Jan. 1957, Tues. 0000 Z, 77.0°S, 43.5°W. We are lying to in the ice again, about 20 miles from Gould Bay. The thin ice forming yesterday solidified around the ship but is no problem. The icebreaker had a hard trip with pressure ridges blocking the way to open water a few miles ahead.

I watched the New Year come in from the flying bridge. They sounded the whistles and siren for a few seconds. Captain Gambacorta had a New Year's party in his large cabin at 1500, serving fruit juice, cake, and hors d'oeuvres. He wants to get us unloaded and to head back as soon as possible. We had a very good veal curry with trimmings for dinner.

2 Jan., Tues. 0000 Z, 77°40'S, 43°15'W. We are still sitting in the ice as is *Staten Island*. Kim, Ed, and I argued whether we come under the Uniform Code of Military Justice while at the station. According to the *Manual of Courts Martial,* any civilian accompanying the military (or with a military community) is covered. Their contention is that while at the station after the ships have left, we are an IGY station and not a military base. I don't believe the Navy looks at it that way.

31

3 Jan., Thurs. We are still stuck. The temperature has been quite warm. The sun came out about 2100 and produced some very beautiful shadow effects. We saw several groups of Adélie penguins. Some near the fantail wandered up and down and then came over when Paul and I called to them. They made quite a racket with their squawks.

4 Jan., Fri. Winds continued from the east, and the ice has shown no signs of opening up. The Coriolis force (in the Southern Hemisphere) keeps the pack ice tight against the ice shelf with an east wind. An Adélie penguin came right up next to the deck and everyone took pictures.

Although people are still treating our situation quite frivolously, there is some tension among us. For instance, this afternoon in the wardroom we almost had a blow up. The tape recorder was playing and there were several differences of opinion as to which selection to play and how loud. Some not entirely humorous remarks regarding shoving books down people's throats, etc., were made but no trouble developed.

[Last week] after the movie we looked at some slides in the wardroom. A little disagreement with some card players ensued about turning off the lights, and two of the pilots nearly came to blows. [Another day] one exchange involved Hugo, and I'm afraid if anyone but he were being baited in such a manner, tempers might have flared. Hugo joked it off; I would have hated to ever see him lose his temper. He is quite pure minded and I had seen him leave the room on several occasions when discussions became too obscene for his taste. Consequently some of the people deliberately bring up such subjects just to watch his reaction.

5 Jan., Sat. We are still stuck.

6 Jan., Sun. Wet snow fell, which covered up a little of the oil, trash, and other filth that has been making the ice around us rather unsightly.

7 Jan., Mon. More snow flurries and temperatures between 25° and 31°F. The time has come when we might be forced to reconsider our plan to get to Cape Adams. We are down to 58% fuel and are burning over 1% a day just sitting. We civilians had a meeting and discussed the possibilities. Hugo and Ed decided to contact Ronne and McDonald and demand a voice in the decision. This might be ignored, but it is all we can do.

8 Jan., Tues. We moved about a mile and towards evening (2100)

32

Staten Island came alongside to give us some fuel. The wind changed to the south and the ice pressure eased. About 1800 the cloud cover blew over and we had sunshine. Around 2200 fog came up and with the sun shining presented a beautiful sight. Although *Staten Island* was just a few feet away, her rigging was nearly obscured, and the misty silhouette of her gun against the hummocky ice surface was striking.

Adélie penguin on pack ice about 25 feet thick in Weddell Sea. Note pressure ridges.

9 Jan, Wed. 0000 Z 77°38'S, 43°02'W. *Staten Island* tried to go ahead but was soon stuck. *Wyandot* moved about 200 ft. Ronne called Hugo [from *Staten Island*] about 1800 and asked him to discuss a new alternative with the scientists. Ronne suggested for our consideration(!) a minimum base at Gould Bay of 18 people or so. There would be no aircraft, and the traverse would have to be self-supporting.

One of the points mentioned in the discussion later with Ronne was the impossibility of any emergency rescue or mechanical aid to traverse people. Ronne said that anyone who felt that this was essential had better not go on the traverse and told of a 1200-mile sled trek he made with one other man.

This particular attitude of Ronne's persisted, with a few exceptions, throughout the next year. It reflected the "heroic" age of Antarctic exploration, and the IGY is generally considered to have

33

ushered in the "scientific" age. Ironically our traverse party became infected with this view, which by 1998 has, fortunately, largely disappeared from the U.S. Antarctic Program.

Hugo, Ed, and Clint had a talk with Ronne the next day, in which Ronne informed them in no uncertain terms that he was boss and that there had been too much discussion already.

10 Jan., Thurs. 0000 Z, 77°37'S, 43°19'W. The sun has been shining most of the day. It is still warm, around freezing. Dufek's sitrep today had the following statement in it:

ALL STATIONS EXCEPT THE WEDDELL SEA AND KNOX COAST MAKING EVERY EFFORT TO COMPLETE DEEP FREEZE II COMMITMENTS ON SCHEDULE.

Perhaps he didn't mean it as strong as it sounds.

11 Jan., Fri. 0000 Z, 77°37'S, 43°20'W. When I went up for breakfast I saw that during the night the ice had opened up and we were sitting in the middle of a polynya. We could see a lead ahead. We started out and were soon making 13 knots.

We had been beset for 11 days. From here west we proceeded into an area previously unexplored by ship, although Ronne made a flight parallel to our track from the west to Gould Bay on his 1946–48 private expedition. He reported a high-elevation area to the south, which he named Edith Ronne Land after his wife, who was also on that expedition.

We approached a 45-mile-long large iceberg that was blocking our path. There was some pack ice around it, but we started to traverse it on the north side. Just before noon on 11 January, a message was received from Dufek ordering us to stop and build the base at the nearest available site. McDonald replied that we were making about 13 knots in open water and expected to arrive at Cape Adams in 36 hours. He requested a reconsideration.

We eventually did build Ellsworth very close to where we were then, but we didn't give in that easily.

About 1700 someone noticed that we were taking water in #2 hold. This is the worst ice damage to the hull so far, as the ship lay to for repairs. In order to get the rupture above the waterline on the starboard side, the D-4 Caterpillar tractor, two LCVPs [landing craft vehicle/personnel], and a smaller boat were suspended out over the port side. This heeled the ship about 10°. A platform was rigged and the men were belayed as the damage was welded.

During the night some whales came around near the welders working down at water level. Everyone was excited; the executive officer ordered the men out and even had a rifleman posted. After a while the whales went away and the work was completed.

Staten Island came alongside and Captains McDonald and Ronne transferred back aboard. Bill Littlewood, Navy oceanographer on *Staten Island*, brought over a jar of bottom samples dredged from the place we've been stuck most of the year. Augie and Ed are making a pebble count, with Paul and me sitting in. One sample at 77°37'S, 43°15'W, had a lot of pebbles in it. Littlewood thought the material had been carried to this location by icebergs. Augie and Ed found mostly quartzite and ferromagnesium rocks, which seemed to indicate a shield origin [a very old crystalline part of a continent].

We knew very little about even the most basic part of the geology of this part of Antarctica in 1957.

In 1958–59 I returned with Bill Littlewood to the Weddell Sea on the icebreaker *Edisto,* a sister ship to the *Staten Island.* I flew in a helicopter to some small nunataks (hills or mountains surrounded by glacial ice) near the eastern edge of the Filchner Ice Shelf to make a gravity measurement and collect geologic samples. I named these the Littlewood Nunataks, after Bill. Recently published geologic interpretation of these samples suggests that this part of Antarctica was attached to North America about a billion years ago, long before the Gondwana continent was formed.

12 Jan., Sat. Another beautiful sunny day. Dufek gave permission to continue westward until blocked by ice, find a site, build the station, and get out. When we were finally under way about 0800 we soon ran out of open water and entered the pack again. We are about 30 miles north of the shelf on the west side of the berg.

Two very large icebergs about 30–45 miles long had blocked our passage. Probably these had, within the previous few years, broken off the Filchner Ice Shelf, which moves forward about 1.2 miles per year (2 km/yr) east of what is now known as Berkner Island. These bergs became grounded on what is now known as Berkner Bank. In 1986 three comparable icebergs calved off the

Filchner Ice Shelf, and in the mid-1990s, two bergs were aground on Berkner Bank, where we had encountered two bergs in 1957.

13 Jan., Sun. 0000 Z, 77°15'S, 45°28'W. All day long we continued through heavy floes. About 1000 another rupture in #2 hold was discovered. This one was a little larger than the last and was letting in 150 gallons per minute. Fortunately nothing was in that area but oil drums. I heard that the water is about 15–18 ft deep in there. About 2100 we finally broke into a lead miles wide and extending west as far as observable. All night long we steamed through open water.

14 Jan., Mon. 0000 Z, 77°28'S, 47°45'W. We proceeded along the Filchner [Ronne] Ice Shelf through open water and pack ice. Morale has improved quite a bit since we hit this open water. Radio traffic is low at present, so wintering-over people can send Class E messages [personal telegrams that we paid for]. The executive officer, Commander Williams, has been censoring them as to any definite information on damage, position, progress, etc.

The aggravating problem of censorship continued to bother us civilians throughout the coming year in any of our personal radio messages. There was no mail. Censorship by the NSF of electronic mail (e-mail) continued to infuriate scientific parties operating out of the U.S. base at McMurdo as recently as 1990. Then the NSF representative would have the e-mail printed out to check it for possible personal messages before it was released for transmission. However, by my latest trip in 1995, technology, the vast bulk of e-mail messages, and common sense had solved these problems. I was able to log into my computer in Denver from a terminal at McMurdo and send and receive messages directly.

15 Jan., Tues. 0000 Z, 76°12'S, 56°52'W. This morning by about 0800 we had reached a point about 42 miles short of Cape Adams and found our way blocked by ice. The barrier in the vicinity is about 120 ft high, which is about 90 ft too high for unloading. Hugo was really down in the mouth; so near and yet so far. McDonald even took a helicopter flight over to Cape Adams.

We discovered that we have damaged our screw further, and vibrations are affecting the reduction gear. They are having difficulties with the steering apparatus. The rupture on the port side was a 5-ft split that was taking water at 200 gallons each minute while we were going slowly or lying to. Our pumps are able to handle this while we are stopped, but at 10 knots the deep tank took in 450 tons of saltwater.

At 2219 the following message regarding our safety was received from Dufek:

YOU ARE NOT TO BE INFLUENCED BY ANYONE'S DE-SIRE TO BREAK A RECORD OR PLACE THE BASE ON LAND. THE SAFETY OF YOUR SHIPS AND MEN MUST BE UPPERMOST IN YOUR MIND AT ALL TIMES. ALSO THAT OF RESUPPLY NEXT YEAR. TIME IS RUNNING OUT.

GLACIER [A NEW, BIGGER ICEBREAKER THAN *STATEN ISLAND*] IS COMMITTED TO KNOX COAST LATE IN SEASON, AND DAMAGE TO *NORTHWIND* AND *ATKA* [WIND CLASS ICEBREAKERS LIKE *STATEN ISLAND*] HAVE REDUCED THE POWER OF EACH TO LESS THAN 70%. YOU ARE ON YOUR OWN.

MY COMMITMENT TO USNC-IGY WAS "OPERA-TIONALLY FEASIBLE." THERE WAS NO PROMISE TO PUT IT AT BOWMAN PENINSULA OR ANY OTHER SPE-CIFIC LOCATION.

And just to make certain we understood his point, he sent the following message at 2314:

YOU ARE DIRECTED TO SELECT A SUITABLE SITE EASILY ACCESSIBLE TO YOU NOW AND BUILD THE BASE.

16 Jan., Wed. We are lying to in open water attempting repair. The hole in port side deep tank of #2 hold has lengthened. It starts about four feet down and was a seven-foot-long crescent-shaped gash, which acts like a scoop while moving forward.

As of 1956, no ship had sunk in the Antarctic since Shackleton's *Endurance* in 1915, so we were not too worried. However, in the 1980s three ships sank in Antarctic seas, two from ice damage in the Ross Sea. We "scientists" should have been more concerned in 1957; I am certain that McDonald and our two ship captains were.

The following message about locating the station was sent to Dufek on 16 January:

ONLY INFLUENCED BY ADVANTAGES WHICH WOULD
ACCRUE BY LOCATING STATION ON LAND AT MAXI-
MUM DISTANCE FROM OTHER IGY STATIONS. INVES-
TIGATION BOWMAN PENINSULA AREA HAS SO FAR
REVEALED THAT CONSTRUCTION [OF] IGY STATION
THERE NOT FEASIBLE DUE LACK OF SUITABLE UN-
LOADING SITES.

AN OFFSHORE LEAD WAS EVENTUALLY DISCOV-
ERED BY WHICH SHIPS COULD HAVE REACHED
AREA. DID NOT WISH TO GIVE UP WITHOUT EXPLOR-
ING ALL POSSIBILITIES.

NOW WITH CLEAR CONSCIENCE WE ARE DI-
RECTING OUR SEARCH BACK TO THE EASTWARD
AND HOPE THAT WE SHALL FIND SOMETHING SUIT-
ABLE ON THE FLOATING SHELF. WIND DIRECTION
WILL STILL BE INFLUENCING SPEED OF SHIP MOVE-
MENTS. WE HAVE POSSIBLE SITE IN MIND NOW.
AREA AROUND GENERAL BELGRANO STATION IS
SATISFACTORY FOR SITE IF WE FIND SHELF LOCA-
TIONS NOT SUITABLE .

Later the following was sent from McDonald to Dufek about
damage to the *Staten Island*:

WHILE PROCEEDING BACK FROM ICEBREAKER, RE-
CON TO EASTWARD WITH *WYANDOT* PARKED IN 20-
MILE WIDE-OPEN WATER AREA NEAR SHELF. *STATEN
ISLAND* LOST ONE BLADE PORT PROP. ICE NO MORE
DIFFICULT THAN SOME ALREADY TRANSITED.
NORTHERLY WINDS HAVE TEMPORARILY CLOSED
PACK TO EASTWARD–*WYANDOT* HAS FOUND BOT-
TOM PORT RUDDER SET ABOUT SIX INCHES AT
TRAILING EDGE BENT.

TWO COURSES OF ACTION APPEAR OPEN NOW.
ONE TO ESTABLISH A SITE ON FIRST FAVORABLE
SHELF, UNLOADING PLATFORM IF ONE CAN BE
FOUND OR CONSTRUCTED; OFF-LOAD CARGO,
READY SHIPS FOR ICE TRANSIT, AND CONSTRUCT
REDUCED STATION. THEN GET OUT FIRST SOUTH-
ERLY WINDS–OTHER COURSE IS TO PROCEED EAST-
WARD DURING SOUTHERLY WIND PERIODS AND
REACH SITE EASTWARD [OF] GOULD BAY AREA, THEN

ESTABLISH STATION IF SUITABLE UNLOADING PLAT-
FORM CAN BE FOUND.

Early that evening *Staten Island* attempted to make a ramp
out of the barrier by firing at it with the five-inch gun. This did
not work, and is my only knowledge of a ship's gun ever being
fired in Antarctica. The next day, we received orders from Dufek
to keep the *Wyandot* and *Staten Island* together and to establish
the IGY station between Belgrano Station and the Greenwich
Meridian.

17 Jan., Thurs. We might be next to the Argentine Base General
Belgrano. Ronne told us that he didn't want us to have any social
intercourse with them.

Some repairs have been made on our hole in the hull at hold #2.
The water was pumped down to seven feet and a collision mat was
placed as a dam. We started underway about 1300 and soon ran out
of lead and into loose pack. A strong south wind came up, and
snow flurries hampered visibility. The pack became a little heavier
and we lay to. Temperatures dropped to 6°F.

Six degrees is quite cold for operations at sea in Antarctic summers with the types of ships we had. In February and early March
1984 on the *S. P. Lee* in the Ross Sea, at the same latitude, we never
encountered temperatures this low.

18 Jan., Fri. Overcast all day as we continued east. Ronne suggested
that we civilians wire Gould on *Curtiss* in the Ross Sea giving our
views on the matter and requesting he request Dufek to let us go
further.

Dr. Lawrence Gould was chairman on the U.S. National Committee for the International Geophysical Year (USNC-IGY). He
was the grand old man of Antarctic geology. He died in 1995 at
98. Gould went to Antarctica with Admiral Byrd in 1928. He led
geologic field parties from Little America II at that time and did
much pioneering geologic mapping. Ronne named Gould Bay
after him on Ronne's 1946 expedition. Gould went on to a prominent scientific career, later becoming president of Carleton College in Minnesota.

At the Antarctic orientation in September 1956, at Davisville, Rhode Island, Gould spoke to all of us heading for Antarctica. I well recall his closing remark, "Remember, if you fall into a crevasse, you'll be in a hell of a lot better shape in 500 years than any of the rest of us!"

McDonald sent the following message from Ronne to Gould. Just before sending it out (to CTF 43), Ronne asked Hugo and Ed to okay it for the scientists.

CAPTAIN RONNE . . . PROPOSES THE FOLLOWING PLAN TO WHICH I CONCUR:

A. REDUCE CB WINTERING PERSONNEL TO 13 KEY MEN.

B. REDUCE AIR UNIT WINTERING PERSONNEL TO ONE PILOT AND TWO MECHANICS.

C. STORE ALL EQUIPMENT AND CARGO NOW ABOARD SHIP AT SITE.

DUE TO CIRCUMSTANCES, SIZE OF ELLSWORTH STATION MUST BE REDUCED. ONLY LIMITED NUMBER OF BUILDINGS ADEQUATELY EQUIPPED. MAXIMUM EXTENT STATION INSTALLATION POSSIBLE BEFORE SHIPS MUST DEPART THIS AREA ABOUT 15 FEB.

A WORKABLE PLAN POSSIBLE WITH NO CURTAILMENT OF IGY SCHEDULED PROGRAM DEPENDING ON LOCATION OF STATION IN LINE WITH YOUR LATEST DIRECTIVE. IF NEAR CAPE NORWEGIA, UNSUITABLE TO TRAVERSE GROUP BECAUSE OF EARLIER WORK BY NOR-SWED-BRIT EXPEDITION. IONOSPHERE PHYSICS PROGRAM WOULD NOT BE JUSTIFIED IN VIEW OF IDENTICAL BRITISH PROGRAM AT HALLEY BAY. FOUR STATIONS WITH METEOROLOGICAL PROGRAM ALREADY EXIST EAST OF BELGRANO BASE.

CDR STEVENS OF CB BELIEVES HE CAN SUPPLY MOST REQUIREMENTS FOR REDUCED WINTERING PERSONNEL. TRAVERSE PARTY CAN FURNISH ITS OWN LOGISTIC SUPPORT AND ONE OTTER AIRPLANE ONLY READIED.

LIMITED RANGE OF OTTER AND INABILITY CARRY WORTHWHILE PAYLOAD EVEN TO AUTHORIZED DISTANCE OF 250 MILES MAKES THIS UNIT OF

NEGLIGIBLE VALUE TO IGY PROGRAM. SCIENTIFIC PERSONNEL, SEABEES, VX-6 UNIT CONCUR IN ABOVE PROPOSAL. BELIEVE GOULD BAY AREA WILL MEET ALL IGY REQUIREMENTS IF ICE CONDITIONS PERMIT ENTRY THERE.

That night, Dufek responded to Captain McDonald:

YOU HAVE PLENTY OF TIME TO BUILD THAT BASE SO TAKE IT EASY. I DEPARTED ATKA BAY LAST SPRING IN *GLACIER* ON 31 MARCH. BEST REGARDS. RADM DUFEK

It was pretty cold, and froze all the sea surface. We proceeded as far as the large icebergs west of Gould Bay when we were stopped. We passed a low area in the shelf that looked like a feasible site, but McDonald has his orders and can't put a base in anywhere along here. The farther east we go the tougher the traverse becomes.

In 1981 the Germans tried to establish von Neumeyer Station in this area but were forced to abandon the effort because of heavy ice and the difficulty of resupply. Instead, that station was built near Cape Norvegia near the Norwegian-British-Swedish 1951–53 station. Germany built a summer station, Filchner Station, near Gould Bay.

19 Jan., Sat. 77°17'S, 45°10'W. The first thing of note today was the following message from Dufek [regarding the reduced station]:

NEGATIVE. SELECT SUITABLE SITE AND BUILD THAT BASE AS PLANNED. GOULD BAY ACCEPTABLE IF SUITABLE. YOU DON'T HAVE TO LEAVE BY 15 FEBRUARY. I WILL TELL YOU WHEN TO LEAVE.[4]

All day we have been negotiating a passage among icebergs. We saw some of the most spectacular scenery down here yet. One berg did not resemble the usual flat-topped tabular ones, but towered many hundreds of feet above us and had many sharp and jagged-looking peaks on it. Through binoculars and telescope I could observe the countless icicles that covered the sides of these floating piles of ice. There are many tension cracks visible. I don't see how forms such as these with large unstable looking blocks on top could develop. There were dirt bands near the base dipping towards the

41

south. These could have been caused by tides but if so the berg must have tipped somehow as the lines were not horizontal. [This iceberg was grounded.]

Staten Island was engaged in some of the toughest icebreaking I've seen so far. She would back off a few ship lengths and then charge forward riding high up on the ice, her bow far in the air. Sometimes this weight would crack the ice beneath, but more often she would have to back off very painfully and start over. Eventually this course was given up and we headed off in a different direction. *Wyandot* managed not to have too much ice contact since the big rip, but we still aren't around those huge bergs that we circumnavigated last week.

20 Jan., Sun. 77°29'S, 45°00'W. Another grey day. We managed to get round that large berg during the night and lay to in a polynya most of the day. The wind was from the north. Ronne transferred back to *Staten Island* and he and McDonald took a flight in to look for a base site. They have found what looks to be an "excellent" one. Unfortunately there were 33 miles of ice between us and it. We tried to move towards evening but eventually gave it up.

I realize now that Captain Gambacorta had probably been having some sleepless nights with worry about his ship sinking beneath his feet, and the responsibility for the safety of the 450 of us onboard. He sent the following message from *Wyandot* to McDonald on *Staten Island*:

REGARDLESS OF BASE SITE BEING AS FAR WEST AS POSSIBLE, WHICH I REALIZE, RECOMMEND THAT THE PRIMARY CONSIDERATION NOW IS SAFETY THIS VESSEL TO GET TO BASE SITE AND TO GET OUT WITHOUT BEING SUBMITTED TO FURTHER HAZARDS WHICH WOULD INCREASE EXTENT OF DAMAGE.

The next day McDonald replied:

I CONCUR. AS YOU KNOW WE CAN'T GO ANY-WHERE UNTIL WE GET BETTER CONDITIONS, AND THE BEST ROUTE OUT SO FAR SEEMS TO GO RIGHT TO BASE SITE. ONCE THERE WE CAN GET YOU UN-LOADED, REPAIRED, AND OUT. THE BREAKER CAN

THEN COME BACK AND FINISH THE JOB. I AM TIRED
TOO OF BEATING AGAINST THIS ICE. BUT THIS IS
NOT A FINAL DECISION. LET'S WAIT AND SEE WHAT
DEVELOPS.

21 Jan., Mon. 0100 Z, 77°34'S. 44°34'W. Another overcast day, quite
cold. We made a little headway during the morning, and reached a
polynya about noon. It snowed off and on all afternoon. I observed
some of the biggest and most perfect snowflakes I've seen yet. We
went into a radio blackout today which was caused by a solar flare.

Frequent radio blackouts were expected at these high latitudes
in the coming year because the IGY was scheduled to coincide
with a solar maximum in the 11-year sunspot cycle. Throughout
the world scientists were preparing to make simultaneous observations of the magnetic field, aurora borealis and australis (northern
and southern lights), ionosphere, etc. In the Antarctic, we could
expect more magnetic storms and bad radio communications than
in lower latitudes.

22 Jan., Tues. 2300 Z, 77°35'S, 44°45'W. We made little progress
today. Winds are out of the south but the pack hasn't opened up.
We are stopped by the ice 15 miles from open water. Radio communication was re-established after the radio blackout.

Lassiter tried to fly in from Punta Arenas yesterday but was turned
back by bad weather. I'm not sure where Lassiter fits in to the plans
of TF 43. I don't believe that VX-6 has, or had until very recently,
any idea that Lassiter might be with us.

That was the end of a mission attempted by Lassiter in the
1956–57 season. Maj. James Lassiter (USAF), chief pilot on Ronne's
private expedition, probably didn't figure in Dufek's plans at all.
The Antarctican Society, in an obituary in March 1993, mentioned
that Lassiter had flown for the CIA. The Antarctic photographic
mission planned with Ronne in 1957 was a CIA operation, probably because mapping was not an IGY program due to the sensitivity of the claims issue. We were operating in an area that is claimed
by U.K., Chile, and Argentina.

23 Jan., Wed. 77°36'S, 44°36'W. This morning a message was received from Dufek ordering us to go to 20°E long. and build the

station. Hugo, Ed, and Jack conferred with Ronne over the radio and decided to send a message to Gould protesting this decision. In a meeting of all the civilians, a message was drafted to send to Ronne for Gould. The last time we did this the message was never sent; Ronne twisted it into a concurrence with his views.

There was a signal flasher on each wing of the bridge, and messages between the ships, when in sight of each other, were commonly sent in Morse code by blinking light. The signalman would open and close a shutter comprised of horizontal metal slats in front of a powerful light about 15 inches in diameter, using a lever on the side.

Our message was flashed to *Staten Island*. When Ronne received it, he apparently became upset, as he asked Lt. (jg) John Dorn (staff communicator and our roommate) to remove it from the file. John replied that he could only do this at the request of McDonald. The latter refused Ronne this favor.

Ed, Hugo, and Jack talked to Ronne again,. who then read them the message he had prepared for Gould, essentially using their arguments. They agreed, and the following was sent with information copies to Albert P. Crary, deputy chief scientist of the U.S. IGY, and Dufek:

WE ARE DIRECTED BY LATEST DISPATCH FROM RADM DUFEK TO ESTABLISH ELLSWORTH STATION BETWEEN 20 WEST AND GREENWICH. WE ARE NOW 20 MILES OFF EASTERN SHORE GOULD BAY MAKING HEADWAY TOWARDS CTG 43.7- [McDonald] SELECTED SITE WHICH MEETS ALL REQUIREMENTS OF IGY AND NAVY. . . .

IGY PERSONNEL ARE IN AGREEMENT WITH THE FOLLOWING, WHICH I SINCERELY CONCUR IN . . . THE ONLY SOLUTION TO JUSTIFY THE EFFORTS AND EXPENDITURES THIS YEAR'S WEDDELL SEA OPERATIONS.

STATION GOULD BAY WOULD BE MORE VALUABLE THAN AT DIRECTED LOCATION 800 MILES TO NORTH, WHERE SEISMOLOGY, GLACIOLOGY, AND TRAVERSE WOULD DUPLICATE WORK OF NORWEGIAN, BRITISH, SWEDISH MAUDHEIM GROUP; AURORA PROJECT WOULD BE IN LESS FAVORABLE AC-

TIVITY ZONE, AND GEOLOGY WOULD BE REPETI-
TIOUS. . . .

WE URGE YOU REQUEST RECONSIDERATION [OF]
RONNE PROPOSAL ON REDUCED STATION SHOULD
TIME EVER BE CONSIDERED LIMITING FACTOR, AND
SET UP ELLSWORTH STATION AT GOULD BAY WHERE
UNLOADING SHIP MOST FEASIBLE. TOO MUCH AT
STAKE NOT TO SUGGEST YOU URGE ADM DUFEK SE-
RIOUS RECONSIDER LATEST DIRECTIVE. WE HAVE
FULL CONFIDENCE IN THE JUDGEMENT OF CTG 43.7.
RONNE SENDS ON BEHALF OF IGY PERSONNEL.

Gambacorta apparently didn't like this because he sent the following message to McDonald:

DO NOT CONCUR. BELIEVE [DUFEK'S MESSAGE] WISE DE-
CISION TO BE ABLE TO GET SHIPS OUT. BELIEVE WE
MAY BE STUCK EAST GOULD BAY EVEN THOUGH
OPEN NOW. HARD GOING PAST THREE DAYS. EXPE-
RIENCE JAN 1–11 AND DAMAGES SUSTAINED THIS
VESSEL SO FAR SUBSTANTIATE ABOVE STATEMENT.
RECOMMEND WE WAIT AND SEE WHEN WE GET
EAST OF GOULD BAY.

The ship's people are getting quite worried about the damage suffered so far. Fred Walker (bosun) came in and told us that the pumps
couldn't handle another hole like that in #2 hold. They are busy all
the time keeping the water level down.

We made slow progress all day, making only about eight miles.

The message to Gould noted an information copy to Albert P.
Crary. He wintered over at Little America for the coming two years
and was acting chief scientist in Antarctica during the winter. He
was in charge of the United States Oversnow Traverse Program as
well as his other duties. Bert, as we knew him, led the Ross Ice
Shelf Traverse in 1957–58, the Victoria Land Traverse in 1958–59,
and the McMurdo–South Pole Traverse in 1960–61. Crary was a
geophysicist-glaciologist and as such was a scientific inspiration to
all of us traverse people.

Bert Crary was the first person to set foot at both the North and
South Poles. He survived crevasses, near plane crashes, and, most

harrowing, a fall into the Ross Sea from the 100-ft-high ice shelf at Little America in 1959.

24 Jan., Thurs. We only made 200 yards again today. Cold and overcast. *Staten Island* passed us from astern on the starboard side this morning and collided her stern into us ripping off our garbage chute and damaging the fence around her flight deck.

In the late evening fog generated and the temperature dropped to 12°F, covering everything with hoar frost.

All ships' garbage in those days, and the not-too-distant past, was dumped over the side, including *Staten Island*'s crashed helicopter. Now dumping of trash, other than sewage, is prohibited in the Antarctic Treaty area and elsewhere in the world by the International Dumping Convention. On my most recent Antarctic cruise in 1988–89, burnable waste was incinerated, and all other trash was shipped back for disposal on land outside of Antarctica.

25 Jan., Fri. Staten Island tried most of the day to break a path, and after supper we started moving slowly. It was cold all day only getting up to 19°F in the late evening. The open water is freezing over every night now, and today it didn't melt.

26 Jan., Sat. A message was received from Dufek ordering us to build the base at the nearest feasible site east of 41°W. By morning we had broken into a lead and after being held up for a while around noon, proceeded to four miles west of 41° west. Gould also sent a message concurring with this directive of Dufek. Apparently our message to Gould had some effect.

At 1700 a boat from *Staten Island* landed on the 20-ft-thick bay ice separating the open lead from the barrier which sloped gently down at this spot. A few miles inland from the ramp is an "excellent" base site. We have finally found a place to build Ellsworth on the floating Filchner Ice Shelf. We are located about 35 miles west of the Argentine General Belgrano Station and about 50 miles west of Shackleton on the east side of a small bay termed Bahia Chica on an Argentine chart, at 77°41'S, 41°10'W. The water is over 2400 ft deep here.

We were over what is now known as the Thiel Trough, west of the deepest part. No one was about to quibble with this location. However, all of the above searching and consideration of various locations were very significant to our planned traverse. The bathymetric soundings we had measured from Ellsworth west across the front of the Filchner (now Ronne) ice shelf to 42 miles from the base of the Antarctic Peninsula were the only data in this area for about two decades. By measuring the elevation of the front of the Ronne ice shelf we were also able to calculate the thickness of the floating ice at about 1000 ft (300 m).

As a result of our party's research and that of Dr. C. Lisignoli at the Argentine Belgrano Base, it was determined that this sloping ramp where we planned to off-load was the result of a high melt rate beneath the Filchner Ice Shelf, which I first reported in a paper in 1968. Because of this ramp, which extended across the entire Filchner Ice Shelf front (but not the Ronne Ice Shelf front west of Gould Bay; see Map 1), it was possible to unload ships. This is the reason Shackleton, Belgrano, and Ellsworth Stations were built so close together.

The station site is about two miles inland. At 2200 the first party from *Wyandot* went ashore. This consisted of Lieutenant Paules and two men. They were very lackadaisically roped up with 3/8 inch manila and carried a long probe and marker flags. If anyone had fallen into a crevasse, he would not have been held in this way by the rope. They flagged out a safe area extending to the bow.

27 Jan., Sun. The sun was out, and the men presented a very colorful picture in their bright yellow-and-green Byrd Cloth parkas and wind pants. The temperature was about 4°F, which is the coldest we have seen yet; this is the closest we have been to the continent. Six men went over to the base site and looked for a trail. They found a few crevasses. Five parties went ashore and commenced to dig pits for "dead men" [two 2-by-8-in. wood beams about 8 ft long] all lashed together and, when frozen in, used to anchor the ship.

One group silhouetted against the skyline looked exactly like grave diggers. Paules asked for volunteers to dig pits for dead men so Hugo, Don, Ed, and I went ashore and dug from 1900 to 2200. The snow was quite dry and we sank in about an inch. About three feet down it became quite consolidated and we had to use a mattock. The temperature was about 0°F, but I worked in just a sweater (long underwear of course).

Our limbo existence will now come to a crashing halt in the activity that I presume will follow in the ensuing days.

The date I first set foot on the Antarctic ice sheet is significant in another aspect, 10 years later (27 January 1967) my second son,

Marc, was born. I was not, however, in Antarctica on that day.

Notes

1. S. E. Morrison, *The European Discovery of North America: The Southern Voyages* (New York: Oxford University Press, 1957).
2. F. Ronne, *Antarctic Conquest: The Story of the Ronne Expedition, 1946–48* (New York: G. P. Putnam's Sons, 1949).
3. This was the first of six Christmases I have spent in Antarctica.
4. Thus ended the reduced station idea, which was very controversial and is not covered in detail here because of space.

3
Fall

For the next two weeks everything moved in a chaotic but deterministic way until the ship's departure on 10 February. In spite of all the plans for a systematic construction of Ellsworth Station by the Seabees taking 40 days, the *Wyandot* was completely unloaded of 11.2 million pounds of cargo, including 5000 drums of fuel, in 11 days. In three more days, Ellsworth Station was either 90% completed (Navy estimate) or 70% completed (Finn Ronne's estimate).

The cargo was hauled to the base site, which was two miles south of the ice front where the *Wyandot* was being unloaded. The scientists worked along with everyone else, first on ice watch and later on construction. Work at the station site comprised 12-hour shifts, which were also assigned to the ship's company as their repair and off-loading schedules permitted. During the next two weeks, temperatures ranged from 30° to –5°F.

On the morning of 28 January, Paul, Hugo, Ed, and I checked the unloading area for cracks and observed a large one at the end next to the ship, forward of the #3 hold. Hugo, Paul, Jim, and I went back about a half mile and probed into a number of crevasses covered over by about three to five feet of snow. One crevasse was right next to the road to the site.

On a floating glacier, such as the area of the Filchner Ice Shelf where we lived and worked, crevasses result from stresses due to spreading and thinning of ice 600–2000 ft thick. Crevasses are usually bridged by snow and are anywhere from a few inches to more than 50 ft wide. Some of the "bridges" collapse, so that the open crevasses are visible. Sagging snow bridges can sometimes be seen from the surface, but better from the air. However, dangerous crevasses may not be visible, even in the best lighting conditions, from the surface or the air.

Snow bridges are sometimes 10 or more feet thick and are safe to cross on foot or vehicle. Many others, however, are quite thin, from a few feet to a few inches, and are easily broken by a person on foot or a vehicle. Crevasses have steep sides that pinch together at a depth greater than you can see, and can be more than 100 ft deep. In 1961, I observed crevasses from the air on the East Antarctic Ice Sheet about 60 miles from the South Pole that appeared to be as much as 100 ft wide. These crevasses must have been several hundred feet deep, which would be the deepest ever reported anywhere. All of the crevasses I directly examined appeared "bottomless"; that is, I lost sight of the still vertical walls because of increasing darkness. Of course, collapsed bridges can sometimes be seen at depth in crevasses. On the oversnow traverse, sometimes we saw three or more such layers of collapsed bridges.

The crevasses we observed on the Filchner Ice Shelf were either long and linear (sometimes curving) or lens-shaped at the surface, only a few times longer than they were wide. Although crevasses can be extremely dangerous, they can also be quite beautiful. (Ed and I spent two months during the summer of 1956 working in a crevassed area on a temperate glacier in Alaska throughout the melt cycle, where we observed snow bridges open and waste away.)

The ice shelf surface at Ellsworth Station was about 130 ft above sea level. There was a sharp break in slope at the boundary between the ramp at the unloading site and the main ice shelf surface; this was marked by hummocks and crevasses that gave the appearance of hills from the ice front at the water's edge. The road from the ship to the station crossed this boundary, which was marked by red flags on crossed bamboo poles.

Except for Finn Ronne, who had made three previous Antarctic expeditions, the Navy personnel had at the time really very little experience in mountaineering, snow and ice techniques, and crevasse operations, which I found shocking. Among the civilian scientific group, Kim and I had extensive rock climbing and mountaineering experience; Ed and I acquired a lot of crevasse and snow experience on the Lemon Creek Glacier in Alaska; Hugo had spent quite some time in the Arctic and in Alaska; and Paul had worked on glaciers. But no one had ever worked with motor vehicles in crevassed areas.

We used a Studebaker Weasel to check for stuck vehicles and to probe for crevasses. The Weasel was a World War II–tracked amphibious vehicle that could theoretically float on water as well as operate on snow. It was about 12 ft long and, for Antarctic use, had an insulated cab. Weasels were fun to drive and could reach speeds of 20–30 mph on smooth snow. However, they were not very durable mechanically and broke through snow bridges more easily than the Sno-Cats.

A Weasel had the throttle and gear-shift controls in the usual places, and was steered by braking the right or left track with levers between the driver's knees. The engine was inside, to the right of the driver, and three passengers could squeeze uncomfortably in the backseat. The Weasels used at all the stations were equipped with "Angry 9" (AN/GRC 9) 7.5-watt radio transceivers mounted behind the driver. All the vehicles, including the Weasels, Sno-Cats, and tractors, were painted bright orange, and the Seabees had stenciled "Fubar Construction Company" on each Navy vehicle.[1]

I caught a ride out to the base site in a Weasel after ice watch the first day. The area at the construction site was as flat in all directions as I have ever seen anywhere. The crew was working on the first two Jamesway huts, an ingeniously useful structure, probably first used by the U.S. Army in the Korean War. At Ellsworth Station, 16 Jamesway huts were quickly set up for the construction crew to live in, and to serve as an emergency camp during the winter should a fire destroy the planned undersnow station. Fire was the greatest threat we would have to worry about during the winter.

The Jamesway hut can be quickly assembled and taken apart, and consists of wooden, hinged arches covered by four-feet-wide insulated fabric panels plus fabric ends equipped with wood doors and covered vestibules. There is a wooden floor, also of boxlike panels about six inches high. When warmed by a diesel fuel space-heater, the hut is quite comfortable.

Jamesway huts are still used in Antarctica in the 1990s for remote field camps and as supplemental summer housing at the South Pole. Because none have been manufactured since the 1950s, they are now carefully taken apart after each field season. There are still Jamesway huts at McMurdo but they are gradually being phased out. This lowly structure has kept many men and women in the U.S. program warm in Antarctica over the past 40 years and will be missed when they are no longer available, probably by 2000.

> *30 Jan., Wed.* This afternoon one of those hot-rod Weasel drivers rolled a sled full of men, and one man's leg was broken. Another man fell into a crevasse but caught himself by his elbows. Someone is going to get killed the way they do things around here!
>
> Paul, Hugo, and I made the Sno-Cats ready, and about 2200 they were hoisted out of the hold by the ship's crane. Paul and I drove them away and parked them.

Unlike the Weasels and D-4 and D-8 tractors, Sno-Cats have a steering wheel like an automobile. Because of the mass of the vehicle and the separately articulated forward and rear pairs of pontoons, hydraulic steering is essential.

> *31 Jan., Thurs.* Paul and I went out to gas up the Sno-Cats about 1030. We started them up and turned the heaters on. While we were pumping fuel into the first vehicle about 100 ft away, we noticed smoke coming out of the other Sno-Cat. I ran back and found that the gasoline heater had caught on fire. The inside was filled with smoke. I opened the back door and threw out burning cardboard. I beat out the flames on the wood floor and fiber wall but couldn't stop the main fire until Ed came up with an extinguisher. Two squirts of carbon tetrachloride did the job. Aside from smoking things up and scorching some paint, the only damage was the wiring on the heater and tubing to the defroster.
>
> Paul came up with the observation that we seem to have Sno-Cats to burn. Paul and I drove the unburned Sno-Cat up to the base for fuel. They handle somewhat sluggishly but take the rough terrain far more smoothly than a Weasel.
>
> We found another crack developing ahead of the ship. We've traced two crevasses crossing the road, which are causing slumping. Although we submit our findings, no one takes any notice. Perhaps nothing will happen. . . .
>
> *1 Feb., Fri.* [At 0300] while a D-4 Cat[erpillar] was scraping snow right at the edge of the shelf next to the ship, a section of shelf about 100 ft long and 20 ft wide broke away and fell into the water carrying the Cat with it. The D-4 was partly submerged but was kept from sinking into the 2400-ft-deep water by the chunk of ice. T. G.

Lowery, who was lowered from the ship in a bosun's chair, quickly attached a cable to the Cat, and it was hoisted out of the water. The driver, Roy Cheeks, had already scrambled out of the Cat, and Jack [the ice warden at the time] threw him a rope and with help quickly scrambled across the floating chunks and up the steep wall. The D-4 and Cheeks were safe.

Paul and I installed radios in the Sno-Cats. We have two Angry 9s with limited range.

In the era of vacuum tubes, these olive-green, heavy, "small" Army radios were about 2 ft high, 1.5 ft wide, and about 7 inches deep. They were strapped into a rack that bolted to the wall. We could listen to a small speaker, or as was normally the case because of vehicle noise, on a pair of headphones. The speaker was always on while the Sno-Cats and Weasels were being driven, and we could hear all the local traffic. After the ships left for the U.S. we traverse people were the only ones generally using radios in vehicles. A microphone on an elastic-coiled wire hung on a hook. On the traverse we used a long wire antenna and a key to send Morse code to try to communicate with Ellsworth Station, but between vehicles a whip antenna mounted on the roof worked well.

2 Feb., Sat. Since the shelf caved in, we stand our ice watches right at the loading site. Consequently, we didn't move around much and were quite cold. The chief petty officers who stand with us are on two-hour watches. They haven't much cold-weather gear and get quite chilled.

I do not think that the *Wyandot* crew were issued Antarctic clothing other than that required for outside shipboard work. Had the *Wyandot* sunk in the ice on its way in or out, as happened to three ships in the 1980s, the more than 200-man ship's company would have been in an imminently serious situation out on the ice floes. Of course, those with Antarctic clothing would have shared, but there was not nearly enough to supply everyone. In addition, there would have been little food and no tents, sleeping bags, or other survival gear. The only—and probably adequate—means of survival would have been to crowd everyone on the *Staten Island*.

The scientists were supplied with six Army duffel bags, each of mostly U.S. Army–issue clothing. I did not receive a field jacket with sleeves long enough for me, and so had to manage the entire year with an old Holubar windbreaker parka over sweaters and long undershirts. My heavy Army bear paw mittens (identical to those used in the U.S. Antarctic Program today) were also too small. I was issued an experimental pair of down mittens with Velcro tape fasteners, which were being used in mountaineering clothing in 1956. We were allowed to keep all this clothing, but the much higher-quality civilian clothing issued since the 1980s is now carefully checked in after return from Antarctica.

> I still haven't found it necessary to wear more than thermal boots, long underwear, one pair of cushion sole socks, GI field pants, sweater, Holubar windbreaker parka, and a balaclava helmet. In spite of the pretty colors of the Byrd Cloth [windproof clothing material] outfits that the Navy supplied everyone, they aren't very windproof as mountaineering garments go.

The Navy parkas were color coded. As I recall, orange was for Seabees, green for ship's company, red for aviators, sky blue for senior officers, and a drab blue-grey for scientists. After the ships departed, we all traded these parkas around, so eventually most of us civilians had one of each color.

> *3 Feb., Sun.* Kim, Jack, and I went out to the base and worked in the afternoon on the foundation to one of the barracks. The weather was warm (about 15°F) and I worked in just a sweater. We had a delicious roast beef dinner in the Jamesway mess hall.
>
> Good news! We civilians are through with ice watch. The ship is about 60% off-loaded. Walking around the base, I was amazed at the vast amount of materiel that has come off that ship. It has piled up over acres of "ground." There are streets laid out, and tractors are constantly moving things around. D-8s drag a train of three or four 10-ton sleds up from the ship. D-4s unload them and bring up the stuff when needed. In spite of various difficulties, building is proceeding a little ahead of schedule. The Clements huts [the permanent base buildings] are going up.

Ellsworth station and all of the other U.S. IGY stations consisted of Clements huts. These were constructed of prefabricated four-by-eight-foot insulated panels, about five inches thick, painted red on the outside, light blue-green on the inside, and held together by metal clips. The floors and ceilings/roofs were of the same type of panels. Each building rested on a steel beam foundation that in turn rested on wood pads four by eight inches placed directly on the leveled snow surface. The buildings were heated by diesel fuel furnaces called jet heaters, with fans forcing the hot air through ducts.

The buildings, food, and fuel caches at Ellsworth and the other undersnow stations at Little America, Byrd, and South Pole were connected by an elaborate system of tunnels. We built tunnels of two-by-four-inch wood frames covered over with burlap and chicken wire. Snow would then be packed around the frames. The original plans were for, at most, two years of operation, and these undersnow bases worked very well during that period. Byrd and South Pole, which operated in the same buildings for a number of additional years, were eventually crushed beneath the accumulating snow load, abandoned, then ultimately replaced.

4 Feb., Mon. Chief Fast, the chief Seabee mechanic, and one of his men drove over from camp to check the Sno-Cats. One nice thing about them is the fact that the engine was built inside the vehicle and can be worked on from inside.

We could not start the Sno-Cats in first gear and shift up to higher gears because the tracks were too tight. Chief Fast told us we should, therefore, start in the gear we intended to drive in. We almost never drove above third gear of the five available. Although very occasionally we drove up to about eight miles per hour, our usual speed was three to five miles per hour because of the rough sastrugi (windblown linear ridges) on the snow surface.

5–6 Feb., Tues.–Wed. We were rudely awakened during the middle of the morning [for] psychological exams by Clint Smith, the physician. I think the results may have been biased by hostile reaction.[2]

After supper, five of us drove out in a Sno-Cat to work. We helped construct the aircraft building. The science building, where we will live, was up and the rooms look luxurious. Everyone is anxious to move off this ship.

Ronne told us to spend more time working on the base. Ed and Hugo have been working on last-minute personal business and did not particularly want to work. Ronne himself just skis around and stays away from the base because "that's the Seabee commander's job."

Kim and I worked second shift on one of the aviation buildings. All but one of the buildings are up in rough form. Eighty-one percent of the cargo has been off-loaded. Both *Wyandot* and *Staten Island* are sending 70 and 50 men/day, respectively, to assist in construction. They are all willing and enthusiastic workers; the infirmary issues each a two-ounce brandy bottle after a 12-hour shift.

7 Feb., Thurs. It was clear and sunny at noon and I worked in only a sweater. By 1900 the temperature had started to drop, and the moisture in the air condensed in the form of microscopic ice crystals. Everything was seen through a golden haze. Eventually the sun was blocked out, and the phenomenon resembled a light fog. The temperature was 6°F at 2130.

Our scientific gear is being unloaded, and the ship was 88% empty at the end of the day. After midnight, we all helped Kim, who had found the panels of his geomagnetism hut, haul these over to the building site. We listened to Voice of America on the radio in the Sno-Cat as we drove back to the ship at 0200. We received Radio Moscow (in English) a few days previously.

9 Feb., Sat. Another sunny day. Ronne told us we have to move out to the base tomorrow. Paul and I went back after supper to pack.

10 Feb., Sun. I woke up early and went to the dentist on *Staten Island*. He pulled my last wisdom tooth as a precaution although I had no problem with it. After a final steak dinner aboard the *Wyandot* we loaded up the Sno-Cats and hauled all our stuff out to the barracks next to the science building, where we will live for the present. It is snowing and blowing hard. A low-pressure area is moving in, and all the ships' company panicked. Everyone was put on 24-hour-a-day construction.

The *Wyandot* left [from where it was unloading] about 2300 tonight. I managed to get a couple of notes written on *Staten Island*. They will leave at noon tomorrow. The men on *Wyandot* had an approved beer party on the "beach" [the unloading site]. The people at the base [Seabees] weren't invited but seemed to come up with beer that was shipped to the station. Things were so rushed that I found time to say goodbye to very few people.

11 Feb., Mon. Everyone was working all night, but some of the civilians spent this time writing letters, so I went to sleep for a while on a bunk in an unfinished building.

About noon the last of the Seabees took off. At 1400 McDonald commissioned Ellsworth in the name of the U.S. Navy and turned it over to Ronne as officer in charge [and also station scientific leader]. We all stood in line, and a flag pole was stuck in a little hole in the snow.

Thirty-nine of us thus officially started to "winter over" in Antarctica. There were 17 Seabees of Detachment Bravo plus Lt. Clint Smith, physician, their officer in charge. There was an 11-man VX-6 air group, the airdales, plus their officer in charge, Lt. Cmdr. Charles J. McCarthy, pilot. Then there were the nine of us IGY scientists, wondering whether we were at a scientific station or a Navy base. Opinions differed.

Chuck McCarthy was officially made executive officer and Ed, deputy station scientific leader. They, with Clint, the physician, had a meeting after a good roast pork dinner and assigned rooms. Paul and Hugo went to live in the glaciology-seismic laboratory next to the radio room; Augie and Jerry were assigned a double in a barracks. Two officers and three chief petty officers occupied the other rooms in the same building. Ed had a single in the science building; and Don and Jack, and Kim and I had the two doubles there, which was quite a lot of space.

There is a lot of work unfinished. Kim's aurora observation tower and the radio tracking dome for the weather balloons aren't complete. Much remains to be done before we are ready for a storm. McDonald stated that 90% of the base was completed, but I would question his definition of "completed." All the supplies were left outside, and much of the tunnel system is unfinished.

12 Feb., Tues. Breakfast was at 0700, work commencing at 0800. We worked all day (until 1800) moving scientific gear into tunnels. Cloudy with wind and snow flurries. No storm. *Wyandot* could have stayed. People are sore about that. Heat in most of the buildings now, including head. Transmitter not working yet. Tooth bothering me. Worked after supper until 2200 fixing up our room. Moved beds and mattresses in. Feel shot. Chuck McCarthy sprained ankle pretty bad two days ago. Is using my ice ax for a crutch. No flying.

13 Feb., Wed. Moved in lockers and built same; hauled boxes and did some electrical work in the galley. Partly cloudy. Bill Sumrall flew as far as Shackleton before weather closed in. Pork chops for lunch and steak for supper. Jack and I troubleshot an oil heater.

For several days, my writing was uncharacteristically terse. I recall my pulled wisdom tooth giving me trouble and remember one particularly long, annoying night when I could not sleep because of it. I was reading *War and Peace* at the time and read a lot that night. We were working very hard those days, entirely on camp work, and were naturally resentful that the Seabee construction team had been pulled out before the station was operating.

I am certain that the ships' captains and Captain McDonald were quite worried having their vessels so deep into the Weddell Sea pack ice this late in the season. The Deep Freeze II Cruise Book reported that the ships crossed the Antarctic Circle, heading north on 16 February, only five days after leaving Ellsworth. They pushed through the pack ice uneventfully but had some very heavy seas. Later we were told that the *Wyandot* took a 70° roll, which I still find hard to believe. The ships were covered with ice, which had to be laboriously chipped off to keep them from capsizing.

At the time, we couldn't have cared less about the ships and wanted to get on with our lives at Ellsworth, with our small, 39-man group in contrast to the 700 men on the *Wyandot* and *Staten Island*. We were sick of shipboard life, and we civilians were sick of the Navy. We soon realized, however, that the Navy was still very much with us.

14 Feb., Thurs. Jack and I spent the day wiring in the breakers and switches for the two auxiliary generators in the garage. Overcast all day. We have not been washing much because the only water available was what we melted ourselves. I didn't get any valentines.

15 Feb., Fri. In the morning I helped Kim move some panels for his geomagnetism building [which Ronne considered nonessential] out to the site for construction. Ronne bawled us out for this at noon—only work on the station itself is to be done.

We changed over to the new galley tonight. Enlisted men eat separately from officers and civilians. . . . We officers and scientists are now eating at a second sitting, the men eating first. Chief Spear told us not to "fraternize with the men." We were gentlemen, he said.

At Ellsworth Station our eating system was unique to the U.S. IGY stations. Officers ate in the galley at a separate time from the enlisted men (called "men") and were served at the table by whoever was assigned the duty as "mess cook" or dishwasher for the current two-week period. In contrast the "men" served themselves in a normal Navy chow line, cafeteria style, which was—and still is—standard at all of the other U.S. stations. This understandably caused a lot of resentment among the men. We nine scientific staff were considered officers, as we had been on the ship. This continued distinction between officers and men symbolized the difference between a Navy base and a U.S. scientific station.

This Navy separation of officers and men goes at least as far back in Antarctic history as the Scott expeditions at the beginning of the twentieth century. Even when Victor Campbell, an officer, and Raymond Priestley, a scientist, spent the winter of 1912 with four others in a survival cave of rock and snow on Inexpressible Island on the Ross Sea coast, they kept this segregation. Priestley was made an honorary Royal Navy officer and together with Campbell and the Navy physician, G. Murray Levick, kept separate with only a line on the floor, from the three enlisted men.

The next day, a snowstorm hit us, with winds around 20–30 knots and temperatures in the high 20°s. Everyone spent all afternoon moving boxes into tunnels. The wet snow stuck to our beards and my glasses. Most of us had started growing beards when we left Punta Arenas and the Navy first allowed beards onboard ship. Finn Ronne was one of the few at Ellsworth (Ed, Jack, Don, Al Spear, Ed Davis the cook, and Grob the baker, also) who did not grow a beard. Paul had come up with a definition that said you had to be able to hold a pencil in it before you could call it a real beard.

Later in my life I wore a beard for 13 years but cut it off when it became mostly grey, at age 52. Afterwards, several young women told me I looked 10 years younger, and except for one trip to Antarctica, I haven't grown it back! I can now understand why Ronne—then age 57—possibly didn't have a beard at Ellsworth.

16 Feb., Sat. The whole IGY crew worked out at the demolition dump [magazine], loading our explosives on two 10-ton sleds to prevent them from drifting over this winter. The weather was partly sunny and no wind. It was warm and very pleasant to work in.

[While on the *Wyandot*] the Navy became aware for the first time that we have gelatin dynamite. Reading the *Blasters Handbook* they were all excited about low-temperature storage and the fact that the dynamite should be turned every 30 days. I too have wondered about the extreme low temperatures it would be subjected to in the winter. The upshot was a message sent to Atlas Powder Company to ask about the turning.

To my knowledge, Atlas never responded. We and other IGY traverse parties used the explosives with no problems. However, during the 1960–61 season when the Navy at old Byrd Station realized that a few tons of the IGY nitroglycerin dynamite had gone through four winters of freezing and thawing in a pile a short distance away, they were quite concerned! As the old station was slowly collapsing beneath the weight of the accumulated snow, there was fear that an explosion could finish the job. The Navy refused to handle these explosives because they considered them unsafe.

I was leader of a three-person geophysical field party there using explosives, so we were requested to dig the 60-lb dynamite boxes out of the snow and load them on a 10-ton sled so they could be moved a much greater distance away. We did this, and as far as I know, the explosives are still there. The concern was that, because nitroglycerin separates out with freezing and thawing, it could become dangerously unstable.

Ed and I planned to use these explosives to send sound waves through the ice and rock to determine their structure. We may not have had a lot of Antarctic experience prior to this trip, but we had had several years' experience working with explosives in the U.S. and during the previous summer on the Lemon Creek Glacier in Alaska.

> We have 3000 lbs of Nitromon (ammonium nitrate) and 6000 lbs of Petrogel (60% nitroglycerin dynamite) and the Navy has about 20 tons of their stuff. Their MK 133 and 135 resemble the Army C-3 and C-4 we used in Alaska and will be a useful supplement for our work. We can use all we want. They have 0.5-lb TNT blocks, which are handy, and 15- and 40-lb shaped charges which might give us some interesting results.

Most of these Navy explosives were "plastic," that is, moldable, of the type used by many terrorists in the past few decades. In the 1950s there was a lot of military surplus food, equipment, and even explosives available for geophysical and other types of scientific research, partly because so much of the research had military funding.

Looking back, we had become not only quite familiar with these explosives, but even casual about their use. Everyone was more casual about using explosives in those days, and in the early 1960s the Navy was even quite willing to fly our explosives out to the field in Antarctica. Although Navy personnel did raise an eyebrow when we flew with both explosives and blasting caps in the same plane, the VX-6 pilots did allow us this. By 1991 geophysicists doing seismic work on the Ross Ice Shelf had a very difficult time getting the same squadron (now called VXE6) to fly explosives in Antarctica.

I had purchased a large selection of paperback books before I left the States and kept them in a makeshift bookcase we made from IGY general supplies. In addition, everyone else brought personal books, which we traded around, and the recreation hall was furnished with a good general library. We also had an excellent scientific and Antarctic library in the science building.

17 Feb., Sun. We continued moving boxes into the tunnels. Weather partly cloudy, quite warm. We had our first movie, *Magambo,* tonight. Grace Kelly still looks good to me. The Navy sent down 300 16-mm movies and projector, which are greatly appreciated. A movie is scheduled for every night in the galley.

A master-at-arms [a Navy policeman] escorts Captain Ronne from his room down to the galley in time for the evening movie as was done for Captain Gambacorta on *Wyandot.* Upon entering the galley, the master-at-arms shouts, "'tention on deck." We are all (including civilians) required to spring briskly (or slovenly) to attention while Ronne is escorted to his specially reserved chair like in the wardroom on *Wyandot.* Needless to say, this makes us "scientists" unhappy. However, Ed suggests we go along with it and other petty things that Ronne dishes out, and save our battles for major issues like the traverse route.

18 Feb., Mon. I strained my back yesterday, and it was quite sore and stiff this morning. Jack and Jerry also strained their backs the other day loading our explosives. The weather cleared, and the temperature dropped from 18°F in the morning to −1° after the movie. We had a colorful almost-sunset. Ed, Kim, Jack, and I worked on tunnel completion. We covered the skeleton with burlap and chicken wire. Snow will be added as weather dictates.

The weather did indeed dictate! As winter came on, the wind blew, the snow drifted up on and over the tunnel structures and covered them. Of course it also drifted through the burlap and into the tunnels and had to be dug out. The original plans called for snow to be bulldozed up against the sides of the tunnel structures, which would have prevented drifting in, but this was another of the many things that were not completed before our ships left.

> The other day Ronne asked Don to fix his jet heater. Don talked with him a lot and has changed from the civilian who hated Ronne most. He now thinks he is not so bad after all.

Although we all had varied relations with Finn Ronne throughout the year, those between Don and Ronne were the most interesting and bizarre.

> Chief [Chief Petty Officer, CPO] Spear has become a little dictator. He has been heard by several people to brag about his power. He is in charge of construction, maintenance, etc.; quite a responsible position.

Al Spear was the actual man in charge of the Seabees under Clint Smith as officer in charge (OINC). He and some of the civilians had clashed, he hadn't bothered me. In fact, I grew to respect Spear's abilities in many areas as the winter progressed.

> Ronne has a pinup girl on his wall, which is distasteful to Hugo. At supper last night, Ronne was kidding him about this and Hugo was quite embarrassed. Con [the helicopter pilot] and Don added to it, and I think Hugo would have left the table if Ronne hadn't been there. There was nothing vulgar by comparison to the [previous] attack [from the officers] on shipboard, but Hugo is too sensitive. He asks for it.

The Navy men had a very large number of fairly chaste (by 1970s–90s standards) pinups on their walls, whereas the scientists at Ellsworth in 1957 had few or none, Interestingly, the psychologists who interviewed us after the winter discovered that we scientists had a lot more headaches than the Navy personnel! Instead of pinup girls on his wall, one of the Navy men had many cutout ads of whiskey bottles. By the 1980s–90s, with many women in Antarctica, there were few or no pinups of naked women on walls at U.S. stations.

19 Feb., Tues. It dropped to –5°F last night and was clear and cold all day. We continued working on tunnels. There is something quite refreshing to me about pounding nails cleanly and solidly into good wood.

Of course a lot of the wood was green and frozen; when the nails bent in the frozen wood, it wasn't so much fun.

20 Feb., Wed. We nailed strips of lath over the burlap on the 500-ft tunnel out to the aircraft shops in the morning. Ronne gave everyone the afternoon off. About 1400 Ronne, Hugo, Paul, Jack, and I jumped in a Weasel and bounced [Ronne drove] down to the "beach" to look for killer whales. These have been seen frequently the past few days by the fellows working on the HO4S helicopter, which is still down there. The sun was shining, the lighting was good, cameras were ready, but no whales appeared.

Ronne instigated a number of contests such as broad jumping, hop, step, and jump, and standing broad jump. He beat most of us at most of them.

We first discovered Ronne's passion to win at games and contests of all kinds, even if he had to cheat. In the broad jumping contest, with Hugo, Paul, and me, he repeatedly kept claiming that we had "stepped across the line," when we hadn't and when he had easily beaten us anyway.

Ronne was in excellent physical shape and kept himself that way all winter. He was about 20 or 30 years older than the rest of us, and his physical prowess was a matter of pride. I have more of an understanding of this today than I did at the time.

21 Feb., Thurs. Ed and I talked to Ronne about our seismic work for this fall. We will try it in Bahia Chica on the fast ice [several-year-old sea ice attached to the ice shelf] south along the barrier for about 10 miles. Our equipment will have to be man-hauled on akios. I thought we were through with that last summer in Alaska!

Akios, now known as banana sleds, were still in common use in the U.S. Antarctic Program in 1995. The only difference between the present version and those used in the 1950s is a slight modification in the rope fasteners to lash cargo down. This very useful piece of equipment is made of white fiberglass and has a white canvas "skirt" to cover cargo.

> We are building narrow tunnels along the north sides of the administration building, barracks, and science building to provide a second exit as an emergency escape hatch. Hugo, Paul, and Jerry, with a few others, have been working on the uncompleted meteorologic tower. Hugo built an A-frame which was being used to haul the heavy equipment up the 20 ft or so off the ground.
>
> It is strange that Don, who on the ship gave the impression of being the biggest goof-off, has been one of the hardest working of the civilians, while Hugo, who always appeared the one most likely to work hard, likes to do things neatly and carefully and sometimes spends more effort than the job is worth.

Hugo Neuburg loved to engineer projects like the A-frame. Although this trait was occasionally a waste of time, it was crucial to our success in more than one instance. But with the meteorological tower, this wasn't the case. Eventually a lot of people just lifted the part-assembled panels of the outer shell up before the A-frame was completed.

> The men have to use the #2 head now, which is just across the tunnel from the science building, and we civilians have to walk about 100 ft past this to the end of the main tunnel to get to the #1 head. Ronne is getting his private head after all; they are hauling and installing the little wooden privy over from the Jamesway village.
>
> We have the most elaborate pit privy I have ever seen. Jet heaters keep the building—which also contains the laundry and [Walter] Cox's [the Navy's photographer] darkroom—quite warm, and one doesn't quite expect the blast of cold air that comes up from below. In the laundry are an automatic washer and a dryer, which makes clothes washing quite simple. Wash days are scheduled because of the limited water—three people each day. This gives each man a turn every two weeks, which isn't too bad. There are showers using melted snow and hot and cold running water.

Nowadays, at McMurdo, there are flush toilets using distilled water! The temperature in the snow beneath the "heads" was about −10°F, which resulted in the building up of "shit trees," as they were known, from the bottom of the snow pit about 10 ft down.

This phenomenon was experienced throughout Antarctica at stations built on snow, but to my knowledge has never been commented on, at least not in writing. At one of the other stations, the shit trees became a problem after sufficient time. This was dealt with using explosives, which created another problem!

At Ellsworth Station and the other U.S. IGY stations on the snow, trash was just dumped and allowed to drift over by blowing snow. Eventually these dumps and the old stations will also flow with the ice off Antarctica and out to sea. This was the fate of Ellsworth more than 10 years ago when it drifted and became part of an iceberg.

Formerly, at McMurdo, the main U.S. base (on land), the Navy hauled broken heavy equipment and other such trash out on the annual sea ice and let it sink in the spring breakup. Now, not only is this not done, but all of the trash in the old garbage dump has been put in cardboard containers or metal drums and shipped out of Antarctica. There are no more skuas (birds) around the McMurdo dump site because no food garbage is disposed of there.

In 1991 at McMurdo they still used paper cups and plates but were trying to cut down on garbage that required burning. Therefore, everyone was instructed not to take food out unless we could carry it in our hands. By 1995 paper cups and plates were mostly gone, and no incineration was done. Today, all nonbiodegradable garbage is shipped out of Antarctica. At Ellsworth, china dishes were used and washed.

22 Feb., Fri. Continued building tunnels. Quite cold, about 1°F at 1000–clear and sunny. It was down to –6°F by 2200. Ronne gave us some bolts of material from the supplies, Byrd Cloth, some alpaca stuff, and rubberized nylon.

Ronne remarked that he couldn't imagine what we could do with the roll of alpaca material. I, tongue in cheek, suggested that it would make nice carpeting for the tunnels. Ronne later commented to someone: "That Behrendt has the strangest ideas!"

I took an Angry 9 radio transceiver out of a Sno-Cat and have it set up on the wall by my bed. I listened, using a beam for an antenna, to Voice of America, BBC, CBC, Radio Moscow, and several German stations. Of course we get a lot of South American stations broadcasting in Spanish. It's interesting to listen to the news (particularly the present Israel-Egypt dispute) from the British, Russian, and U.S. points of view.

23 Feb., Sat. Ed, Kim, and I built the access to the aurora tower at the rear of the science building. This involved a lot of climbing around and pounding nails from flimsy supports about 20 ft above the "ground." The temperature was around 3°F. Holiday routine commenced at 1400, but we worked until we finished at 1730.

North side of Ellsworth Station shortly after completion. Buildings are separated from gunny cloth–covered storage "tunnels." Aurora tower with Plexiglas domes is immediately in front of science building. Sno-Cat at right.

The aurora tower was about 30 ft above the original snow surface at the height of the three small Plexiglas domes on top. It was supported by four strong aluminum poles at the corners strengthened by guy cables. A vertical shaft about eight feet square, made of plywood, allowed access from the tunnel behind the science building via an aluminum ladder. Kim learned the stunt of sliding down the ladder by holding the sides with mittened hands and feet. Several of us regular visitors to the tower acquired this technique as well.

24 Feb., Sun. No work, so I slept until 1000 today. Paul, Hugo, and I skied over to Bahia Chica, about half a mile west of the station, and out on the bay ice [several-year-old sea ice, also called fast ice] for about two miles. We found a good site for the seismic spread as far from the barrier as possible. There were a lot of pressure ridges and hummocks close to the barrier. We found a place where a nice slope is at about 15° from the ice shelf to the bay ice. Ronne came skiing up at this point and took us over to an area [of recently frozen ice] where seawater was seeping up, and warned us.

After we passed through a narrow band of rough ice, we found a smooth, flat, snow surface. We skied out to less than 100 ft from the water's edge where the soft new sea ice was three inches thick. The temperature was in the 20°s, and the sky was overcast. This made it difficult to see where one was going–it was almost a whiteout. We put in about eight miles.

A "whiteout" is a common optical phenomenon in Antarctica, resulting from an overcast sky over the featureless snow surface. This results in multiple reflection and scattering of the light so that no shadows or definition of the snow surface or horizon are visible. The air, however, is clear; there is no fog or falling snow, and distant people or vehicles are visible. An unidentified object can be quite confusing in appearance. For example, I once mistook a dark beer can on the snow about six feet in front of me for a building a half mile away.

Walking or driving over invisible sastrugi in a whiteout is quite confusing. When flying, or driving over the snow in crevassed areas, whiteouts are very dangerous. I once heard of flying in a whiteout compared to being inside a Ping-Pong ball.

Before coming to Antarctica, I had skied only once since high school. It was a cross-country, backpacking trip in the Porcupine Mountains of the Michigan Upper Peninsula in 1955, where I suffered the only serious frostbite of my life. I spent two weeks in a hospital, but fortunately didn't lose the first two toes from each foot, which I well might have done, for gangrene had set in. Needless to say, after that experience, I was always extremely careful in Antarctica.

25 Feb., Mon. Ed and I started setting up the seismic equipment in the glaciology-seismology lab. The day was clear and cold. Temperatures dropped from 0°F at noon to –27° by midnight.

The ham station [amateur radio] is set up. Chief [Kenneth] Kent, who is in charge, finally made his first ham contacts in the States. Paul phoned his girl in Los Angeles. Ronne has made a new law: No one goes in the communications rooms, including the ham room, except Kent and the two operators. No one else uses the ham equipment. We were told at the Davisville orientation that we could all participate in the ham program if we wanted to.

The procedure was to make a radio contact on the state-of-the-art, single–side band, 1000-watt transceiver, with a ham in the States. That operator would connect the radio using a "phone patch" to a telephone and place a collect call to a particular individual, who paid only U.S. domestic long-distance charges. These phone patches at the seven U.S. stations were purely a volunteer effort by the hams in the States. Many of these operators were eager to contact Antarctica, as this was the first year that U.S. ham stations in Antarctica were operating. Unfortunately, in addition to being a great morale boost when we got through to our families and loved ones, the ham station at Ellsworth caused a great deal of strife and discontent.

[A few weeks later . . .] Mac has been trying to get Grob a patch with his wife in Wausau for several days but she is never at home. This afternoon he tried and found she was at her mother's home, but someone there refused to accept the charge so the call wasn't put through. This shook Grob up a bit.

Probably the person who answered the call thought the charges were calculated directly from Antarctica.

Personal calls were not very private. Not only the radio operators at both ends heard the conversations, but anyone listening in ("reading the mail") on the ham frequencies did as well. During the IGY there was a lot of interest in Antarctica within the U.S., unlike today, so it was only human nature to listen in. One had to say "over" at the end of each transmission (as in, "I love you, over."), but we all craved these phone patches.[3]

No license was required to operate ham radios in Antarctica because we were not operating in the U.S. This non-national status of Antarctica was particularly curious in pre–Antarctic Treaty years but still basically continues to this day. There are many strange legal anomalies because of the U.S. status of "nonclaimant" in

Antarctica. For example, U.S. and state laws on drug possession, air traffic control, and, until 1993, the National Environmental Policy Act regarding the National Science Foundation program do not apply there. I imagine a good U.S. lawyer could get a civilian defendant off from a murder charge in Antarctica. But the claimant countries–Argentina, Australia, Chile, France, New Zealand, Norway, and the U.K.–each view their claimed areas of Antarctica as part of their sovereign territories, subject to their respective laws.

"Hamgrams" were short personal radio messages sent through ham operators and the Red Cross in the States to our friends and families. We could also receive answers in the same way. Because of poor radio communications and other reasons, these were relatively rare. Hamgrams were a very important morale-boosting factor during the winter and a major preoccupation of us all, along with phone patches.

When we civilians wished to send a hamgram, we were required to take it in to Ronne so he could read it and censor out anything he didn't like. Consequently, we didn't put any comments in about the growing problems we were having with him. Of course, we resented this censoring greatly, particularly considering that we had no way to mail or receive letters.

While preparing this book, I found one of my handwritten hamgrams with "OK, F.R." scrawled in Ronne's familiar initials at the bottom. As it was a personal message to a woman, I still resent this invasion of my privacy. Ronne must have had a slight guilty conscience about censoring all our hamgrams because he explained the necessity at least three times to various IGY people. Nonetheless, the procedure continued throughout the year. The Navy personnel were censored as well.

26–27 Feb., Tues.–Wed. Ed and I worked two days getting gear together for our seismic work.

The scientists are getting disturbed that we can't work on our own programs. Aside from Ed and me for the past two days, everyone is still on general work. The emergency stuff is done and while much work remains, I think it is time to think of the IGY program. Mac told Hugo that he considers this a Navy base with some IGY scientists here, too.

The Navy people just found out that they would not get the per diem allowance they had expected. This amounts to about $40 a month for the men and $150 month for the officers. This was quite a shock, as many had drawn these funds in advance and are now in the hole all this money. Five of the men drank two cases of beer, brooding over their troubles.[4]

28 Feb., Thurs. Ed and I drove a Weasel with the Arctic 10-man tent and other [nonseismic] gear down to the ramp. We dragged an akio, wearing man-haul harnesses west across the tidal crack separating the ice shelf from the bay ice, through hummocks for a little over a mile. It was clear and the sun was shining brightly, but it was quite cold. I almost frostbit my ear on the shady side, in spite of the fact

View from air looking south along Bahia Chica. Seismic refraction profile was measured for several miles near corniced edge along the 130-ft-elevation surface of the ice shelf. Tide crack separates fast ice to west (right) from Filchner Ice Shelf. Killer whales hunted along the tide crack.

that we were working hard enough that we were comfortable with parkas open and scarves off. Ed stepped into a crack between the sea ice and the several-year-old bay ice, hurting his chest when he fell. We set the tent up a few hundred yards in from this crack. We hurried back at 1240 and were almost late for chow.

The temperature dropped to –17°F. We have been having the sun dip beneath the horizon around midnight for a couple of weeks now. The Pole Station, where the sun still is above the horizon 24 hours/day, recorded –69°F yesterday. I imagine that they will go well below –100°F this winter.

E. Thiel man-hauling akio on fast ice in Bahia Chica.

The South Pole Station had been established entirely by air just a few weeks earlier. No one had set foot there until Dufek, with Lt. Cmdr. C. "Gus" Shinn, pilot, landed in a Navy R4D airplane on skis on 31 October 1956, since the Amundsen and Scott parties in 1911 and 1912, respectively. This was the first winter people had ever spent at the South Pole or anywhere else on the high Antarctic ice sheet, and no one knew how cold it might get.

At the South Pole Station, Dr. Paul Siple, station scientific leader at 48, was much senior, with many years of scientific experience to 24-year old Lt.(jg) Jack Tuck, the Navy officer in charge. Although Siple was originally concerned about the dual command, there were no problems because he was really in charge. I knew both Siple and Tuck only slightly but was impressed by both. Although I am sure they had their difficult times that first winter at the Pole, from everything I heard first- and secondhand from the men who wintered there, Siple was an inspiring leader and morale was high.

1 March, Fri. Ed, Hugo, Paul, Aug, Kim, and I all helped Don and Jack with their 68-ft antenna. We saw Marlon Brando in Shakespeare's *Julius Caesar* tonight. Most of the Navy people, including Ronne, walked out during the showing. It was the second time I've seen it.

2 March, Sat. Ed, Hugo, Paul, Aug, and I took a Weasel, all the seis-

71

mic gear, and several hundred pounds of explosives out this morning. The tidal crack was wider, and there was very thin ice at our crossing. Two akios were loaded to 500–600 pounds each. We crossed on snowshoes and, with a long line, dragged the sleds over. Aug and I took the instruments, and the rest took the second sled loaded with explosives, cables, etc. We really struggled and strained to drag our loads through the hummocks to our tent. We arrived exhausted about 1300 and cooked up some 5-in-1's.

Army 5-in-1 rations provided canned food for five men for one day in each 50-lb case. They were not particularly tasty. Interestingly, 5-in-1 rations each contained five packs of cigarettes.

About 1350 Ronne and Spear showed up, Ronne on skis. He came into the tent and accused us of loafing, "having a picnic." We had just about knocked ourselves out pulling the sleds out and were in no mood for talk like this. He said he had been on the hill where we parked the Weasels for an hour and we had been in the tent all that time. Aug and I argued with him and I guess I surprised everyone, including Ronne from what they said later, with the vehemence of my words.[5] This was the first such stand I've taken. Up to now I have not committed myself much in discussions. . . . Hugo, trying to ease the situation, said in his usual cheerful voice, "Have some lima beans, Finn."

Spear and Ronne took off after about 10–15 minutes. Ronne was sore mainly because he had come out to get blast pictures and we weren't ready to shoot. He is a very suspicious man and doesn't trust the integrity of anyone (particularly us). It is impossible to argue with him because he ignores anything you say if he doesn't have a good answer, and brings up another point. Finally, he just walks away in the middle of the discussion.

To really cap off a discouraging day, we found shortly thereafter that we had forgotten the connecting cables for the instruments. We laid out the 2300-ft spread of cables and geophones [miniature seismographs] and headed back to camp, which we reached about 1715. All five of us were quite discouraged at Ronne's attitude today, and I was the most angry I've been in the past couple of years. I worked up to it after Ronne had left. The cable omission could only be blamed on us (me specifically).

3 March, Sun. The weather started out sunny and clear but clouded up about 1000. When we arrived down at the tidal crack we found it was too wide to cross safely, so Aug and I went back for an aluminum ladder which we used as a bridge. Suddenly, Aug, who was bending over with his back to the crack doing something, heard a loud splash right behind him. He turned and saw the snout of a killer whale (orca) sticking up about 6 ft into the air not 30 ft from him. It gave him quite a start. Three killer whales were working their way along the crack and came up breaking through the ice not more than 20 ft from our bridge. We took pictures and watched them for a few minutes until they passed on. No one wanted to be the first across the bridge with these hungry animals swimming around beneath. I understand that one way these animals hunt is to smash through the ice and dump their prey into the water.

This was more dangerous than we realized at the time. We were really on thin ice–literally, only a few inches of weak salt-filled "new ice" near the edge of the tidal crack–and to a killer whale beneath, we probably looked in silhouette about the same as a penguin.

We finally reached the tent about 1300 with another sled of explosives. Paul and Augie dug down seven feet through snow and then

Killer whales (orcas), which became a hazard to seismologists, crossing tide crack in which they are swimming (Photo by N. Aughenbaugh).

drilled down another six feet through ice. They loaded the hole with 25 lbs of explosives, and we prepared to fire. The wind or something was making much "noise" on our instruments. We decided to shoot anyway, but the charge misfired. We tried again with no result. By this time it was 1900. . . . We didn't get back until after 2000, so we missed chow.

Ronne insinuated that we were all loafing out there; he bawled Ed out for not being out of camp by 0800. Everyone else was on a holiday routine because it was Sunday. Ed told him that at present we could get along with four men. A few minutes later Ronne came into the galley where Augie and I were raiding the icebox. He told Aug that Dr. Thiel said he didn't need him out there and that he would stay in camp and work on wiring tomorrow. All the rest of the IGY people are on their own programs now. Aug told him that his contract said he was an "assistant seismologist" and that he wasn't hired as a common laborer. Ronne told him that he didn't like his attitude and that he didn't cooperate like the rest of the group. This made Aug (and me) really angry, and he made a few bitter remarks. He asked Ronne when he could fly over to Shackleton to talk to their geologist about the local geology (Hugo had flown to Shackleton earlier today to discuss the Sno-Cats). Ronne said he could tell him all about the geology. Augie said he wanted to hear it from a geologist. About this point I walked out.

Aug is in a bad position because he really doesn't have a project of his own, so Ronne wants to make him a general flunky. Despite his contract, Ronne thinks he is a geologist; and since there is no surface geology here he has no scientific work to do. Actually, he was hired to work as part of the traverse team on glaciology, seismology, and any geology that happened to be available.

Neither geology nor mapping was part of the IGY Antarctic program because of the political sensitivity and possible claims issue. Actually a number of the glaciologists in the various national expeditions had geologic training, and the geophysicists, like Ed and me, had done our previous work primarily on geologic problems.

It was down to −18°F tonight and −72°F at the Pole; their diesel fuel is freezing.

4 March, Mon. Ed, Paul, Aug, and I worked on the bay ice while Hugo started his glaciology work.

This was one of the frequent, clever compromises that Ed worked throughout the winter to deflect Ronne. We really only needed four people and because Ronne wouldn't push Hugo around at this time, he could work on his program without Ronne objecting.

It was sunny, −14°F, with a 30-knot southeast wind when we arrived at the tidal crack. Snow was blowing, the surface was hard and free of loose snow. It was bitterly cold. We saw the killer whales in the crack at a greater distance than yesterday. The crack was too wide to bridge safely with the ladder so we returned to camp for a plywood rowboat and some warmer clothes. About 1100 we made it across using the boat; the weather had clouded up but the wind was still blowing. We had our Coleman stove roaring away but still couldn't get the tent very warm. The instruments and batteries were so cold that everything soon became covered with ice due to condensation from the water vapor put out from the stove. Even the galvanometers in the camera were covered with frost. I put four hand warmers inside the oscillograph camera, which warmed things up.

We shot two charges of military explosives next to the tent, but the records were unreadable due to electrical noise. Because of extreme condensation we cannot operate the seismic equipment successfully under these conditions. We walked back to the crack and found that the wind had changed and blown the bay ice in.

5 March, Tues. Paul, Ed, Augie, and I went out to get the seismic equipment on the ice. The crack was wider than we had seen it yet, and we were glad we had the boat. The temperature was in the 20°s with a low overcast. Visibility was poor and became very bad around noon.

We loaded the instruments on one akio, and the four of us pulled it back. We heard some whales blowing in the open sea [the winds had carried the new ice out] a few hundred yards to the west. We went over and saw two whales bigger than killer whales, perhaps minkes, with a more curved dorsal fin and at least 40 ft long. They seemed to be after a couple of emperor penguins. They apparently caught them, because as we started hauling we heard the most loud and terrified squawking voices. Soon they stopped.

I now question whether the whales that we saw hunted penguins for food.

We hauled one load to the crack by noon, and in the afternoon dragged the rest over in two more trips. Again the wind had shifted [to the southwest] and the crack was now narrow enough that we could get across with the ladder.

In my journal I wrote that the wind that closed the crack was from the southwest. However, wind from that direction would not have closed the crack. Most likely it was tidal currents, which changed direction four times a day, that were opening and closing the tidal crack. Although the bay ice and ice shelf were both floating, the approximately 100-times-greater thickness of the ice shelf would have meant a tidal current along this boundary.

> We took a 600-ft-long, one-inch-diameter rope and tied up three akios, the boat, and ladder in a single file with the other end attached to the Weasel up the slope. Although the rope broke halfway up the hill, we eventually managed to take them up in two trips from this point. We walked in to chow about 1830.

Life wasn't all work and strife. Don and Jack had two state-of-the-art Ampex tape recorders, very high-fi, which cost about $600 each—big money in 1956—and a good speaker. Don put the opera *La Boheme* on tape, and we sat around listening. We didn't have anything in the line of soft drinks in camp, but Don swiped us a case of tomato juice. Kim and I sat on the freshly tiled deck listening to music and drinking tomato juice; a very pleasant evening. We heard *La Boheme* many, many times during the next eight months, and I really grew to love the music—fortunately. I became intimately acquainted with the plot and still go to see a performance whenever there is one in Denver or Central City.

> Ronne gave Ed a sketch map of his proposed traverse route. He has it planned for 65 field days with a start by working over to Shackleton, following the route of the Transantarctic Expedition. Then we would head west into Edith Ronne land and finally cut northeast back to near Gould Bay. He thought we could not get far inland because of heavy crevassing.
>
> This plan is not too satisfactory, and some of the people don't like it. I think that it may not be too bad. If we can use the British road to get a jump off farther inland, we should take advantage of this. I think we should go farther west and let our relief fly out and work back. This would extend the traverse time by perhaps another 60 days.

I find Ronne's proposal interesting now, because we all apparently forgot about it in the arguments about the traverse route later that winter and the following spring. At those times, Ronne appeared to not want us to traverse southwest, and we argued for this direction.

6 March, Wed. Ed and I spent [four] days installing the equipment in a Sno-Cat. We will really have a roomy lab to work in. There will be about 1000 lbs of stuff with just the seismic gear, batteries, gravity meter. The maximum load specified for the vehicle is 1500 lbs.

Ronne called Hugo, Ed, and Jack into his room after chow. He wants all the scientists to go back on camp work. Ronne wants Hugo and Paul to move into the science building.

After the movie the nine of us had a meeting in the ionosphere lab, which occupies the end of the science building closest to the main tunnel. We decided that we would not go back on camp work because our programs were too far behind already. As a group he can't force us to, nor can he send in a bad report about all the IGY people. Hugo and Paul will stay. The space they are living in is part of the seismic-glaciology lab. At worst we will make the room back into a lab, if they are forced out. I've decided there is no future in letting Ronne get me angry. I will try to ignore his pettier actions.

Fortunately Carl Eklund saved our science. Dr. Carl R. Eklund, biologist, was the station scientific leader at Wilkes Station. He was well liked and respected by the IGY and general scientific community. During the U.S. Antarctic Service Expedition (1939–41) Eklund wintered over at East Base with Finn Ronne. During that expedition the two made a significant dog-sled journey south along George VI Sound and showed that Alexander I Island is separated from the Antarctic Peninsula.

7 March, Thurs. Ronne called Ed in this morning and showed him a science sitrep Eklund sent out from Wilkes Station. They are really doing work there. Glaciology is especially far ahead. They obviously have been working full time on their programs since they landed (later even than us).

Ronne is sending out a sitrep and wants to say as much as possible about our work, but since we have been off camp work only a week, he can't say much. At any rate we are working on our own programs today with Ronne's agreement. I think Eklund's report influenced this. Everything is competitive with Ronne; he has told Ed that he wants us to produce the most scientific work of any station.

Paul and Hugo are still in their room, but Spear took their door off this morning. Hugo and Paul met Ronne in the tunnel and Hugo asked him in so many words why he [Ronne] could have a door when they could not. Ronne blew up and swore at them. Hugo's image of Ronne is now completely shattered. He now thinks that "Ronne is a psychopath."

The scientists and enlisted men had green curtains covering their doorways, but the officers all had wood doors. At McMurdo today, all of the doors to personal rooms, with the exception of some dormitory bunk rooms, have locks.

Don had a son 27 February but only found out yesterday, so there was a little party in the iono lab. Cigars, beer, and *La Boheme;* Mimi died.

8 March, Fri. Hugo broke out the maps of the known coastal area along the Weddell Sea, and now we have some wall decorations. Jack has been playing three- and four-part music with his recorder by using two tape recorders. It sounds pretty good.

9 March, Sat. It was Mac's birthday, and Grob baked a cake for him and all the birthdays in February and March. This was served at the movie. Afterwards a number of the men including Mac and Con came over and continued the party. Mac left early. About 2330 I went to bed. After that things became pretty rowdy. Don, Jack, and Kim were full of party spirits. At one point . . . Con, Don, and others led the group over to sing "Rock-a-Bye Baby" to Hugo. Greaney mustered everyone in the tunnel and marched them counting cadence over to Hugo's. Apparently Ronne heard them.

10 March, Sun. Ronne is perturbed about the party Saturday night. We had a session with him after noon chow at which he laid down the law. No fraternization with enlisted men. No visiting their quarters or they ours. Curfew at 2300; no one in the tunnels after that except while working. Men muster at 0700. IGY muster at 0745. No drinking with the men. The men are being held responsible under the Uniform Code of Military Justice, and he threatened us with stopping our salaries. Aug was quite upset and argued violently with Ronne. Ronne put up a memo in the chow hall on the new regime with a list of everyone's name to initial.

The next day, he told Ed that the IGY people had better sign. Only Hugo had done so. Most of us hadn't yet, but I imagined we would be doing so soon.

Liquor has always been a problem to some in Antarctica. Ronne would have preferred not to have any at all at Ellsworth, but the

Navy had sent an abundant supply. At other stations, people were allowed to buy a certain ration, as in the U.S. Antarctic Program today, and drink it at their discretion. Ronne, however, did not allow any alcohol except beer to be freely available, because he thought people would just get drunk. From time to time he would authorize a party with plenty of liquor, and many *would* get drunk, which just proved Ronne's point. He would then get upset and stop all alcohol. After a few weeks the cycle would start again, and we had some very rowdy parties.

There were one or two men who quietly drank too much, who somehow managed to obtain an adequate supply to support their habit.

> *11–15 March, Mon.–Fri.* Ed and I are having difficulties with electronic noise in the seismic equipment that we can't get rid of. We moved some of our seismic gear into Jack's lab so we could use his oscilloscope. It is discouraging not being able to get this trouble licked, but at least we are learning a little about the circuits.

We worked on the noise difficulty all week. By Friday, we had narrowed the problem down to a power supply unit called a dynamotor.

Jack and Don were the best electronic experts we had, but they were busy with their own work with the C-4 ionosounder. This instrument would generate the signal, which measured the height of layers in the ionosphere from reflections of a sweep of radio frequencies. The six-by-three-by-three prism of vacuum tubes and wires was shipped untested, with no circuit diagrams. When Jack and Don first set it up, not surprisingly, it did not work. They painstakingly and laboriously traced and diagrammed the circuits and made the ionosounder operational.

> Con and Sumrall are being moved out of barracks #1 and into their own addition to the administration building, which was just built. This will keep them from being contaminated by enlisted men.

Con Jaburg and Willie Sumrall's door opened to the outside, so really they had their own separate building, about 12 by 16 ft. However, this put all of the five officers under the same roof.

I washed my clothes, including, for the first time, my field trousers I had worn every day since the ship landed in January. I was issued only two pairs of these Army "many pocket" field trousers for the entire year. I kept one new pair in reserve and wore the other for all outside work, with long underwear beneath. Eventually these became so worn that I no longer dared to wash them; they just became more dirty, greasy, and tattered through the winter.

> Ronne called Kim, Ed, and Jack in. He wants a library-conference room in the science building which will take up Kim's lab. Kim argued with Ronne, who told him off. According to Ronne, "Kim was sarcastic, overpaid, too young, no experience, and little training." Kim almost lost his temper and was then forced to apologize, which drew more vituperation from Ronne. Kim was completely demoralized. Ronne referred to Kim as having "a mature beard on an immature face." Actually Kim has appeared to me to be one of the most conscientious of our group. He has several of his own projects in addition to the specified one and has been working very hard trying to get set up before dark.
>
> I received a Class E telegram from the folks, a most welcome morale booster.
>
> Five people from Shackleton flew over for supper Thursday. They were Dr. Vivian "Bunny" Fuchs, Goeffery Pratt, seismologist, David Pratt (no relation), an engineer who modified their Sno-Cats, George Lowe, a New Zealand mountaineer (who was on the Everest Expedition) and John Lewis, pilot. Fuchs first met Ronne at Marguerite Bay in 1948, at East Base, which Ronne used for his private expedition.

Dr. Vivian Fuchs, geologist, was the leader of the Commonwealth Transantarctic Expedition (TAE). Their group had established Shackleton Station about 50 miles east of Ellsworth on the Filchner Ice Shelf a year earlier. Fuchs became director of the British Antarctic Survey. He was later knighted for leading the TAE.

> It was very interesting to talk to them and we all wished we could have had more than an hour to chat. Fuchs told Ed about flat-lying strata with coal seams, which he tentatively identified as Jurassic in age from plant fossils.

Geologists now know that these mountains are part of the Transantarctic Mountains, which show similar rock layers extending across the continent from the Ross Sea area to Africa, which broke away from this part of Antarctica about 175 million years ago.

> The Shackleton people have two men out 25 miles from their depot whom they left with 9 days' food 10 days ago. Due to bad weather they haven't been able to get back. They will try to get in tomorrow and have asked us to support them. The Brits all wore different gear and bright-colored caps and sweaters which contrasted pleasantly with our olive drab appearance.

From the 1960s through the 1990s, the official clothing issued in the U.S. Antarctic Program has included bright red parkas and red wool lumberjack shirts. Nowadays people bring their own various colored clothing as well, which all makes for a more "normal" appearance than our military olive drab.

> We had steak, and Dave Pratt asked if we always ate this well. When we said yes, he told us that other than a little frozen mutton, they were living on canned and dehydrated food entirely.
>
> The British have a much more experienced group in Antarctic living than we do. One fellow has spent four years in the Arctic and two in Antarctica. They are using an Otter aircraft like ours but are allowing a much greater range than the 250 miles VX-6 is restricted to. They have no search-and-rescue facilities if this plane goes down beyond the range of their small Auster plane.[6]
>
> Kim has a plan for using parallactic photography for aurora height determination, for which he needs the help of the people at Shackleton Station. Kim and Ronne presented this plan to the British, which they agreed to help with. Kim gave them the necessary material.
>
> *16 March, Sat.* Ed and Hugo are accompanying Ronne on a flight into the area we may traverse to look at the terrain. This is the first long flight.

This flight was a significant exploration.

> Ed, Hugo, Ronne, Mac, and Willie Sumrall left in the Otter about 1145 and flew at 160 until 1440 at 70 knots. They reversed course and returned to camp at 1630. What they saw didn't look too encouraging. There is a large crack about a mile wide and 250 ft deep that runs east-west for many miles about 25 miles south of here.

Later, this crack, or rift, was named the Grand Chasm by the British at Shackleton Station. Fuchs discovered the east end of the Grand Chasm (clouds obscured the area to the west) on 31 January 1956, on a reconnaissance flight from Shackleton. Although this discovery had been made more than a year earlier, we were not aware of the Grand Chasm until our flight this day. If we had been aware, I wonder if Ellsworth Station would have been placed on the Filchner Ice Shelf.

> There is much crevassing, and it looks like we will have a hard time getting out of this area in the spring. They saw nothing to indicate anything but ice shelf, and their altimeter showed something in the range of 200 ft. At almost 200 miles south, they observed the east-west-trending ice escarpment rising up to high land with visible mountains to the south.

The results of this flight gave us something to argue and think about all the coming winter. I worked on the equipment the day Ed was flying. I replaced a condenser we had checked several days prior in the dynamotor, and the equipment worked. I spent the rest of the day putting the gear back together and reinstalling it in the Sno-Cat, I was keeping my fingers crossed until we could get a good record in the field before I'd really believe we had our troubles licked.

We had no spare condenser, but I obtained a different type from the Navy and wired part of it in. This repair was actually a significant accomplishment. Without this piece of equipment we could not have measured ice thickness along our traverse.

> The wind picked up in the afternoon and blew about 30 knots all night. Much snow blew through the burlap walls and drifted up in the tunnel. The hatch blew off Kim's tower twice.
>
> Jerry and his boys are having troubles with the small radios and balloons. They have had three successful flights, called radio-sondes, and about seven failures.

The meteorological program called for launching hydrogen-filled balloons carrying small instruments connected to radio transmitters to measure pressure and temperature. Using the directional tracking antenna in the "raydome" at the south edge of the camp, elevation from pressure, and direction (azimuth and vertical angle) were measured as the balloon rose to about 40,000 ft before it burst from expansion. The data were recorded as a time record, which gave wind speed and direction at all elevation levels of the ascent.

17 March, Sun. A memorial service was held in the newly completed rec hall for Admiral Byrd, who died 11 March, as at all U.S. Antarctic stations today. Ronne spoke as the only person who knew Byrd and, considering his dislike for the man, was quite fair and unhypocritical in what he said. Jack, who is a lay reader in the Episcopal Church, ran the brief service.

About 1730 Ron Brown [Brownie], the helicopter mechanic, came into Con's room. He was sore because Clint had bawled him out for swearing and he had more or less told him off. Davis, the cook, kicked him out of the chow hall where he was working because he was putting clean plates on a dirty table. About 1930 Cox and Con came around checking to see if any of us were out in a Weasel. Brownie had said, "I'm going to Shackleton," and had apparently taken off in a Weasel, as one was missing. A most unorganized search commenced with people running around in the dark looking for fresh Weasel tracks in the snow.

This search was really quite bizarre, with most people in the camp going off in all directions in the dark in Weasels and on foot. Ronne led one small group. I was in a Weasel looking for tracks by making a large circle around the entire perimeter, beyond the usual traveled area. Eventually we probably would have found the tracks, but someone had an even better idea of counting the lights of the Weasels driving apparently aimlessly around.

There were five Weasels searching but six sets of headlights! Obviously Brown and the missing Weasel were in the group. Taking an educated guess that the most distant set of lights belonged to the missing vehicle, someone drove out to that Weasel, and there was the missing man. He was driving along at a great rate and was chased down. Apparently he was just out for a ride.

As we were all in radio communication, the search was called off and we came in. It was humorous after the event but could have been quite serious, particularly considering that there were crevasses in the vicinity.

18 March, Mon. Ed, Augie, and I went out to the tidal crack and laid out a spread on the thin ice of the seismic cables connected to geophones. The Sno-Cat was well up the slope on the edge of the ice shelf, so the geophones were on the top of the ice shelf and also on the thin new sea ice. The cables were thus in a T shape. We fired two shots in the water with about two pounds of explosive [ammonium nitrate] each and received very good bottom and other reflections. These are the first records we have made in Antarctica.

In our standard seismic operation, we spread out two 1200-ft cables and attached geophones, or "jugs," to each of 12 pairs of wire connectors at 100-ft intervals. We shot off explosive charges in a hand-drilled hole about four inches in diameter and anywhere from about 6–45 ft (2–15 m) deep. Charge size varied greatly from a pound or two for a reflection (echo) from the sea bottom or ice-rock interface to 1000 lbs for long distances from the shot to the recording system. When the geophones on the snow surface vibrated in response to the reflected sound (seismic) wave, a small voltage was generated and received at the recording instruments. Half the measured time from the shot to the recorded reflection, multiplied by the velocity of sound in the ice and snow, which we measured independently, gave the ice thickness or the combined ice and water thickness on the floating ice shelf.

The seismic equipment was state of the art in 1956, but quite primitive by 1990s standards. Because each of the 24 amplifiers had about 10 vacuum tubes, each aluminum case of six weighed about 50 lbs. Another 50-lb case contained the control unit; still another converted 24 volts to high voltage. We did not have digital recording equipment or even tape recorders, but used an oscillograph camera weighing about 70 lbs and using photo recording paper.

The photographic solutions developed each seismic record as soon as it was measured. A miniature "darkroom" on which the camera rested was used to develop the records. Access to the darkroom was through an opaque sleeve into which the developing hand and arm was placed to reach the three developing tanks. This in turn required plenty of water (preferably warm), chemicals, etc. After developing and fixing, the 8-inch-wide, 4- to 10-foot-long paper records required careful washing and drying in the

Sno-Cat, by draping them on a wire line fashioned out of a lead to a blasting cap, or indoors at Ellsworth.

It was not unusual to have a record freeze immediately after I removed one from the tank to examine it after each shot. When I noticed that the developer was turning my right hand brown, I obtained some surgical gloves from Clint Smith, the Navy physician, which solved the problem. I was assigned by Ed to do all of the seismic instrument operation during this Antarctic trip. Several years later, when I was the boss, I assigned someone else to this job.

For this reflection measurement of depth to the bottom of the ice shelf and to the sea bottom, we recorded the time to about 0.001 seconds' accuracy of the seismic waves for the various reflections (echoes).[7] Using the seismic velocity in seawater, snow, and ice, we could determine the ice shelf thickness and the depth to the seafloor. At this location the water was 2597 ft (792 m) deep and the ice shelf was 760 ft (232 m) thick. The surface elevation on the top of the ice shelf was 138 ft (42 m).

> Ronne told Ed this noon [I overheard from my room] that he would take Augie off the traverse if he didn't shape up. He said a lot more derogatory things about him. Ed protested but Ronne made it clear that he would decide. Apparently we will have little to say regarding routes, etc., on traverse. Aug, when Ed told him, said he would sue if he were removed from our group, because that is what he was hired for.
>
> The strong wind Saturday night blew a lot of snow through the burlap walls of the tunnels. The long (about 500-ft) aircraft tunnel is filled to the top in several places and is impassable.

Brownie had to dig the tunnel clear, as punishment for his Weasel ride on Sunday night. When snow banked up on the sides, the tunnels would be OK, and we could walk safely between the buildings, essentially "indoors." The strong winds we were regularly experiencing were rapidly drifting up the entire station.

> *19 March, Tues.* In the morning we fired another reflection shot in at the tidal crack. Kent went out with us this morning to see how our gear operates. He sure is out of shape, as that walk up the ramp just about did him in.

What I didn't stop to realize is that we five traverse people were really getting in excellent shape. Ed and Aug were 28, I was 24, and Paul was 22. Hugo was the old man, at 36.

> After noon Paul, Hugo, and Ed in a Weasel went south along the edge of Bahia Chica to fire a long-distance [refraction] shot. Aug stayed with me as I worked at the instruments. Our two Sno-Cats were in radio contact. About 200 yards south of us the Weasel was stopped when a snow bridge over a crevasse sagged suddenly. Everything was OK, and they managed to back up. . . .
> This was our first serious encounter with Antarctic crevasses. Farther on, about 1.5 miles, they got out to investigate the edge of the barrier. Ahead of them and out of sight over the slope the cornice edge broke off with loud noises and plumes of snow. They retreated.

A cornice is a curved edge of a vertical ice cliff, built out by windblown snow. Cornices thin to a feather edge, but may appear quite solid when standing on the upper convex surface. They can be very weak and easily break off the edge of the ice front about 100 ft above the sea or sea ice below. Bert Crary fell into the Ross Sea in 1958 at Little America, when a cornice broke between him and his assistant, Steve den Hartog, while making an oceanographic measurement in the Ross Sea; he survived. Three men in a Weasel were lost when they drove over the corniced ice shelf edge in poor visibility at Maudheim, on the Norwegian-British-Swedish Expedition a few years earlier.

We observed cornices from the *Wyandot* all along the ice front of the Filchner and more particularly the Ronne (as it is now known) Ice Shelf. We also saw cornices all along the ice front of Bahia Chica from the surface of the ice shelf as the edge curved around to the south and from the bay ice we had been working on earlier.

We also saw many drifted-over collapsed cornices while working on the bay ice along the tidal crack. Snow bridges can re-form over crevasses after collapse, for example, by windblown snow building cornices out from the sides until they meet and join. As with crevasses, the elegant curve of a cornice can be quite beautiful when seen in the right combination of light and shadow.

> About two miles south a vain search was made for a feasible place to load a charge. Finally they came back to a ramp about .75 mile

south of us and fired a case of Petrogel, which I recorded. We will
have problems finding a location for our next shot.

I now realize that this drive along the edge of the ice shelf was
really quite dangerous, and that we were really very naive.

Such a large charge (60 lbs) was required because shooting in
snow rather than water resulted in a great loss of seismic energy.
We sent a radio signal from the shot to the recording instruments,
which I operated, to measure the time it took for the sound waves
to travel through the snow, ice, water, and rock to the instruments.

20 March, Wed. Clear and cold, about −25°F. After noon chow Ed,
Aug, and I drove south in the Sno-Cat along the barrier edge of
Bahia Chica for about six miles. We left the vehicle for about an
hour and roped up on snowshoes and searched for a ramp down to
the bay ice. There was a stiff 10–20-knot wind that made us glad we
had our face masks, although my glasses fogged up.

This was about the only time that we ever wore face masks because of the condensation and freezing problem.

We approached the edge and found a cornice cliff instead of a ramp.
The hummocked bay ice 100 ft below was a spectacular sight against
the late afternoon sun and blue sky. The sun was setting at 1800 as
we headed back; the equinox is at midnight. It was −30°F when I
turned in at 2230. There was a faint aurora [the first that I noted in
my journal].

The days were rapidly getting shorter during these weeks. At
the latitude of Ellsworth, the transition from the first sunsets in late
February to the last sight of the sun for the winter on about 26
April was about nine weeks. At the South Pole this takes place on
the equinox, with an extra day or so for refraction.

21 March, Thurs. The Weasel wouldn't start (it was −30°F), but the
Sno-Cat ran fine. This is probably because of the 24-volt electrical
system contrasted to 6 volts in the Weasel. By the time the Weasel
was going and we picked up a load of Petrogel, it was noon. Con
asked to come along, so he rode in the Sno-Cat with me. We drove
out to a point where we could see to direct Paul and Ed by radio as
they drove around to a ramp across an indentation in the barrier.

Visibility was poor, and they couldn't see the edge of the ice cliff, but working together we managed to get them to the ramp.

Con drove the Sno-Cat back to our seismic spread about eight miles from the ramp and we contacted them. They were stuck in a partially collapsed snow bridge over a crevasse. Ed walked around to the sled to examine the situation and fell in up to his waist. They managed to unhook the sled and back out; they then dragged the sled upslope with a rope. Again we contacted them and Paul said, "I am looking out the door straight down 40 ft into a crevasse that we are straddling. This makes me very unhappy."

They drove across and decided that it was dangerous to work there without a third man. I suggested that they fire a charge in the crevasse. They shot 300 lbs of Petrogel, but I didn't record any energy on the geophones from that distance.

22 March, Fri. We helped the glaciologists this afternoon. I volunteered to dig. We took temperature observations at various depths in the two-meter-deep pit and filled density tubes with snow. Paul measured the snow stratigraphy and I copied the data. It was –24°F, and this was very cold work as we weren't moving much. My feet were chilled in my thermal boots.

My big problem in the cold is to keep my nose from freezing and my glasses from fogging, which happens when I pull my parka hood forward. These aims appear to be mutually exclusive at present.

The food has really been excellent and diversified. Ed Davis is a very good cook and Dick Grob a fine baker. We have lots of cake, pie, and other pastry in addition to plenty of delicious bread.

23 March, Sat. Aug and I took off at 1000 in the Sno-Cat to go to the seismic spread and survey while the others went for dynamite and headed for the ramp. Shortly we became unable to make radio contact, although we could hear them fine. We began to slow down, although the engine was running well. We came to a stop and discovered that the clutch had burned out. This probably came from starting from a stop in each gear. About 40 minutes later the boys came along and when appraised of the situation, headed back.

Hugo and Ed came back in a D-4, and we hitched up arriving back in camp about 1730. We will have to improvise a clutch, as we don't have a spare.

How casually I treated the greatest vehicle disaster of our stay in Antarctica!

That night, we had a bull session in the science building. We felt that our rights as civilians were slowly being encroached upon and that we needed to take some action to protect them.

24 March., Sun. Holiday Routine so we slept in. After noon Hugo drove the D-4 and towed me out to the spread in the seismic Sno-Cat with the burned-out clutch, while Ed, Aug, and Paul headed for the ramp. They fired 450 lbs of Petrogel at 1730 and I recorded a record 20 seconds long. The paper comes out at 21 inches per second, so I had my hands full.

The recording paper came out of a slit in the bottom of the seismic camera, and I caught it in my right hand inserted in the developing box below.

25 March, Mon. Clear, cold, and windy again. We went out to the spread after noon chow. Ed, Aug, and Paul left me at the broken-down Sno-Cat parked at the seismic spread and proceeded on to the shot point. The boys slid about 280 lbs of explosives over the edge of a cliff intending to drop them into the tidal crack. This caught on a ledge above the bay ice and they could not retrieve it, so the shot was fired there. I spent most of the afternoon just waiting in the Sno-Cat.

26 March, Tues. Ed and I worked on seismic records. It was −38°F this afternoon while Hugo, Paul, and Aug were surveying. Ice fog about 1600, which made it impossible so they didn't accomplish much. Their Weasel wouldn't start, so they walked about two miles in.

27 March, Wed. Paul, Ed, and I went out early to shoot a refraction shot at two miles. We had a lot of trouble with the radios due to snow static as we had 20-knot winds. This resulted from blowing snow against the antenna. We could produce a half-inch spark from the static charge built up in this way across a gap created by disconnecting the antenna.

The others found a new ramp down to the sea ice, while I waited to record. After chow, with Aug added to our complement, we returned and shot two shots. The heater in the Sno-Cat wasn't working properly, and it didn't get above 25°F inside so wasn't too comfortable.

We took up the geophone spread and cables. By this time it was getting dark. It was quite cold (−25°F) with a high wind, and tears even froze our eyelashes together. I thought of Robert Service's poem "The Cremation of Sam McGee," where he noted, "It got so cold that the lids they froze so sometimes we couldn't see." In digging up geophones I accidentally cut the 24-conductor cable with the shovel in two places, so we will have to repair that before we can set up again.

Hugo drove out in a D-4 to tow the Sno-Cat in and dropped the tractor about four feet into a crevasse. Paul drove him right back while we continued our work. He tried to get some help from Spear directly rather than going to Ronne. Ronne was mad and chewed him out for this. Hugo then blamed Ed for not going to Ronne instead of him.

After supper Ed, Hugo, Paul, Aug, Spear, and Davis went out in a D-8 and rescued the D-4 without much trouble. We pulled the Sno-Cat back to camp, using a Weasel with no crevasse problems.

Lassiter will bring 11 men with him when he flies down in September.

Maj. James Lassiter (USAF) had tried to fly in from South America the previous summer, but because of our delays, had eventually given up and returned to the U.S. This is my first mention of Lassiter's plans for the 1957–58 season. The casual way I noted this in my journal indicates that we knew all along that the Lassiter mission was on for the following summer. This is significant, because it was apparently a classified operation at this time.

28 March, Thurs. We saw *Tight Little Island* tonight. It is interesting to note the reactions of the various groups. Most of the Navy people walked out tonight while it is usually the civilians that either walk out or don't come to the Navy fare.

I see I had some elitist tendencies in those days, not because we walked out frequently, but because I chose to comment on this in my journal!

29 March, Fri. The rec hall is in operation now with Ping-Pong, shuffle board, pool tables. Jack and Don are helping set up the station hi-fi set for the rec hall.

This was before the days of stereo, and all the music provided was on 33⅓ rpm LP records. For a while we had the turntable and amplifier in the science building, so they recorded some of Jack's records of organ and band music on tape.

We had a good auroral display, the most spectacular I have ever seen. There were even reds in it.

Because I grew up in Wisconsin, I was used to northern lights, but this phenomenon was unfamiliar to most people at Ellsworth. They were not particularly interested. As we worked outside most days in the dark winter, we saw aurora each clear day.

30 March, Sat. I sent a hamgram out tonight, and when I took it in to Ronne to censor, he showed me some model dog sleds he is making. He has been working on them since his 1940 expedition. I said, "Well, I suppose if you don't finish them now you'll finish them on the next expedition." He replied, "If I don't finish now, they'll never get finished."

He showed me a plate he painted and a wastebasket, similarly decorated. His phonograph was playing "Pictures at an Exhibition," and when I remarked that I liked that selection he picked up the envelope and said, "Oh that's what it is." He has a painting of *Kista Dan* [the Antarctic ship] on his wall that I like very much. It is a copy he picked up in Valparaiso.

31 March, Sun. We took the day off. This is the second day we haven't worked since the ships left. It is much warmer (–15°F), and the sky is overcast.

Obviously our perspective on what was "warm" was changing as the winter approached.

We had a church service at 1000 and only six people showed up beside Jack and May, who ran the show—[Fred] Dyrdal, Paul, Hugo, Aug, Kim, and me.

Back when the ship had just sailed from the U.S., I wrote down a brief description of my fellow civilians. Now that I had come to know them better I thought I'd write more.

Don Skidmore is very intelligent. He has led an interesting life, spending some time in the merchant marine and has studied for various vocations, including nursing. He graduated from college last June in business administration. He has been working as administrative assistant to the vice president of National Radio Company. His vitriolic wit and cynical mockery of other people's weaknesses have made him some enemies. The things he mocks most in others are the traits which he himself possesses and when this is pointed out, will readily admit it. Don misses his family very much; if it weren't for this he would enjoy it here more. He is a very hard worker and picks up new skills easily.

Don is not the sort to stab his buddies in the back, although he has a way of getting into the confidence of superiors. He never shows any reverence or respect for position and delights in insulting people, which trait Ronne ate right up. He can be very humorous at times. I think one of the funniest sights I've seen was his clowned-up rendition of "I'm a Little Teapot" at that infamous party several weeks ago.

Jack Brown is a very interesting person. He is one of the tallest men here and one of the quietest. He and Don make, at first appearance, an incongruous team, but of all people I think he has one of the best temperaments for working with Don. He is one of the older men (around 30) and left a good job which he has held for several years at DuPont in Wilmington. He is single and graduated from Cornell with a bachelor's degree in physics with a minor in English literature. He is a deeply religious man, but doesn't flaunt it. He is a lay reader in the Episcopal Church.

Jack spent several years in the Navy during World War II as an electronics technician, stationed in Chicago. He plays the organ and the piano quite well, and also is very good on the recorder. He has a quiet sense of humor that sometimes sparkles out at unexpected moments. Although he is not at all cold and reserved, he has said less and made less known about his personal life than any of us. Don is very loyal to Jack and thinks a great deal of him. Jack is a very considerate person and goes out of his way to do things for people. He hasn't made known his reasons for coming down here, but as he took a cut in pay, and from his general nature, I would judge there to be a bit of romance for the unknown in his soul.

Jerry Fierle is a very likable person. He is short (about 5 ft, 2 in.) and is 35 years old. He has spent 13 years working for the Weather Bureau, mostly in Alaska and of northern Canada. He homesteaded a place in Alaska for a few years. He married a girl who, to judge from her picture, is all or part Indian; she died giving birth to a son six years ago. This boy lives with Jerry's brother in Texas. It is since his wife's death that he has spent time at the isolated stations. I think he still mourns for his wife; he showed me her picture and her small hunting knife which he brought with him.

Jerry never went to college. He spent the war in the Navy coming out as a chief petty officer, (or "chief"). He is a GS 9 and a Navy-educated man as far as his profession (meteorology) goes. He constantly smokes a pipe or cigar. At first glance he is quite irascible; however, he is a very considerate person, both to the boys who work with him and to the people he lives with (e.g., he would always make a point on the ship of waking Aug and me for breakfast if we overslept).

He has no use for Ronne and the feeling is reciprocated. Jerry goes his way and Ronne lets him alone. I gather that he has acquired a reputation for not being pushed around in his Weather Bureau. He lives with Augie in the barracks next door. Jerry will apply to stay over a second tour—if Ronne isn't base commander.

Kim Malville, 22, has been working very hard at his program. He is the only person in his discipline here and has had to work alone on all his installations [we all helped him on heavy work]. He is the second youngest of our group and is probably the most intelligent. He has a tongue-in-cheek sense of humor and can really string people along without their realizing it. He has reached the point with me that I told him I refuse to believe anything he says. Kim has a girl, who is a sophomore. He didn't hear from her for quite a while and it sort of got to him, but he has received two hamgrams recently which raised his spirits.

Kim is quite well read, and he, Jack, and I have had some good games of "Who Am I?" He has a temper, which is not easily roused (at least he doesn't show it), but which Ronne has triggered several times. He doesn't smoke and drinks only occasionally.

Paul Walker, 22, is engaged to a girl who is coming into an income of $60,000/year, which was unknown to him until after they were engaged. He has spent two summers in Greenland and a couple working in Glacier National Park. He is the most easygoing and good-natured of the IGY people. Paul has more glaciology experience than Hugo, and from what I've observed this fall is quite familiar with snow (crevasses, etc.). He and Hugo are the "expert" Sno-Cat mechanics, having taken a five-day training course at the Tucker factory at Medford, Oregon. He is a good roommate for Hugo, as he is probably the only one who could put up with him.

Hugo Neuburg is a real character. He is 36 years old and comes from Yonkers, N.Y. His father immigrated from Germany, and Hugo has inherited a German background. When he was a child he was quite sickly so his parents sent him to Germany for several years where he regained his health. Because of this, probably, physical fitness has become almost an obsession with him. He is probably the strongest person on the base. He is very careful about what he eats. On the ship he worked out at calisthenics more than anyone.

Hugo brought his own supply of vitamin pills.

Hugo has been on several cosmic ray expeditions including one to the Galapagos Islands, and two summers on Mt. Wrangell in Alaska. He was one of the members of the Fletcher Polar Basin Expedition. He and another man were to be landed at the North Pole with dogs and sleds. They planed to trek to Baffin Island, making various scientific observations (including continuous sounding of the Arctic Ocean with a line). They were not allowed to buy gas for their plane when they arrived in Thule, Greenland, however, and that ended the expedition.

In many respects, although he is well educated, Hugo is quite naive, almost simple. He is very "pure in heart" and is one of the kindest and most thoughtful people I have met. He has a very different sense of humor and does not get a lot of jokes but really enjoys those he does get the point of. He always is chuckling and laughing at something the rest don't think is that funny, and this annoys many people and several mock him. He doesn't appear to notice this, however.

Hugo is, in spite of his age and travels, quite ingenuous in his relations with others, which gives him some difficulty. He has little or no sophistication in the art of conversation and, consequently, subtleties and innuendoes pass by unnoticed. While he is inherently good-natured, he has no tact when disagreeing with someone, which has seriously hindered his relations with Ronne. He must feel very lonely and unhappy at times, although he manages to hide it quite well. Sometimes, however, he looks quite tragic.

Hugo is a member of the Explorers Club, as is Ronne, and he met Ronne there.[8] Apparently he was impressed by him (it is easy, as he can be very charming), because he almost worshipped him at the start. Now since he has seen that Ronne is not the great god he held him to be, his idol has been smashed. He is now one of the most bitterly anti-Ronne people and really feels frustrated as far as these arguments go.

Hugo loves to figure jobs out in advance, and always seems to do things the hard way. Because he is strong, he sometimes forgets everyone else isn't his equal. At other times he overengineers simple projects. He is meticulously clean and neat in all his actions and habits, and I think that the fact that I am not always so, bothers him. He gets a great kick and shock out of the way I splash hypo [a photographic solution] wildly about inside the Sno-Cat when I pull a record out of the developing box to examine it.

Notes

1. Fubar was a common World War II acronym meaning "fucked up beyond all recognition."
2. Among a battery of questions, we were asked to rank our peer work group, that is, the civilians.
3. In stark contrast, during my latest trip to Antarctica in 1995, occasionally at McMurdo I would pick up the phone on my desk and make an inexpensive ($.90/minute) call to the U.S. directly through a satellite link.
4. Every Navy man wintering over was a volunteer, and some had come to Antarctica primarily for the money.
5. My outburst must have made a lasting impression on Ronne because he referred to it in his book about our expedition, *Antarctic Command.*
6. I realize now, and perhaps Fuchs anticipated it then, that in an emergency beyond their capabilities, they could have expected search-and-rescue support from the U.S. program.
7. We recorded reflections through the ice shelf from the ice-water interface; through the ice shelf to the sea bottom and back through the water and ice shelf; the reflection through the water only from the sea bottom; and through the water only from the sea surface to the sea bottom to the bottom of the ice shelf, back to the sea bottom and back to the surface. It was a unique experiment because this was the only place where we could work on both the ice-shelf surface and the sea-ice surface at essentially the same point.
8. Possibly for this reason I delayed joining the Explorers Club until 1978.

4
Winter Begins

We were settling in to our home beneath the snow at Ellsworth. I recall becoming quite comfortable in the station and as the food was great, felt completely at home. As the Antarctic winter approached, it was quite interesting outdoors to see the rapid changes. Much scientific work followed, but for the sake of brevity, I present only parts of it here.

> *1 April, Mon.* We commenced Winter Routine: Breakfast (for us officers) 0830–0850, noon chow 1300, supper, 1745, movie, 1915. This is a real "loaf and smoke" routine, as the Navy men call it.

> *2 April, Tues.* We have the most complete library of Antarctic literature . . . that I've ever seen. All the classics by Scott, Amundsen, Shackleton, Byrd, Ellsworth, and Mawson, in addition to the most up-to-date stuff available. James Cook's works on the South Pacific (1768–71) (including charts) are also here. There are scientific journals from the past few years. In addition to technical books in all our fields, we have books on ornithology, geography, climatology, photography, and history. German and French dictionaries in addition to *Webster's Collegiate* are but a part of the shelf of technical reference handbooks. I only hope I read part of this.
>   Kevin Walton's and Jennie Darlington's books are here but not Ronne's.

Jenny Darlington's *My Antarctic Honeymoon* is an account of the winter at East Base during Finn Ronne's private expedition, when Jenny and Edith (Jackie) Ronne were the first women to winter over in Antarctica. This book is quite critical of Ronne, as noted previously. Kevin Walton wintered over the same season with the UK Falkland Islands Dependencies Survey, also at Marguerite Bay, close to Ronne's base. Walton wrote a book, *Two Years in Antarctica,* in which he, too, was quite critical of Ronne, particularly his policy of nonfraternization between the British and the Americans.

We have an electric piano in our library, and everyone has fun with it. Jack can play quite well and provides much enjoyable listening.

3 April, Wed. Storming outside all day. Winds up to 40 knots, but not too cold.

4 April, Thurs. It was amazingly warm today, 22°F. A lot of snow had blown through the burlap, and we all had to shovel our entrances out. It was overcast and visibility was poor when we went out and set up a seismic reflection spread about four miles east of camp. We fired three shots. I have been having trouble sleeping the past few nights. I feel tired after supper so I sleep until the movie at 1900. Then I feel wide awake at midnight.

5 April, Fri. We have been in a radio blackout for the past five days, and Kim's magnetograph shows a magnetic storm in progress.

6 April, Sat. Ronne is getting upset with us because Don hasn't been getting up at 0830. Don feels that we should be free to choose our own schedule as long as we are doing our work. We slept in late this morning, and Ronne came in and woke Don. He chewed him out. The rest of us were in the sack but rolled out quickly. Ed explained to him later that he had said we could sleep on Saturday. Ronne had forgotten this and at any rate didn't want it in the future.

We had an inspection at 1100. Ed made it quite clear when these inspections were planned that we didn't want to stand inspection like Navy people. Ronne agreed to this, and supposedly the place is inspected only for fire hazards. Holiday Routine in the afternoon.

7 April, Sun. The only Navy person at church was Chief May who helped with the service. All the civilians were there except Jerry and Don. Jack (who preached) doesn't like it that the Navy doesn't show. Basically the only reason most of the civilians came is to show support for Jack's efforts.

Jack continued these services for two more weeks. After Easter, 21 April, there was no more church at Ellsworth.

After supper Paul, Aug, Ed, Don, and I played Monopoly.

It's interesting to see how we civilians move up and down on Ronne's list. Don, who was his favorite a few weeks ago, is near the bottom, and Paul, who was low is now in #1 position. I have moved up from near the bottom to somewhere in the middle. This is reflected in the seating at mess. We officer types all sit at one long table. Ronne sits at the head with McCarthy and Con on either side. Clint, Ed, Sumrall, and Jack are next. Kim, Paul, and I follow. Don and Hugo are down near the other end, and the very end is occupied by Jerry and Aug. For a long time Aug sat at the end opposite of Ronne, but now he takes a side chair. This is the present arrangement, but it varies from week to week. The middle is more or less neutral. Don, who a few weeks ago liked Ronne, now hates his guts.

8 April, Mon. Aug, Ed, and I picked up the seismic spread. The sun is very low on the horizon these days, and due to the thin ground fog there were pale rainbows ("sun dogs") on either side of it.

We received the positions of the other non-U.S. continental Antarctic stations on 8 April. The British, Chilean, and Argentine Palmer Peninsula Stations were not included.[1]

9 April, Tues. Hugo and Paul worked all day taking the clutch out of the Sno-Cat. Walt Davis, the Navy mechanic, said the whole clutch assembly would have to be replaced.[2] While the clutch was being removed, Ed and I rewired our battery-charging system. We moved the seismic batteries to the starboard side so the weight would be better distributed.

Each Sno-Cat came equipped with two oversize 12-volt batteries wired in series for the 24-volt system. In addition we required two additional 175-pound, 12-volt batteries to power the 24-volt, 24-channel seismic system because the vacuum tubes drew so much current.

Despite our repeated requests, Ronne refused to ask James Lassiter to bring a replacement clutch. Thus began a conflict with Ronne that lasted for the next six months. In early winter, he had started communicating with us through memos, which I religiously copied into my journal. We, in turn, responded in the same way, but the whole process got entirely out of hand as the winter progressed. There were numerous memos back and forth from Ed and Hugo to Ronne on the subject of the clutch. Ronne often communicated with Lassiter, via ham radio, and repeatedly stated that Lassiter should not fly the clutch down. Believing the clutch replacement was essential, we managed to get direct and "secret" communication through to Bert Crary, the chief scientist at Little America, about it. Vivian Fuchs, at Shackleton, offered to have his mechanic attempt to retemper the burned-out clutch springs, but this did not prove feasible.

10 April, Wed. Ronne, Ed, and Don had a discussion about the IGY people working on mess duty, etc. We do not want to unless the other officers (namely Clint, Con, and Willie) do also. Our contracts stated that if this is deemed necessary by the station scientific leader "for the safety, health, and welfare of the station," we would share household duties.

At Little America during this same winter when the Navy captain there suggested to Bert Crary that the scientists take turns washing dishes, Bert was reported to have said, "Fine, let us two take the first shift," or words to that effect, whereupon the subject was permanently dropped. At Ellsworth, mess duty, or "mess cooking," was a full-time two-week assignment, at the expense of other duties. Mess cooking did not involve cooking or food handling, only cleanup chores and waiting tables for the officers. No officers or chief petty officers were assigned mess cooking duty at Ellsworth. But at other stations everyone took turns for one meal at a time.

Early this morning (about 0300) the hot water heater set fire to the men's head. The fire alarm system installed yesterday afternoon detected it and the generator watch put it out.

Fire, the greatest hazard we faced during the winter, did result, but fortunately there were no injuries in this case. At the Soviet station, Mirny, several years later, six men were killed while trapped in a burning building. Snow had blocked the rear entrance, and the fire started at the other end of the building. All of our buildings at Ellsworth were widely separated, and both front and rear entrances were kept free of drifted snow. The doors opened inward so one could probably always push out even through snowdrifts. Eventually, of course, the buildings and connecting tunnels drifted over, and we were living totally under the snow with buildings connected by the tunnels.

We had the Navy's sewing machine tonight, and several of us tried our hands at repairing our clothes.

11 April, Thurs. It is getting dark very early these days.

As the winter night approached, we went out progressively later and came indoors earlier. When it finally was dark all day, we went back to going outside after breakfast, took a meal break at noon, and worked again until just before supper.

12 April, Fri. I received two hamgrams this morning, which were quite welcome. . . . Dave [my brother] is getting married. I wrote answers to these and took them in to get them cleared (censored) by the Captain after the movie.

Ronne never actually did change or remove anything we wrote, but of course we never included anything about our troubles that he could object to. He would read each item of correspondence while we waited in front of him. As leader of both the IGY and Navy groups, Ronne had antagonized almost everyone by this point and didn't have any friends. Consequently, he took these opportunities of checking what we wrote to converse individually with us. These talks were interesting, but the procedure was humiliating.

By now, Hugo was really low in Ronne's esteem, mostly because he pooh-poohed Ronne's tent design rather untactfully. Ronne had prepared a quite carefully drawn scale plan across which Hugo had written, "Rejected by Neuburg." This was the design of the tent that Finn's father, Martin Ronne, made for Amundsen's historic dog-sled journey to the South Pole in 1911–12, so naturally he felt personally insulted by Hugo's rejection.

[Ronne] doesn't think we will get very far on traverse, and doesn't expect a clutch replacement. He thinks we take too many pictures.

I carried a collapsible Kodak Retina IIa in my pocket every day for the entire year and took several thousand Kodachrome slides and black-and-white pictures. I developed the black-and-white film and made prints at Ellsworth.

He told me to tell Ed to come in for a talk. Later Ed told me he thought Ronne had the tape recorder on.

Clear with a moon tonight. It was quite beautiful so I took a couple of pictures.

13 April, Sat. Ed and I tiled the foyer of the science building this morning.

We had previously tiled our own rooms and the rest of the open areas in the science building, so by this time our space and the rest of the station was quite livable. The U.S. IGY stations were probably the most luxurious up to that time in Antarctic history, which did a lot for winter morale.

There was a station party with birthday cake, hors d'oeuvres, and punch spiked with bourbon, which somehow became stronger as the evening progressed. Paul, Ed, Kim, Jack, Don, and I had an interesting philosophical discussion on the merits of religion and churches, which lasted until nearly 0300.

Kim sent a story to his folks when the ship left, for publication with some West Coast magazine. They cleared it with IGY but not the Navy; today Kim received a message from CHINFO (chief of information, a Navy position) pointing out that it should have been cleared with them.

Even from today's perspective there is an understandable tendency of those in authority in remote field situations (or even in the White House) to attempt to control release of information that might embarrass or reflect badly on them. Usually some "security" excuse is used, but also usually the average American finds a way to circumvent the restriction. For example, in 1990 at McMurdo, the National Science Foundation complained about a lower level civilian employee of the contractor, Antarctic Support Activities, writing freelance articles, which she mailed to the *Washington Post.*

14–23 April, Sun.–Tues. The temperature ranged from −10°F to −30°F. We saw a beautiful sunset about 1430 [19 Apr.]. Ronne talked to Paul Siple, at the South Pole; they had −89°F. The sitreps from the other stations have come in. Byrd Station reported temperatures down to −68°F. They haven't completed their aurora tower yet. Wilkes reported an ice cap station established for meteorology and glaciology 50 miles from the main camp at 4000 ft elevation.

We awoke 16 April to find blowing snow in the tunnels and rips in the burlap. Winds held from the high 20s to around 40 knots at night. Ronne told us at a meeting after breakfast that we had been doing our own work long enough and that we should do some camp work. No one objected to this, but we didn't like the threatening way he said it. Ed defended our right to our work. As he was walking out he turned to Augie and said, "I know you don't like this." This took us all, and especially Aug, by surprise. He retorted with, "You're always accusing me of things I didn't say, you varmint!" which Ronne ignored as he closed the door.

We spent parts of several days shoveling snow in tunnels and entrances to buildings and repairing the holes in the tunnel burlap. Ed and I shoveled a lot of snow that had blown to the science tunnel, including a large pile partially blocking the entrance to the short tunnel to Ronne's door. Later, Ronne complained to Al Spear that, "they wouldn't even do me a favor and shovel out my entrance. I had to do it myself." Spear replied, "Well, I think they are pissed off at you."

I took two altimeters and measured the elevation difference from the seismic shot point to our main bench mark. This was the first time I had been outside on the south side of camp since our big winds. The sides of the tunnels are covered up to the roof. I looked at our Sno-Cat . . . parked about 200 yards south of the garage out in the open. There was no drift around it. . . . Very little snow blew inside. About 40 ft to the north (leeward side) there was a long, about 50-ft, narrow drift caused by the Sno-Cat. The fact that the body is up in the air above the tracks produced this effect, I believe. I think we can leave the Sno-Cats out in the open safely all winter. The rest of the vehicles are parked close together near the garage and are quite drifted in. A couple of Weasels are almost covered.

Apparently the Navy people did not notice the drifting, and there were serious problems resulting from this at the end of the winter.

Ed and I took a Weasel and went down to the ramp to the sea ice in Bahia Chica where our spread was to measure an altimeter profile. Hugo had warned us that the lower part had broken off, so we were roped up. I was in the lead. Visibility was very poor, near whiteout, as I made my way down. I could barely make out that I was nearing the edge of the barrier. Below I could see the frozen-over tidal crack, but there was nothing I could use as a reference to tell how far up I was. I tested the edge with my ice ax and it crumbled, so I lay on my belly and looked over. I reached down with my ax and was able to touch firm bottom. The cliff was only three feet high and I stepped down. Ed got quite a charge out of the whole affair and I was disgusted. He confided to me later that he was glad I was first. It really is quite impossible to judge depth and height and distance under whiteout conditions.

When Ed told Ronne that Jerry was the best qualified meteorology man here, with 13 years in the Weather Bureau, Ronne was surprised. He called Jerry for their first talk. When asked what his job was, Jerry replied that he is showing the Navy how to use their equipment and "doing things they can't do." When Ronne said that they should have more visits, Jerry told him he was too busy.

Jack and Don finally got their C-4 ionosphere recorder operative. The C-4 was used to measure the height of various layers of the ionosphere. Four to twelve times an hour, it put out a blaring sweep-frequency radio transmission, which lasted 15 seconds. This noise could be heard on every speaker, including tape recorders, phonographs, and even our electric piano, and also the main radio receivers in camp. This meant that when our radio operators would communicate back and forth with the Navy using Morse code, the C-4 destroyed all radio contact during that 15-second interval. Every piece of electronic equipment in camp picked up this noise.

We opened the office supplies. There is a fantastic amount. We have 100 one-pound boxes of rubber bands, and three cases of 8½-by-11-inch tablets. Thousands of pencils but only one roll of masking tape. Two typewriters, two Friden [mechanical] calculators, and two adding machines.

A number of the men have shaved their beards off including Chuck McCarthy, who had the best one.

One Saturday Con Jaburg, the helicopter pilot, came in with a bottle of rye, which he had been working on since early evening [20 April]. Ed, Jack, and Kim helped him finish it off. We all sat around Jack's room. Con is a very interesting fellow. Sir John Ross (the Arctic explorer) and Sir James Clark Ross are ancestors of his. Con is quite well read, and his taste in music is good. He is a lieutenant with eight years' service. Con tries to hide the fact that he has any cultural background, particularly when with his Navy buddies, as on the ship. He has a tape recorder and brought a good selection of music including jazz and operatic arias. He changed his mind about coming down here but was unable to unvolunteer.

Jack and I recorded "Damnation of Faust" until 0230 one morning in the rec hall. I printed pictures one Sunday afternoon. I just finished reading the best-written Antarctic book I've seen yet, *The Antarctic Problem* by E. W. Hunter Cristie. It discusses the history of

N. Aughenbaugh fueling Weasel. Weasels were used for seismic and glaciology work around Ellsworth Station.

this sector of the continent and the dispute between Chile, Argentina, and Great Britain over competing claims. One night I read Orwell's *Animal Farm* before going to sleep.

Ed, Jack, Kim, and I sat up until 0200 another night arguing whether a physical phenomenon could exist if it could not be measured, and whether men like Einstein deserve the fame they have received or whether the great discoveries credited to them were just the result of their scientific environment and would have to have been made by someone at that time anyway.

We had a discussion the other day in which I asked how many of us would have come here if we could have seen how things were going to be. I wasn't too surprised to find that Ed and I are the only ones. Really, in spite of all our bitching, things are quite pleasant. I'm more upset about getting fat and the fact that my sheets have shrunk to the point where they won't fit around my mattress than I am about anything else. Otherwise I'm quite happy and content. All these other happenings will make quite interesting and humorous memories in the future.

24 April, Wed. Jack's boss in Little America called him up for a [voice] talk on the Navy channel. Reception was too poor to converse. Ronne was quite surprised . . . and pointed out again that we can't talk business by ham.

This ham gear was state-of-the-art single side band, which the Navy was not yet using in 1956. Although the hams were used for recreation purposes only, they still worked better for voice communication at all of the Antarctic stations than the official Navy radios. For messages during the IGY period, including all of those quoted in this book, the Navy relied on manual key-operated equipment. Chuck Forlidas and Bob Haskill were the Navy operators who had to send, by hand, and receive, by ear, all of these messages using Morse code.

Although Ronne typically didn't allow us to have ham contacts with scientists in the program, he finally allowed Jack and Don to speak to their boss in Little America. Unlike Ellsworth, Little America had ham contacts every day all over Antarctica and talked to Shackleton constantly. After Crary had returned to Little America from a week in the field doing seismic work, and was close to the radio, Ed, who was with Jack and Don, hoped Crary would ask to speak to him, but he didn't ask for fear of Ronne's reprisal.

24 April, Wed. We helped Jack and Don set up their whistler antenna . . . an all-wood mast about 35 ft long which we stood up in a hole 8 ft deep. There are no guy lines.

The whistlers we observed in Antarctica are caused by lightning strikes in the Northern Hemisphere resulting in a "signal" that travels along magnetic lines of force to the conjugate point in the Southern Hemisphere. Due to dispersion, it sounds like a whistle. Soon Jack was recording whistlers on their fine tape recorders.

25 April, Thurs. I feel I don't get enough exercise on these days we work in, and I have trouble getting to sleep at midnight (probably because I sleep an hour after supper). Tonight I took a walk around the camp about 2200. The sky was overcast but I managed to keep my footing among the sastrugi, which are so compacted that one does not wade through them but walks on the surface.[3]

26 April, Fri. The sun came up today in spite of Hugo's calculations that it had set for the last time yesterday. It was visible for about three minutes. There was a mirage effect when examined through binoculars and dark filter; an image could be seen above the sun. Everyone was out taking pictures. Hugo maintained that the whole thing was a "very interesting phenomenon." The temperature was quite warm (above 0°F).

27 April, Sat. A few days ago, Augie took Darlington's book to read, and now several of the enlisted men have read it. Clint (not knowing it was in circulation) said it would be bad if it got into enlisted men's hands. Spear was joking about sending a hamgram to Jennie Darlington telling how he enjoyed the book; I can imagine how Ronne would like that.

At breakfast today (before the Captain's arrival) Ken Kent returned Darlington's book, *My Antarctic Honeymoon,* to Don. He had it beneath his shirt, but Ronne saw and recognized it while he was leaving. Ed Davis, the cook, came in just after breakfast and Don lent him the book, signing for it in his own name. A few minutes later Ronne came in with blood in his eye and called Ed into the library. A moment later he called Don in and made him get it back from Davis. Ronne was really mad and Don sort of lost his temper, too. Kim and I were in the iono lab but couldn't help hearing, because they were both shouting. Don, realizing he couldn't argue about the book, blew up about one of Ronne's statements. . . . "You can call me a liar behind my back, but don't call me a liar to my face!" Gaining more control he shouted, "Are you through?" When Ronne said, "Yes," [Don] stalked out of the room. . . . Ronne told Ed to remove that book from the library; Ronne also told Ed that none of the enlisted men were allowed to read or use the books in our library. I don't believe he knows that there are at least two other copies in camp.

While we were sitting in the galley late tonight for our usual snack, we saw that the floor beneath the stove was burning. Fuel oil had dripped down and had caught fire. The blaze was put out quickly by Ed Davis. This is the third (fourth, counting the Sno-Cat) fire, and all were caused by defective heaters or stoves.

28 April, Sun. No church today. About noon, while I was sleeping, the Captain asked Don and Ed up to his room. Don was restricted from use of the rec hall for two weeks. This punishment and its acceptance by all of us is one more tacit admission that we are on a Navy base. . . .

Kim and I took the bunk beds apart, and now his is against the wall separating us from Don and Jack. The lighting and the tile give a much more pleasant aspect to the room.

Paul has not heard from his girlfriend for a month and has sent three hamgrams with no answer. This is getting him down, and he is pretty discouraged about everything here as a result.

For a few days, we have had a phantom in camp who posts notes in various places constructed from words and letters cut out of magazines. Tonight during the movie, someone pinned a blood-stained note to the Captain's door with a bloody knife saying, "The Phantom strikes!" Instead of taking it as a joke and not mentioning it, Ronne really blew up.

Con was in our place playing Scrabble and Mac came in to get him. They held a board of inquiry, consisting of Con, Mac, and Clint. All the men who did not attend the movie were rounded up and grilled individually. Don, Jack, and I were all sleeping during this time, but no civilians were questioned. In fact, we officially know nothing of the incident.

Men are now speaking of the buddy system, and joking about not going to the head alone. Most of the men took the whole thing as a good joke. As Ed put it, we should be concerned, because the more dissension we had in camp, the more difficult our work would be; but still it was funny.

29 April, Mon. Our warm spell continued with temperatures around 0°F and overcast. Almost everybody was at the movie tonight. Everyone is jokingly accusing each other of being the Phantom. The word is that the sleuths found a thumb print on the knife.

30 April, Tues. Chief May announced he would go on mess duty. He told the Captain that he couldn't spare any of his men for the job and would do it himself. Ronne would not permit him to do mess duty as a chief petty officer, but insisted on one of May's aerographers. This forced them to cut down to one weather balloon launch (radio-sonde) per day instead of two. Ronne called Jerry in to discuss this; the resulting explosion drove Mac out of the building and caused Clint to try and quiet them three times. Ronne mentioned that they should be able to operate twice daily with four men, and Jerry pointed out that they only had three. They went around for a while on Jerry's working on his own IGY program rather than helping the Navy. "Fearless" [Aug's nickname for Jerry] pointed out that he has done their work for so long, that he is way behind on his own.

Jerry was the one person among us that Ronne couldn't intimidate. He had spent World War II on a destroyer in the Indian Ocean. As a result of Jerry's clash with Ronne, Aug greeted Don at dinner that night with "Hello Number Two," referring to Jerry replacing Don as number one on Ronne's hate list. Aug was now in third place.

Up until a few weeks ago the men all liked Ronne, and their enmity was directed mainly at Spear and Clint. Partially through his own actions, and possibly Darlington's book, Ronne is now cordially disliked by the men. All the Navy people including officers don't think Ronne acts befitting to a "four striper." Any time he has a notice posted, signed with his name and "Captain USN," someone always pencils in an "R" [for "Reserve"], the correct designation in his case, after the "N."

Spear on the other hand is now more popular with the men and is really close to being, as he boasted soon after we landed, the "most powerful man in camp." Thus far, he has Ronne and Clint afraid of him because he is their means of controlling the men. He has managed to become instead of the most detested person in camp, fairly well liked by both civilians and enlisted men.

1 May, Wed. Crary sent us a message asking whether any of the glaciology-seismic people wanted to stay a second season. None did, but we all were interested in coming down the summer of 1958–59. We drafted a reply which stated this and included our names. Ed took the reply to Crary in to Ronne and had to listen to his troubles for 45 minutes. Ed said, "If he continues this way all winter, I think he is mentally unbalanced." Ronne drafted his own message in answer to Crary but he refused to list our names.

Ronne sent a coded message to Odishaw [executive director of the U.S. National Committee for the IGY (USNC-IGY)] about us which ran along the following lines: "Orange is uncooperative, a menace to morale, —— [all derogatory statements]. [Pear and other fruit code names], the good expeditioners are working hard to produce results in their disciplines. Specific recommendations will follow."

I later found that this message refers specifically to the traverse people and that Augie is the one being blasted. I think that is most unfair and underhanded. Ed tried to dissuade him and defended Augie to no avail.

Siple sent a long dispatch out protesting the restrictions on use of ham and Navy radio for general IGY use and exchange of information. Apparently they had been having trouble with Little America Station. I hope it does some good. Mac thought it was a lot of hogwash. Two messages came in [on 5 May] authorizing us to use ham gear for discussions among IGY personnel.

Paul talked with his girl by phone patch, and is almost convinced she still loves him. I received a hamgram.

By this time it was dark outside most of the day. Ed and I spent our scientific working days on various seismic experiments around

109

Ellsworth when the weather was good, and inside interpreting our records on bad days.

2 May, Thurs. We saw the 1937 movie *Captains Courageous,* with Spencer Tracy. I think this is the best sailing movie I've ever seen.

3 May, Fri. Ed and Hugo exchanged memos with Ronne and finally convinced him to send a message to Crary in Little America on the subject of the Sno-Cat clutch. In it Ronne added,

> THEY ALSO HAVE RUMOR OF CONFIDENTIAL NA-
> TURE THAT INDEPENDENT GROUP MAY LAND HERE
> LATTER PART OCT/NOV AND HAVE THEM DELIVER
> THEIR SPARE CLUTCH WEIGHING 38 LBS NET. I HAVE
> NO KNOWLEDGE SUCH OPERATION. RONNE.

Ronne's remark about having no knowledge of the delivery was a flat-out lie. In his message, he alluded to the Lassiter Air Force party, which was always a bit mysterious. I now think that Ronne did not mention Lassiter's name in the message because this CIA mission was probably classified. Although we all knew about it and Ronne freely discussed it, it was still always a bit murky.

During this time, the U.S. was concerned about cold war matters and was secretly considering making a claim to the entire Antarctic continent. The Lassiter mapping mission was probably related to the U.S. claim interest, although nothing was formally pursued. The Antarctic Treaty, signed in 1959 by the 12 acting Antarctic countries, froze the claims issue but did not resolve it. As noted earlier, the U.S. and U.S.S.R. maintained at the time that they each had a "basis for a claim"; the U.S. and Russia still do.

The temperature was 11°F. Paul and Aug dug about six feet of the deep pit, but although they have it covered I expect that it filled in tonight because we had 50-knot winds.

The IGY glaciology program called for construction of a deep snow pit to measure snow accumulation, temperature, snow density, and other characteristics. Under Hugo's direction, this was the glaciologists' major project for the winter. Paul and Aug started on 3 May, and the project took until August to complete. Ed and I started helping on 27 May and continued to the end.

A heavy canvas pyramid "tent" was built over the 10-ft-by-10-ft (3-by-3-m) square opening at the top. There was a bright electric light at the bottom, which in the white reflecting snow provided plenty of illumination. Hugo designed the pit to incline at 75° and taper to about 6 ft by 6 ft (2 by 2 m) at the bottom. At each 3-m-depth increase, the glaciologists would spent a few days making observations, while Ed and I worked on other projects.

At the South Pole Station, a snow "mine" was dug at a shallow angle, and the snow melted for water. Ellsworth was the only station to have a deep pit dug outside during the winter. Ours was located about a quarter-mile east of the station, away from camp interference, and eventually reached a depth of 31 m (about 110 ft). Hugo designed 3-ft-wide plywood platforms, placed about 17-ft intervals, to stand and work on. Semicircular holes were cut at one end, and the more than 100-ft wire rope ladder, with aluminum rungs, passed down through these along the right side of the pit looking down. We would stand on the platforms to work, and they gave us the illusion of security in climbing up and down.

Hugo and Paul made their measurements from the continually deepening bottom as the pit was being dug, so there was no danger of their falling. At the top, the pit was dug into fairly compacted snow, called firn, that densified nearly to ice by the bottom. As the pit gradually deepened, we gradually grew used to climbing up and down the ladder. Later when the pit was deep, only a few visitors ever had the courage to climb up and down.

Although outdoor temperatures at the pit site were quite cold and the wind made working on the surface difficult in the dark with lots of blowing snow, it was relatively comfortable in the pit itself. Here there was no wind, and the temperature was the mean annual temperature in the Ellsworth area (about −10°F). Paul and Hugo worked at the bottom stripped to their long undershirts while digging. Snow was hauled out in a large rectangular wooden box called the "bucket" by a one-inch-diameter manila rope run through a block and tackle suspended at the top, and pulled up by a Weasel. The bucket, with crude runners on one side, was raised and lowered using the Weasel, along the 75° inclined wall next to the platforms.

The three of us working at the top would disconnect the bucket, pull it away, and dump the snow. During most of the digging, I drove the Weasel. When Augie signaled me to stop by waving his hand silhouetted against the light from the tent, I would climb out to help. I would trudge towards Ed and Aug frequently though the blowing snow and the strong south wind were stinging my face. By that time they would be hitched up with waist and shoulder straps, and I would put on my waist loop.

At a voice signal, we would heave our weight against the canvas straps and the heavy bucket would start to move. We pulled it about a hundred feet laboriously over the snow and dumped it at the end of the row of earlier hauls. The snow was too cold for the box to slide easily. At −40°F the friction was so high, it seemed like pulling along a sand beach. It took the three of us to overturn the bucket and get the snow properly dumped in place. We then pulled the bucket back, hitched it to the block and tackle, and I carefully lowered it down into the pit guided by Augie's waving arm.

By the time the heavy bucket reached the bottom, Paul and Hugo were ready to fill it again. The process was repeated over and over throughout a typical workday. Six years later when I read Aleksandr Isayevich Solzhenitsyn's *One Day in the Life of Ivan Denisovich,* his description of working in the winter dark in the Siberian Gulag brought back memories of digging the pit.

The glaciologists collected snow samples at close intervals for measurements of density; they measured the stratigraphy for determination of annual accumulation, studied grain size, and made other observations. Even though there was no wind in the pit, this relatively inactive work at about −10°F inside was very chilling; Hugo, Paul, and Aug wore their warmest clothes for it.

Our routine during the pit-digging was to go out about and work two hours. We would then go into the station for coffee. During these days of total darkness, the coffee break was essential to get a bit of warmth, light, and most importantly, fresh pastry with lots of butter to snack on. We shouldn't have been drinking so much coffee while working outside at such low temperatures, though, because coffee is a diuretic, which became apparent on our short quarter-mile hike back to the pit! I learned this for the first time that winter, but drank coffee anyway—for the psychological boost it provided, I suppose.

At noon we would eat a huge meal, after which I usually took a half-hour nap. Mid-afternoon coffee and snack was followed at

1700 by another huge meal. I usually napped for a couple of hours after that and stayed up most of the night with coffee and half a dozen slices of toast dripping with butter at midnight. I could not get to sleep until about 0400 or 0500 and would then race to breakfast at the last minute (0830) and force down some cooked cereal and then sleepily head outside to work. I noted about this time that I was still having insomnia even when I didn't take a nap after supper, but that many others in camp did, too. In fact, about half the camp wandered about all night during the winter. I tried to skip breakfast a few times when working outside but found I was too chilled by coffee-break time. I suppose I was eating more than 5000 calories/day. I gained about 35 lbs to about 210 lbs, which helped keep me warm.

> *4 May, Sat.* Paul and I spent the afternoon printing Aug's killer whale pictures. They came out quite well. I had a phone patch home through a ham in Minneapolis, but the radio band dropped out before Grob and Ed could make a contact. Chuck McCarthy, who operated the radio, thinks my mother has "the sweetest voice" and surprisingly clear for a woman on the radio.

This was the first mention of my getting a phone patch. My journal shows that I only received two until late September when communications were better.

> *5 May, Sun.* I was awakened by Don at 1030 and after consuming two steaks I set out together with Don, Hugo, and Ed about 1130 for a short hike. We wore snowshoes and carried ice axes and a rope. The temperature was −26°F, but there was no wind and it was quite comfortable. The sky was clear at first but became overcast. We walked down to where the ships landed. The edge has broken off almost as far as the dead men [the ship mooring points]. There is still a lot of debris lying around. I never thought I'd find an old beer can in the Antarctic, but I did today.
>
> We left the landing site and headed west around the point and down the coast of Bahia Chica to our old seismic work ramp. To our knowledge no one has been along here before. There were numerous crevasses, and the surface was quite irregular. We passed a very good example of the doughnut-shaped "blowouts" with a snow cone in the center, that Aug is interested in studying. This one was about 20 ft deep, with the cone about 50 ft high. It was too dark to take any pictures.

After Hugo stepped through snow bridges three times and Don and I once apiece, we decided to rope up. When we neared the foot of our ramp to the tidal crack we found another section had cracked off forming a crevasse about 40 inches wide with the downhill edge about a foot lower. Don jumped across but Hugo, after looking down in it for a while, decided his sore back wasn't up to it so he unroped and waited for us. Ed jumped and then warned me about the taut rope between us. Fortunately I slid forward a couple of feet when he hit the end directly over the crevasse. I jumped over and we examined the tidal crack.

As usual the new sea ice was mushy near the crack and sticky back away, due to the salt leaching out. When we climbed back up hill, I managed to step across the gap, and Hugo and I pulled Don and Ed over with the rope. We returned to camp, much refreshed by our walk, about 1400.

Two men died in a crevasse near the base at McMurdo several years ago on just such a Sunday afternoon excursion. However, we were fairly experienced with crevasses by this time, and were roped up, so there was no particular risk to us.

I read Albert Camus' *The Rebel* and am reading Vilhjálmur Stefánsson's *Arctic Manual*. Don, Aug, Paul, and I played bridge for the first time since the ship left.

6 May, Mon. Ronne sent another press release which is full of the distortions which I am now convinced that everyone who writes for the public about Antarctica is guilty of, e.g.: "Suns rays dipped below the surface 24 April to return until latter part August. Those who braved elements topside –37°, 18-mile wind witnessed beautiful sight whole northern heaven aflame." It was actually about 0° to –5°F with little wind, and we just saw a little color where the sun was.

"Temperature hovers between –26° and –40°." Actually the range has been around 10° to –10°F the past couple of weeks. . . .

After chow Ed and I set up one of the two-man tents supplied by the Navy. It is pretty nice but too heavy for backpacking.

There was an external frame which supported the tent using elastic bungee cord, the first of this type I had seen.

7 May, Tues. It was about –14°F most of the day, so Ed and I decided to sleep [out] in it. . . . I slept in a single bag with my trousers under me until about 0400 by which I became a little chilly, so I put the outer part of the double bag on and slept well. I found out later the low for the night was −43°F, which is the coldest so far. Ed used an air mattress and a different type of double, but was a little cold. Hugo, not to be outdone, slept out in the open [without a tent] near the pit on his coat in a double bag.

We were furnished with double Army mummy-type sleeping bags consisting of 40% down and 60% feathers enclosed in a strong cotton fabric. The outer bag had a nylon lining so the inner bag could slide easily. These were too heavy for backpacking but excellent for our needs. The feathers did not compress as 100% down would have and were thus better on the snow with slight insulation beneath the bags.

In 1957 we did not have foam mats or 1990s' type of small air mattresses. I was never cold in a double bag although this particular night was probably as cold as I ever encountered camping out in Antarctica in 12 trips. By contrast, one sunny summer "night" in December 1991, it was 76°F due to solar radiation inside a small tent at about 6000 ft elevation on the West Antarctic Ice Sheet.

We were awakened at 0855 by Augie. My flashlight batteries had frozen, so I couldn't see my watch and we overslept. When we came in we found Kim, Jack, and Don still asleep. Hugo had overslept, so Paul, Aug, and Jerry were the only ones who made it to the mess hall.

Jerry was sitting at one of the side tables having coffee, and Ronne was at the end of the long table. The group at Jerry's end was discussing green coconuts, and Jerry remarked in his usual language about the laxative properties thereof. Ronne didn't appreciate this and said, "I don't have to listen to that kind of talk while I'm eating." Jerry replied, "I told you before that I'm not going to change my way of talking. If you don't like it, eat quick and get out." This somewhat disturbed the Captain, and he told Jerry to come to his office at 1030. Jerry told him he was too busy at that time. Ronne came in and told Ed about it and asked him to bring Jerry in at 1130. They went in and Jerry was ordered to stay away from movies for two weeks.

After lunch Ronne brought in a memorandum in which he pointed out that we civilians came under the Uniform Code of Military Justice (UCMJ) while at this station.

Jerry came to the movie tonight and if looks could kill, Ronne would have felled him. Ronne gave Jerry a written statement that he was judged guilty of disrespect to the commanding officer as specified under certain sections of the UCMJ and as commanding officer, he was restricting Jerry from the privilege of attending the movies for two weeks. It stated he would be ejected forcibly if necessary, Al Spear was appointed master at arms by authorization posted in the chow hall to enforce the sentence.

Even today, I think it was a very grave error to have both the position of chief scientist and Navy officer in charge vested in the same person. Ronne played one role or the other depending on its convenience in the situation. Of course we civilian scientists learned to play that game effectively, too! I was quite comfortable talking to senior officers like Ronne (or later Admiral David Tyree at McMurdo), pilots, or enlisted men who had something I needed for my work (e.g., food supplies or mechanical help). If I was told to go through the chain of command, I always played the dumb, inexperienced civilian. However, we all took advantage of whatever "officer" perks our status entitled us to. Eventually these perks became zero at Ellsworth but were useful in future years on Navy ships and at McMurdo and Byrd as long as the Navy ran the U.S. Antarctic Program. The NSF, which has run the program since the 1970s, knows quite well how to deal with would-be prima donna scientists.

> *8 May, Wed.* The temperature went down to −45° by 2100. This is the coldest I've ever seen it. The stars are out by 1300 now. The people at the Pole Station have lost an average of 16 lbs apiece and are quite concerned about it. They all suffer from insomnia. It is −70°F in their tunnels.

> *9 May, Thurs.* At about 1700 this afternoon Captain Dickey in Little America, Ronne's commanding officer in Antarctica . . . called Ronne on the Navy circuit. It so happened that Paul was in his room and overheard the whole conversation. It also happened that Ed, Don, and Jack overheard it on Jack's receiver.
> The gist of the conversation was that we come under the UCMJ only where damage or theft of equipment is involved or where personal life is endangered. Dickey said, "As near as I can make out, the same rules that apply to Navy technicians apply to them. I don't mean to imply that all are Navy technicians." A few minutes later

Ronne came in to us and asked for the information that [IGY] gave us [with our contracts]. He said, "I just talked to Captain Dickey and he told me that you are all Navy technicians and therefore come under the UCMJ."

Con had heard this end of Ronne's conversation with Dickey on his tape recorder. The Navy transmitters put out so much power that various pieces of electronic equipment in addition to radio receivers around the base picked it up. Consequently Ronne's numerous "secret" conversations throughout the winter were commonly heard at Ellsworth on hi-fi phonographs and tape recorders. Ronne assured Dickey repeatedly that everything was under control and asked him to hold the report that he had sent in on Jerry's "court martial" at Little America. Ronne said that Jerry wouldn't need his copy of the report, but Jerry refused to give it back.

Ronne saw my prints of Augie's whale pictures on Don's wall. He came to me and said, "Did you develop those there whale pictures?" I said I had, and he asked, "Do you have the negatives?" As a matter of fact I still did, but Aug had specifically and emphatically stated that anyone could have prints except Ronne. I hedgingly replied, "Augie took those; I had color film in my camera." I took the negatives back to Aug.

About 1600 I hiked out to the pit. The moon is three-quarters full and it is clear and very beautiful outside.

Working outdoors throughout the winter gave us a perspective on the *Sturm und Drang* inside the station, which helped get us through the winter.

10 May, Fri. The temperature dropped down to –67°F at the pit and about –65°F in camp this morning and stayed in the 60s all day with a 10-knot breeze. I thought it was supposed to be calm at temperatures this low.

This was the coldest temperature measured at Ellsworth during the winter, although May was not the coldest month. Normally in Antarctica August and September are the coldest.

I walked out to the pit, and later in the afternoon Ed and I took a walk. I was quite comfortable in my thermal boots and Holubar

117

parka with a sweater and a long undershirt under it. I fixed the hood so I could button my fur-trimmed hood inside. I wore my field trousers, long johns, and a pair of wind pants, but was a little cold in the legs. I still haven't found a solution to the glasses-frosting problem. I wore a face mask, which kept my nose from freezing.

Aside from Walt Davis, who operates the tractors (one diesel D-4 is kept running continuously), none of the Navy people spends much time outdoors. Paul, Aug, and Hugo spend more time out than anyone. The temperature in the tunnels is −53°F.

Spear kidded Don in the garage about what "the Old Man" was going to do when he found out we listened to his conversation on Don and Jack's radio. Don denied any such occurrence.

As it turned out, "the Old Man" never found out, and the comment only showed my paranoia! Eventually, more or less everyone—civilian, officer, or enlisted man—felt he could speak freely about almost anything without fear that it would be reported to Ronne. The dynamics between Ronne and the rest of us were heating up as we got into the winter. I'm sure this would have happened with Ronne and a similar isolated group of independent, young civilian "scientists" and Navy personnel anywhere, but the fact that almost everyone at Ellsworth stayed indoors 24 hours a day only made our situation worse.

11 May, Sat. Ronne wants to put Aug, Paul, Don, and me on mess duty to "raise the men's morale." I wouldn't mind the idea if the officers of similar rank and the other IGYs were also put on. Ronne says it wouldn't look right for officers [Con, Clint, and Willie] to do this kind of work.

We are officer status when it suits his purposes and apparently lose any such rights and privileges when he wishes it. We GS 9s are the equal of a full lieutenant, or so Ronne said in Davisville, and we were informed on the *Wyandot.* GS 11 corresponds to a lieutenant commander.

Jack, Hugo, and Ed had a meeting with Ronne about his mess duty plan. As Ed described it to me, the discussion was carried on in Ronne's frustratingly illogical manner. Whenever a point is raised that Ronne can't argue down, he doesn't answer but changes the subject. Two of us will be off scientific work for two weeks at a time (probably it will be me and either Paul or Aug first). The chiefs and officers will apparently not take their turn. Ronne refused to [address] that point when Ed brought it up, and changed the subject. He told Hugo to give him the name of Aug or Paul as the man he could spare. Hugo said he couldn't spare anyone, Ed said he couldn't spare me, and Jack answered the same for Don. Ronne told him to appoint someone and Hugo asked for that order in writing. Ronne blew up at this and Ed said, "That's all right, Hugo. We have witnesses."

This made the Captain really hit the ceiling; he accused them of trying to "get him." Hugo said, "Let's not get excited," and Ronne answered, his voice raised a couple of octaves, "Who's excited, who's excited?" He is the most impossible man to argue with I have ever met!

After the movie (Grace Kelly in *Dial M for Murder*) the May party was held, with a birthday cake for those whose birthdays are in May, which included me. Hannah got his eye blacked in the party festivities.

12 May, Sun. About −40°F with a 30-knot wind, rather unpleasant. Ronne told the cooks that Paul and I would be working for them. Ed told him at breakfast that we wanted a written directive and Ronne got mad. He said he would furnish one. We waited all afternoon and evening but nothing showed up.

13 May, Mon. When we came in to breakfast at 0830 as usual, we were met with many black looks [we hadn't reported to mess cooking]. After breakfast we started shoveling out our back porch and repairing the tunnel. The wind was 40 knots at −35°F, and it was quite miserable.

Later in the winter the drifts completely covered the tunnels and we were sheltered from the weather completely as we worked or walked between the buildings "inside."

About 0930 Ronne descended upon us. This time he had a written directive which not only put Paul and me on mess cooking, but changed the IGY meal hours to coincide with the men.

To: Dr. E. Thiel, Deput. St. Sc. Leader
Subj: Household and Maintenance Duties

1. Effective immediately in accordance with Ref[erence 2] you are directed to furnish two IGY civilian personnel for mess cooking under the supervision of E. Davis, CS 1. They will be on duty two consecutive weeks commencing 0745 on 14 May 1957.
2. All IGY personnel will eat with the general mess, breakfast

0800 to 0825; lunch 1230 to 1255; and dinner 1700 to 1725.
3. Upon completion of this duty, another directive will be forth-
coming in regard to assignment of personnel for maintenance
and housekeeping duties. Finn Ronne

Ronne said we shouldn't take any more coffee breaks but wrote a
memo rescinding this later in the day. Ronne and the other four
officers now have their own private sitting. This new arrangement
was greeted enthusiastically by the men, particularly the fact that
we now are subject to mess duty. . . .

Our objection to this detail is not that we feel we are above that
sort of labor but that it hinders our scientific work and we feel that
the officers should take their turn if we do. Be that as it may, Paul
and I are now rising at 0700 and working until supper dishes are
finished. This sounds like a long day but actually it is only about six
working hours as we get a couple of hours off between meals. I
wash and Paul wipes. I think everyone else is more upset at this
situation than we are.

Ronne asked Dick Grob [the baker] how Paul and I were working. He appeared to be either surprised and/or disappointed to find
that we were working hard and cheerfully. Paul and I have washed
so many dishes in our lives that this doesn't seem particularly unpleasant. . . .[4]

The rest of the IGYs spent the day writing memoranda to Ronne
and receiving answers. One follows:

From: IGY Scientific Discipline Leaders
To: Capt. Finn Ronne
Subject: Performance of Maintenance and Household Duties by
IGY Personnel

In your directive . . . to the Dep. St. Sc. Ldr, . . . you have ordered him to supply two IGY scientists to perform mess duty
for two weeks beginning today; you quote Reference 2 as your
authority for so doing.

   In as much as we, in one accord, have advised you against
such action because of the serious curtailment of the IGY scientific program, which would necessarily result from such action,
we respectfully bring to your attention the following section of
OPNAV pp. 21–100 A Regulations Governing U.S. Navy Technicians: "Section III part 9. Special Orders Regarding Technicians: (e) Technicians shall be allowed to carry out duties to which
they have been assigned by the sponsoring Bureau or Office,

and when necessary, shall have Naval personnel designated by the commanding officer to assist in the execution of these duties, and should not be required to perform routine Naval duties which would interfere with the basic orders."

Because of the conflicting views prescribed in these two references, we request clarification from higher authority.

CC: A. P. Crary, M. G. Morgan, H. Wexler, N. J. Oliver, H. Odishaw

At one point today, Ronne mentioned to Hugo, . . . "You are all keeping diaries and writing down everything I say. But you won't put anything over on me because I'm keeping a diary, too."

We were all basically healthy during our winter in Antarctica. There were no illnesses, as is typical for an isolated group there. However, there were various minor injuries that were exceptions to the rule. When Spear heated a closed can of plastic wood on a space heater, the can blew up and sprayed the stuff in his eyes. The cornea of his right eye and both lids were burned. Spear had both eyes bandaged and was led around by McCauley for a few days until the bandages were removed. A few days later, Ed Davis and Greaney were wrestling around and Greaney fell and twisted his leg around a table leg reinjuring on old injury.

The temperature at the Pole was down to −100.2°F the other day. We saw *How Green Was My Valley*. No hamgrams have gone out for three weeks now.

14 May, Tues. We had to shovel snow drifted into the galley tunnel for a couple hours this morning instead of our two-hour break.

15 May, Wed. Hannah changed the camp wiring around a few days ago enabling the generators to be operated safely without constant supervision. This increased the power noise in the whistler receiver. Jack told Ronne that for the whistler program to be feasible that they would have to set up the generator under the old system, which included a generator watch. Ronne cried on his shoulder for an hour about the inequities of the IGY people. As a result, a memo from Ronne was delivered . . . : "Two enlisted men will participate in the re-established watch, and it is hereby requested that you furnish one IGY person or persons to cover a period of watch standing in the generator room. The IGY person or persons selected by you should report to Hannah during the working hours on 16 May for instructions. This new watch will commence on May 17, 1957 at 0830."

This shook everyone up, and while Paul and I were cleaning up supper, the rest had a meeting to discuss policy. This means that one-third of the scientific staff will be taken off scientific work.

The movie tonight was *The Caine Mutiny* with Humphrey Bogart. Some of the similarities between Queeg and our Captain are too close for joking; almost everyone, except Ronne, noticed this.

I finished Stefánsson's *Arctic Manual* and am reading *Gods Graves and Scholars* by Ceram.

16 May, Thurs. Ed went to Ronne and asked him if he were granting our request of 13 May for clarification by higher authority. He also asked if we would be allowed to use the ham gear. Ronne answered, "No!" to both questions. He said, "All you have to do is follow orders and see that they are carried out." Thereupon Ed presented him with the two following and walked out.

16 May 1957
Captain Finn Ronne
Station Scientific Leader
Ellsworth Station Antarctica

Dear Capt. Ronne:

As deputy station scientific leader I have two responsibilities: (a) loyalty to you and your program of administration, (b) loyalty to the IGY scientific program. At present the two responsibilities are in sharp conflict. The force of your directives placing one-third of the scientific personnel on camp maintenance will result in a serious curtailment of the scientific program; I cannot in clear conscience endorse such a decision. I also cannot approve the strict communication censorship which exists on this station. From time to time I have made suggestions concerning replacement of the Sno-Cat clutch, operation of the amateur radio equipment, the equitable distribution of mess duty, etc., but my suggestions are never accepted. It would seem that my position as deputy station scientific leader is merely a convenient means for you to issue directives to the scientists.

Under the circumstances, I tender my resignation as deputy station scientific leader.

Very truly yours,
Edward Thiel

16 May 1957
To: Capt. Finn Ronne
From: IGY Personnel
Subject: Curtailment of scientific program

We, the entire scientific staff at Ellsworth Station officially protest your actions (ref. memos of May 13 and May 15), knowing
that a serious curtailment of the IGY program must result. We
therefore cannot comply with your request (ref. memo of May
15 [about the generator watch]) until we obtain a voice contact
with Deputy Chief Scientist A. P. Crary.

IGY Scientific Staff Ellsworth Station

Ed's letter of resignation was never forwarded to higher IGY
authorities and eventually quietly forgotten, officially. However, it
was discussed at an all-day meeting of the nine scientific personnel
at the National Academy of Sciences at which we were "debriefed"
on the day we arrived back in the U.S.

At this point things had come to a head. We as a group were
refusing to comply with Ronne's directives and he was adamant.
We insisted on a voice communication with Bert Crary (as chief
scientist in the winter in Antarctica). Essentially we were going on
strike, although no one used this term.

At 1000 Ronne came in and called Jack out for a talk. He spent an
hour and forty-five minutes with the Captain in which Ronne ranted
about the unity of the group. Jack insisted that we are not refusing
point blank to cooperate, but that we thought things could be ironed
out if we could talk to Crary. Mac and Clint came in as well. The
conversation was repeated individually with Hugo and Ed.

Hugo corroborated Jack's statement about a contact with Crary
being essential and that Ed was the man to talk. Ronne told him
that he and Paul would have to leave their room during any conversation with Crary. Hugo said something about censorship, which
made Ronne almost lose control of himself. He denied any censorship vehemently. Apparently Ronne feels a little guilty on this point
so is quite touchy about it. He grabbed Hugo's arm, and Hugo said
he almost hit Ronne.

Ronne consented to a voice contact with Crary. He showed Ed,
Jack, and Hugo the dispatch he had prepared. Ed said it was not
acceptable and Hugo told him, "No gentleman would send a message like that."

17 May, Fri. About 1645 a contact with Little America was made and the battle began. Hugo had already tipped us off in the science building and the radio and tape recorder were running. Jack and Don taped the whole conversation, and Kim and Don sat up late getting it typed up.

In the following transcripts, all of Ronne's repetition appears exactly as it was recorded. The tape recordings capture in Ronne and Ed's exact words the tense atmosphere at the station at this time. I doubt that many recordings like this have been made at a wintering-over Antarctic station. We had state-of-the-art technical capabilities within our IGY group. The word "nerd" had recently been invented by Dr. Seuss; we all were nerds.

RONNE: This is Ronne. We have sent you a message this morning regarding IGY personnel. It is actually not as serious as it appears from the message. However, I would like you to make a decision on the message with regards to the IGY personnel for extremely limited duty as indicated in my message to you. They do not wish to participate in any activity whatsoever. They maintain that it is below their dignity to participate, for example in mess duty, which has never been asked of them before last Monday. But, the basic policy that should be determined by you is whether or not I am permitted to have them perform extremely limited duty–if it is within my prerogative to have them perform extremely limited duty outside the IGY work, provided it, in my opinion, does not interfere with the IGY program. That is all. Over to you.

CRARY [this transmission was poorly understood on the tape recording using the receiver in the ionolab]: This is Crary. Hello, Finn.——certain things in the operational plan————the civilian personnel will not normally be assigned maintenance duties——— it is not the intention they will be assigned normal military duties——if you construe this is unusual you have every right to ask the civilians to do military duties————you should remember, however, you don't undermine the scientific program————personally my feelings are————we should volunteer to work the same hours as the military personnel————

RONNE: . . . Now, I will put Dr. Thiel on the line and he has his view which is exactly contrary, and considerably confused according to the directives that I referred to in my dispatch, as well as the situation here. I have gone into the work program, and they

124

have lots of time to do other things except assist slightly in the work that I ask them to do. Here is Dr. Thiel.

THIEL: This is Ed Thiel. I have four points to discuss this afternoon [but was allowed to discuss only one]. I do not concur with the message Captain Ronne sent you this morning. It presents a one-sided view. Difficulties here have led to my resignation as deputy station scientific leader. I cannot maintain both loyalty to Captain Ronne and loyalty to the IGY program when it requires hurting that program to the extent of taking three of our nine men for base work. This is a matter for policy decision, and we ask for your decision. I speak for all nine of the scientists–all nine–the unanimous viewpoint.

The first point I wish to discuss is base maintenance. For mess duty Captain Ronne has requested four men in two shifts lasting two weeks apiece, a total loss of two man months. We . . . have two men on mess duty now. This has forced me to abandon the seismic study. . . . This program was abandoned. Abandoned because of the two traverse people now on mess duty. Our deep pit program is now lagging. Captain Ronne feels that two or three men are sufficient to dig this pit. I feel four or five are needed to dig the pit. I would like to see the entire traverse party on the pit.

Admiral Dufek's letter dated 1 August 1956 states "shall be equitable shared." Captain Ronne places great emphasis on the "shall" and ignores the "equitable." He has exempted many of the enlisted men, all chiefs, and all officers from mess duty. Do we have officer status? The dish washing would be a bad blow to IGY morale at this station. We have put in many hours to do nonscientific work [discusses generator watch of one man full time, until the ships come in next summer.] To meet his present requirements would mean we would have to use one-third of our personnel. I feel that there are 30 men here to support the nine of us. My opinion is that they can do without our going on mess duty or generator watch.

We pledge our whole-hearted support in emergencies as in the past. That was the first of four points I wish to discuss. We request your opinion on whether we must serve mess duty and whether or not it shall be equitable, that is, involves all personnel on this station except ranking officers. That is the first of four points. Over to you.

CRARY [reception again poor; excerpts follow]: Finn———your message———but I do not feel your———am piecing it together———say in reply, I am sorry difficult time———program watch———sacrifice to time————and from our experience here it is————necessary to shut down on his program————manning the generator uses all the time he has————the rest of the program————he has every right to do so rather than shut down on his program————in regard to the other trouble————operation should be equitable————station should contribute————operational plan———decided———emergency————perhaps I didn't cover all your questions.

RONNE: Crary, this is Ronne speaking again. I will have to correct the false statements. I will have to correct the false statements. I will have to correct the false statements by Dr. Thiel. They are false! We have two IGY men on mess duty right now. They will finish a week from Sunday. They will finish a week from Sunday. I do not intend to have any IGY men on duty until Neuburg has completed his deep pit. I do not intend to have any IGY men on duty until Neuburg has completed his deep pit. That was the first false statement by Dr. Thiel because he does not know. I told him that. They make up false statements among themselves not according to the facts. The second false statement he issued was about the generator watch. That generator watch by IGY personnel is not, is not intended to last until the ship comes in. It is only to last for about two months. That means there are still five men available to dig the deep pit, but as he said it is a human question, and unless I get authority to work it out in the best interests of the IGY program, no settlement can be made with Dr. Thiel, because these disputes will keep going on.

Furthermore he mentioned that all the military personnel here are not doing anything. Radio operators are on watch 12 and 14 hours every day, and the other men are all working hard. We still have lots of equipment in the tunnels not even opened. As soon as that equipment has been cleared away and snow cleared out of the tunnels, I will have an additional enlisted man available for generator watch so all of the statements made by Dr. Thiel are absolutely false. He does not know the facts! He is talking only from the talk he has had with the other IGY people. That is about all I have on the subject, but I can assure you that the seismic work that he outlined–it will be going on without any delay whatsoever.

Involved here is a morale problem that he and his associates have not the slightest conception of. They have done much to make it harder for me to keep up a good morale. I will come back to the basic principle again–that I be allowed to have them perform extremely limited duties without going into details. The authority was invested in me and the responsibility is entirely my own. I shall do the utmost to see that the IGY program is not being retarded or curtailed in any way whatsoever. Over to you, Crary.

Capt. E. W. Dickey was the Navy officer in charge of all Navy personnel and operations during the winter on Antarctica, and was Captain Ronne's Navy commanding officer in his capacity as officer in charge of the "Navy" Ellsworth Station. Although Ronne used his unique situation of being both station scientific leader and Navy officer in charge to his advantage, in this case it worked against him. Both he and Ed thought that this voice contact was with Crary only, as requested, and were unaware that Dickey was listening beside Crary in Little America. You never can tell who is listening when you talk on the radio. As we later learned there were people in the U.S. listening, too.

DICKEY: This is Captain Dickey——point of view of the Navy representing Admiral Dufek——We are committed to supporting the IGY. As far as officers and CPO's for mess cooking, as far as I see it there is no need for them. Of course they are all ready to go if they are needed. I know they are, here. Is it really necessary?

    The work should go according to seniority. I'm sure they all have mature judgement, but if they refuse they are all going to answer for it. The military are definitely going to have to answer for it any way you look at it. This is an IGY expedition down here, and I know the Navy would never want it said we wouldn't support this operation down here. And we are going to be held responsible if the IGY is mistreated——and I'm sure you have the same thing in mind, that you have done a good job here—— and let's see if you can work it out yourself and get more——I'm sorry the communication is so bad, but does that make any sense to you? Over.

RONNE: Captain, this is Ronne speaking. This is Ronne speaking. Yes, it makes sense to me. Yes, it makes sense to me, but unfortunately it does not make sense to the nine IGY men here. They have their own union. If you can hear me, I will repeat a few phrases I said in my last conversation. The statements by Dr. Thiel about generator watch by IGY until the ship returns is false–false! The statement that IGY men will be on mess duty for months is false. The statement that IGY men will be on mess duty for months is false. The statement that the deep pit program is being hampered is false. The statement that the deep pit program is being hampered is false. It will not. The work will go on as before.

Ronne had refused five times to let Ed talk again and ordered Ed out when Captain Dickey came on. We found out that Ed was outside the radio room, and Don got so mad he ran up and started shouting about these injustices. He yelled when Ed told him Ronne wouldn't let him in: "I'm going to kill that bastard!" Ed finally went back in and told Ronne he had to talk. Ronne gave him permission to discuss the Sno-Cat clutch only. Ed started to talk but the band dropped out.

> Ronne accused us of forming a union of the 9 IGY people stronger than "the United Mine Workers."

Although he had referred to the nine of us having a union, the colorful phrase about the United Mine Workers does not show up on the tape transcript, which I obtained a copy of several months later. This is how myths get started, because that is what we all believed had been said. About three weeks later, Hugo made a sign with "United Mine Workers" at the top and "Weddell Local" at the bottom. He put this up at the top of the pit inside the tent.

> Ronne called Jack later in the evening. To Jack he appeared a beaten man, but I can't believe that. He told Jack that when Paul and I finish our mess job there will be no more camp work for the civilians. Jack and Ed are willing to let things cool down. Most of the men listened on the radio in the rec hall. Ronne kicked everyone in camp out of the communications building but almost everyone heard this side of it. They really are mad at Ed.

> *18 May, Sat.* [my 25th birthday] Ronne sent the following to Little America. I never thought I'd see him admit an error; I hope things will be better from now on.

> PASS TO CRARY. EXPRESS APPRECIATION, YOUR CLARIFICATION OF IGY DUTIES THIS STATION. THIS HAD CAUSED SOME MISUNDERSTANDING DUE TO WRONG INTERPRETATION ON MY PART. ALL IS NOW CORRECTED AND RUNNING SMOOTHLY.

BEST REGARDS,
RONNE

A few days later Ronne called Spear in and asked him a list of questions about need for civilians on base maintenance, etc. He recorded the whole conversation and gave Al a list of prepared statements as answers to read. These recordings were made of other people, some quite openly. It would be historically interesting if these tapes are still available somewhere.

19 May, Sun. Kent sent some hamgrams out for the first time since 4 May and received some in. I received a couple.

All the water that we use in the kitchen (galley) we get from a snow-melting tank in one corner. The drifts are now high enough around camp that Walt Davis pushes a pile of snow up every couple of days to the roofs of the heads and the galley with a D-8. The snow melter below is filled by Paul or me about four times a day via a chute from the roof. The only heat is that of the room. From there it is pumped to the water heaters, showers, washing machines, and faucets. There is running water only in the two heads and the galley. Because the nozzle for the fuel injection system of the hot water heater in the galley was lost when it was installed, this apparatus is not useable. All hot water in the galley is obtained by heating it on the stove or from the steam jacket of the coffee urn.

This is another example of the routine ingenuity of the Navy and IGY people throughout the year. I mention only casually a few of these makeshift repairs and inventions because we came to take them for granted. Jack and Don had to trace the circuits of the six-foot-high C-4 ionospheric recorder because no diagrams were available at the time of shipment. I improvised a totally different condenser in repairing the high voltage power supply for the seismic gear, etc. We really had a talented group—all volunteers— extending to Wally Cox, who was a really creative photographer, Ed Davis the cook, and Dick Grob the baker. Eventually the generator watch problem was solved by more ingenuity.

The baker at the South Pole needed still more ingenuity. The elevation there is about 9600 ft but at a pressure elevation of nearly 12,000 ft. The experienced Navy baker sent there had never tried his craft higher than sea level. I recall that someone in the States had to find recipes for bread, cakes, etc. corrected for this eleva-tion and send them in messages.

About the coldest temperature measured at the Pole in the win-ter of 1957 was –116°F. Earlier that season at a higher elevation than the South Pole the U.S.S.R. also established Vostok Station on the polar plateau. This was the first winter that any interior stations had been operated in Antarctica and no one knew what to expect. The world record low temperature of –126.9°F was recorded at Vostok on 24 August 1960.

20 May, Mon. Warm (about 5°F) and windy. Mathis cut my hair. Everyone has been kidding me about it. Apparently it wasn't such a hot job. This is my first haircut since early January before the ships landed.

21 May, Tues. The Captain came up to me in the head this afternoon and thanked me (and Paul, who wasn't there) for mess cooking. He told me, we have done more to raise morale than anyone. After supper he asked me if I wanted a phone patch and said Mac would get me one. Unfortunately the band dropped out.

At present the tentative [ship] itinerary is *Wyandot* to B.A. [Buenos Aires] and thence to Santos, Brazil. Ed, Kim, Paul, and I are think-ing of jumping ship and touring north and across the Andes by railroad. Then up the west coast to Caracas. From there no one is sure where.

We had hoped that if we stayed out of the U.S. for 18 months, not counting transit on the high seas, our income would be exempt from federal taxes. We never actually stayed out of the country that long, partly because we were not sure it would work. How-ever, several men of the scientific groups at other U.S. Antarctic stations did. This point was controversial. Although Antarctica is outside the U.S., it is not recognized by the U.S. as being a part of any other country. Eventually courts ruled that Antarctica has a "high seas" status for tax purposes, so no Americans working there are exempt from U.S. taxes.

22 May, Wed. Warm (5°F), overcast. We saw another *Victory at Sea* at the movie tonight. The Navy films contain many chapters of this television series, about World War II, which I enjoy; there is an original score by Richard Rogers.

23 May, Thurs. The wind began to blow in the afternoon (10°F) at between 40 and 50 knots. We saw *On the Waterfront* in the evening.

24 May, Fri. Winds up to 55 knots out of northeast all day. Davis couldn't see to drive the D-8, so water was short. Shoveling snow into the galley hatch was quite a project. Hannah put two spotlights on Kim's tower, but I could barely see them through the blowing snow. I went up in the aurora tower and looked out a hatch in the side. It was quite a sight to see the driving, swirling snow lighted by the floods as it swept past. I think that most of camp will be drifted over when this storm is over.

The tower was quivering and humming like a sailboat running before the wind on a full plane. The guy cables to the tower were slack on the leeward side. I keep telling Kim it will blow over if we have a strong wind out of due north or south. Kim's tower is really coming along nicely.[5] He built a bunk and has a mattress up near the ceiling on the east end. There he counts meteors through a pair of binoculars mounted in the roof. He sleeps up there in the afternoon; it's quieter.

These curious meteor observations were an official part of our program because of a report from one of the Byrd expeditions that a very high number of meteors were seen during the winter. However, the IGY observations showed this not to be the case. Probably the earlier report was based on some optical or mental illusion resulting from staring too long at the night sky.

Hugo and Aug became lost trying to find their way out to the pit and had to return to camp and start over before they could find it.

This could have been quite serious. A few years later a man disappeared at Byrd Station in the winter walking in blowing snow from a building outside the station, and his body was never found.

I wonder what is happening to the planes. They are not covered but are only protected from four sides, which I would think would encourage drifting. I think it would have been better to remove the wings and tie the planes down out in the open.

The Sno-Cats are out in the open, away from camp, but the Navy vehicles are parked all together close to the buildings and many are completely covered. I think this is quite foolish planning, particularly since we had plenty of warning from the first few small winds.

Very few people get outdoors at all anymore; our traverse party digging the pit and Walt Davis and the weather balloon launch crew are the only people who regularly do. I don't believe Kent, Mac, Clint, or Ronne have been out in a month, yet these are the people who sit in the ham shack and tell people how terrible the Antarctic is. Paul heard Clint tell someone on the radio that conditions are so bad that it is only possible to spend a few minutes at a time outside. I heard the Captain jokingly state that he isn't going outside until the sun comes up. It is now dark 24 hours a day. It gets a little lighter towards noon, but stars are still visible.

25 May, Sat. There is a lot more drifting around camp. The water for the galley today was melted from slabs, one by five feet long, that I cut from a long drift on the roof.

Ronne sent out another press release. It was nauseating, filled with distortions like "huge rift, three miles across, 250 ft deep extending east-west for hundreds of miles." "Dwellers of ice entombed Ellsworth Station are getting ready to roll out of their sleeping bags and start day." Only a couple civilians use sleeping bags rather than sheets and blankets and Ronne has complained about this.

"Killer whale packs several dozen still poke pointed heads up through ordinary ice floes. . . . Their mouthful of teeth and snorting sound makes one tremble because they will attack human beings every opportunity. They are the man eaters of Antarctica, wild beasts of the sea. I thought they had withdrawn long ago." No one has seen a killer whale since we quit our seismic work at the tidal crack.

"Your breath gives hissing reverberation. Moisture you exhale immediately freeze. Ice crystals grind together as they leave nostrils or mouth. One of the strangest things about cold temperatures." I have yet to observe any phenomenon like this.

Ed has been removed from the list of people who receive dispatches so [that] the IGY people don't see anything anymore.

Somehow we still managed to "see" a lot.

From what I have managed to pick up in the galley today, Don got pretty high with some of the men in the rec hall last night. He spent all day in bed.

"High" in those days referred to drinking alcohol. In the 1970s and early 1980s there was pot at McMurdo, the South Pole, and some of the field parties; but use of that became quite low, if not nonexistent, by the 1990s. Booze continues to be the main problem of drug abuse in Antarctica, as it was to a small extent during our winter at Ellsworth. However, by 1995 even alcohol use was way down at McMurdo. Probably this is partly the result of the presence of a number of grey-haired men and women and only a few Navy people, who are quite young.

26 May, Sun. I hiked out towards the explosive magazine for a mile or so by myself this afternoon. It was overcast with a little wind. Visibility was poor but it was quite warm. It is really quite lonely out there when one gets beyond sight of the lights of camp. I'm glad I had a compass. Everything is grey and black; there was absolutely nothing visible except the snow. Although it was night, there was light enough to see oneself, the antennas, etc., when they were near.

As I walked across the snow, every so often I would cross an area underlain by hoar frost, or depth-hoar, as it is sometimes called. This is an air space left under several inches of snow by recrystallization. My weight would collapse it with an indescribable noise somewhere between a crunch and a sigh over a wide area. As a snow bridge over a crevasse sounds like that when the hoar frost on the underside falls off, one tends to be wary of such sounds. In spite of the fact that we know any crevasses in this area are safely bridged, I still can't get used to the sound of the depth hoar collapsing. I am not alone in this feeling, however.

I lay down on my back on the snow for a few minutes and just contemplated the sky. All of the troubles we are having seem so petty when facing the real Antarctica.

27 May, Mon. Paul and I finished up mess cooking after the supper dishes last night. We joined the boys in the pit today.

By this time my beard was about four inches long, and it helped keep my face warm. However, the balaclava helmet I wore always froze to my beard from condensation from my breath. Icicles would routinely form from my nostrils. All of the others who worked outdoors were in a similar situation. I finally partially kept my nose from freezing by use of a "nose jock," a Navy piece of clothing that provided some protection to my upper cheeks and the top of my nose. I wore "waffle weave" long underwear, a heavy sweater, my Holubar windbreaker, field pants, wind pants, cushion-sole wool socks, white rubber thermal boots (the identical boots called "bunny boots" in the 1990s), and "bear paw" mittens (too small) with knit liners. The mittens were tied to a web strap and would dangle from my neck if I took them off.

Mathis had lent me more or less permanently his VX-6 fur hood of the type that is independent of a coat. I wore this under my parka more easily than the one issued with my too-small-to-wear field jacket. The fur trim was a great help in keeping my face warm. Still, our noses and cheeks suffered minor frostbite regularly and gave our faces the appearance of sunburn even though it was dark out all the time. It is 1998 now, and I have this very useful fur hood hanging ready to put on, in my cabin at 10,500 ft in the Colorado Rockies.

28 May, Tues. We dug the pit down to six meters in the morning, but it already looks quite impressive. Our present technique consists of Paul and Hugo digging and filling the wooden bucket Hugo made. I suggested dumping the snow right next to the tent and getting Davis in a D-8 to push it away when a pile accumulated. Ronne has told Hugo that they cannot use Navy equipment or personnel in the pit construction, so that is out. We had to work to get a Weasel.

Ed and I were dismissed from the pit while the rest make their glaciology measurements. Ed typed three copies of the recording of the talk with Crary. He needs a copy because Ronne has accused him of lying to Crary, and there is no telling what he has quoted Ed as saying in his [Ronne's] log.

Apparently Don and Ronne are on speaking terms again. He told Don that he thinks he made a mistake in letting Ed talk to Crary. He said that everyone in Antarctica was listening to it. He knows that the talk was recorded, and he asked Jack to destroy the tape.

29 May, Wed. I continued computing today.

I used the term "computing" very loosely. We had a Friden electric-powered mechanical calculator with which I was reducing seismic data. Times have changed since then. When I was in a remote field camp in Antarctica in 1991–92 we had 15 computer terminals (including 5 workstations) for 13 scientific personnel operating in a Jamesway hut, although some of us were living in tents.

After morning coffee Aug and Paul took a Weasel and went out looking for their accumulation stakes, so I helped Hugo by standing in the bottom of the pit recording stratigraphy. Interesting but cold, although it was only –10°F, because I wasn't moving around.

Snow accumulation levels were measured in two ways during IGY in Antarctica. Actual measurements were made, as Paul and Aug were doing, by putting out a network of stakes over a several-mile-wide area well away from the station to avoid errors caused by drifting. The other method was to measure the thickness of identifiable annual layers in the deep snow pit, shallow snow pits dug on the oversnow traverses, and using hand-drilled snow cores about 30 ft deep, also on the traverses.

Ronne gave Ed and Hugo a memo this noon about the traverse preparations and the clutch replacements, which stated in part: "I know of no flights coming in here and first ships will be here on 10 January 1958."

E. Thiel reducing data with Friden calculator in science building. Frost gravity meter to right of chair.

Tonight Jack happened to be listening on his receiver and heard Forlidas talking to "Taffy," Shackleton's operator. Forlidas explained that "there is interference here at one minute past the hour, five minutes past, 15 past, 30 past, 40 past, 55 past, 59 past, and on the hour. It is the ionosphere people, and we can't make them stop."

It was amusing to listen to Taffy in his very English voice conversing with Forlidas' southern drawl.

30 May, Thurs. (Memorial Day) Holiday Routine so I slept in until 1130.

31 May, Fri. I received three hamgrams. I stayed up and read until 0430 this morning and took a nap tonight from 1730 to 2200. Hugo is still taking data; at this rate we'll never finish the pit. Snow has been melting on the roof and dripping through the cracks between panels that haven't been sealed with tape. Hoar frost is growing on the ceiling of the tunnels.

1 June, Sat. [In the deep pit] Hugo, Paul, and Aug are cutting out snow blocks for tritium analysis by the AEC [Atomic Energy Commission].

These snow blocks were for nuclear bomb fallout studies. One of the jobs of the glaciologists was also to take surface snow samples as soon as the ship landed and send them back for fallout analysis. Radioactive fallout was measured in Antarctic snow from nuclear tests, which were conducted in the air in those days. Ironically that air testing period still provides a good marker horizon to measure snow accumulation all over Antarctica and Greenland, whatever the radiation from those tests did to our bodies. The Chernobyl incident had as great a measurable effect in Antarctic snow as the 1964 peak bomb test year.

Con, Jack, and Ed came over to our room this afternoon and drank beer and talked. Jack read some Thurber, which put Ed to sleep. He doesn't appreciate that kind of humor. Tonight Con dressed up in a suit and tie for a joke. It was strange to see.

2 June, Sun. It is −40°F. today. We have been taking vitamin pills to keep us healthy, etc. Poor Ed apparently never learned how to take a pill because he goes through a real ordeal every day, and everyone sweats him through each time. It's quite painful to observe (either aurally or visually).

Scurvy was a great problem on the early expeditions and probably contributed to the death of the Scott party on their return from the South Pole in 1912. By the IGY, however, with the ample

136

supply of frozen fresh meat, fruit, and vegetables, the issue was not even considered. This was before the concept of megavitamins as a dietary supplement, but small doses of vitamins were recommended by the Navy medical experts of that day.

For working outdoors, that is, outside the base in the dark, I wore a warm pair of insulated rubber thermal boots. However, inside the base I always had on a pair of heavy box-toed Army ski boots. These were plenty warm for walking in the tunnels at –40°F, and not too hot indoors. As no one else wore these, and because they made quite a loud noise when walking on the hollow wood floors, Hugo hung the nickname "Walking Thunder" on me. Apparently it was apropos.

> *3 June, Mon.* It warmed up gradually from –19°F at 0900 to –4°F at 1700. We dug all day; I operated the Weasel. Hugo and I put up safety lines for the people at the edge of the pit to snap into with a carabiner, and Hugo installed the wire rope ladder with aluminum rungs. A 50-ft length folds up quite small and weighs about 10 lbs.
>
> I took two hamgrams in to get them cleared by the Captain tonight about 2200.

As mentioned previously, Ronne used the ritual of censoring our hamgrams to strike up conversations and unload his troubles. He may not have realized that we always discussed these sessions among ourselves afterwards. I suppose he was quite lonely that winter. He was about 20 years older than the next oldest people at the station. He constantly spoke negatively about someone or other, so eventually–and frequently–we all were criticized by Ronne to each other.

> At first he was just friendly and thanked me again for mess cooking. Then he started in on the troubles we've had and went over everything that has happened, even Jerry's run-in with him. He told me Jerry said, "Go to hell!" and "Fuck you!"
>
> Ronne blames Ed for everything and says he has a record of all that happened and signed statements by witnesses. Apparently the memos Ed and Hugo have been answering him with have really gotten to him; he showed me one which really upset him. Ed's talk with Crary upset him, too. . . .
>
> He thinks that we will all fail in our scientific program and that while we were subject to mess cooking, etc., we could use that as

our excuse. Now we are all on our own and have no such excuses. It isn't conceivable to him that we might prefer it that way. He talked about the traverse quite a bit (he doesn't have much hope for us there) and kept stressing the point that if we get through the heavily crevassed area surrounding us for about 30 miles, we will have pretty easy going to the southeast. (He mentioned "southeast" several times.) We would much prefer southwest as that would tend to tie us in with the other traverses. I can see that we will have a lot more trouble before the traverse begins.

Ed certainly is in a difficult position. Ronne is trying, by talks like the one tonight, to turn the rest of the civilians against Ed, and I don't think he will be successful. I said to Ronne in parting tonight, "Well, Captain, it's a long winter."

While Ronne and I were talking, he felt a tremor in the shelf, although I didn't notice it. Paul, over in his room, also felt it. Eventually the shelf did break off. Charles Swithinbank of the British Antarctic Survey told me about 20 years later that some of their scientists saw part of Ellsworth Station in the cliff of an iceberg drifting in the Weddell Sea. The front of the Filchner Ice Shelf advances more than a mile (about 2 km) each year, and bergs regularly break off.

4 June, Tues. 15–20 knot wind at –26°F–rather hard on the face. The moon is up almost half full. Quite clear. We excavated all morning and in the afternoon put the first 2½-ft-wide platform at 17 ft down.

I printed up a picture of Jerry Fierle clowning with a cigar in his mouth. Someone had put up a photo of Toulouse Lautrec, from the movie with Jose Ferrer, and labeled it Fierle (he is quite short). I cut the face out of my print and pasted it on the other with a rather humorous result that everyone got a kick out of.

Clint and Mac mixed up some martinis using ethanol (190 proof) for gin and Chilean white wine for vermouth. They almost burned the insides out of their throats until they diluted it. Together with Con, they came over, and a cocktail party was held in the ionolab. They must be quite sick of beer.

5 June, Wed. Temperature was –36°F and the wind died so it wasn't too bad working. The moon gave me enough light to see where we were hauling the snow.

6 June, Thurs. We dug down to a depth of a little more than nine meters today. It was –45°F with a 20-knot south wind which frostbit our faces in a few seconds of facing it directly. With balaclava wool helmets, fur hoods, and facing into the wind as little as possible, we managed without too much trouble. I found it necessary to leave my glasses in the Weasel when I got out to help haul the bucket of snow, as they frosted up immediately if I pulled my balaclava over my nose.

I was very nearsighted and could barely see without the glasses.

The tip of my nose was nipped yesterday, and it was quite painful and tender today. Mac mentioned the other night in all seriousness that he thought it would be a good idea to check out with him when we go out to the pit. Some of these people are so afraid of the dark that they don't even know what it is like outside.

7 June, Fri. Paul, Aug, and Hugo spent the day taking data in the pit. It was about −10°F at the bottom and Paul . . . became miserably cold just standing, rather than digging. He said there was ice inside his thermal boots.

Ronne is writing a report consisting of several pages about each of us civilians for Navy or IGY.

I think now that this was material for Ronne's book, but my comment shows our paranoia.

Several days ago [Ronne] called Don in and asked him about Jack, and yesterday Jack was asked to describe Don. I think he is working on me now because tonight when I came into the galley for coffee he asked me how tall I was. He thought I was the tallest person at the station, but I thought Jack was. When Carl Crouse came around on fire watch, someone suggested we measure Jack, Carl, and me. The results: #1 Behrendt 6 ft, 3¼ in., #2 Brown 6 ft, 2¾ in., and #3 Crouse 6 ft., 2 in.

I slept from 1800–2300 and stayed up until 0530. Con and Jack spent several hours chatting and drinking beer in our room tonight until 0330. Con mentioned he felt insulted by the fact that three of the five officers here are restricted from the radio area. After several requests by Ed and others, we received some of the other stations' scientific sitreps a few days ago.

8 June, Sat. There was an official party tonight in the rec hall. Clint furnished two bottles of whiskey (limited because of the Captain's orders) which went fast, but there was lots of beer. Everyone was given 20 poker chips and various games were played (bingo, pool, blackjack). I returned about midnight from reading and joined a poker game with Mathis and Greaney; I was lucky and won most of their chips. Forlidas took the 14 Jack had left, and within an hour he and I were the only ones left. We counted up our winnings and found he had about 200; I had 157. Willie Sumrall had won 105 at bingo and retired earlier. The prizes were 1st $15, 2nd $10, and 3rd $5.

We actually had no cash at Ellsworth, so these prizes were only credit at Ship Stores. However, I bought a nice electric razor, which I never used that winter, for my prize.

9 June, Sun. I finished Gould's book *Cold;* it was quite enjoyable and expresses feelings towards the Antarctic that are similar to my own.

10 June, Mon. We resumed our digging. The temp. was –33°F with a 25-knot wind from the south that made it rather painful to face. Several of us have been nipped in the nose, but this is no worse than sunburn.

The moon is up and full now, and it is really quite beautiful out. Visibility is perfect and we don't even need the lights of the Weasel to drive by. Around noon on these clear days, a reddish tinge is visible on the northern horizon even though we are only 11 days from the shortest day. The stars are extremely brilliant and distinct, although when the moon is highest some of the fainter ones are not visible.

Don recorded a couple of songs from some Asian or Near East stations today (he couldn't understand the language). They are rather interesting and a welcome change from Fats Domino. Paul and I printed pictures until 0400. I helped Con print up some pictures he and Willie took of each other.

I had more experience in developing and printing film than anyone at Ellsworth, except Wally Cox, so I frequently gave pictures to people or helped them process their own.

11 June, Tues. The wind diminished all day and the temperature was around –46°F. It was more comfortable today than Monday. The moon is so bright that the color of the clothes and the Weasel were quite apparent. I loaded Kodachrome 12 into my camera and shot a few pictures. Paul and Hugo are now using a mattock to chop the very hard firn, as it is impossible to push a shovel in.

Kim and the Captain had a long talk in which Ronne cried on his shoulder about all the usual subjects and a few more. He only wants to be nice to everyone, yet everybody is always coming up with some new trouble as fast as he settled the previous one. He still harps on Ed's talk with Crary and Hugo's shooting movies on the plane ride last fall [which he objected to at the time]. Ronne told Kim he wasn't "writing a book this time because nothing is going on." Ronne exclaimed to Kim about "all these people and only one small traverse in the field!"

Four years later, Ronne's *Antarctic Command* was published, in which he gave us all hell! We were angry but not surprised.

Ronne's small, private 1946–48 expedition had several field parties with dog teams supported by air. When we went to Antarctica during the 1956–57 austral summer, the only field programs carried south by the 12 ships were the three (Ellsworth, Byrd, and Little America) oversnow traverse parties. Starting in the following season, during the IGY, other field parties began operating near Little America and in later years, farther out of McMurdo and Byrd Stations. Therefore, during our two summer seasons essentially all of the logistic effort of the U.S. program for science field parties was in support of three geophysical-glaciological traverses. There was a massive logistic field effort involving D-8 tractor trains called "swings" to support Byrd Station from Little America. The South Pole Station then, as now, was totally supported by air.

Ronne can't see why the government will put money into Antarctic programs that don't have any application towards exploiting any wealth which this continent may possess. He has so many troubles here that he can't concentrate on his writing. He almost had a nervous breakdown after his last expedition.

He would like to organize (but not come down on) an expedition in the future to do more mapping using the abandoned IGY stations. However, he does not think these buildings will stand up under many years accumulation of snow.

Ronne was right. The U.S. IGY stations built on the snow were Ellsworth, Little America, Byrd, and South Pole. They were planned to last only two winters, but Ellsworth lasted four (two by the U.S. and two by Argentina), Byrd five, and the original South Pole—with only about four to five inches of snow per year accumula-

Tent over deep pit in moonlight. N. Aughenbaugh at right.

tion—lasted some years longer. I spent time at Byrd Station in the summers of 1960–61 and 1961–62 and saw how the station was collapsing by the weight of the heavy overlying drifts. McMurdo, Hallett, and Wilkes Stations were built on rock, and in the summers the snow melted away. A few of the original buildings remain at McMurdo today.

> Ronne thinks we should be working on the traverse plans now rather than on the pit. The people next winter can do that. We should be packing food and planning it. I agree with him here, but every time I have mentioned this, it has not met with much enthusiasm.
>
> Ronne, in his conversation with Kim, even went into the past and told how Byrd always tried to block him. The idea of what later became the East Base of the U.S. Antarctic Service Expedition was his originally, but Roosevelt didn't know of him when he heard of it and called Byrd in, and Byrd took it over. When he took his own expedition to East Base at Stonington Island . . . Byrd fought against his getting support in Washington.

East Base, which has not been used since Ronne's expedition, was designated a Historic Site at an Antarctic Treaty Consultative Meeting in about 1990. It is the first U.S. station on bedrock in

Antarctica, and therefore the only early one that remains. Byrd's various Little Americas on the Ross Ice Shelf were crushed by snow load and ultimately drifted out to sea like Ellsworth. The politically correct view today (with the exception of a preserved Australian station) is that bases or buildings built before World War II are "historic," and those built later are trash and must be destroyed and the debris removed.

Mac came in and cried on Jack's shoulder (with the help of a case of beer). He told Ronne that he considers it an insult to the officers of this base that they are restricted from the radio room. Ronne, who can't afford to have Mac against him, too, agreed to let him run things his own way and that the officers could go in the radio (and ham) areas. As Mac was leaving, Ronne added that this did not apply to Clint Smith, as he wanted him to get up in the morning.

12 June, Wed. It was down to −51°F early but was up to −29°F later this morning. It was so warm that we worked with our hoods back, and I had my parka unzipped. I left my wind pants at home after noon but found to my dismay that the temperature was dropping fast. The cold came in through all the holes in my trousers and made me unhappy. The temperature was down in the −40s°F when we quit for the day.

13 June, Thurs. The temperature was in the low −50s°F all day, but it was quite calm and therefore comfortable. The snow is not slippery at these temperatures, so moving the box [snow bucket] from the pit is like dragging it over sand. This morning there was a red glow on the northern horizon and a ring around the moon. Sea smoke, indicating open leads in the ocean, was visible in a few places. These leads must be constantly changing, as the fog appears in a different place every few days.

"Sea smoke" refers to water vapor from the relatively warm open sea so exposed, condensing in the frigid air as a local fog. When backlit against the orange glow of the sun below the horizon, sea smoke was quite beautiful.

We finished 12 m depth before coffee this afternoon, and now the glaciologists will take over the pit. Aug is having trouble hearing their shouts as he stands in front of the tent directing me as I raise and lower the bucket with the Weasel. It seems as though the snow is absorbing the sound of their voices.

Ed talked to Geoffrey Pratt, the seismologist at Shackleton at 2100, and we heard the conversation on the radio in the iono lab. Pratt said that he had done a little reflection work and discussed his results with Ed. Ronne was right there and had previously told Ed to make it short. He reiterated his previous statement that he saw little need for future contacts. Taffy, their operator, said something about them having frequent contacts with the Argentine Base Belgrano (35 miles away, between Ellsworth and Shackleton) and asked us if we contacted them. Ronne told Kim that we are not going to talk to Belgrano. "We don't want to have anything to do with them; the British don't either." Hugo knows a glaciologist over there who he met in Greenland and has wanted to talk to for some time. Small chance!

Paul was over in the evening, and he and Kim discussed their women until I fell asleep about 0100.

14 June, Fri. I have been studying glaciological reports of the United States Antarctic Service Expedition (USAS) in 1939–41. The USAS had two bases: West Base at Little America on the Ross Ice Shelf and East Base on the Antarctic Peninsula.

The USAS, in the Division of Territories and Island Possessions of the U.S. Department of Interior, was meant to be a permanent agency representing U.S. interests in Antarctica. World War II interrupted this, and all personnel were removed from Antarctica in February 1941. I attempted to find out what happened to the USAS after the war but found nothing. Although not funded and with no personnel, the USAS may still be a legally authorized federal agency.

Mac came in and had a little talk with Ed about the support VX-6 will give us. Ed explained that he and/or Hugo should be on the flights that we shall need to determine a route. He told Mac quite definitely that while we all recognize and hope to make use of Ronne's experience, he [Ed] and Hugo will determine where the traverse will go.

There are 26,000 gallons of avgas [aviation gasoline] (of which Mac says Lassiter can have only 10,000). Ed mentioned that Ronne might sacrifice the traverse program to give Lassiter more gas. Mac told of a message received today stating that the station CO [commanding officer] has direct authority over all Navy operation except VX-6. Mac talked of flying fuel to us every couple of days. Mac told me that the Otter burns approximately 30 gallons/hour (in its single engine) and can average about 90 mph. This means that 16,000 gallons should be far in excess of our needs.

Four days later, Mac received a message from his superior in VX-6 stating that he was not authorized to make any commitment of avgas. This meant Lassiter couldn't use VX-6 gas, and perhaps wouldn't come down. Ronne ran around in circles trying to figure a way of circumventing this. Ed asked the rhetorical question, "How many gallons of gas would he want for a new clutch?"

The question of avgas use persisted through the winter and into the spring. The issue became very political with Ronne making "secret" phone patches to Washington to go over Rear Admiral Dufek's head, to get authorization for use by Lassiter. Hugo and Paul, whose room was separated from the ham shack by only a quarter-inch plywood wall, heard many of these conversations while they "slept" because we were two hours ahead of Washington. All of this, of course, had a great impact on plans for our long oversnow traverse.

15 June, Sat. The temperature was up to 8°F last night with a wind, which was a rise of over 60°F in 24 hours. I cleaned the head this morning and then slept most of the day until 1600. I had been up reading until 0530 in the morning. Ronne had brought some tracing paper over so I traced Ed's copy of the *Wyandot* navigator's chart of the edge of the shelf.

Our early papers in 1958–59 using *Wyandot* and *Staten Island* data and our preliminary traverse results were the first scientific publications from this part of Antarctica.

I went over and talked with Augie and Jerry for a few hours. When I returned I found Paul and Ed in our room, so we four chatted until 0200. Paul talked with the Captain today, and Ronne told him he doesn't think we will get through the crevassed area. He said Hugo will head right back for camp at the first snow bridge we have to cross. He, in his usual fashion of orally brooding over past events, even went back to the inefficiency of the seismologists out on the bay ice at the end of February. He thinks it is too dangerous for us to go out there–killer whales will attack us.

145

16 June, Sun. It was 3°F outside with a strong wind. I stayed up until 0500 reading and slept until 1230. Ronne, Don, Paul, and I played bridge in the library this afternoon. Don and I won by 90 points, but the Captain called it a draw. When we added up the score, Ronne said he should get another hundred points because he had a hundred honors in his first hand (which he hadn't mentioned before).

Despite all of the tensions in the camp, we continued these occasional Sunday bridge games with Ronne during the winter. These were enjoyable, and because Don, Paul, and I were among the most junior scientists, Ronne felt he was not compromising his power struggles with Ed and Hugo.

Walt Davis [the Seabee mechanic] dropped in our room in the afternoon, and Paul and Ed were there, too. We talked about the vehicles on traverse and about the Navy for a couple hours. Walt referred to the fleet sailors as "the canoe club."

17 June, Mon. Crary suggested, in a message from Little America, that Ed and I do some tidal work with the gravity meter. Kim commenced our two hourly gravity observations at 0045. Ed took over at 0845 and I finished up at 1645.

We used the gravity meter to measure the rise and fall of the floating ice shelf with the tide. Unlike the seismic equipment, "land" gravity meters in use today are essentially the same as those used in the IGY. A gravity meter, or gravimeter, is a weight on an extremely sensitive spring. Very slight variations in gravity can be measured by adjusting the spring length with a delicate screw to keep the "stretch" the same. The number of turns of the screw is the measurement of the change in gravity. Because the instrument is so sensitive, the internal temperature has to be kept constant by a thermostat and a battery-powered heater. We were measuring differences in gravity at Ellsworth to better than one part in ten million accuracy. This is about the effect of a change in elevation of one foot in air. We would take turns reading the meter every two hours for a month. The gravity meter was placed on a tripod in the science library, so we took the readings in comfort. Kim and Jack joked that this appeared to be the only place in the science building that had "gravity."

146

We had to average the moving needle every five seconds for five minutes, as viewed through a telescope eyepiece, because of low-frequency wave motion of the floating ice shelf in response to waves on the ocean. The gravimeter acted as a seismograph. During the traverse, as we progressed inland on the ice shelf, this wave motion rapidly decreased with distance from the ice front (front of ice shelf). We planned to measure gravity on the traverse to determine ice thickness between seismic reflection stations.

The rise and fall of the floating ice shelf of about six feet twice a day with the tide was measurable by the relative decrease and increase of gravity, respectively. These measurements simultaneously at Little America and Ellsworth in the IGY were the first tidal determinations published in the Ross and Weddell Seas well away from land in the essentially "open" sea.

We appear to have a tidal period of somewhere around 12 hours here as an approximation after one day of observation.

Mac, Con, Hugo, Ed, and I had a meeting to discuss helicopter air support for the traverse. Ronne came in to get some supplies and looked somewhat surprised when he saw us all sitting around the table studying a map. He didn't say anything at that time.

The next day Ronne complained to Mac about having that meeting without him; the "key figure," as Ronne put it to Mac, was absent. Mac told him that he had initiated the meeting and hadn't asked the Captain because Ed and Hugo were the ones going on the traverse. Two weeks later Ronne told Ed that he didn't want us to have any more meetings discussing the traverse unless he was there.

Squabbles between the officers and the enlisted were common, and some men gave their officers the silent treatment, However, everyone talked to the scientists, and the science building was a favorite hangout for many.

18 June, Tues. The wind we had Monday ran drifts all over the pit area and formed lots of sastrugi. This made it very difficult to drag the bucket around. The moon is dying fast, and we had ground fog so visibility was poor and we were stumbling all the time and falling frequently. The temperature was in the –20s°F with a gradually in-

creasing wind. We spent the morning putting in our second platform about 35 ft down in the pit.

I showed Paul how to rappel. It is amazing and somewhat discon-
certing that a group such as ours, which has spent and will spend
lots of time in crevassed areas, knows as little about rope handling
and associated techniques as we do. I am the only person who even
knows how to tie into the middle of a rope. Hugo practiced a little
crevasse rescue technique in Greenland this summer, but I believe
that no one besides he and I know anything about removing a person from a crevasse. Ed asked Kim to be our alternate or replacement in case any of the five traverse people becomes a casualty;
Kim accepted.

I had had a lot of rope-handling experience in about four years
of rock climbing and a little mountaineering, including a few hours
of practicing crevasse rescues hanging from cliffs and tree branches.
When Ed and I had spent the previous summer on the Lemon
Creek Glacier in Alaska, we worked on foot in crevasses constantly,
while frequently roped up, but never practiced or needed a rescue.

Since the mid-1960s, a very good field safety program has been
run by the NSF at McMurdo, providing at least rudimentary in-
struction in crevasse rescue and other snow survival techniques for
all personnel who might find themselves in survival situations. I
have taken this 36-hour course in Antarctica a couple of times (as
recently as 1990) and relearned a few things I had forgotten. Camping out, building snow shelters, etc., prevents panic and gives people
new to Antarctica confidence that they can survive in these conditions.

Jack is operating the C-4 [ionosounder] every five minutes and is really
making the radio operators' lives difficult. There is a Special World
Interval, and all over the world right now IGY ionosphere stations are
taking readings at precisely the same time.

19 June, Wed. There was a lot of blowing snow with a 25-knot wind and
−20°F, but it was clear above. The sky was full of stars; they are very
bright down here. The Southern Cross was directly overhead, and I
could see Orion upside down (to my more boreal accustomed eyes)
along the northern horizon. Today the drifting snow is covering the
sastrugi and filling in the areas between the piles of snow we have been
dumping. Some windy days there is little or no blowing snow, while
on others there is a lot. I wonder why, as little ever actually falls.

The Captain was joking with Paul about how they beat Don and me at bridge on Sunday. I think he actually believes that they did win by this time. He cannot stand to lose at any game. Hardly anyone in camp (including all the officers) will play Ping-Pong with him because they say he cheats.

I spent the evening patching my old parka—the sleeves are getting pretty holey. This morning I had tried one of the brightly colored anoraks they issued us but the wind went right through it.

Kim installed a pair of sound powered telephones between the tower and our room. Now if there is a spectacular aurora for me to photograph he can let me know.

20 June, Thurs. We had strong southerly winds (about 30–35 knots) with very much blowing snow at about –25°F. Clint came in with psychological tests again. They didn't go into our opinions of specific individuals in our working groups as the last ones did, so we all took them.

We disliked peer evaluations and had agreed amongst ourselves that we would not participate in this part as we had done on the ship.

21 June, Fri. The wind had dropped and the temperature was down to –28°F today when we reached the pit. Hugo wanted to get to 15 m today, so he didn't putter around as much as usual and we hauled 25 buckets out.

Paul actually dug most of the snow in this eventually 100-ft-deep pit, while Hugo did the design and detail work. It was eventually exactly three meters square at the top, and tapered to two, exactly, at the bottom. Because there is less than half as much snow per meter dug at two-by-two meters square than three-by-three meters, digging proceeded progressively faster as the pit deepened even though the snow had hardened almost to ice. The Ellsworth pit was Hugo's masterpiece and the deepest dug in Antarctica in the IGY.

Ronne came out to the pit in the morning, just as we were pulling and loading up. He stuck his head inside the tent. While we were dragging the box away, he saw Hugo's UMW sign because he called down and asked him if he needed any "mine workers." He left before we returned and couldn't have spent more than a half a minute out there.

22 June, Sat. (Mid-Winter Day) Holiday Routine for this truly Antarctic celebration. We are at the halfway mark not only in the cycle of the sun but in total time on this cruise. It's all downhill now. Time has certainly gone by rapidly; there are so many things that I wanted to do that I haven't found time for yet.

I had gone to bed early the night before because I intended to get up early and print pictures. However, I slept in until 1030 at which time I had brunch [steak and eggs]. This afternoon I went into Jack's room and listened to a recording of *Don Juan in Hell* with Agnes Moorehead, Charles Laughton, and Charles Boyer.

The Captain came in and invited Don, Jack, and Ed over to his place for a little party. They had some champagne to celebrate this day. He didn't invite any other civilians although Kim, Paul, and I were all in the science building when he asked the others. Con and Mac were invited but not Willie and Clint. This seemed gross bad manners to the rest of us, and we have been kidding the three who attended the little soiree of selling their souls for a little champagne. We had a very good Christmas-type dinner this evening. Shrimp cocktail, turkey, ham, three vegetables, stuffing, two kinds of pie, ice cream, lemonade, coffee, olives, etc. Very fine meal!

About 2330 a group retired to our room and Jack read some Dylan Thomas to us. I was sitting on Kim's bed with Paul who was dropping his ashes into Kim's upturned bed lamp. Kim was in my chair, and Ed and Jack were sitting on my bed. The reading drove Paul to sleep, and Ed started reading Hemingway. Don began to play band music in the next room as loud as the machine would go. It was a very amusing scene.

Notes

1. Argentina-General Belgrano	75°8'S, 28°48'W
Australia-Mawson	67°36'S, 62°53'E
Davis Base (Vestfold Hills)	68°22'S, 77°55'E
France-Dumont Durville	66°40'S, 140°01'E
Charcot	69°21'S, 139°02'E (alt. 2400 m)
Japan-Showa Base	
Ongul Island E. Side	
Lutzow-Holm Bay	69°02'S, 29°36'E
New Zealand-Scott	77°50'S, 166°44'E
USSR Mirny	66°34'S, 92°54'E
Bunger Hills	66°16'S, 100°44'E

Pioneerskaya	69°44'S, 95°20'E (alt. 8800 ft.)
Vostok	81°00'S, 110°00'E (approx.)
Sovietskaya	82°00'S, 50°00'E (approx.)
United Kingdom, Halley Bay	77°31'S, 26°36'W
Shackleton	77°57'S, 37°16'W

2. We had no real mechanic at Ellsworth Station assigned to the traverse, unlike the two traverses planned out of Little America and Byrd Stations.
3. Throughout the winter the sastrugi built up, reaching heights of about three feet around Ellsworth.
4. I supported myself for a while as an undergrad at the University of Wisconsin by washing dishes at the student union.
5. All Kim's equipment was mounted under the three domes. Four jet heater tubes ran up from the heater at one end of the building, and a fan at each dome kept them from frosting. A 5000-watt electric heater furnished auxiliary heat, and it was quite comfortable.

5
The Long Night Goes On and On and On...

As the winter continued, our collective state of mind deteriorated. Fortunately the quality of the food did not.

Mac told Jack that apparently Ed and Ronne's ham radio conversation with Crary regarding mess duties was heard in Washington, D.C., and other places. Mac had talked to a physician in Louisiana and a ham in Washington D.C., the very next day or two who said that he had either heard the conversation himself or had heard about it. The doctor wanted to know if we needed his help. Apparently, he thought that Ronne had some mental problems. For that matter, he probably wondered if we *all* were in need of a bit of psychotherapy! The narrative continues as we worked on the deep pit and lived beneath the snow.

23 June, Sun. We played bridge all afternoon. This time Ronne and I stood Don and Paul and we won (about 900–250). Ronne still tried to claim a win for last week but didn't get too upset when Don and I told him he was wrong. Don told him he had a very convenient memory and only remembered what he wanted to. Ronne was in a very jovial mood because he'd won, so he just laughed.

Just before the movie, while I was taking a gravity reading, Ronne came in and went over a news release with Kim, on the aurora program. He borrowed our thesaurus a few days ago. Kim told him he thought it was too flowery. Ronne agreed but said that's the way the public wants it. The movie interrupted their chat, and they resumed it exactly two hours later while I was taking another reading. Kim tried to tame him down but to no avail. Ronne described red rings around the moon, which nobody has seen, and depicted the aurora as being all colors of the spectrum. Kim did manage to stop this last statement; the only colors he (or anyone) has seen are green and very occasionally red. The Captain changed his statement to "a symphony of color passing in review." Kim told him that "symphonies don't pass in review." So he changed it to "a symphony of color parading in review." All this time in the background [on the tape recorder] I could hear Faust riding down to hell accompanied by Berlioz' music at full volume and Mephistopheles' "Hop! Hop!" The whole thing was so hilarious I had to restrain myself to keep from laughing.

24 June, Mon. A few days ago, Hugo . . . reiterated his statement that I could plan the food for the traverse. Aug offered to help. If I am given a free hand, I think I can get a reasonable menu from our supplies of three pounds/person/day. I dug out the invoices for the traverse food sent us, and broke the lists down into different types. We have a lot of 5-in-1's and canned vegetables. There is a goodly amount of dehydrated stuff, too, including pork chops, bacon, and steak, which I have never tried. I think we can make a satisfactory diet from the stuff, although how much weight we can allow for food will be a determining factor. We have frozen-fresh meat and vegetables, too.

I soon realized that food weight was insignificant on the traverse. We burned one gallon of fuel per Sno-Cat per mile traveled. At 7 lbs per gallon, that equaled 420 lbs of fuel per day for two Sno-Cats traveling 30 miles per day. Even if we used 4–5 lbs of food per day per person, counting packaging, that would only amount to 20–25 lbs per day of food for the five of us.

In the afternoon Ronne was down in the garage, and Al Spear asked him if there couldn't be two showings of the movie because the men didn't enjoy it much under the present atmosphere of restraint. (Ronne has been issuing orders through his officers regarding catcalling, talking, etc.) The Captain lost his temper at this. There absolutely wouldn't be two showings. "The men all hate me," he said. He was through with appeasing them. In the future he would order court martial for offenses. He walked across the room to where Jim Ray was working, oblivious to the preceding, and asked, "Do you hate me?" This took Ray completely by surprise. He couldn't think what to answer so he said, "I'm neutral." Ronne didn't like this and yelled at him for a while.

I now wonder where I heard the account described in the preceding paragraph. I doubt that Spear or Ray told me. This is illustrative of how gossip traveled around the station!

Lewis tried to send a hamgram out today. Mac had OK'd it but Ronne found it in the radio room and jumped on it. Lewis had told his wife that he thought it was impossible to get a phone patch with her. (She's in the Washington area and Ronne has had about 13 patches through Washington, D.C.). He also told her to buy Darlington's *My Antarctic Honeymoon*. Ronne wouldn't send [the hamgram] . . . and chewed him out for 30 minutes.

I couldn't sleep, so Kim and I talked mountaineering over the telephone to his tower until 0430.

25 June, Tues. I spent the day studying reports of the Antarctic Service Expedition. Russell Frazier and Paul Siple discussed some interesting effects of acclimation on the human body with which I was unfamiliar. They reported diminished circulation in the extremities due to vasoconstriction and dehydration of subcutaneous tissue.

There was also a report by Siple about windchill, a term he "invented" on this expedition. He published the first chart of windchill—temperature compared to wind speed—in the USAS reports.

The reason Jerry has been rather cool towards some of the scientists in this building and hasn't spent much time here is that he thinks he was discriminated against because he wasn't "quite good enough" to live in the science building. Originally there were to be three of us in each room, but Don objected so violently that it was decided to put two people in that barracks. I think Jerry thinks we look down upon him and don't accept him as one of us because he doesn't have a college education.

The hot water system in the men's head is not functioning, so they are permitted to use our head from 1600 to 1900.

Again this strange segregation of "men" from "officers." It seems almost as bad in retrospect as at Scott's base at Cape Evans during the Terra Nova Expedition in 1910–13. Nowadays at the new barracks at McMurdo and at remote field camps, men's and women's bathroom facilities are housed together, with just doors at McMurdo for privacy.

26 June, Wed. The temperature was in the −30s°F with a wind that increased all day up to around 25 knots. There was a lot of blowing snow which made visibility very poor. We nearly had an accident because of this. I was pulling a load out when Aug changed his hand signal from "pull back" to "stop." I couldn't see him well enough silhouetted against the light from the tent covering the pit to realize he had changed, and I pulled the bucket up until it hit the top. Fortunately I stopped about then and there was no serious damage. If the rope had broken, the full bucket would have fallen on Paul and Hugo below; if not, I would have pulled the tent down.

There have been a number of fatalities over the years at U.S. and other Antarctic stations in "industrial" types of accidents like this.

27 June, Thurs. We took gravity readings every hour because the moon is in first quarter. . . . As I was taking the 0800–1600 readings, this meant I had to run in from the pit each time. It was –50°F at 0900 but warmed gradually throughout the day. There was no wind so it was quite pleasant.

I am amused at this remark. Of course it was pleasant if I walked indoors and warmed up every hour!

Clint told Hugo about a meeting held Tuesday. The situation in the administration building where Clint, Mac, and Ronne lived had reached the point where neither Mac nor Clint were speaking with Ronne. Ronne has been talking against Clint to Spear and giving him (a chief) orders to give to Clint (a full lieutenant). Al Spear was fed up and called a meeting of the three officers in Ronne's office. He told Ronne that he objected to conspiring with him against Clint (his own superior officer) and wanted to get the situation cleared up. Was he to put a chair out for Clint at the movie or not?

Even though the three live in the same building, they don't walk down to the movie together. Clint was quite surprised at Spear's audacity. Ronne was shaken, too, but couldn't say much–he depends on Al too much. There is a fair amount of truth in Al's statement of several months ago that he is the most powerful man on this base.

Haskill and Don have been drinking and boxing in the rec hall tonight. They came over here about 2330 where Con, Mac, and Jack have been consuming beer in the iono lab. I imagine Ronne would be disconcerted if he were to come in now and see his officers, enlisted men, and scientists sitting around drinking together.

Our jet heater hasn't been working right for several weeks, and the afternoon it overheated and almost caused a fire. The tubes started scorching, and smoke was coming from somewhere. Fortunately we noticed it and shut the power off.

How casually I—and all of us—treated potentially life-threatening incidents like this and the near accident with the Weasel pulling up the heavy bucket filled with snow. Our somewhat cavalier attitude persisted through the year regarding fires, explosions, crevasses, aircraft incidents, etc. Perhaps this is why it is best to send young men and women to winter over in Antarctica. I'm still not particularly disconcerted when these incidents happen around me today in Antarctica, but I am a damn sight more aware of their potential seriousness!

We are now measuring temperature at the pit several times a day for Jerry.

The temperatures at the pit, about a quarter-mile east of the station, were usually 2° to 3°F colder than the "official" temperature at the station because of the "heat island" effect of the station. This is why it is so difficult to obtain reliable determinations of climatic warming by studying longtime temperature records in Antarctica or anywhere else in the world. Jerry recognized this and tried to correct for it by the observations outside at the pit, away from the station.

> *28 June, Fri.* It was about −30°F with a strong south wind. Paul, Aug, Hugo, and I spent the morning putting in another platform in the pit. Davis leaned over while working outdoors on a D-8 and ran a vertical projecting rod into his eye. Half his cornea was scraped, and though Clint thought he will have no permanent effects, he is in quite a bit of pain. [Luckily, his eye healed in a week.]
> Ed received a message from Crary relaying a message describing the seismic program at Mirny [USSR]. They have run a reflection profile for 275 km, getting ice thicknesses ranging from 800 to 2250 m. Thus far they have accomplished more than the three U.S. seismic teams have, but they came down a year before the U.S.

In 1963 at a scientific meeting in the U.S., I met the Soviet geophysicist, Andrei Kapitsa, who made these ice-thickness measurements at Mirny, and we have continued casual contact over the years. In 1994, at a pleasant dinner in Frascati, Italy, with Kapitsa and his wife, he pointed out that we are now almost as far removed in time from this IGY period as we were then from the era of Scott and Amundsen (1911–12). Time flies when you're having fun!

> Beiszer has been painting up cups with personal decorations for VX-6 people. I gave him my old plastic mug that I picked up on the Yukon River trip two years ago. . . . I am making him an 8 by 10 print of a picture I took of him at a party several months ago. He painted the cup for me with an appropriate design suggested by Aug.

Beiszer decorated the cup with a humorously painted dog's head. At one time Ronne had referred to me as a shaggy St. Bernard, and described me as such in his book. I still use the cup when camping in Colorado, but the painting has long since worn off.

> I received a hamgram from the folks.

> *29 June, Sat.* It was warmer (about −12°F) with a fairly strong east wind today, but it actually felt colder than Thursday's −50°F. We dug as usual.
>
> I am reading *The White Desert* by John Giaever–the story of the Norwegian, British, Swedish expedition at Cape Norvegia (Maudheim), 1949–52. He discusses the wintering party thus:

> > One thing certain is that a wintering party may be exposed to mental as well as physical strain of utmost severity. . . . I agree that the choice of men is enormously important. . . . I have seen the most cheerful of optimists fall into a state of melancholy, brooding, and homesickness during a polar winter, and I have seen the most talkative and hearty fellows turn sulky and silent and limp. Yes, the very sturdiest of them have become unnerved and even have shown fear of the dark. Often one makes a wrong choice. But good fellows who are sportsmen, thoroughly interested and in good health–can usually manage without any difficulty.
> >
> > My experience is that an expedition leader will hold his own provided he does not fish for popularity. It will be his plain and very unpleasant duty to act as the scapegoat for criticism in order to obviate disputes among the members of the party. It is

better for the whole group to be unanimous in their fury against the leader than to quarrel among themselves.

I think Don has passed the peak in his current phase of popularity with Ronne. At least, he didn't score any points last night at 2315 when he woke the Captain up to get him to OK a hamgram. I heard Ronne lecturing him on the subject in the iono lab tonight. Ronne said it was midnight and reminded [Don] of the 2300 curfew.

Several times recently when I (and Jack and Don) have been reading in bed late, Kim has brought us toast and something to drink from the galley. He is quite thoughtful, occasionally.

I more or less systematically photographed each of the men at Ellsworth. Wally Cox, the Navy photographer, also took pictures but in a professional capacity. Still, everyone seemed to get a kick out of my informal black-and-white photos taken with existing light.

I dropped in on Willie Sumrall and took his picture. He was reading *Lee's Lieutenants*. He has the biggest collection of pinups in camp. Willie is the youngest of the officers (just 21) and he made "jg" [lieutenant, junior grade] only a few weeks ago. He is from Sumrall, Mississippi. His three main interests are women, flying, and the Confederate States of America. He quit reading *Gone With the Wind* after only a hundred pages because "there wasn't enough sex and the South was losing." He spends a lot of time by himself and doesn't have any close friends. He and Con (they room together) get along fairly well, but Con comes down to the science building for his social life.

Willie has put on a man-of-the-world cynical attitude towards life, but can really be friendly when you talk to him alone. He seemed quite pleased that I wanted to get his picture, and we had an enjoyable hour's conversation—mostly about flying (his interest) in Alaska (mine). I feel that he is probably quite lonely down here, but he doesn't show it much. He has no duties at present and keeps pretty much to himself, which must give him lots of time for thinking. He has a rather quick temper and is a strong "white supremacist."

30 June, Sun. Clint called the traverse people together in his room in the afternoon and talked to us about some of the health problems we can take care of ourselves in the summer in the field. This is the first of a series of such get-togethers. Today the subject was teeth. Many people . . . have reported trouble with old fillings dropping out or giving pain when exposed to cold air. Already the doctor at Pole (and I think Byrd) has reported such difficulties. We practiced on the extracted examples obtained from the dentist on *Staten Island.* Clint also discussed snow blindness, sunburn, eye injuries, boils, etc.

Kim gave a lecture on the aurora in the library tonight. He posted a note announcing it on the bulletin board yesterday. Ronne was all shook up that he wasn't consulted and mentioned it to Don and to Ed today. Clint, Con, Mac, Al Spear, Jack, Hugo, Paul, Ed, and I attended. Afterwards we went over for coffee and Ronne came in. He didn't say anything but was obviously incensed as he loudly dragged the officers' table away from the wall and slammed a chair down on the floor. Ed was the last of us to leave, and Ronne cornered him and told him that this shouldn't have happened. Ed told him it was Kim's talk, and the Captain said he wanted to talk to Kim. Ronne can't have anything go on that he doesn't have some say over.

1 July, Mon. Too windy outside to dig. Kim gave the second part of his lecture. Earlier Kim went up and talked to Ronne about a message he wanted to send out and then said, "Oh, by the way, I'm going to give another lecture tonight." This was just what Ronne had been waiting for, and he gave vent to his spleen with another of his usual diatribes against doing anything without consulting him. . . . "Mac and Con have no college education, and Willie has had only two years. Only Clint and I have a college education. They are the ones who would appreciate such lectures. You can't expect people with lowclass backgrounds like the men—you can tell that by the vulgar way they talk—to be interested in something like this unless it is given a buildup. Why, I would have personally asked each man to go. But, you people want your own show so the nine of you can get in your own little group and have your lectures."

Although Kim told Ronne that he would be very welcome to attend the lectures and perhaps even learn something, Ronne remained adamant. I showed Kim what I wrote, and he asked me to read it to Con. Con didn't much like Ronne's slap at his education and suggested that for the next lecture we try and get as many men to come as possible. He thought he could get the VX-6 men to come by asking, "Do you want to get the Captain mad?" This wasn't exactly the reason we wanted people to attend, but it did have amusing possibilities.

On 1 July, the IGY officially began. It ran for 18 months, and I recall the comic strip "Pogo" commenting on this strange "year."

2 July, Tues. Augie and I hiked out to measure accumulation and/or ablation [decrease] at stakes put in several months ago. When we went out at 0900, we saw a good auroral display with several showings of red. It was clear, fairly calm, and –39°F.

Kim continued his lectures on the aurora for two hours. Our group had dwindled to Jack, Ed, Hugo, Aug, Mac, Con, and myself. It began to get really interesting tonight. Con and Mac followed it through the Lyman and Balmer series, stumbled through the Fraunhofer lines, but beat a retreat at the Milne mechanism. Kim and I were discussing the lack of an academic atmosphere here, as one gets used to in a university group. Tonight was the first example of this mood we have had here; it is somewhat disappointing that we haven't done this more often.

In contrast, the academic atmosphere at McMurdo in the summertime has always been pretty good. This is probably because of a large number of relatively senior scientists passing through. There is frequently a critical mass sufficient for lively, if possibly only multidisciplinary, discussion. Nowadays, when I and others are asked to give popular or scientific talks about our research, these events are usually quite well attended by people of all job descriptions at the base. In 1990, when I finished a presentation to several hundred people on 200 million years of Antarctic rifting, complete with color slides, it was followed by a spirited question-and-answer period. I told that group how appreciative I was for their interest. After all, their only purpose in Antarctica was to help support the scientific program, and yet I felt, and continue to feel strongly, an obligation to help explain our work. Most of the researchers feel this way, and it helps morale and, therefore, the program as well.

3 July, Wed. I began studying Robin's report of the seismic work done on the Norwegian-British-Swedish Expedition at Maudheim in 1949–52.

Dr. Gordon Robin, an Australian who emigrated to Britain, essentially pioneered the seismic method we used on the Antarctic ice during the IGY and the following decade of the oversnow traverse program. Robin later became director of Scott Polar Research Institute, where he served for many years. He and I met and became friends. He is now retired, but was hale and hearty when I last saw him in London in 1992.

I continued studying the Maudheim group reports. This expedition was the prototype for the IGY oversnow traverse program. They had only three Weasels as their mechanized transport, and no planes. They had a lot of mechanical trouble. One day they laid a cache at 45 miles and returned. Another day they drove in from 130 miles out. [They lost one Weasel and three men over the front of the ice shelf.]

Aug and I went out in the Weasel to the farthest stakes a few miles east to measure accumulation. It was really a wonderful feeling to be driving around out in the open country away from camp. All we could see of it was a faint gleam from the light on Kim's tower. We could see and sometimes follow the tracks made one and two months ago in these measurements. Almost all of the stakes read negative accumulation, and the few that read positive were in small drifts.

The wind in the winter was removing possibly more snow than was actually falling because the main snow accumulation occurred in the summer. However, firnification of the snow causes actual lowering of the snow surface, which may have been the cause of the "negative" accumulation observations.

The snow surface has changed quite a bit in the past six months. Where formerly it was quite soft for several inches and skis and snowshoes were handy, now it is quite hard with many more sastrugi. Last summer one could sleep in a Weasel cruising at 15 mph but now a 10 mph ride practically shakes one's teeth loose. We didn't find all the stakes before supper and went out after chow for another one and a half hours in order to complete the job.

We have been going through a Weasel in about three days of operation. Walt Davis thinks it is impossible to run equipment continuously at these temperatures. He has been kept busy on three Weasels in rotation for us since we began the pit. I think it is the Weasels that can't stand up at these low temperatures rather than any vehicle, because people back home in Wisconsin operate cars, trucks, etc., all winter and frequently in temperatures in the $-20°$ to $-40°F$, range without these disastrous results. I can't see how these Weasels (particularly with our limited ability as mechanics) could stand up on traverse.

Monday Walt begins mess cooking for two weeks and will be unable to do any mechanical work.

This was just another instance of the way in which the inefficient dishwashing procedure impacted our scientific activities.

It was party night in the ionosphere lab. Ed, Kim, Paul, and I weren't in the right spirit and spent most of the time in our room. Mac, Con, Clint, Jack, with May, Brownie (Ron Brown), and Carl Crouse present for a time, comprised the party. Martinis were served. At one point in the serious discussion stage Jack dug out a copy of the *Psychology of Abnormal People* by J.J.B. Morgan, Ph.D., and began reading aloud.

This selection . . . was very popular with the audience and, in my opinion, is a pretty good description of Finn Ronne:

Typical pre-holiday or Saturday evening in science building. Left foreground: R. Brown, face partly hidden; center (left to right): C. Jaburg, J. Brown, J. Malville; in back: D. Skidmore.

Compensation (for inferiority feelings) can take the form of not exalting ourselves, but of degrading others and the end result a raising of our relative status will be the same, in either case. The urge for authority is probably a compensating mechanism based on this background. Such individuals crave authoritative position, but make the most tactless executives that one could well find. A good way to determine whether a person has a tendency to develop such a compensation is to vest him with a little authority and notice how he behaves under it. Any tendency to compensate will be shown by an assumption of dignity and authority out of proportion to the weight of office. The person soon loses sight of the fact that an executive position is for the purpose of increasing cooperation and productivity, and thinks that its main function is to have his subordinates bow and scrape before him. Most of the pleas for obedience that we hear are expressions of a supposed executive, who insists on manifesting his authority, having lost sight of the fact that obedience is a secondary product of mutual cooperation.

On the other hand we have persons who do not try so much to exalt themselves but to degrade others. This leads to the well-known practice of gossiping, scandalmongering, muckraking, and all the other forms that defamation of others may take. The reason that such practices are followed with impunity to the person most interested in spreading vilifying news is that, in too many cases he is able to find incidents that are partly, true. The hearer is at once absorbed by the news and the slanderer escapes unnoticed.

As I write now in 1997, I wonder how much of the second paragraph of the quotation from Morgan's book could have been applied to those of us in the scientific group. Certainly none of us was in any particular position of authority, but we were obviously not above "gossiping, scandalmongering, [and] muckraking."

4 July, Thurs. Holiday Routine. The Captain came over and we played bridge in the afternoon. I was just getting up at 1230 when he arrived, and he kidded me about his having eaten two meals while I hadn't eaten any. I mentioned that I hadn't gone to bed until 0300. He said he knew we were having a party over here because Mac didn't get in until then. He and Don beat Paul and me.

5 July, Fri. After noon I showed Clint how to make and then helped him in the manufacture of hydrochloric acid. I then made a determination of its strength (using $AgNO_3$). . . .
Ronne came in and asked Ed if Mac and Con and Jack disturbed him (or us) with their parties. They generally are pretty quiet (com-

pared to Don) but occasionally keep Ed awake. He realized that Ronne was hoping he would complain so as to take action against any future occurrences. Ed told him he wasn't bothered. Ronne mentioned something about 2300 curfew.

By this time no one paid any attention to the 11 P.M. curfew, and people were wandering around the station 24 hours a day. Everyone's sleep habits became disarranged; so, as there was always coffee, cocoa, bread for toast, and other food in the galley, there were always a few people eating or drinking there.

Clint played host, after the movie, to Ed, Hugo, Jack, Kim, Mac, and me in his room, . . . and we started on a USAFI [United States Armed Forces Institute] course in music appreciation. We listened to Mendelssohn's Violin Concerto in E-flat, op. 64.

There were a number of courses available through the University of Wisconsin Extension Service. The music course was particularly good.

At one point I left to take a gravity reading, and didn't shut the front door of the building as quietly as I could have. Hugo also left to get his sewing. I apparently disturbed Ronne, who ran out from his room and caught Hugo when he returned. He bawled him out for slamming doors at 2300.

Although we were well supplied with clothes, mending was an ongoing necessity that we all had to succumb to occasionally. Some, such as I, eventually looked pretty ragged.

6 July, Sat. There was a 20–25-knot wind with temperatures around –15°F all day. The moon is coming up again, so in a few days we will have bright light to work in. On moonless days our light comes (except for a little twilight around noon) entirely from the stars with the southern cross directly overhead. Of course we have the Weasel headlights.

We received the sitreps from the other stations and found that, as of 1 July, Little America had their pit down 18 m, we were at 17, Wilkes was at 10, and Byrd was at 8 m. Ronne has been telling people around here that the pit doesn't have to be completed until 1960. He wants us to work on the traverse. Time and again he has stated to us that Antarctic expeditions complete only about 20% of their scheduled work and we will be no exception, so therefore give up the pit for now. He may be right about the 20%, but one certainly doesn't tackle a program with the defeatist attitude of completing only a fifth of it.

We completed a lot more than 20%–in fact, almost all that was planned, and a lot that had not been, including the tidal measurements.

7 July, Sun. Paul woke me at 1230 for another bridge game with the Captain. Don and I really pounded them. Before the game Ronne told Don that we shouldn't get coffee and rolls from the galley, as food wasn't to be taken out of the chow hall. Don didn't have an opportunity to tell me, so . . . I asked them each individually if they wanted some coffee. Ronne declined. When I returned he made quite a point of telling me of his dislike of this practice. (I have seen him do this himself at night numerous times, when he doesn't want to sit in there with us.)

After the movie we had our second lesson in the music course. We all took turns reading the text, and Clint ran the phonograph. We took the quizzes on rhythm and harmony, and finished off by listening to several Chopin nocturnes, a short bit of Villa-Lobos, and *Swan Lake.* Augie was also there tonight. Ronne wasn't invited and therefore doesn't like the existence of the group. Don wouldn't come because he said, "I would if Ronne had been invited. There is no point in looking for trouble." My, how times have changed!

I think Clint started these sessions now, just to antagonize Ronne; when we are over there we can hear . . . the Captain start his hi-hi set. I sometimes actually feel sorry for Ronne. He has no friends on this base at all and must be very lonely as a result. He has lots of free time on his hands in which to brood. Although he always sits at his own table when he comes to the chow hall at night and finds us there, he occasionally is sitting talking with the men when we come in. Part of the reason for his success in losing friends and alienating people is that he has talked against every individual here (at least once) to somebody and that somebody always repeats the story to everyone else.

Ronne has had Clint's name removed from the distribution list of dispatches. Now Mac and Ronne are the only ones who officially see the messages, with the exception of IGY sitreps and warnings which we now get.

8 July, Mon. Mac told us that he warned Ronne that "he will really be in trouble when he gets back now." Ronne excitedly asked, "What for, what for?" Mac informed him that it is against Navy regulations to withhold messages from Clint [as officer in charge of the Seabee detachment]. Clint will now receive copies of all non-IGY messages.

Jack and I were having coffee later when Chuck Forlidas, one of the two radio operators, joined us. He told us that Ronne had given him and Haskill an oral order not to give "Dr." Smith any of the dispatches except those addressed to him personally. Forlidas and Haskill complied with the order, and although several messages concerned Clint's work, they were not given to him. In turn, Ronne gave Haskill and Forlidas a written statement reprimanding the two for *not* giving Clint the dispatches. Perhaps unbeknownst to Ronne, the two men had kept an official log, and they recorded Ronne's order withholding messages from Clint.

Mac came in and told Ed and me that Lassiter is coming down about 10 November and bringing 12 men (including himself) and staying over until March. Mac says he can't give them any avgas unless he gets specific authorization from the commanding officer of VX-6. But, as Hugo put it, "Ronne doesn't name all these mountains in Antarctica for nothing." I'm sure Ronne's influence will get him authorization.

9 July, Tues. It warmed up to –30°F, and some snow fell for an hour or so in the morning. This is one of the few such times it has snowed this winter.

Clint was over tonight talking with Ed and me. According to him, Ronne was talking about the traverse at supper. He keeps talking our chances of success down and enlarges on our ineptness and inexperience.

No one had any experience at driving vehicles across the Antarctic ice sheet prior to the IGY except the short traverse of the Norwegian-British-Swedish Expedition, referred to previously, which used Weasels. The short Weasels, with a relatively high "ground" pressure, were not very safe in crevasses compared to Sno-Cats, although safety in crevasses is a relative term.

Ronne said we probably wouldn't get any seismic work done farther than 20 miles around camp. He said it was impossible for us to go southwest, as the crevasses are too bad. The Captain talked about Lassiter's mission also, Clint said. Ronne's scheme called for only 8 men, and he doesn't see why Lassiter is bringing 12. Ronne admitted (boasted) that he had planned the operation himself.

I have often wondered whether Ronne had, in fact, planned the mission. Jim Lassiter seemed quite capable of planning and promoting an operation like this, and my impression is that he was every bit as smooth an operator around Washington, D.C., as Ronne. More likely, each man used the other for his own purposes. Such things even occur in the U.S. Antarctic Program today!

Ed, Kim, and I were discussing . . . our traverse into the unexplored area to the southwest of Ellsworth. . . . In 1947 Ronne made two flights into this area. One was south, following the curve of the Palmer [now Antarctic] Peninsula along the Orville Escarpment.[1] To the right he could see the Ellsworth Highland and to the left was the Filchner [now Ronne] Ice Shelf. They were forced to turn back before they saw anything else.

The second flight was east along the edge of the Filchner [Ronne] Ice Shelf. They flew as far east as Gould Bay (which Ronne named) but not far enough to see Moltke Nunatak (near Shackleton Base), probably around the site of Belgrano (I). On their return they headed south for about 30 miles. On this leg Ronne recorded an altimeter reading of about 700 ft; they saw no features in the snow surface. Upon this information alone, Edith Ronne Land was named and discovered.

I now think that Ronne measured the high surface of Berkner Island, which was discovered and mapped on our IGY expedition.

When Ed, Hugo, Ronne, and Mac flew south last fall, slightly east of Ronne's 1947 flight, they saw nothing to indicate anything but ice shelf, and their altimeter showed something in the range of 200 ft. It was almost 200 miles south before they observed the east-west-trending ice escarpment rising up to high land with visible mountains to the south. [See Chapter 3 for the discussion of the traverse route on 5 March.]

10 July, Wed. I received a hamgram today. Poor Paul hasn't heard from his fiancee since 4 June. He feels pretty low. We dug down to 21 m.

The Pole sitrep came in, and Ronne made a point of asking everyone to read it. They are short-handed (only 18 in all) and lose a man day when on general camp work. I wonder if we are going through last May's hassle [about the scientists being assigned to mess cooking] all over again.

11 July, Thurs. Kim took a hamgram up for Ronne to censor . . . and the Captain asked him what he plans to do when the sun comes up. Kim has lots to do and he told the Captain so. Ronne said, "We're going to try some of what they are doing at the Pole Station." Kim asked what he had in mind and Ronne told him, "mess duty." Ronne added, "The ships are coming the 10th of January. You will be sure glad when they do."

At 0300 Hugo, with Forlidas operating the radio, talked to Verne Anderson (chief glaciologist) and Mario Giovinetto (assistant glaciologist) at Byrd Station. He told Verne, "Major Jimmy Lassiter is flying down on Nov. 10. Tell Crary (at Little America) to send a message to Washington to Odishaw to get a Sno-Cat clutch sent down."

They contact Little America frequently and said they would relay it. Hugo told them that we couldn't contact Crary and that we are under a "dictatorial censorship" as regards to communication. Mario Giovinetto asked if we had been in contact with Belgrano. They talk to them occasionally. Mario, who is an Argentine, told us that they (the Argentines at Belgrano) have a good deal of knowledge of crevasses in our area. It seems rather odd that we can't find what the Argentines, 35 miles away, know about our area, while the people at Byrd Station can.

12 July, Fri. At the close of the regular schedule from McMurdo last night, the operator told Haskill of an accident they had yesterday. A helicopter crashed, killing one VX-6 man and critically injuring three other people.

Nelson R. Cole was the man killed. There were six in the aircraft. The plane burst into flames when it hit. Although the report said the man was killed instantly, I imagine he burned to death because two men were dragged out, but flames kept the would-be rescuers from getting Cole out.

Today helicopters do not fly at night in the U.S. Antarctic Program during the winter.

A message came in from the acting secretary of USNC-IGY in Washington: EVERY EFFORT IS BEING MADE TO MAKE

EARLY DELIVERY CLUTCH ASSEMBLY UNIT TO ELLS-
WORTH STA FOR 57–58 TRAVERSE. SEVERAL MODES OF
DELIVERY ARE BEING INVESTIGATED. WILL ADVISE.
ODISHAW. This is the most encouraging bit of news we have had
in months.

Hugo, Ed, and Ronne had a meeting to discuss the traverse tonight. Ed persuaded him [Ronne] to consent to at least one more
recon flight at an azimuth of about 190°F. Ronne still doesn't want
Hugo along. Ronne told them our food must be all packaged and
our mogas [automotive gas] must be hauled over to the airstrip.
Ronne remained adamant in his veto of any conversation with the
Argentines at Belgrano Base. Ronne agreed to a route slightly west
of south, if possible, but doubted the chances of getting very far. He
thinks we may not get out of the immediate area. Ed pointed out
that if we couldn't get through and the people next year do, it will
make us look pretty bad. That was a telling point and Ronne appreciated it.

13 July, Sat. The following message came in:

FROM: COMNAVSUPFOR ANTARCTICA 111938 Z
ACTION: LITTLE AMERICA
INFO: ELLSWORTH STA, BYRD STA

IGY FOR CRARY. REEVALUATION AND DETAILED
STUDY OF COORDINATED AIR SUPPORT FOR ALL
PHASES OF 57–58 SCIENTIFIC PROGRAM UNDER WAY
HERE. FULL SUPPORT OF TRAVERSE . . . APPEARS POS-
SIBLE. TRAVERSE RESUPPLY, ESPECIALLY AT ELL-
SWORTH, REQUIRES CAREFUL PLANNING. DESIRE
STATEMENT YOUR LATEST THINKING ON TRAVERSE
SUPPORT. ARE YOU PLANNING ADVANCE DEPOT
LAYING OR RESUPPLY AT FIELD PARTY? ODISHAW.

It is interesting that this message was directed to Albert Crary
at Little America and sent to Ellsworth for our information only. It
is apparent that Hugh Odishaw and the other IGY leaders in Washington assumed that Crary, not Ronne–even for Ellsworth–was
the decision maker in Antarctica regarding the traverse and its lo-
gistical support.

I read Shaw's *Mrs Warren's Profession* this afternoon and am now
reading *Grapes of Wrath*. When Kim came to bed this morning he
piled a stack of my pocket books in a condition of unstable equilib-

rium on a sloping surface next to the head of my bed. I was dreaming that I was walking through a door when suddenly I was jumped from behind. I woke to find pocket books all over me. I decided to return the favor and piled a stack of heavy books from the library on the rail at the head of his bed, and set my alarm clock for 1115. Unfortunately, when he reached for the clock, the books didn't fall. I shall have to devise something more subtle.

No wonder Finn Ronne thought of us as "college kids." My son Marc, reading this and other similar passages of my journal, when he was about 25 years old, was quite amused at these antics of Kim, me, and 22-year-old Paul at a similar or younger age. He has always known Kim and me as "old" adults throughout his life.

14 July, Sun. The Captain came over, and he and I beat Paul and Don at bridge. These games are very trying, but interesting. It seems that poor Paul is always on the losing side.

Clint lectured us on cold injuries. He told us some things that are direct contradictions to advice given me by other doctors. This phase of medicine is quite new and there are controversial points.

Because I had spent two weeks in the hospital in 1955 with frostbitten toes, I viewed cold injuries with more than an academic interest.

15 July, Mon. The temperature was −10°F with a very strong northeast wind. There was more blowing snow than we have had yet; visibility was very poor. Aug had to signal me with a light as I drove the Weasel pulling the bucket of snow up from the pit. To add to the fun, the Weasel heater was packed full of snow and was therefore inoperable.

Paul would commonly ride up and down from the bottom of the pit to help pull by standing on the large wooden bucket used to remove the snow. He would partly balance himself by letting the moving rope of the block and tackle run through his mittened hands. By this time the pit was about 70 ft deep.

We had a near accident this afternoon when Paul rode down on the bucket. About 20 ft down, the leg of his wind pants were caught in the pulley on the bucket, jammed, and stopped the rope from going through. Meanwhile, I kept on going another 20–30 ft before Aug stopped me. This left Paul with only his jammed cuff keeping him from a free drop to the bottom. He managed to reach the ladder along the side and hung on while I backed up and released him. We started down again, and a little farther on I heard a funny noise in the tracks. I climbed out and found about 12 ft of rope wound around under the starboard track. The rope had caught in the snow, and the combined weight of Paul and the bucket had not pulled it through so I ran over the accumulating slack. By this time Paul had enough. He stepped off the box and went down the ladder. When I backed up, the 12 ft of slack, of course, went out with a rush and the bucket took a fall and bounced up and down on the rope quite vigorously.

Fortunately everything held, because otherwise the heavy bucket would have hit Paul and Hugo at the bottom of the pit.

Kent spent two hours sending a hamgram from Ronne to Lowell Thomas [a well-known radio broadcaster]. It was about 300 words long, and practically a press release. Ronne won't let us send anything over 50 words and not more than one per week.

16 July, Tues. The wind continued strong, at about –18°F. Much blowing snow. We dug in the morning and installed another platform after noon. About 1000, as he passed the radio shack on a trip in, Hugo heard Mac and Haskill discussing a glaciology roundtable discussion among the stations, scheduled for 0900. No one had told Hugo. He became very angry and sounded off to Haskill and Mac, blaming Ronne. He was furious when he came back to the pit.

At 1030 Haskill came out and told us that they had contacted Little America on the ham set and Hugo could discuss his glaciological problems with Crary and Peter Schoek [aurora observer at Little America]. We all went in, and Ed, Aug, and I listened on Don and Jack's receiver. Mac ran the set. Hugo told Crary that Ronne was not intending to allow him on any recon flight, but wanted to take a photographer in his place. Crary told him that both he and Ed [as co-leaders of the traverse] should be on these flights and that there should be plenty of flights so pictures can be taken also. He said he hoped a flight from Little America could bring our clutch over. They talked quite a while about the pit program and a little about the traverse program.

The idea of the chief glaciologist and chief geophysicist as coleaders of the traverses did not work very well in actuality and was subsequently discontinued. At Little America there was no doubt that Bert Crary, a geophysicist-glaciologist, was the leader; and at Byrd, Charlie Bentley, a more senior geophysicist with a brand-new Ph.D., was the real leader. The co-leadership of Ed and Hugo worked reasonably well because of their accommodating personalities—and the united front we had to present to Ronne—but there was no question that Ed Thiel was the senior scientist of the two. When the going was really tough on the traverse, most serious decisions were essentially made by consensus of the five of us.

When I led a traverse in 1961–62, it was my fourth trip to Antarctica and no one else had, for example, any experience working with Sno-Cats in crevasses. I was then the only party leader.

The following message copied to Ellsworth, from Crary to Odishaw in Washington, came in this afternoon:

IGY NO. 16 YOUR 111938 Z [ODISHAW'S MESSAGE TO CRARY WE RECEIVED 13 JULY] DETAILS TRAVERSE SUPPORT PLANNING, EXCLUSIVE OF RECON FLIGHTS NECESSARY IN ADVANCE OF PARTY, AS FOLLOWS. . . . SNO-CAT LOADS 300 GALLONS PER . . . SUFFICIENT FOR 300 MILES TRAVERSE OR THREE WEEKS' OPERATION. . . . TRAVERSE PARTY WILL NOTIFY LITTLE AMERICA WHEN HALF OF GAS HAS BEEN CONSUMED. FLIGHT CAN THEN BE MADE ANY TIME WITHIN FOLLOWING WEEK, LANDING AT SNO-CATS WHICH CAN EASILY BE LOCATED BY RADAR. THIS PROCESS COULD AVOID SEARCHING FOR CACHES, WAITING FOR PLANES, AND LANDING ON UNEXAMINED SURFACES.

FOR BYRD PARTY SIMILAR PROCESS PLANNED R4D OPERATING FM BYRD STATION. THIS WILL REQUIRE AVGAS FROM MCMURDO EARLY SPRING DELIVERY. FOR ELLSWORTH SIMILAR PROCESS CAN BE NEXT OPERATION OR THERE WILL BE SERIOUS CURTAILMENT WITHOUT R4D OR SIMILAR TYPE PLANE. TIE TO OR NEAR EASTERN POINT BYRD STA TRAVERSE MOST DESIRABLE . . . BUT IMPOSSIBLE WITH PRESENT TYPE AIRCRAFT. IN VIEW ALSO OF URGENT NEED FOR SNO-CAT CLUTCH ASSEMBLY STRONGLY URGE THIS PROBLEM OF R4D ASSIGNMENT . . . BE RECONSIDERED.

None of the three traverse parties ever seriously considered laying fuel caches in advance.

> Ronne brought this in after supper. He is upset over it, probably because there definitely would be no gas for Lassiter with an R4D (same as DC-3 or USAF C-47) over here.
>
> Ronne told Ed and Hugo he is thinking of sending in a message telling them it would be unnecessary to send an R4D, because we won't be able to get the vehicles beyond the large crevasses 30 miles out. If we really can't get out (and we haven't admitted the possibility as yet), there will be some questions asked in Washington as to why the station was put here.

As apparent from our attitude, we only ascribed the worst motives to Ronne in his constant discouragement of our most ambitious traverse plans. I still believe he wanted to save aircraft fuel for Lassiter, at the expense of the traverse, but I also now realize he had a real concern about our safety. Establishing Ellsworth on the Filchner Ice Shelf, instead of at the junction of the Ronne Ice Shelf and the Antarctic Peninsula as originally planned, made the Filchner Ice Shelf Traverse extremely difficult and hazardous. It was not until the late 1980s that the British and Germans begin to make extensive surface geophysical measurements on the Filchner-Ronne Ice Shelf system, using light aircraft and airlifted snowmobiles and lightweight geophysical (seismic) equipment.

> *17 July, Wed.* The wind was howling at 40 knots and Walt Davis couldn't start the Weasel so we worked indoors. I spent most of the day sewing small red trail flags to mark our route with on traverse.

I asked someone to take a picture of me using the camp sewing machine, which the *Milwaukee Journal* eventually published with a number of my other photographs. People in the States found it quite interesting in the 1950s that a man could use a sewing machine.

> Kim, Cox, Con, Beiszer are the committee to plan the format for Ellsworth's pages in the Operation Deep Freeze cruise book.

Our activities at Ellsworth were covered in the Operation Deep Freeze II (1956–57) and III (1957–58) books. Although the Navy has almost completely phased out its support for the United States Antarctic Program (USAP) in the 1990s, they still used the term "Operation Deep Freeze," at least to 1995. The Operation Deep Freeze cruise books are similar to a high school yearbook with many photographs and names of everyone in the ships' crews and those who wintered over in the U.S. IGY program.[2] All of the vital statistics for the names and locations of stations, ships, their itineraries, etc., are included. The cruise books were primarily paid for by the Navy ships' crews and station personnel and also by us scientific personnel. These unpretentious books are essentially unavailable, except in personal libraries. Both books sit on my desk as I write, and they have been an invaluable reference.

At our music appreciation course, we learned about the scherzo trio form. Clint produced a bottle of Old Methuselah (bourbon), which several of those present enjoyed.

18 July, Thurs. Fourteen IGY people have volunteered for a second year: Crary, Cromie, Dalrymple, Taylor, Hanson, Hough, Landolt, Giovinetto, Morenay, Johns, Davis, Morris, Hale, and Glasgal. It seems significant that Ellsworth is the only station with no volunteers for a second term.

Ronne sent the following out today:

TO: IGY WASH D.C., INFO COMNAVSUPFOR ANTARCTICA/COMNAV UNITS ANTARCTICA/LITTLE AMERICA STA NR 181721Z IGY NO. 41. REFERENCE LITTLE AMERICA 151950 Z [CRARY'S MESSAGE TO ODISHAW RECEIVED 16 JULY].

CURTAILMENT OF TRAVERSE HERE LIKELY DUE STATION LOCATION ON CAPE WITH HEAVILY CREVASSED AREA SOUTHWARD FOR 50 MILES. HERE A 3-MILE-WIDE RIFT, 250 FT DEEP, AND 100 MILES OR MORE LONG IN EAST-WEST DIR. BLOCKS ENTRY INLAND . . . ABOUT 80°30'S WHERE STEEP CREVASSE-FILLED ESCARPMENT RISES TO 4000 FT AND MORE IN ELEVATION [NOW KNOWN AS BERKNER ISLAND]. EARLIEST AIR RECON FLIGHTS WILL DETERMINE TYPE TERRAIN WESTERLY FOR PASSAGE VICINITY ESCARPMENT, THUS CLARIFY POSSIBILITY TIE TO OR NEAR EASTERN POINT OF BYRD STATION TRAVERSE.

OUR MAIN OBJECTIVE TO REACH INLAND AREA FOR

POSSIBLE TRAVERSE WILL BE BY TWO METHODS, (A) FIND SAFE TRAIL THROUGH CREVASSES FOR 50-MILES AIRLINE DISTANCE TO SNOW RAMP ACROSS RIFT OR (B) FIND SAFE TRAIL THROUGH CREVASSES TO REACH SHACKLETON STATION AND FOLLOW THEIR ROUTE SOUTH TO SMOOTH CREVASSE-FREE AREA. . . . SHOULD R4D BE UNAVAILABLE, AM CONFIDENT LASSITER WILL SUPPORT TRAVERSE IF NEEDED BEYOND CAPACITY AIRCRAFT NOW HERE. UTMOST EFFORTS WILL BE EXERTED TOWARDS SUCCESSFUL FIELDWORK.

That rift, named Grand Chasm by the British party at Shackleton, is only about 50 miles long from the estimates of Hugo, Ed, and McCarthy.

Ronne came over to find out some things about the magnetic field of the earth, for something he is writing, but Kim was in the tower. He told me to have Malville (he never calls anyone by his first name) come up and see him. Kim, when he came down from his tower (still not mollified over Ronne's reaction to his lecture), said Ronne could come down here if he wanted to talk to him. After the movie Ronne came over. Paul, Don, Ed, Kim, and I were talking in the library. The conversation went something like this:

RONNE (with smile): Say, Malville, I wonder if you could tell me something about the changes with the magnetic field?

KIM (also smiling): Well, Captain, you should have come to my lectures; I discussed it all there.

RONNE (smile disappears; replaced by usual set look around mouth): Thiel told me that they were caused by sunspots and solar flares.

KIM (moment of indecision): That's right.

(Long pause. Skidmore, Walker, and Behrendt resume conversation.)

At this Ronne turned and stalked out the back door (the closest). He has trouble managing the handle during which time no one says anything.

ED: Well, Kim, you just lost a point there.

BEHRENDT: All the scientists just lost a point.

Ronne was quite disturbed I am sure over the "rudeness of that young college kid."

19 July, Fri. It was dropped down to –52°F by quitting time. We dug down to 24 m by noon. The sky was very clear, and there was a very bright red glow on the northern horizon. Although it will be a month before we see the sun again, it looked like it would rise today. Everything was tinged a beautiful lavender. This is one point upon which the extravagances of most writers on the Antarctic are justified. It was really beautiful. There must be an open lead next to the ice front because rose-colored clouds of sea smoke obscured the horizon itself.

Working outside gave us a perspective on the petty, and not so petty, conflicts within. It was during our outside work that I developed an appreciation for the beauty of Antarctica that will last throughout my life.

At our music course tonight we studied polyphonic music and the fugal form. Wednesday we took up the minuet (scherzo and trio).

20 July, Sat. The following was received from Crary at Little America [about damage to the Sno-Cat]:

TRAVERSE SNO-CAT DRIVE AXLE ASSEMBLY DAMAGED IN ATTEMPT MOVE VEHICLE TO GARAGE FOR TRAVERSE PREPARATION. VEHICLE HAD NOT BEEN MOVED SINCE MID-MARCH. TRACKS WERE DUG CLEAR AND MOTOR STARTED. IN FIRST ATTEMPT TO MOVE VEHICLE, RING AND PINION GEARS BOTH FRONT AND REAR WERE BROKEN. REQUEST FOLLOWING ITEMS BE SENT FIRST AVAILABLE AIRCRAFT IN OCTOBER.

This message is of course of great interest to the five of us. I am forced to admit that this message was received by us with mixed emotions. Naturally we are sympathetic, but at the same time there is the negative sort of comfort [*Schadenfreude!*] in the knowledge that we are not the only people to have trouble with the Sno-Cats. I can personally sympathize with the poor fellow who let the clutch out and felt everything break. It is fortunate that this happened at Little America (where replacement by air is easy) rather than here.

Ellsworth Station was the most inaccessible of the U.S. Antarctic stations including the South Pole. The flight in and out by Lassiter with two C-47s in 1957–58 was the only U.S. flight from outside the continent to land on the Filchner-Ronne ice front during the period from the 1950s to the early 1980s that I know of. I carried out several widely spaced geophysical survey flights over the Filchner-Ronne Ice Shelf and Berkner Island in 1963–64 and 1978 based at Byrd Station and McMurdo respectively, but no landings.

21 July, Sun. I slept all morning and we played bridge this afternoon. Ronne and Don beat Paul and me. Clint lectured us about strains and sprains today. Paul had a phone patch with his folks; he thinks he may not be wiped out with Carol after all. His spirits rose considerably. We studied the sonata form tonight and concentrated on the first movement of Beethoven's Fifth Symphony. High winds all day today—much drifting.

22 July, Mon. Winds up to 35 knots; we didn't work in the pit. I didn't get to sleep until 0600. I worked on flag making all day, but was quite sleepy. Hugo gave a talk on glaciology.

23 July, Tues. Warm (about –7°F) and little wind. It took Aug and me until coffee break to dig the drifted snow of this last storm away from the front of the tent. Paul lectured on glacial flow in the evening and we had an interesting and lively discussion.

After the movie, the Captain called Kim in; he told him of a new photographic processing arrangement which caused problems. Kim replied, "This is typical of the support that the IGY is receiving from the Navy." Ronne answered that IGY wasn't supporting the Navy very well either. Kim replied that we (IGY) were down here to do scientific work, not to support the Navy. At this, Ronne lost his temper and began shouting at Kim. Mac and Clint could hear him in their rooms. He told him that he was going on mess duty next summer. Kim answered that he had a program to carry out, and that he (Ronne) personally and the Navy in particular would be judged by the quality of the scientific work accomplished. Ronne shouted things about "the gall of a young college kid" talking to him that way. Clint was all excited and cornered Kim to get him to repeat the parts he had missed.

We were all keeping diaries. Someday some future Roland Huntford can collect all of these diaries and write a "true" (or *Roshamon*) history of this year at Ellsworth.

24 July, Wed. About –25°F with no wind and consequently very pleasant working conditions. The pit is narrower now (2 by 2 m) so we managed to get 150 cm deeper today, which bought us to 27 m depth. We had five visitors out at various occasions today. Only Butler and Larson had nerve enough to climb down the rope ladder to the bottom. It is a bit scary to climb down the first time, I imagine. We became used to it gradually as it deepened.

We studied the song form in the final lesson in the USAFI music course. Paul received a hamgram from his girl tonight, which will make him an easier person to live with. He has been under quite a strain as the last he heard was on 3 June.

25 July, Thurs. Ronne isn't speaking to Kim anymore. [Kim] wasn't sure the first time, but when he met Ronne in the passage outside the radio room, smiled, and said, "Good evening, Captain," the Captain didn't say a word, but just glared at him.

I was doing a little thinking about this trip tonight and came up with the following . . . which seemed pertinent. In listing characteristics desirable and/or necessary for scientists on an expedition of the present type, in addition to physical and professional qualifications and perhaps more important, is a personal integrity such that no matter how difficult and trying the situation may become, the primary goal (the scientific program) remains paramount in the mind and is conscientiously worked towards even at the expense of alienating the support personnel or undergoing constant strife. We are very fortunate in that the nine of us seem to possess this qualification. We are also fortunate (in fact, the situation would be unbearable without it) in spite of personal feuds, to have built up a trust in each other such that we are not afraid that every statement we make will be relayed to the Captain. This is the only thing that separates the atmosphere here from that of a totalitarian police state.

26 July, Fri. Ronne brought the following information copy to Ellsworth of a message from Washington to Little America about the Ellsworth traverse support:

COMNAVSUPFOR [DUFEK] ADVISES ALL AVAILABLE R4D AIRCRAFT ALREADY FULLY COMMITTED TO SUPPORT IGY ROSS SEA AREA OPERATIONS. . . . HOWEVER ARRANGEMENTS ARE BEING INVESTIGATED FOR LASSITER LONG-RANGE AIRCRAFT TO BE BASED AT ELLSWORTH SUBSEQUENT TO OCT 25. THESE TWO AIRCRAFT CAN AUGMENT OTTER SUPPORT AND THUS INCREASE TRAVERSE CAPABILITY IN ADDITION TO PERFORMING PLANNED LASSITER PROGRAM. USE OF 11,000 GALLONS AVGAS AT ELLSWORTH STA IS CONSIGNED TO IGY AND MUST BE

USED FOR IGY TRAVERSE SUPPORT. COMNAV-
SUPFOR ADVISED THAT REMAINING 15,000 GALLONS
RESERVED FOR SAR [SEARCH AND RESCUE] PURPOSES
UNTIL RELEASED FOR OTHER PURPOSES BY COM-
NAVSUPFOR. YOUR OPINION REQUESTED TO RE-
VISE PLANNED 57–58 TRAVERSE PATH AS FOLLOWS:
ELLSWORTH STATION TO 81°S, 75°W TO 77°20'S, 71°30'W
(MOUNT HASSAGE) TO ELLSWORTH STA.

Ronne said that the route suggested is "absurd." Ronne was quite
disturbed about the reference to the SAR avgas limitation. He was
so upset that he made the slip of telling Ed that Lassiter "needs a
minimum of 15,000 gallons of avgas for his program."

Ronne sent out the following dispatch to Washington in the
afternoon which he brought in to Ed:

UNABLE DETERMINE EXTENT AND DIRECTION FOR
TRAVERSE PARTY TRAVEL UNTIL FIRST RECON
FLIGHT MADE ON COURSE DUE SOUTH FOR 175
MILES. . . . ARE NOT CERTAIN OF CHANCES GETTING
INLAND ON SURFACE. . . . UNLESS LASSITER OBTAINS
PERMISSION USE GAS BEYOND THAT ASSIGNED IGY,
SEE NO PURPOSE HIM COMING.

About a month later, early in the morning, Ronne received two
phone patches about the avgas. Hugo, while lying in his bed trying
to sleep, heard this side of an hour-long talk with Ronne's wife. Apparently someone in Washington with initials "J.C.K." had been
pulling strings to get the avgas allocated to Lassiter with some success. Ronne specified that Lassiter was to bring nothing extra. J.C.K.
was probably someone connected with Lassiter's CIA mission.

On 5 September a dispatch came in from Dufek stating that
15,000 gallons of avgas were to be saved for search and rescue and
could not be used before 15 December. The other 11,000 gallons
were to be used as Ronne saw fit. Mac interpreted this as blanket
authorization for Ronne to give Lassiter gas. He and the other officers had kidded us traverse people about being "wiped out."
Apparently Ronne got through to J.C.K.

On 8 September, Ronne had a phone patch with Lassiter. Hugo
and Paul lying awake in their beds heard the talk. Lassiter asked if
he should bring the Sno-Cat clutch, and Ronne told him no, that

the people at Shackleton were fixing everything up for us. Meanwhile Ronne had told us that they probably would not get it fixed and that we had better plan on using Weasels. Needless to say, his numerous orders to Lassiter not to bring the clutch displeased us traverse people greatly.

I worked on flags again today. Con talked a few minutes on jazz tonight and we heard a few examples followed by Benjamin Britten's "Young People's Guide to the Orchestra."

27 July, Sat. Ed, Don, and I spent the afternoon shoveling snow out of the tunnel in back of the science building. The temperature was in the –50s°F all day. I received a hamgram.

There was no official station party this month, but everyone had been building up to the state of mind where some sort of party was inevitable. The airdales started this afternoon out in their buildings and continued on into the night.

This was the most raucous party of the winter.

During the movie McCarthy came into the galley from the rear and stood slopping beer around on people. Crouse, who was splashed, attempted to throw some at him but sprayed Ronne instead. The Captain, who can't stand a scene in front of a large audience, showed amazing forbearance. Shortly thereafter Mac got down on his hands and knees and crawled under all the tables on the left up to the front of the room whispering to each person he came to, "Shh!–I don't want the Captain to see me." There was a lot of disturbance by the time he neared the door whereupon he shouted, "Goddamn it, shut up!"

Later in the airdale building, Haskill somersaulted into a bucket of water and came up with the pail on his head. He took a running headlong dive at the space heater and knocked it about six feet across the room, cutting a four-inch gash in the top of his head. He staggered down to see Clint, who took three stitches in the scalp. Haskill was temporarily quiet but kept asking for the Captain to say a prayer for him.

I was drinking coffee in the galley when in walked Haskill with a can of beer in his hand. He cut a very comical figure with his skull bandage of surgical tubing, his handlebar moustache, and his hair sticking out behind his ears.

Ed and I decided to pay a visit to the aircraft building. Some VX-6 people, Forlidas and Jack (who was changing the whistler tape) were there. Pretty soon Haskill showed up and got into a wrestling match with Mac in the course of which his bandage was pulled off. About this point Ed and I left. By the time we got back another party was going in the rec hall.

All the civilians were out of the festivities tonight. Jack stayed up with Con and Mac but not drinking much when I last saw him. Paul was over at our house. Hugo spent the evening out in the cold tunnel taking pictures of snow blocks from the pit.

28 July, Sun. The temperature was around –60°F all day. I was awakened at 0500 for a phone patch with the folks. It was good to hear their voices. They asked if I hear much news down here. This made me pause and think about how really isolated from the rest of the world we are. No, we don't hear much news, mainly because we don't make much effort to. The radio on my wall developed troubles months ago and I never even felt much incentive to repair it. The occasional bits of news we do hear is largely meaningless, out of context with what preceded it. The main thing is that, other than personal news of friends and families, which we get through hamgrams, we are not much interested in what goes on in the outside world. News of the other Antarctic stations is much more eagerly sought after.

Ronne came over, and Don and I edged him and Paul out by 150 points at bridge. He was in his "genial-ornery" mood. He told Paul and me, "You aren't in Dutch anymore because it looks like Lassiter isn't coming down." We didn't know what to make of this cryptic remark and I asked him why Lassiter wasn't coming. He mumbled something about it being too involved to go into but that it had something to do with Navy–Air Force politics. Navy doesn't want Air Force interfering in their theater of operation.

Because the Lassiter (USAF) mission was a CIA operation, the politics involved the Navy, Air Force, and CIA, as well as Ronne's personal agenda. I was pretty naive in those days about such things. After more than 40 additional years of Antarctic experience, I must admit I have participated in similar bureaucratic exercises. I realize that all of us active Antarctic scientists, and others, have our hidden agendas both nationally and internationally. It is partly the reason I have sat through so many boring Antarctic Treaty Consultative Meetings.

Clint lectured us on fractures in the afternoon. This is one of the more likely injuries we may have to cope with on traverse. In the evening at music, we listened to three selections of Prokofiev: Classical Symphony, *Peter and the Wolf,* and a violin concerto. I am forced to admit that he isn't my favorite composer.

29 July, Mon. It warmed up to −54°F today with a 20-knot wind which made visibility poor. However, we dug in the morning and the last platform went in after lunch. I must be getting more acclimatized all the time because a month ago I wasn't able to do much at −30°F with a 20-knot wind without freezing my nose. I can now manage with difficulty at −50°F. The wind, of course, makes all the difference in the world. Ed gave a lecture on earthquake seismology tonight.

Ronne brought in an information copy to Ellsworth of the following dispatch from Crary in Little America to Washington: CONCUR YOUR REVISED ELLSWORTH STA 57–58 TRAVERSE PATH [TO MEET THE BYRD TRAVERSE ROUTE]. MOST IMPORTANT ASSISTANCE BE GIVEN IN SETTING UP INLAND GAS CACHES. This sounds as if they are ignoring Ronne's repeated statements about the impossibility of getting very far here.

Ed and Hugo had a talk about work in the pit. Crary specified that the pit was to be 20–30 m deep. Hugo with his usual thoroughness wants to get an extra 5 m (to 35) which would take at least another week. Hugo stated quite emphatically that he is in charge of the pit and that they would go deeper. Ed pointed out that he and I were sacrificing our program, and that he was not to count on our help beyond the end of July. Hugo said he would do it himself if no one would help. Ed told him to stop acting like Ronne.

I realize that I recorded this little spat partly because it was so exceptional. Ed and Hugo had to get along with each other comfortably to make our traverse successful. I am sure I could not have gotten along with Hugo nearly as well had I been in Ed's position.

30 July, Tues. The wind was up to 30 knots, and there was more blowing snow than we have had yet this winter, so digging was out. When I went out at 1300 to shut off the Weasel and "seal it up," I could barely see the light on Kim's tower from the garage entrance. I worked on trail flags.

Ronne stopped me in the tunnel this afternoon and asked me if I had heard any complaints about our phone patches Sunday morning. He said that people were saying that he talked for an hour and 50 minutes but that it was not so. He really is shook up about people knowing how long he talked. Ken had it written in the ham log that he talked for an hour and 50 minutes.

After supper Don, Kim, and I planned a "Ronne Rating" to keep track of current and past positions on Ronne's hate list. We set up a system of 10 grades on an exponential scale with the lowest numbers being the most hated. It was decided that #1 (10 on a scale of 100 points) was the case where Ronne "completely lost control" of himself with the person in question. Number 10, or 100 points, was the position known as "Golden," which Jack occupies in the Captain's mind. We each rated everyone and averaged the results to get our present positions. I am 86, which is between #8 ("nonentity") and #9 ("nice fellow"). From #8 to #1 are the most esteemed positions (i.e., where Ronne dislikes one to a greater or lesser degree). Don was rated about 90.

After the movie Ronne came in and asked Don if he had been complaining and spreading talk about him talking for an hour and 50 minutes to his wife Sunday. He told Don he only talked for 50 minutes. Don said that he hadn't but that just for the record he knew that Ronne had talked an hour and 40 minutes at least. Don said that at 0545 he had turned on their receiver to get the time, for their ionosphere clock had heard him talking then. At this Ronne blew up and shouted that this was none of Don's "goddamn business." He went on to rant about not talking that long and besides, "It's none of your goddamn business if I did!"

When Ronne turned to stalk out, Don told him that he was leaving because, "You're afraid of me!" Ronne was about incoherent by this time but he managed to state that he wasn't afraid and to mumble more threats. Don told him, "If you are not afraid, stay and discuss this," but Ronne was leaving.

We all went into the library to hear Ed's second lecture on seismology. First, however, we re-evaluated Don's Ronne Rating from about 90 up to 15, which currently places him at the head of the list.

Both Augie and Paul had given hamgrams to Ronne to censor within the first five minutes after his scene with Don, and both reported him very distraught.

I realize now that these battles must have been unbelievably distressing and frustrating for Ronne because, unlike the rest of us, he was the leader and had no one to commiserate with. I noted the "goddamn" above because Ronne normally never used any expletives and was quite fastidious in his speech, around us at least. He didn't care for the generally vulgar way he considered that the enlisted men talked.

By this time we had become so used to Seabee English that I don't recall noticing it anymore. For instance, a Japanese friend and colleague, Hiromu Shimizu, who wintered over at Byrd Station a couple of years later, learned all of his fluent spoken English among the Navy Seabees at the station. He apparently never learned any other English term for "wastebasket" other than "shit can." He had a few difficulties when he went from a year in Antarctica to a year at the Ohio State University in 1962. Nowadays, of course, this would not cause any problems at a university. The colorful Seabee vocabulary, as spoken by some of the men, seemed to require "fuck" to be used at least once a sentence as in, "It's six o'fucking clock."

Clint, Con, Don, Paul, Ed, Kim, Hugo, and I all sat around in the library for two hours while Jack was with Ronne, waiting for the outcome of their conversation about his fight with Don. To while the time away we had an interesting, if academic, discussion on sexual intercourse.

Jack came in about midnight and gave us an account of his talk. He had stood up for Don and had pointed out that Ronne had taken unfair advantage of the privileges that his rank and position put within his reach. He got to the shouting stage with Jack, too: "It's none of their damn business if I talk for five hours." However, he even grudgingly admitted that he had talked for an hour and fifty minutes. He can't afford to lose the only shoulder he still has to cry on, so the conversation ended with Jack still having a Ronne Rating of 90 plus. Ronne talked about the Uniform Code of Military Justice (UCMJ) and wants to restrict Don from the movies and rec hall for two weeks for "disrespect." Jack pointed out that Captain Dickey in Little America had told Ronne that he couldn't treat civilians this way under UCMJ, and Ronne admitted this was so.

31 July, Wed. Calm and down to −49°F by 1700. It was clear and quite light around noon.

McCarthy is planning to dig out his aircraft, which are pretty well buried in snow. One of the wings on the Otter is crumpled. It isn't known whether the fuselage is all right or not. Fortunately there is a spare wing for each plane.

Ed went in to see Ronne, who was still in a heated state. Ronne covered several points. He told Ed that we will not receive help with vehicle maintenance and repair including starting the Weasel in the morning.

Starting the Weasel involved heating it with a Hermann Nelson aircraft engine preheater. This gasoline-powered heater was used for vehicles of all types and provided heat through flexible ducts as needed to specific locations. Actually, Walt Davis, the mechanic, was doing this because he was outside early every day moving snow around with the D-4 tractor, and because he was a really nice guy inside a gruff exterior. He saved our bacon on numerous occasions.

Walt Davis told me he wanted no part of the dispute between Ronne and us. "The Old Man can bust me right down to a seaman if he wants!"

Ronne informed Ed that he is keeping record of our "poor cooperation" including tape recordings. "You will hear voices you recognize when you get back to Washington." Malville (when his winter program is complete) will stand mess duty "if its the last thing I do as leader of this base." Hamgrams are a privilege not a right. Therefore privilege can be withdrawn same as for movies and rec hall.

Mac told us that Ronne took the pile of hamgrams into his room this afternoon and later brought it back to the radio room. Ronne had removed three hamgrams that Augie had put in and two that Kim had submitted, intending not to send them. I don't see why he persecutes Augie so much. Mac remonstrated with him on this action, pointing out that he is hurting the people back in the States who expect to hear from Kim and Aug. This scored with the Captain, and he said he'd hold them out a couple of days and think about it. Kim and Aug aren't doing anything until they see if he returns them. Officially they don't even know they are not in the pile. Ronne wasn't (isn't) even intending to tell them their messages are not going out. This is the most demoralizing and cruel thing he has done yet. Unfortunately he has found the spot, for the first time, where he can really hurt most of us. I wonder if he would withhold incoming messages. Paul told Mac, before we knew that any messages had been withdrawn, that he will resign on the spot if Ronne would do that to him.

I notice throughout I used the expression "the States" or "back in the States." In McMurdo in 1995 I commonly heard people refer to "back in the World."

Notes

1. The Antarctic Peninsula was then called the Palmer Peninsula on U.S. maps, Graham Land on British maps, Bernardo O'Higgins Land on Chilean maps, and San Martin Land by the Argentines.
2. The activities during the 1956–58 period of this book are covered in the volumes Operation Deep Freeze II (ed. J. E. Oglesby, JOC), 1957, and III (ed. M. P. Beebe, Lt. [jg]), 1958 (Paoli, Penn.: Dorville Corp.).

6
The Sun Returns

Finally the major work of the glaciologists was completed. Now we could move on to other activities.

View near vertically down 100-ft-deep pit. Platforms and wire rope ladder at right.

1 Aug., Thurs. We finished digging the pit today. The final depth is 100 ft, or 31 m. We had very pleasant working conditions, no wind, and quite warm (about −33°F) all day. I am reading *The Rain Cave,* and I like it. Paul talked on the tape recorder for Ronne's CBS interview series and even sang a song accompanied by his uke. We have been kidding him about this. Paul relaxed from the strain of the pit digging tonight and drank a little too much BuMed brandy.

This Navy Bureau of Medicine brandy, in two-ounce bottles, was supplied to the medical officers and, although not particularly good, was frequently available. There seems to have been a large quantity at Ellsworth.

> Ronne has been talking up our refusal to volunteer to "mess cook" among the enlisted men in order to turn them against us, but other than a few congenital "sand crab" haters he hasn't made much progress. If he wants to "divide and rule," he should never have moved us in to mess with the men. When you get to know a man and eat with him everyday, you are more apt to like him than dislike him.

"Sand crab" was the derogatory slang term the Seabees used for civilians on a base. The scientific people were all called sand crabs, or just "crabs," at the IGY Antarctic stations. By 1960, at McMurdo, the term was "farp," for fellow of the Antarctic research program. In the early 1990s the scientists at McMurdo were known as "beakers," but most of us who passed through that station quickly never heard it used. I read it first in a *New York Times* article, although I was in McMurdo in 1990 and 1991. I've frequently noticed that a slang term printed in a newspaper develops a life of its own. By 1995 the term "beaker" was not heard much around McMurdo, but I did hear it used out at a field camp by an "old timer" Antarctic Support Associates man who had three to five years' Antarctic experience.

> Ronne chewed Con out for calling enlisted men by their first names. He asked, "You were an enlisted man once. Did officers ever call you by your first name?" Con told him, "Yes." Ronne countered with "Well, you never hear Mac (the only man on the base who Ronne calls by his first name and at that uses his nickname) addressing enlisted men by their first names." Con disagreed here, too, but Ronne wouldn't accept this. At supper tonight, when Mac called across the room to Grob, "These are good biscuits, Dick," Ronne wouldn't meet Con's eye.
> Ronne gave up trying to keep the civilians from calling the enlisted men by their first names long ago. He is the only one we aren't on a first-name basis with. Hugo, who knew Ronne in the Explorers Club, still calls him "Finn," which I don't think Ronne likes.

> *2 Aug., Fri.* We studied J. S. Bach tonight and listened to some of his organ music (including the Toccata and Fugue in D Minor) and the

2nd and 3rd Brandenburg Concerti. I really enjoyed the latter, particularly #2.

Kim got Kent to admit that "someone" had removed his hamgrams from the file to send out. I brought the subject up to Ed that I (and most of the rest of the GS 9's) think that he and Jack have a responsibility . . . to try and get Ronne to release these hamgrams if he holds them up indefinitely. He didn't look at it that way and that everyone should fight his own battles and that it took a "lot of crust" for someone to ask another person to fight them for him.

Ed had resigned as deputy station scientific leader in May, but the rest of us never really accepted that and thought Ed should have been our intermediary with Ronne. Ed apparently did not see it that way.

3 Aug., Sat. We cleaned up the science building and took the afternoon off. I slept. Thirty-five-knot winds at −35°F all day. It will drift in all that the airdales dug out around their aircraft yesterday.

Public opinion persuaded the Captain to consent to another party tonight. At first he wanted an organized games, etc., and nearly nonalcoholic type of affair. Con, Mac, and Jack didn't think the men would like this, but Ronne disagreed with them and said he would ask the men personally what kind of a party they wanted. He did this all morning and at noon came up with the great idea of letting the men plan their party the way they like and have a goodly amount of liquor. There were 10 fifths [a fifth was 4/5ths of a quart before metrification in the late 1970s] of bourbon allotted, but this time it wasn't put in the punch, so I enjoyed a number of cups. Chief May dispensed the booze with no limit to anyone but still kept control of the bottles so no one could hog it all. Everyone enjoyed himself, and there was lots to eat. Consequently even Ronne was happy.

4 Aug., Sun. The Captain and I beat Paul and Don today at bridge. We practiced splints and treatment of fractures this afternoon. At music tonight we heard more Bach (including part of his Christmas Oratorio). Filet mignon for supper (typical Sunday dinner).

There was no more filet mignon in the U.S. Antarctic Program at McMurdo, in the summer at least, in the Navy mess in the 1980s and 1990s, as Antarctica apparently wasn't considered a hardship post anymore. As of 1992–93 the contractor, Antarctic Support

Associates, took over the food service at all three U.S. stations. The reviews were mixed when I was at McMurdo in January 1995. Now there is vegetarian and nonvegetarian food at all meals, and a lot of pasta. When I heard some complaints about no fresh eggs for a week or so, I commented to the complainers, "Yeah, life is tough in Antarctica!"

> *5 Aug., Mon.* I took my physical exam, which included a blood-pressure determination and weighing. Beiszer gave me a haircut tonight. It may not be the best job I've ever had but it is probably the shortest.

Those of us who were working outdoors in the winter were, not surprisingly, in great physical shape although we did put on weight. I was up to my highest weight ever at about 210–215 lbs. The extra fat helped us in the cold, I think. By the end of the traverse, I was down to about 175 lbs.

As for my haircut, it was a mistake to take off so much. I really felt the cold, despite my balaclava helmet and pile-lined fur parka hood. For a time, Augie, Don, and Paul didn't cut their hair at all during the year at Ellsworth, which we others became used to. Ronne, who was balding, disliked long hair and beards, but didn't make any particular effort to control us on this subject.

Long hair on men was quite unusual in the United States in the 1950s but ubiquitous in the 1960s and early 1970s, and is still commonplace, even in the 1990s, in Boulder and elsewhere. At McMurdo, South Pole, and summer field camps in 1995, I noticed few beards, but a number of men wore their long hair in pony tails.

> Augie gave a very good lecture on Antarctic geology after the movie.
>
> Ed and I went out to the airdale area and took some pictures of the buried Otters. The Otter with the damaged wing has been shoveled partly clear, but only the windshield and part of the engine cowling are visible on the other aircraft. There was a lot of color in the north, and the lighting was quite interesting.
>
> *6 Aug., Tues.* Ed and I took the Weasel and went out to the pit with the gravimeter to measure the vertical gradient. We read from top to bottom and back to top in the morning and repeated after noon. Although it was only −30°F and −10°F at the bottom of the pit, I was colder today, especially my feet, than I have been all winter. This

Part of Otter aircraft buried in drifted snow. Fuselage was warped and destroyed.

was mainly due to the inactivity while taking the readings. Five minutes reading while hardly moving a muscle slowed up my circulation down to the point where I nipped my nose pretty badly when I went outside to the Weasel.

This is about the coldest I recall having been in all my trips to Antarctica. We needed five minutes to take a single measurement because the floating ice shelf was constantly in motion at the micro level that we could observe with the gravimeter, which as I noted previously acted as a seismograph.

Ronne, Mac, and Con traveled on foot down to the sea today. They found open water a ways out. We have had open water off and on all winter as evidenced by sea smoke to the north on numerous occasions.

At Ellsworth in the 1957 winter, the strong winds kept blowing the new ice away from the front of the ice shelf every few days.

Cox and Ronne shot movies of Ed and me taking gravity observations after supper. The bright light (or something) gave me a headache. Augie finished up his lecture discussing the geology of West Antarctica tonight.

The only thing known of the geology of West Antarctica in 1957 was a little about the northern Antarctic Peninsula and the coastal area of Marie Byrd Land close to the Ross Ice Shelf. Although a few mountain ranges had been sighted in West Antarctica by Ellsworth and Ronne, none had been visited on the surface. Ellsworth had seen the northernmost peaks of the Sentinel Mountain Range, in the Ellsworth Mountains, but the highest, main part had been obscured by clouds at the time of his 1935 flight. Most of West Antarctica had not been flown over or explored at all. This changed rapidly during the following summer and over the next few years.

> It was enjoyable to see the physicists like Jack and Kim (who have glibly thrown all sorts of high-sounding language at people like Paul and Aug) squirm under a few geologic terms. It seems rather ironic that, although geology isn't one of the fields of the IGY, we have four out of the nine scientists with geology degrees.
>
> *7 Aug., Wed.* A good share of the morning was wasted by Ronne and Cox taking movies. I was the subject. We dug out the seismic gear and dragged it over to the library and set it up.

The seismic equipment and all of our scientific supplies, food, etc., was stored in the tunnels connecting the buildings and between the buildings. By this time the drifts had covered the entire station and only the aurora tower and the fiberglass dome, called radome, protecting the weather balloon tracking antenna projected on aluminum posts above the surface. At the end of the winter parts of the tops of the buildings could still be seen, but by the end of the second winter all were buried.

> Con and Clint told us of a discussion at their mess tonight. Con asked Ronne what were the economic possibilities (mining specifically) down here. Ronne told him there were none, and all this talk about it was just talk. Con said, "That's what Augie said in his lecture last night." At this Ronne did a 180-degree-phase shift and stated that Aughenbaugh didn't know what he was talking about. "I can tell you" he said (a favorite expression of his) pointing his finger for emphasis, and then proceeded to tell about all the ore deposits in the Antarctic, particularly copper in the Palmer Peninsula (which apparently had been found on his expedition). Augie had discussed

Meteorology radome and buried camp in late winter.

all this in his lecture and had found his information in the geologic papers published by the geologists on Ronne's and on other expeditions. There are ore minerals but not of high enough grade or quantity to warrant exploitation at present. Similar low-grade ores are not being mined in the U.S. today. Augie (mostly through his reading down here) knows more about Antarctic geology than 99% of the geologists in the U.S.

The controversy surrounding mining in Antarctica is still alive in the 1990s. During the negotiation of the Convention on the Regulation of Antarctic Mineral Resource Activities (CRAMRA) in the 1980s, environmental groups like Greenpeace and the Antarctic and Southern Ocean Coalition made a lot of noise about the danger to the fragile Antarctic ecosystem that mining would bring. However, throughout this period the international mining industry was not at all interested in Antarctica. Most mines, except for gold, have been closed in the U.S. because of low prices. CRAMRA was adopted by consensus of the Antarctic Treaty in 1988 but never was ratified. CRAMRA was essentially rewritten (with the claimant nation accommodation removed) into the Environmental Protocol to the Antarctic Treaty, which was signed in 1991.

There was some interest in offshore oil by the petroleum industry after the OPEC oil boycott of 1973 tripled prices, which led to the negotiation of CRAMRA. By 1991 the price of oil was so low that the industry did not try to block the prohibition in the Environmental Protocol against future oil and mineral activities, except for scientific research in Antarctica. I published a number of papers on this subject along with other colleagues, which may have helped persuade industry and government that there are no economic petroleum and mineral resources in Antarctica.

The Environmental Protocol was adopted by consensus of the 25 Antarctic Treaty consultative parties and signed in 1991. The protocol entered into force in 1998 when it was ratified by each of the parties in the Antarctic Treaty at the time of its adoption.

8 Aug., Thurs. We started checking out the seismic gear this morning. Don refused to pose for Ronne's movies, so he and the Captain

F. Ronne recording sound for his movie in ionolab in science building.

had another talk. Don must have learned a lot in his several years as an attendant in various mental hospitals, because he made a deal with the Captain whereby he gets to operate the ham set in return for posing for the movies.

I printed pictures tonight. The only bulb that was sent down with Kim's enlarger burned out last week. Hugo built a replacement by soldering another size bulb into the base of the burned bulb. It isn't the best, but it works.

Hugo's real talents can be seen again in this sort of painstaking improvisation. This attribute could be occasionally exasperating, but Hugo several times saved the day on more important things than the enlarger bulb.

> *9 Aug., Fri.* It was too windy so we worked inside. I spent the day making a photocopy of Bentley's report on the seismic work he did in Greenland.

This was before the days of true photocopying machines, so we resorted to using several tedious ways of copying the various memos, messages, and documents, including cameras and seismic photographic paper. The lowest-tech but very reliable method was simply hand copying short items into my journal.

> Don thinks that the Captain put Kim's and Augie's hamgrams back in the pile to be sent, but not Don's own. Perhaps this is due to messages such as Augie received and the one that came in from the Navy as regards Crouse. It seems that his family hasn't heard from him since we have been here, and they questioned the Navy. Clint mentioned that other messages had been coming in from families asking to hear from various people. Don received a Class E from his wife this afternoon asking why she hasn't heard from him. Don wrote a Class E in reply in which he asked her to make an appointment for him in April with Senator Saltonstall. [Don had requested this in the hamgram that Ronne pulled out.] He mentioned that he couldn't tell her about the situation here and that some of the men haven't contacted their families yet.

Ronne didn't like Don's message and asked him to change it. Don replied, "It's my wife and my message." Ronne mentioned that he couldn't let anything derogatory to the station be sent out and told Don that people might think something was wrong. However, he ultimately approved the message under pressure.

> *10 Aug., Sat.* Ed and I went out and checked over our Sno-Cat. There is a little snow around two of the tracks, but otherwise there is no real trouble. Some of the Weasels are actually lost; they are buried so deep. The Sno-Cat engine is all covered with snow blown in through the grill in front. In this respect the Weasel is far better designed. Although the Sno-Cat engine is actually inside the cab, it

is insulated from it so there is no heating of the vehicle by the engine.

Eventually, we convinced the Tucker Company to modify the Sno-Cat design. When I used three new vehicles for a traverse I led in 1961, the engine was completely inside the elongated box-shaped cab. The heat of the engine then warmed the inside quite effectively.

The airdales are now working seven days a week digging the planes out. Starting Monday everyone fuels his own house.

Throughout the winter until this time the VX-6 enlisted men, who had little aircraft-related work to do, had done the onerous job of dragging 55-gallon drums of diesel fuel on an akio through-out the station through the tunnels and hand-pumping them into the tanks at each end of each building, which supplied the jet heaters.

11 Aug., Sun. I slept until noon. Ronne decided not to play bridge with us today. He said he was too busy.

In retrospect, with all the tension we were experiencing, it seems amazing that we managed to keep up these bridge games with Ronne all winter. The last we played with him was 4 August.

Tonight we saw *Random Harvest* with Ronald Coleman and Greer Garson. One of our better pictures. We started Beethoven (Moon-light Sonata, *Egmont and Leonora* no. 3 overtures) in our course.
   Clint lectured us on appendicitis and the methods of treatment we could employ on traverse.

Fortunately, we had no appendicitis problems on the traverse. However, I had appendicitis in Antarctica in November 1960 at Byrd Station during a 12-day radio blackout. Because they couldn't fly planes to evacuate me to McMurdo for surgery, the physician treated me with penicillin. I recovered, though, and continued my geophysical fieldwork for the rest of the summer season. The fol-lowing year, I had my appendix removed before returning to the Antarctic fieldwork.

2 Aug., Mon. There was a 20-knot wind at −56°F. Ed, Paul, Aug, and I carried all the traverse food from the science tunnel to the now-empty tunnel adjoining the science building. Aug and I spent the rest of the day opening boxes and calculating menus. It was −27°F in the tunnel, and we both became quite cold. I couldn't keep my feet warm due to lack of activity. It is warmer working outdoors or in the pit. It felt good to be working at food planning again. I have always enjoyed this type of work and have done a lot of it in the past five years.

I volunteered to plan the food and be the main cook on the traverse. As a "poor starving student," I had found I was fed the best on camping and mountaineering trips when I managed the food. This Antarctic duty was an easy continuation.

13 Aug., Tues. Aug and I finished sorting and separating out what we want. Our inventory runs as follows:

TYPE OF FOOD	DAYS SUPPLY
milk (Carnation Instant–the best)	80
cream (for coffee)	80
curry (powder)	80
pudding (Royal instant)	28
cereal (farina and oatmeal)	70 (*more unopened*)
dried fruit	32
Minute Rice	28
tea (powdered)	80
fruit juice	169
potatoes (granule)	56
sugar	72 (*lbs*)
salt and pepper	80
corned beef	24
spaghetti	14
bacon (canned, fried)	14
lunch meat (Spam)	14
ham (canned)	24
soups (unlimited, instant powders)	80
ice cream (plenty of Tastie Freeze)	80
dehydrated steaks and pork chops (canned)	30
butter (canned)	288
frozen meat (stew, ground beef, tenderloin strip steaks)	80 45
crackers (C-ration type)	*hundreds of lbs*
dehydrated cheese	80

I obtained a few emergency trail rations from Ed Davis [the cook] and examined them. They are not too palatable, consisting of meat bars, chocolate, raisins, fruitcake, cereal bars, soup, crackers, cocoa, etc. The approximately 40-ounce ration contains about 6000 calories. Weight could be cut some without diminishing calories too much. They also have a vitamin pill and a fuel tablet. Most people think the meat bar unfit to eat, but I think I could get along all right on them if I had to.

Don, Jack, Paul, and I played pinochle. Don and I really get in violent arguments at cards, and it's hard on the other players. I guess the winter is telling. Fortunately we forget our fights–until the next game.

Don told Kent off as regards the ham gear tonight. There are 50 hamgrams piling up to go out, and none have gone out for nearly a month. Don wrote a several-page report on the ham gear situation and gave it to Ronne the next day. Kent told Ronne that either he or Don would have to go as regards ham operation. Kent went. Don is now in charge of the ham station, and Kent is on daytime work of maintaining equipment. I can't help thinking of Don's statement on 29 July to Ronne: "You are afraid of me!"

Paul received a hamgram from his folks today, which indicates that his fiancee may not be that anymore. He is pretty discouraged, but is trying to put on a blasé front. He sent a Class E to her today with a blunt query as to the situation.

Aug, Con, Kim, Ed, Paul, and I spent a couple of hours sitting around our room discussing women, Washington, D.C., women, IGY staff in Washington, female secretaries for IGY [there was one called Yum Yum], and geology.

14 Aug., Wed. It has been getting colder all along. The past two weeks have averaged in the –40s° and –50s°F with lots of wind.

It is interesting that although it was colder now but just as dark outside as at the same time before the solstice, many more people were working outside. The psychological effect of the approaching spring and first sunrise after the long winter (it was still winter) made everyone anxious to rush the season.

Aug and I sorted all the food. It was –38°F in the tunnel, and we couldn't find any of our boots that would keep our feet warm, inactive as we were. Ed and Kim were kidding me about wearing heavy clothes in the tunnel (normally in going to the galley, head, etc., we wore regular indoor clothes).

We did not wear hats, jackets, or mittens when walking between the buildings in the tunnels. Our wet hair and beards would freeze. I usually wore long underwear, army wool shirt, khaki wash pants, and heavy army ski boots with one pair of wool socks inside.

I'm reading an excellent book by Dr. R. B. Robertson (a psychiatrist) called *Of Whales and Men*. In it he discusses the sex life of the South Georgia wintering-over people. As his statements sum up the conditions pretty well here, I will quote him:

> There was an insatiable demand among the isolated men for pornographic literature. . . . Masturbation, my informants all agreed, was rampant. . . . We went on to talk of homosexuality. From the chatter of the three observant and intelligent men, the impression I got (an impression later confirmed by my own ob-

I am reading on bed in room. Angry 9 radio mounted on wall. Sound-powered phone connected to aurora tower. Note clips holding panels of wall together; silver tape prevents snow blowing through crack.

> servation) was that physical homosexuality was so rare as to be almost nonexistent . . . a thing one cannot say about isolated groups of soldiers or sailors under other circumstances. On the other hand, evidence of repressed homosexuality was apparent wherever one looked. Every little group had its member distin-

guished for his ability to tell dirty stories, the bulk of which had
a homosexual coloring, to which his companions listened with
relish. Every group also had its delicate effeminate member to
whom the rough whale men showed more consideration and
kindliness than they did to one another. Maybe it's overstretch-
ing an analytic interpretation to see repressed homosexuality in
such harmless behavior, as it may be to see something significant in the whalemen's tendency, when they are drunk, to paw
and wrestle with one another.

I am very much impressed by *Of Whales and Men*. I wish someone
would write a book like that on an Antarctic expedition. Our men
were pretty well screened.

In my journal, I implied that there were no homosexual men
at Ellsworth. I now think this shows my naiveté. I have known gay
men in the present-day U.S. Antarctic Program, and I assume they
were there during IGY. Of course in 1957, any gay man at Ellsworth
was strictly in the closet. In more recent years I have known people
in Antarctica who were gay or lesbian, but no one who knew of
this paid it any attention. At McMurdo in January 1995 I noticed
one man wearing a pink triangle "gay pride" T-shirt in the mess
hall. The main difference today is the albeit limited outlet for het-
erosexual activity. I heard a song on the local McMurdo FM station in 1989, "If you can't be with the one you love, love the one
you're with." I first saw condoms for sale in the Ship Stores at
McMurdo in 1984, but later these were dispensed more privately,
through the medical department, I assume. I was recently told by a
woman in Boulder that she had heard that the expression "ice wives"
was common in McMurdo in 1996. This idiom was news to me.

15 Aug., Thurs. Ed, Augie, and I have mostly completed the packing
of our traverse food. I divided it into four 30-day lots (A, B, C, and
D). A will go with us. B and C will be flown out, and D will be for
our replacements. A and B are packed in cardboard boxes, but we
ran out of boxes before we finished. We will have to wait for the rest
until more beer is consumed.

Two days ago we treated everyone with cookies from our traverse
supplies. We mixed up some of the dehydrated cheese we have for
traverse and served it at afternoon coffee. All the traverse people
liked it, but the rest of the men thought it was terrible. Yesterday we
tried our three varieties of "soup, dehydrated." The onion is very

good, the cream of potato is good, and the lima bean is pretty bad. These are the handiest soup concentrates I've seen yet. No cooking is required at all; one just pours the contents of an envelope into eight ounces of hot water and stirs.

This was the first time we had seen soup packets that did not require cooking, and they were not generally available in stores at home in 1956. We did eat a lot of onion and potato soup on the traverse.

Aug and I hauled all the emergency trail rations we would take on traverse out from the main food tunnel behind the galley and into the field where they would be out of the way. In spite of the dehydrated nature of this food, it still ran to over four pounds/person/day–mainly due to the packaging.

The weather people put the last of a certain vacuum tube in their radio-sonde tracking instrument. When this goes, they will have to track balloons visually from Kim's tower. This will cut their height down from 60,000+ ft to about 30,000.

No vacuum tubes are available in the U.S. anymore, but I heard on National Public Radio in 1993 that a U.S. Weather Bureau instrument being used today couldn't be repaired without a vacuum tube from Russia.

The Navy radio gear is working excellently, now that the antenna has been fixed. I sent out a Class E message today, and Ronne made me withdraw the hamgram I had in the pile. There are over 50 piled up. Chuck Forlidas received some hamgrams from Little America and ham frequencies with it. Officially, of course, it was on the ham gear.

We had a good aurora tonight, and Ed and Paul were out taking pictures. I ran over to the glaciology lab (slipping in the tunnel and banging my knee on the deck en route) and borrowed their tripod for my camera. Hugo was in his room loading his camera and planning to use the tripod himself. He was quite disturbed at me with just cause, I must admit. By the time I went outside, the display was fading. I took a picture for about five minutes and then relinquished the tripod to Hugo. The display came back quite brightly while he was out, but his camera froze. Tomorrow I'll have to try and straighten things out with him. I wish he wasn't so damn polite and had told me, "No, you can't use the tripod." He will let people walk over him and then play the martyr about it.

The sun will rise one of these days. In a publicity dispatch Willie Sumrall (PIO, public information officer) quotes Walt May as announcing the sun's rise on 16 Aug. Hugo made a number of calculations and posted a notice on the bulletin board stating Old Sol's ETA (estimated time of arrival) for 17 Aug. It will be interesting to see who is right.

16 Aug., Fri. Clear, calm, and cold, about –50°F. The sun (or maybe not the sun–there is some discussion about it) peeped over the horizon at 1136. Don and Hugo who were out repairing the ham antenna (one leg has been down for months) observed it. Even the Captain came out in his fur parka. How different a day from the 10°F temperature when it last set in April. Ronne sent out another of his glorified press releases. He mentions that few people braved the "–56" weather where "10-mile winds lashed their faces."

Paul heard from his ex-fiancee by hamgram. He is feeling pretty low. That's about the worst thing one could have happen when down here. I'm glad I didn't get myself that involved.

17 Aug., Sat. The airdales [have] one plane dug out and staked down on the "air strip." They have dug enough away from their second aircraft to observe that it is telescoped slightly. It is not repairable. It seems quite unforgivable that a commanding officer who has spent three previous winters in the Antarctic could allow planes to be stored like ours were. There is a third Otter still uncrated, so with a wing replacement on the first one, there will be two operational aircraft. Ronne told Hugo that if anything happens to one of the remaining two Otters, the traverse will have to be canceled.

Ronne is now telling people that he warned Mac about storing the airplanes the way he did. As a matter of fact, he didn't, but he wants to clear himself of this fiasco and leave McCarthy responsible.

I don't remember how I would have known that he did not warn Mac, and it may not be so. We were so ready to blame Ronne for everything that we were getting as bad as he was. There was blame enough to go around regarding the damage to the planes.

It was quite apparent to those of us who went outdoors as the winter was approaching that anything stored near the structures built as frames for the tunnels would be drifted over. We moved the Sno-Cats well away from the station as soon as we stopped using them in the fall. Obviously neither Ronne nor McCarthy ever examined the drifting aircraft early in the winter when they could have been easily moved. Of course, McCarthy, as OIC (officer in charge) of VX-6, would have had to take responsibility for this. One Otter cost $85,000 in 1957. A used Twin-Otter in the mid-1980s sold for about $1 million, and a new ski-equipped Hercules LC-130 cost the National Science Foundation more than $40 million in the 1990s. However, $85,000 seemed a lot of money to me in 1957.

> I have been having headaches a lot lately. I wonder if we are getting slight carbon monoxide poisoning.

I realize now that my headaches were probably tension headaches; they were common in others of the scientific group as it turned out. Writing in my journal was not apparently sufficient release.

> It is Paul's birthday tomorrow (23), so the boys had a party in Jack's room tonight.
>
> *18 Aug., Sun.* Last night about 2200 the wind shifted to northeast and clouded. The temperature rose abruptly from –45°F to 2°F. I went out about 0300 this morning for a minute and the warm wind felt like a summer breeze. At breakfast Aug and Walt Davis thought it would be a good idea to take advantage of the weather and move the Sno-Cat without the clutch to the pit for our seismic work. There was a near whiteout. The temperature was up to 6°F. . . .
>
> At first aid today we practiced traction splinting. Berlioz was the composer and *Romeo and Juliet* as the selection at the meeting of the "Chamber Music Society of Upper Ellsworth," as Chief May has called us. I received a hamgram from home.
>
> *19 Aug., Mon.* Continued warm (about 2°F), calm, and overcast. Hugo wanted to survey this morning, so Ed and I drove out about three miles east of camp to locate a range pole for him. It was so warm that I just wore my sweater and a hood.
>
> There were seven phone patches tonight as the new administration took over. Kent is telling everyone that the band is beginning to come in, and everyone will give Skidmore et al. credit.

He was probably right, as the ham communication improved at least partially because the sun coming up changed the ionosphere to better conditions.

20 Aug., Tues. Another eight phone patches and three hamgrams out. At 0900 the traverse group was gathered in Hugo's room waiting for the ham roundtable on traverse work. Ronne was of course waiting in the radio room. Ed went in but Ronne told him that there was Navy traffic and ordered him out. He followed him out and told him that he would let him know when they could get through. Ed said he would wait in the lab. Ronne said, "You can wait all day if you like." Upon reconsideration he told Ed that he should go to work. Ed answered that this was his discipline and he would wait there. Ronne got a little warm and went on about how "you . . . people are always like this" and ordered (in his capacity as station scientific leader) Ed to go to work. Ed answered that he would work on data right there. Ronne left; he didn't know that the other four of us were behind the curtain in Hugo's room.

A few minutes later Kent came in and told Ed that they could listen even if they couldn't transmit, so Ed and Hugo went in. The speaker was on, so I sat at the seismic table and copied the conversation. Crary discussed testing the crevasse detector [with which the traverses were supplied], which they aren't familiar with either. They are going to mount the seismic gear in one Sno-Cat, crevasse detector in the second, and cooking and other gear in the third. They have mechanical troubles with all three vehicles at present.

Finally our Navy traffic was completed and Kent contacted KC4USA and KC4USB (Little America and Byrd). Ronne opened the conversation by mentioning the following points: (1) We would have a recon flight to see if it is possible to get through to the west and meet the Byrd people; (2) one Otter is completely damaged, one is flyable, and one is in the crate. If either of the latter two is damaged, it will limit the support of traverse. We are surrounded by crevasses to the south and east. He had doubts about our ability to get through.

Ed talked then and said the large crevasse was about ¾ mile wide and 40 miles long rather than the 150 miles Ronne had mentioned. Ronne started accusing Ed of telling untruths at this point. Ed mentioned some doubt about the possibility of getting the clutch repaired–stated we are still hoping for a flight in with a replacement. Ed asked what they were using for sleeping, etc. Ronne started loudly abusing Ed for behaving like "Boy Scouts." He said, "Why ask him? My God, you have a man with four years' experience right next to you!" Crary answered that they planned to sleep in their Sno-Cats and do their cooking outside.

Ronne objected to Ed discussing the geographical situation. He maintains that it is his job to pick a route for the traverse. They went over to his room and continued their discussion. Ed argued that he and Hugo have written statements that it is their responsibility to pick a route. Ronne stated that this only applies to the general direction and extent and that he is to determine the exact route. He repeated that it is Hugo's job to find a route for the first 50 miles and that only Ed will go on the longer flights.

The Captain says he told Mac not to unpack the other plane or start flying until October. Ronne is talking about the equinoxial storms and 100-knot winds we can expect.

Weather in the spring appears to be much worse in the Antarctic Peninsula in the area of East Base where Ronne had spent his previous two expeditions. In 1990 and 1991 there were several-week delays due to weather in October in the Antarctic Peninsula for small twin-engine aircraft with which I was involved in aeromagnetic surveys.

We spent the afternoon mounting the seismic gear in the Sno-Cat. The wind was up pretty high, and the temperature had dropped to –16°F. All the light fluffy new snow which had accumulated since Sunday blew away. I needed a part for an antenna mast base, so I scrounged one from one of the Jamesway huts. These buildings are not drifted over much.

Lewis, Hugo, Greaney, and I got into a discussion on Darwin's theory of evolution vs. religion tonight. I thought such discussions had died out 50 years ago but Dave Greaney was the dissenting orator. [This was another example of my naiveté.]

21 Aug., Wed. We had a very beautiful day with a north wind at –16°F. The sun is definitely here now. It was above the horizon for the past several days. We began our seismic work in the pit. The results are tolerable, but we have timing difficulties. Ronne came running out because he wanted to know where the IGY photoflood bulbs were. He made Ed go in and show him. Jim Hanna rolled a fuel drum down his leg and onto his ankle. Clint x-rayed it and found it was only a bad sprain. We heard Schumann's 2nd Symphony and a quartet tonight; I don't enjoy Schumann much. I received two hamgrams from [my brother] Dave. He is in Austria now.

This last entry represents a typical group of non sequiturs, characteristic of my journal on the rare occasion when I did not have something specific to write about.

22 Aug., Thurs. Pit seismic work all day. Ronne came out and sat in the Sno-Cat while we ran one record. Ed was in the pit and Augie operated the blaster.

We were shooting blasting caps in the wall at 2.5-m spacing and measuring the time it takes for the sound to get to the surface. From this, we determine the compressional- and shear-wave velocities in the snow at these intervals to relate it to density and snow accumulation.

We don't bother with coffee breaks anymore. When you are doing work you enjoy, time goes by too rapidly.

23 Aug., Fri. Overcast and about –22°F. A sign-up sheet asking for orders for the wintering-over cruise book was posted. In addition there was a column for suggestions as to a dedication. One of the entries was "Jenny Darlington" and other derogatory comments. This really got to the Captain, as is quite understandable. Ronne took the list of suggested dedications for the cruise book list and began to compare handwriting samples in another "stolen strawberries" case in an attempt to find out who "stabbed me in the back."

This reference to "stolen strawberries" is an incident in Wouk's *The Caine Mutiny,* which most of us had read, and which seemed applicable at many times during this year.

24 Aug., Sat. We took more seismic data today than we have so far down here. This doesn't say much for nearly a whole year's work. We ran out of caps this morning, and Ed and I went out to the magazine to get some more. We have them on a sled near (but not too near) the explosives about a mile to the north of camp. Although it was clear overhead; there was so much blowing snow that visibility was quite poor. We lost sight of camp quite soon. Ed and I couldn't agree on where the sleds were, so we spread out to search.

Usually it doesn't really seem like Antarctica around here, but today it was quite apparent. It was bitter cold, and I had a hard time keeping my face from freezing. About –45°F with a strong wind, so I was cursing Harry Francis and his clothing selection that didn't provide me with a large enough parka hood or mittens. It seemed quite impressive with the only things visible being the sastrugi, a few ice hummocks, the blowing snow, and the dim figure of Ed in the distance.

After wandering around a bit we finally found the sled and picked up the caps. We followed an old Weasel track from the caps back to camp. It was weather in which one could easily have become lost. Since the winter set in, the snow surface has become quite hard, and one does not hear the collapse of depth-hoar layers that was so noticeable last summer.

I was listening on the radio in the Sno-Cat this morning to a meteorology discussion between Shackleton, South Ice (their inland station 250 miles south of Shackleton), and Halley Bay which came in loud and clear. I heard Shackleton tell South Ice that they would probably see them within a week, so they must be flying already.

There was another party tonight. Ed Davis really goes to a lot of work to prepare food for these affairs. There was a regular smorgasbord with three kinds of sandwiches, olives, sardines, cheese, peanut butter, pickles, popcorn, punch (unspiked), and various fruit juices. Walt May was bartender again serving Old Methuselah (bourbon) as desired. It was a very quiet party as parties go down here.

With no sex and little alcohol available at the IGY Antarctic stations, the Navy did an excellent job of providing lots of food and cooks of a quality to prepare it well. At Byrd Station this same winter, some of their food never reached them by the summer tractor trains that supplied that station. Consequently, although we had a much more difficult time during the winter in our interpersonal relations because of Ronne, we sublimated by eating well. The Byrd Station group was congenial, but ate much more poorly. They had a ration of only a few cans of beer apiece for the entire year.

It is hard . . . to get in a real party mood without some feminine companionship. Most of our work and life down here has been such a completely masculine atmosphere that a woman would seem out of place, but absence of the gentler sex is painfully apparent at parties or during holidays. There is a false, hollow, artificial ring to any pretension of normal celebrations. Take Christmas aboard the *Wyandot*. We had a tree, presents, and a turkey dinner, but the Christmas spirit was certainly lacking. I'm sure next Christmas when we are on traverse and it will be just another day for us, it will be a more pleasant occasion. It will be good to see a woman again.

In contrast to the year at Ellsworth, the presence of women in all parts of the operations now, including remote field parties, makes for a much more civilized and normal existence. Prior to going to Antarctica, all of my camping, mountaineering, backpacking, and canoeing trips at University of Wisconsin had included at least one-third women, so the Navy's exclusion of women from Antarctica until the late 1960s seemed very strange.

25 Aug., Sun. I spent most of the day reading. Clint lectured on burn treatment today. We listened to Mendelssohn's Scottish Symphony at the Chamber Music Society of Upper Ellsworth.

Don made an outline map of the U.S. in which he wrote everyone's name in the area that they wanted phone patches but omitted Ronne's name. Ronne took the map out of the ham shack and called Don in this afternoon. He wanted to know why his name wasn't on it. Don told him that he'd made the statement, "I can get a phone patch anytime I want," and he therefore hadn't deemed it necessary to mark him down also. He then wrote the Captain's name down [on the map]. Ronne didn't like this and crossed it out. He abruptly changed the subject and asked Don if he had written Jenny Darlington's name on the suggested dedication list [for the cruise books]. Don admitted that he had. Ronne then accused him, "After all I've done for you, you stab me in the back." Don asked him just what he had done for him. Ronne told him that his wife had been putting things about Don into the papers. Don told him that he didn't want any publicity. Ronne then got off on the subject of Mrs. Darlington. He asked why of all people, he [Don] had to pick the one person he was at odds with. Actually Don had done it just as a joke and to needle Ronne a bit, but he told him he thought her book had done a lot for morale at this base. Ronne called her "that slut." He said that she had been "picked up in a bar." Ronne said that Darlington was a millionaire and had spent $10,000 just to get that book published, and that his wife had to get someone else to write it for her.

Ronne told Don that he was glad to know where they stood with each other. Don told him the men wouldn't make fun of him if he didn't take it so seriously. Ronne answered that he was the last person on the base that any of the men would make fun of. He accused Don, "You hate me." Don answered, "You sound just like my little boy when he can't have his own way," and walked out.

26 Aug., Mon. There have been 30-odd phone patches since Skidmore et al. took over administration of the ham gear a week ago. The hamgrams are moving now, too.

A good ham contact was made with Wilkes Station. Ronne talked with Carl Eklund and told him that he is "having trouble with the sand crabs" (civilians). Hugo talked with Dick Cameron (glaciologist), Paul talked with Molholm (asst. glaciologist), and Kim talked to Ralph Glasgal, the aurora man. The latter asked Kim if he had read *My Antarctic Honeymoon* (I imagine it was included in all the station libraries). Kim answered that he had and that it was too kind to our Captain. He told him it had been on our library shelf for a couple of months until there was a "book burning" and it was removed by Ronne.

Paul talked to his ex-fiancee this morning. She is getting married in a couple of weeks. Paul is in a "women are no damn good" sort of mood. Ed lectured tonight on the method [barometric altimeters] we will use on traverse to determine our elevation. Ronne brought in the following memo to Ed:

To: IGY Civilians

It is now certain that Major James Lassiter will come to Ellsworth Station toward latter part of October or early November. You may desire to receive a letter on that flight. If so, you may indicate name and address from whom you wish to receive a letter. My closest contact in Wash. [his wife] will then contact the person and make certain the letter gets on the plane.

Finn Ronne

He remarked, "Of course, you can ask Jenny Darlington to send your letters rather than my wife, if you want."

27 Aug., Tues. It was about −45°F all day with a 10-knot wind. We ran out of movies that we haven't seen before. I worked on flags this morning and on food this afternoon. Ed Davis is giving us a lot of extras from the galley.

The most useful thing we received was an unlimited supply of frozen beef tenderloins in about seven-pound pieces.

Don was running the ham gear this morning early and talked to the Pole. Siple wondered if Ronne was around. The Captain was notified and came into the ham shack. He jerked the headphones off Don's head and ordered him out. These were Don's own headphones and he doesn't let other people use them. He sadly shook his head from side to side. Ronne shouted something to the effect of, "You don't run this outfit." Don and Forlidas left the radio room but not before they turned the Navy transmitter on to the ham frequency. This caused an unpleasant oscillation that made conversation impossible. They went and had a cup of coffee so that if Ronne started calling for help they wouldn't be around to assist. The Captain gave up pretty soon.

Hugo gave a lecture on the method we plan to determine our position while on traverse. I found it quite informative.

I knew nothing of celestial navigation, nor did anyone else on the traverse other than Hugo.

28 Aug., Wed. About −55°F with 15 knots of wind, when I went out to help drill this morning. All during the dark months when it was warmer outside, only a few people ventured out, and as I remarked to Augie this morning, "We had the world to ourselves." Now that it is light again, many people are going out. It was far more comfortable during June than it is now.

The hole in the bottom of the pit is 82 ft (24 m) deep; consequently we have a drill rod extending almost all the way up the 100-ft (31-m) deep pit when we pull it out every 1.5 ft (50 cm) to get the core. The whole operation is, of course, done by hand and there is a rope running through a block [pulley] to suspend the snaky string of 1-m-long rods. The bottom of the hole is well below sea level now and is at last in ice. A preferred orientation of the bubbles in the ice has been observed, but unfortunately there is no way that the core can be oriented.

Ed and I went out and helped Hugo and Augie drill the last meter tonight and finished about 2030. We have the deepest snow pit that any of us have ever heard of and definitely the deepest at present in Antarctica. We also have one of the deepest hand-drilled holes.

A few months later the glaciologists at Wilkes Station beat us with a 115-ft (35-m) deep pit. There was a sort of competition going on among the pit diggers.

We all fuel the jet heaters in our own areas now that the VX-6 people are working on their aircraft again. Our jet heater burns about 80 gallons of fuel oil per week. This keeps half of this building and the aurora tower warm. I wonder how far 80 gallons goes towards heating a house in the States?

My brother's home in Wisconsin required about 40 gallons/week during a particularly cold spell in January 1994, so the answer is about two weeks.

Con and Willie [both officers] have to fuel the Captain's heater, which they dislike on principle. Last week Con spilled some oil and didn't wipe it up. Ronne slipped in it and took a good pratfall. Of course, he chewed Con out and told him to clean it up; Con didn't. That night a cartoon depicting this event with appropriate comments appeared. Naturally the Captain didn't like it.

29 Aug., Thurs. Clear, −45°F with increasing winds up to 25 knots. Ed and I finished shooting the drill hole for velocity determinations in the morning and spent the afternoon changing the spread for reflection shooting. It was bitter cold; I imagine that few people have ever done exploration seismic work under these conditions.

We fired small charges up the drill hole, after the glaciologists were through with it, and recorded the shots on geophones on the surface and at several levels in the wall of the pit. We used photographic solutions to develop our seismic records and had to mix them in hot water and carry them out in one-gallon thermos jugs. I would roll six or eight feet of paper back and forth in the developing solution. This cooled through the working period so that I would start developing for only a quarter of a minute or so with my hand in the tank beneath the seismic camera. By the time we were finished, the solutions were so cold that it took up to six or seven minutes to develop a record.

I lay down when we came in, planning to nap until midnight and then go over in the rec hall and listen to records. I awoke at 0800 in the morning.

30 Aug., Fri. It was warmer (about −35°F), overcast, with a 30-knot north wind. There was so much blowing snow we were forced to quit.

This was an amazing contrast to the weather we had been having.

31 Aug., Sat. About −30°F and calm, overcast. We tried three more shots in the pit this morning but couldn't get a reflection. [I now realize we were having seismic noise problems with the cold snow at this time of winter.] After lunch we took up our spread. We had nine geophones in groups of three in the pit, which meant much entanglement of cable up and down the walls. This gave us some trouble, and I climbed up and down the ladder about three times before we managed to reel it all up.

I recall an amusing incident associated with reeling up the 1200-ft cable. I worked at the bottom of the pit and Ed at the top. I suggested that he reel from the top taking up the dangling loops. He wanted to cut loose all of the cable and have me reel it from the bottom. He won, but the instant Ed cut the ties the cable fell into a horrible tangle at the bottom of the pit. There was no way two men could have worked together to untangle the wuzzle, but at least Ed had the grace to stand shivering at the top while I spent a long time getting it sorted out. The amusing part to me is that I apparently chose not to describe it in my journal.

I am reading Mark Twain's *Life on the Mississippi*. A very quiet Saturday night. The author's discussion of the upper river and the area around Lake Pepin and Maiden Rock almost made me homesick for Wisconsin.

1 Sept., Sun. Clear and −50°F. I spent most of the day reading. About 1530 I went out and took some pictures of the sunset.

Clint lectured on shock today, and I learned several interesting things. He isn't showing us how to give blood transfusions, but we will be able to administer Dextran infusions intravenously. We finished with Mendelssohn and took up Brahms tonight (First Symphony).

Ronne added his own note to the end of the monthly scientific sitrep, "STATION SCIENTIFIC LEADER EXPRESS GRATIFICATION ON ENTHUSIASTIC ENDEAVOR BY IGY PERSONNEL TO OBTAIN MAXIMUM RESULTS AND THE MILITARY GROUP'S SPLENDID EVER-READY COOPERATION ENABLING IGY GROUP DEVOTE ENTIRE TIME ON THEIR OWN WORK."

It seems that this statement would make any reader wonder what other work we might have been doing, other than what we were paid to do.

2 Sept., Mon. (Labor Day) Holiday Routine so we all slept in. I spent the day reading.

3 Sept., Tues. We commenced Summer Routine today. Breakfast 0715–0745, lunch 1130–1200, supper 1715–1745. (Officers 30 minutes later.)

Minus 40°F with blowing snow. Ed had me repair the seismic cable, which had several loose connections. I set up in the library and soon had cable strewn around the room. While I was out for a

214

few minutes, Ronne came in looking for a desk lamp. Don gave him the only one available, which had no shade. He then had the gall to come in and take the shade off my lamp, which I had taken out in the library. When I returned and saw this I stalked up to Ronne's room and asked for it back. He started one of those interminable discussions and/or lectures of his which covered every subject and evaded the question of my lamp shade. He maintained that we had no right to a bed lamp (being none for Navy people) and that here were men in camp without any. He blustered on about the poor attitude of civilians, traverse planning, recommending we don't get our bonus, and mess duty, etc., etc. I sat by, not saying much. By dinnertime we were miles away from the shade. Mac came in to talk to Ronne, and I went to eat.

I was the center of attraction and was thoroughly reviled and despised for not getting the shade back. After lunch Don and Kim, who like everyone else in camp were enjoying the whole affair immensely, took my bed lamp off the wall and shortened the cord to about two feet. I took this up and told Ronne he could have it but that I wanted my shade back. Of course he didn't want the other lamp and replied with . . . "I can't use that." I must have looked determined because he said, "You'll get your shade back." At that moment Don burst in with more turmoil about Spear throwing his boxes out (or some such thing). I stood there while they went at it and finally Ronne repeated, "I'll give your shade back" and motioned me out. Five minutes later Spear brought the shade in.

4 Sept., Wed. It was blowing too hard to drive out with the Sno-Cat. I cleaned the head and shoveled out our back entrance. Ed and I dug a 5000-ft reel of zip cord [standardized conductor "lamp" cord that we used to fire shots] out of our seismic gear pile in the tunnel and lugged it to the Sno-Cat. It was a most unwieldy load.

Paul has been measuring the densities of the deep drill-hole cores and has been having all sorts of difficulties. He came up with a reading of .918 when the maximum theoretical density for pure ice is .917. After some finagling he worked it down to .680, which is too low. Finally he devised a new procedure and came up with .87, which he swears is correct. These densities are quite critical and important in our seismic velocity studies.

Ed noticed that Ronne spoke to me in a quite different tone of voice than he usually uses with me. He is still mad that he didn't get his own way with the lamp shade. He has ordered Don to get him a lamp shade now.

I lay down (after a game of hearts) at 1900 for a nap until music time. I didn't wake up until 0730 the next morning.

5 Sept., Thurs. Winds about 25 knots with much blowing snow. Poor visibility.

A cartoon entitled "All the-Brothers Were Valiant" [the name of a movie we had seen] appeared on the (unofficial) bulletin board in the galley tonight. In the center of the three-feet-square sheet was an octopus with bloodshot eyes. All around were small figures engaged in fighting it, representing the nine IGY people. In order that there would be no mistake in identification, the heads were faces cut from photographs.

In one corner was Jerry standing on a pile of chopped-up octopus arms making a V for Victory sign (he has a cigar in his mouth). He is wearing a Superman suit with hero medals and "The Phantom" written across the back. He has a sword.

Augie is standing near him saying, "Let's go fight some more octopus. He's my hero."

Kim is hacking at an arm with a sword saying, "So you won't come to my lectures."

Ed is standing, sunk up to his knees, in the ground (where he has been pounded), feeling the lump on his head and saying, "Maybe your method is best Golden Boy; have patience." His sword is broken and an arm of the octopus is beating him with a club.

Golden Boy (Jack) is deftly parrying a thrust with his sword and is a gleaming knight in shining armor saying, "I think my way is better." He is illuminated by a desk lamp held in one tentacle of the octopus at which a St. Bernard dog (me) is barking. A voice to one side is saying, "Sic 'em Walking-Thunder."

Don is sitting on the head of the beast picking petals off a daisy saying, "I like him. I don't like him. I like him. I don't . . ." A sign points to him saying, "two-week cycle."

Hugo is standing nearby with a slide rule in his hand wearing his patched field trousers and plaid shirt, across the front of which is written, "Explorers Club." He holds a letter in his hand which reads, "To Simon (Simon Legree), Well done, John L. Lewis" [the well-known president of the United Mine Workers]. He is asking, "Why does he fight me?"

In the upper left-hand corner is Paul, lying in bed with his feet sticking up out of the covers saying, "It's all so tiring." Several of the octopus arms have been hacked off.

This cartoon was greeted with more enthusiasm than any so far. Unfortunately after the movie and before Ronne had seen it, Hugo took it down to have it inked in. I'm afraid that it will have lost its impact by the time Ronne sees it now. It was the work of Augie, Jerry, and Beiszer.

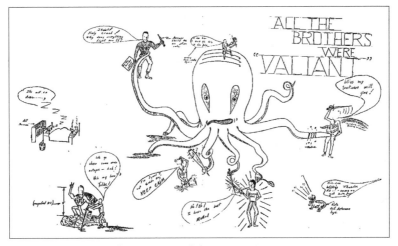

Cartoon of F. Ronne and science group fighting.

A week and a half later, the cartoon "All the Brothers Were Valiant" appeared in the mess hall, redrawn in ink. Ronne saw it and mentioned that he wanted it. Before he could get it, Kim had quietly taken it down and posted it in our library. Jack took the cartoon down and put it away. We didn't think it was a good idea for Ronne to get it, as he apparently wanted it for evidence. Today, Jack Brown has the cartoon.

> *6 Sept., Fri.* Warm (about −15°F), with northeast winds gradually increasing to 25 knots by 1700. High overcast. We finally hauled the Sno-Cat out to [the location we unimaginatively called] Point A where we intend to set up our seismic recording spread of geophones. The hydraulic steering was frozen up so I had a difficult time steering.

This was about two miles east of the camp, and we planned a several-week experiment where we would shoot a series of explosive charges to the south to study the seismic velocity in the ice shelf and bedrock beneath the seafloor. The other traverse people would help.

> Ed and I took the Weasel and loaded explosives from the magazine sleds. There is very little drifting out there. I'm certainly glad we put the dynamite into the sleds up off the snow. The pack ice is back in against the ice front and no leads are visible.

217

7 Sept., Sat. About –6°F with 20-knot winds. When we were ready to go, the Weasel was found to have a broken distributor shaft; at present there are no Weasels operable in camp. After lunch Hugo, Paul, Aug, Don, Kim, Ed, and I went out to dig up the traverse sleds.

Hannah has been running a temperature and has been in bed for the past five days now. Presumably flu; I thought that there were no diseases in Antarctica. Camp sprained his weak ankle a week ago on the icy boards in the tunnel. He is now hobbling around in a cast.

After a game of hearts I went to bed at 1900 for a nap and didn't wake up until 0930 the next morning.

My sleeping habits were obviously changing, as noted in previous journal entries, as the sun rose, and I was apparently working physically harder outdoors.

8 Sept., Sun. Much blowing snow outside and temperatures down in the –30s°F. I spent the day studying geophysics. The Byrd sitrep came in. Included in it is the following interesting point from Chuck Bentley: "TRAVERSE SEISMIC AND GRAVITY SUMMARY [LITTLE AMERICA TO BYRD STATION]. ICE THICKNESS PROFILE: GRAVITY AND SEISMIC REFLECTION DEPTHS IN GOOD AGREEMENT. ROCK RELIEF VERY RUGGED. LOWEST POINT 1400 M BELOW SEA LEVEL, HIGHEST 30 M ABOVE. MAXIMUM ICE THICKNESS 2600 M, AVERAGE 1650 M."

This is quite interesting because it reopens the old question of a below–sea level trough separating East and West Antarctica. The traverses next summer should shed more light on this subject. How ironic it would be if Marie Byrd Land and Edith Ronne Land were both a couple of thousand feet below sea level.

They are! At least the bedrock elevation below the ice sheet is. However, there is no major trough connecting the Ross and Filchner-Ronne Ice Shelf areas.

Mac told me that Ronne has me quoted in his log as admitting that we nine civilians have a "pact" against him. Six months ago this lie would have infuriated me; now it just irks me. It is just what one expects these days. I can't argue against it because he can write anything in his log the same as I can in mine. Unfortunately more people will see his writing.

Ronne published *Antarctic Command* about this expedition in 1961. *Antarctica My Destiny,* his last book published in 1979, covered the IGY year as well. I waited 40 years to publish my version.

Ronne had a radio talk with Fuchs over at Shackleton at 1700. Paul and Hugo listened in their room. Con and others listened in the rec hall where the conversation came blaring through on the phonograph. As the men have run a line into the galley speaker from the record player, it was also avidly listened to in the chow hall as we ate supper. Ronne discussed bringing the clutch over to Shackleton when the planes are flying. He told them that Lassiter was flying down and that he could ask him to bring several letters and a small package for each of the people at Shackleton. (And yet he refuses to ask him to bring a clutch.)

After the movie tonight there was a meeting in the library with Ronne, Mac, and the five traverse people. Ed brought up a number of points on logistics. Would he [Ronne] please ask Lassiter to bring a clutch replacement when he comes? Round and round and round we went. I can well imagine that Ronne is sick of hearing this request. He said at one point, "Lassiter isn't interested in your traverse. He has his own program to think of. He doesn't care how far you get." I pointed out that Lassiter is human and it wouldn't hurt to ask him. He ignored all such arguments and kept changing the subject. Several times he stood up as if to walk out and Ed stood up, too, and kept right on talking.

I argued more than I have with him since that day in the tent out on the bay ice. Fortunately I've become a little more used to his method of carrying on a "discussion" (i.e., to shout louder and to change the subject when a point is made that can't be controverted) and am not so worried about losing my temper and saying things I'd regret (I hope).

In the course of all this it came out that Ronne didn't send Augie's name in to have a letter from his folks sent down via Lassiter. How small can that man get! Then Augie asked permission to take pictures from the air of the ice trough he is studying and has surveyed. Ronne was noncommittal but obviously disliked granting permission. There was quite an argument on this point. Ronne kept going off on tangents (e.g., Why did you burn out the clutch? or, Why didn't you see that you have all the traverse supplies before you left the states?). Augie and on one occasion I kept steering him back to the question, but he refused to give a definite answer.

Finally, the smoke cleared with nothing settled. Ronne accused us of calling him over just to ask him pointed questions requiring a yes-no answer. Mac asked what he should do if, when the planes get flying, Augie asks to go up and get a picture of the trough. Ronne grudgingly said OK. Thus something constructive did come out of all the hassle.

9 Sept., Mon. It was quite warm (–20°F) with little wind. No Weasel, so I spent the afternoon helping Don, Chuck Forlidas, and Bob Haskill work on the transmission line to the rhombic antenna for the ham gear. Con gave a very interesting evening lecture tonight on the Otter aircraft and particularly on the helicopter (H04S-3).

10 Sept., Tues. Again no Weasel so we loaded up an akio with solutions, lunch, etc., and walked out to A. It was overcast and calm, about –20°F. We got about 15 shots off. It is a leisurely 30-minute walk with an empty sled.

Don, on the ham gear, talked to an Al Sears in Houston early in the morning. He wants to get a recorded interview with Ed and me to take to the S.E.G. meeting in November (both of us are members of the Society of Exploration Geophysicists). On Friday, Ed and I were wakened by Don about 0200 to talk to Sears.

A year later we made the first scientific presentation of our traverse results at the annual S.E.G. meeting.

11 Sept., Wed. A sunny day but with 20-knot winds at –30°F, so it was a bit unpleasant working outside. The visibility was so poor (blowing snow) that the only way we found our way out to A and back was on old Weasel tracks. We could see none of the flags until we were right next to one. The heater in the seismic Sno-Cat wasn't working right so it didn't get very warm inside. We received the following:

To: IGY Civilian Personnel
From: Commanding Officer Ellsworth Station
Subject: Sanitary Conditions, Inspection of

1. Your attention is directed to Dr. C. Smith, Medical Officer's memorandum of 10 September regarding sanitary conditions at this station.
2. Accordingly there will be no urinating in the passageway behind the Science Building or in the immediate vicinity of the door leading to the outside. This notice is specifically directed towards those living in the science building and/or any visitors frequenting the area.

Finn Ronne, Captain, USNR
Commanding

This is a classic memo, which I thought needed to be published here. Actually no one urinated in the passageway, but we scientists and officers commonly did so outside the tunnel outdoors behind the science building. The alternative was a 100-ft trek down the tunnel system to the officer's head past the enlisted men's head, which we were not allowed to use.

I laid down at 1900 for a nap and didn't wake up until 0700 the next morning.

12 Sept., Thurs. Twenty-five-knot winds and −40°F today, so we stayed home and worked up some of the records we have been shooting lately. Lots of memos, dispatches, etc. The following was received at 1000:

FM: IGY WASH DC
ACTION: ELLSWORTH STA
INFO: LITTLE AMERICA STATION/COMNAVSUP
FOR ANTARCTICA COMNAVUNITS ANTARCTICA/
REPCOMNAVSUPFOR ANTARCTICA CHRISTCHURCH
NZ 102034 Z
YOUR 261830 Z JULY [RONNE TO ODISHAW 26 JULY].

ADVISE IF ADDITIONAL INFORMATION AVAILABLE REGARDING FEASIBLE ROUTE INLAND FOR PROPOSED TRAVERSE. LASSITER ADVISES ADDITIONAL 25,000 GALLONS AVGAS WILL BE TRANSPORTED TO ELLSWORTH STATION FOR HIS USE. ALSO LASSITER WILL TRANSPORT SPARE SNO-CAT CLUTCH.

Needless to say the message from IGY produced much jubilation amongst us five "United Mine Workers." Ronne made it quite apparent by his attitude that he didn't like this bit of news. He told Hugo when he gave his copy to him that now maybe we would "stop all the bitching."

About the end of November, Jim Lassiter told me that he and "Dr. Odishaw" had had some strong words about the clutch. Odishaw had tried to order Lassiter to bring our spare clutch down, pointing out that all this was part of IGY. Lassiter held very strongly to his position that his program was independent of any other.

Finally Odishaw gave up and Lassiter agreed to bring the clutch—as a favor, not because he was ordered to. Of course Odishaw was only responding to all of the efforts we had gone through during the winter to communicate about the clutch replacement.

Ronne sent the following dispatch out:

FROM: ELLSWORTH STA 122051 Z
ACTION: IGY WASH DC
INFO: COMNAVUNITS ANTARCTICA– COMNAV-SUPFOR ANTARCTICA REP COMNAVSUPFOR ANT-ARCTICA CHRISTCHURCH NZ LITTLE AMERICA
YOUR 102034 Z [THE PREVIOUS MESSAGE].

NO FURTHER INFO AVAILABLE FEASIBLE ROUTE IN-LAND FOR TRAVERSE PARTY. HOPE IMPROVEMENT WEATHER MAKE RECON FLIGHT POSSIBLE BY 10 OCT. NETWORK CREVASSES SOUTHWEST AND WEST PRECLUDES DOUBT ON SAFE PASSAGE THROUGH TO 50-MILE RIFT. HOWEVER, UTMOST EFFORT WILL BE MADE TO GET TRAVERSE PARTY SAFELY INLAND. YOU WILL BE NOTIFIED IMMEDIATELY ON RESULT OF FLIGHTS.

Jack sent out a resupply list to the head of the ionosphere physics program, Dr. M. G. Morgan at Dartmouth. Morgan in an earlier message had mentioned that he might visit Ellsworth with the resupply ship. In closing Jack added the following note: "FERVENTLY HOPE YOU CAN VISIT WITH RESUPPLY TO OBSERVE FIRSTHAND ACTIVITY HERE–INCLUDING CALIGULAS RAIN." Ronne asked Don what "Caligulas rain" meant [of course, it was deliberately not spelled "Caligula's reign"] and Don told him it was a dawn chorus [a geophysical term] named after a Roman emperor.

13 Sept., Fri. Aug, Ed, and I drove out in the finally repaired Weasel and did some seismic refraction work. The heater in the Sno-Cat crapped out and barely warmed the temperature up to 20°F inside. Needless to say this made the developing of records somewhat arduous. The wet records would freeze while I had them out examining them. Most discouraging work, but we did get two good records.

After lunch, I found a spare fuel control valve for the heater, which I installed with much difficulty, due to cold hands and the poor design of the Sno-Cat, which makes it very hard to get at the various installations for servicing them. The temperature was –30°F with a 15-knot breeze, and I had to work outside reaching in through the front of the vehicle to get at the heater. We took the three 175-lb seismic batteries in to charge them tonight because the voltage regulator and/or alternator has been working inefficiently.

14 Sept., Sat. Paul, Aug, Ed, and I drove out to Point A in the morning. Ed and I chained off 1500 m and put flags marking future shot points at 300-m intervals. It was −40° [C and F are the same at −40°] with a high overcast. When we finished we accompanied Paul and Aug on down the line for a couple of miles as they measured their accumulation stakes. There has been little or no accumulation in the past two weeks, and the old raised Weasel tracks in the snow are evidence of wind erosion. The sastrugi are bigger and harder than ever. Weasel riding is an extremely rough experience these days.

After lunch Ed and I drove up to the magazines and loaded a sled up with about 1500 lbs of 133 [No. 133, also known as C-3, is a military plastic explosive] and Petrogel. We also threw on three 40-lb military-shaped charges to experiment with.

There was a party tonight in the rec hall, but I read and went to bed early.

15 Sept., Sun. I got up at 0930 and after breakfast, spent the day reading and listening to music in the rec hall—Berlioz' *Requiem* and part of Handel's *Messiah*. I read two books today and started a third. Clint has had a library book, *The Life of Greece,* a 700-page epic by Will Durant, which I want to read. I asked him when he would finish, and he said probably not before the traverse. I borrowed it for a week but everyone thinks I won't get it read in that time; it is rather meaty.

Hugo talked to Crary over the ham gear, with Ronne standing by. Hugo's point this time was that he wanted to go on the recon flight for the traverse. There was the usual prologue by Ronne and the usual fighting in the background. Crary took the usual attitude (he knows what is going on here) of not giving Ronne any orders or reprimands but saying, "I'm sure you can work this out among yourselves, but the way we are doing it over here is . . ."

When they finished, Ronne and Hugo went over to Ronne's office and had another big fight. Hugo accused him of deliberately lying to antagonize the men against us. He also told Ronne that, "You are not my boss—Crary is." (Not true—Ronne is our boss at this station.) They shouted at each other and finally Hugo walked out.

Ronne talked to Shackleton again. As usual his voice came booming in on the hi-fi set and on the speakers in the barracks and chow hall. He is offering to have Lassiter bring down some parts they need and fly them out to them in the field, if they have left Shackleton already.

16 Sept., Mon. I had a phone patch home this morning at 0530. It sure was great to talk to the folks!

I had my only two previous phone patches on 4 May and 28 July.

Ed strained his back fueling the heater. He went up to see Clint about it and Ronne wanted to talk to him. Ronne went over all the past history as usual. He showed Ed a letter from Gould instructing him to write a fitness report on each of us. These reports will be on file at the National Academy of Sciences. He implied that these reports would be derogatory on us. He thinks that they must have sent all the "bad eggs" to him. His main gripe is still our uncooperation as regards to mess duty. Paul and I sat around waiting to go to work all morning, until about 1030 when it was too late.

Ed told me two things that Ronne mentioned in his talk with him which he did not see fit to tell the group. He told me so I could record them here: (1) Ronne asked Ed to withdraw his resignation as deputy station scientific leader. He told Ed that he hasn't sent it in to Washington yet. Ed told him that as things seem to be running smoothly at present and since he will be leaving here soon, he doesn't see any reason to change his earlier decision. Besides, he told Ronne, he feels that the reasons forcing this resignation will probably be felt in the future. I think Ronne doesn't want that letter of resignation to appear in Washington; (2) he mentioned to Ed that "it was a good thing Aughenbaugh didn't submit his parents' address when Ronne offered to have Lassiter bring one letter apiece for us." He said that he would have crossed his name off the list anyway. Ed told me he said, "I'm not doing any favors for him."

After lunch Paul, Ed, and I went out to Point A. The heater still isn't working very well and it was about 11°F inside the Sno-Cat. The wet records froze faster than I could write the data on them.

17 Sept., Tues. Forty below with 29-knot south wind. The company that manufactured the Sno-Cat heater is named South Wind; they probably did not have this wind in mind!

This afternoon the wind dropped so Aug, Kim, . . . and I drove out to Point A and changed the spread. The cables were so drifted in with snow that I had to very gingerly dig long sections out with a shovel. Our new line now runs north 330 m. As the ice edge curves south to the east of camp, the end of our spread is only a thousand yards or less from the edge, and there are hummocks quite close. We climbed up one and observed a large depression sloping towards the ice front. The sun was shining and although it was quite cold, it was exhilarating to see some local relief even if it was only 50 ft. We didn't have a rope with us or we would have gone down to the edge.

18 Sept., Wed. I had a phone patch with Ruth early this morning. The weather was bad. Twenty-five-to 30-knot winds at about −38°F with much blowing snow. We stayed in camp and I spent the day sewing flags.

Al Spear is on a [mandatory] diet (as are other people), and it is amusing to watch him calculate his calories and decide how much food he can eat at each meal. He is allowed about 900 calories/day. I sat down next to him with a morning snack of six pieces of toast dripping with butter and he remarked woefully, "That's more than I can eat all day!"

19 Sept., Thurs. Bad weather continued so I kept on at the flag production.

20 Sept., Fri. Several days ago, Clint and Willie heard Shackleton and Halley Bay talking on the radio. Someone is very sick at Halley Bay and they have been having medical conferences with London. Today the Auster aircraft at Shackleton tried to fly up there, but was forced down by darkness–somewhere.

Thus, we became aware of an ordeal with which we were only peripherally involved but which we kept close track of with some concern in the coming days.

Aug, Ed, and I spent the day drilling shot holes about 25 ft (8 m) deep.

We drilled all of our holes with a hand-operated SIPRE (U.S. Army Snow Ice and Permafrost Research and Engineering lab) coring auger, which took about a 3-inch-diameter core. We had to pull up the 1-m-long core barrel three times per meter because the snow and firn cuttings filled the barrel. As we could only lift about three or four of the 1-m aluminum rods over our head in removing the core barrel, we had to take the drill string apart this often. Two of us could drill an 8–10-m hole but we needed three to drill 45 ft (about 15 m) for our deepest shot holes.

Ronne ordered Don to get him a phone patch last night. Don got everyone else in that area, including himself, patches before Ronne (Ronne had one patch already this week), and then the band went out before he put him through. Ronne became very angry at this and had a long talk with Mac about it. Tonight after the movie he called Don up to his room. Mac was there, too.

Clint, Willie, Con, Ed, Kim, Hugo, Aug, and I were in Clint's room listening to records. Of course we shut the machine off to hear the fireworks. Clint and Willie removed their shoes and hid in the medical stock room (which has a common wall with Ronne's room) to listen.

The conversation started relatively peacefully. Ronne accused Don of "disloyalty, disobedience, and disrespect" in not getting him a patch. Don explained that he had made a mistake and that he would get him a patch tonight. Ronne told him that in the Navy there were no "mistakes" and that a Captain's wish was a command. He told Don that he was "canceled." Don asked what he meant and Ronne told him that he couldn't operate the ham gear any more.

From this point on, voices and tempers rose exponentially. Don said, "You made a bargain!" Ronne had taken movies of Don in return for which Don was made operator. "Give me the pictures!" After this both talked at the same time. Don shouted, "You're the most selfish person I've ever met. If you give me a sensible order I'll listen to it." He accused Ronne of stealing base supplies. "You even stole John Behrendt's personal lamp!" he shouted and walked out slamming the door. "I did not; I took the lamp in the library!" Ronne shouted after him. "Oh, go to hell," Don said, as he strode across the sick bay.

Meanwhile, Ed had jumped up and gone into the stock room with Clint and Willie to listen better. When Don walked out it took them by surprise. There was a mad stampede back to Clint's room and they burst through the door stumbling over each other, as Don was coming across the room.

We hardly had time to catch our collective breaths when Don came in again and walked back to Ronne's room. "I don't want to have anything more to do with you the rest of the time I'm down at this base!" he told the Captain. "I'll have you thrown in irons!" screamed Ronne . . . nearly beside himself with rage. "Bull shit!" said Don and walked out, again slamming the three doors in his path so hard that the building shook.

This made Don a hero in most people's eyes. Unfortunately it seems to me that he cut off his nose to spite his face. Perhaps he could have cajoled the Captain into letting him stay in the ham shack by offering enough phone patches. It's hurting the whole camp to have him out. In the past week everyone on base that has wanted to, has had phone patches. Unfortunately it is not easy to control one's tongue when enraged by Captain Ronne.

21 Sept., Sat. At 0000 this morning Fuchs, at Shackleton, called Ronne. Don, Kim, and I listened. Fuchs explained the situation of their downed aircraft. The doctor and a pilot set out for Halley Bay but couldn't find it due to fog. They think they overshot and turned around and tried to fly back but were overtaken by dark, and landed for the night. They have 15 days' food, two sleeping bags, but no tent. They plan to try and fly to Halley Bay in the morning. They don't know where they are, but are about a half mile in from the edge of the ice shelf. Fuchs stated that their Otter won't be ready to fly for three days and wanted to know if we could help if needed. Ronne replied (with Mac there also) that our plane is ready to go.

Visibility was bad when we drove out to work and became worse all day. The only way I was able to drive in the afternoon was to follow old tracks. I had to have my head out the window looking at the tracks directly alongside; I could only drive five miles/hour. A dark spot appeared in the distance ahead, and Ed thought it was the aurora tower. It turned out to be a beer can about 20 ft ahead of us. The whiteout plays tricks on one's eyes.

Ronne told Ed tonight to tell me that he didn't steal my lamp shade. He took it unknowingly off the lamp in the library. . . .

Ronne had a long talk with Paul tonight. He told Paul that he (Paul) and I would be the only people whom he would not report as having broken their contracts. Ronne told him that they shouldn't have sent a man of his rank to this station because they don't have the facilities to take proper care of him here (e.g., usually captains have their private mess). He repeated his well-known remark, "I didn't get these four stripes for nothing!"

Although we were not aware of it, Finn Ronne had quite a controversial reputation around Washington as a result of his earlier expedition, and I now wonder if he was sent to Ellsworth, the most isolated U.S. IGY station, to get him out of the way. I think George Dufek did not want Ronne around the McMurdo–Little America–Byrd–Hallett–South Pole circuit of stations. According to Paul Siple (in *90° South*), Admiral Richard Byrd was treated pretty poorly by the Navy people at McMurdo in Deep Freeze I in 1956–57; he was not wanted around anymore by the "real Navy." I imagine Ronne received some of the same treatment, as he suggested in his book, *Antarctic Command.* Of course Finn Ronne wanted to explore Edith Ronne Land further, which made Ellsworth the logical place, so the Navy (Dufek) was probably pleased to give him this assignment. The highest-ranking officers at Byrd, South Pole, Wilkes, and Hallett were only lieutenants (two stripes).

Hugo reports that Ronne had three phone patches tonight.

22 Sept., Sun. Blowing snow and warm (about –5°F). I spent the day reading Will Durant. I didn't finish the book, but Clint offered to let me have it another week.

23 Sept., Mon. Warm (up to 17°F at noon) with falling snow and whiteout. The visibility was so poor that it took Ed, Aug, and me 45 minutes to drive in for lunch. At one point we found ourselves at a flag on our shot point line running south when we thought we were heading (and had started) west. Fortunately I had my compass, and by a combination of dead reckoning and getting out and walking circles around the Weasel, we managed to work our way slowly down our east-west flag line into camp. We were late for chow and had to eat what the officers had left in their serving bowls.

We obtained some pretty good records today, including reflections off the ocean bottom.

About this time Kim and Ronne exchanged a series of long memos where Kim tried to explain how much important work he needed to do, and Ronne specified that Kim would be scheduled for two two-week periods of mess duty.

Someone posted the following on our library bulletin board: "The horror of that moment," the King went on, "I shall never, never forget!" "You will, though," the queen said, "if you don't make a memorandum of it." Lewis Carroll

24 Sept., Tues. The temperature was up to 20°F today, and it was very comfortable working outdoors. We fired a lot of shots off up to our 1500-m flag. The snow surface has changed with all the new snow that has fallen within the past two days. It is now soft and about nine inches deep. I drove the Weasel in at 15 mph today. Skis or snowshoes would be handy.

Don has been operating the ham gear surreptitiously at night in spite of Ronne's orders. The other operators are not doing much operating in sympathy with Don's dismissal. Ronne told Ed tonight that if Don shapes up, he can be ham operator again and if not, he may put him on mess duty.

25 Sept., Wed. Paul, Ed, and I drove out this morning, loaded a sled up with explosive at Point A and headed south for 3 km. It was still pretty poor visibility, and we spent a lot of time finding our way. We drilled a hole and after lunch we got shots off at 1.5 and 3 km. By quitting time it had cleared quite a bit. This is the first look I've had on a clear day warm enough to use binoculars out that way, and I could see for miles around.

A talk with Fuchs tonight disclosed that the downed Auster is presumably still sitting, waiting in this weather. The Shackleton people won't have their Otter ready for two or three more days. The present plan is for Ronne, Mac, and Con to fly to Shackleton tomorrow, pick up Dr. Fuchs, and proceed to Halley Bay (about 250 miles from here).

26 Sept., Thurs. Overcast and poor visibility so no flights.

Because the clutch was out, we could only use the seismic Sno-Cat as a laboratory for the seismic system, which filled up about half the space inside. I would run the engine to charge batteries and operate the heater and lights. It was still dark part of the working day. I recall eating meat bars cold for lunch. These were essentially pemmican and consisted of cooked, dried, generic meat with about 50% added fat and some mild seasoning and came sealed in aluminum foil. In the 1990s in health-conscious Boulder these would be considered not very politically correct. Generally meat bars were used in Antarctica in the 1950s and 1960s to make a stew or "hoosh," but we used them mainly as a lunch or snack, warmed or cold. I rather enjoyed them, but my body craved fat because of working in these low temperatures. It never was very warm in the Sno-Cat during the winter, even with the heater operating full blast.

I would spend many hours on a day such as this reading in the Sno-Cat while I waited for the shot to be prepared by the others some distance away. They would hand drill a shot 30–45 ft deep, load the charge in it, and then fire it. They then sent a radio signal to me, which I would record along with the seismic waves to determine the exact instant that the shot was fired. By measuring the seismic energy at the 2300-ft spread of 24 geophones connected to the cables, we could determine the sound velocity in the ice shelf and in the rock beneath the seafloor, as well as depth of the various layers.

We fired two shots off at 4.5 km with poor results. The first was 140 pounds of Navy plastic explosive (133), and the second was a shaped charge. I operated the instruments so saw neither. We had a near accident when the 40-lb shaped charge was fired. This comes in a funnel-shaped assembly with a steel jacket. Aug and Ed set it up on its small stand in the bottom of the crater left by the 140-lb shot. They fired from the Weasel about 40 ft away. The charge was not in line of sight due to the crater. When it went off, it blew two windows out of the Weasel, cracked the glass in three more, blew all the doors and the overhead hatches open, and riddled the upper foot of the starboard side with shrapnel from the metal canister. If they had fired it on the surface in line of sight, someone might have been killed by the small pieces of steel that pierced the metal sides. Fortunately all the shrapnel went over the heads of Aug and Ed. Needless to say, we will be more careful with shaped charges next time.

The Weasel was turned over by the blast, Augie told me in 1995; the two of them managed to roll it upright.

The normal procedure we had developed was to make a radio contact after each shot. After this shot I called for a long time before I raised them. When I got through, they mumbled something about some difficulty, but I didn't realize how bad it was until they picked me up at the Sno-Cat to return to the station.

We came in early and spent the rest of the afternoon repairing the Weasel.

Walt Davis, the Navy mechanic, was usually grumpy at us for the way we were hard on the vehicles. He really chewed Ed and Augie out this time after he slowly took a look around the damaged Weasel and noted the blown-out windows, the cracked glass, and the shrapnel holes. However, he even did some of the repairs. Davis didn't tell Ronne either nor did anyone else. We all kept pretty quiet about this incident.

Ronne gave orders that he wanted a phone patch tonight. He happened to be sitting in the ham shack with Mac who was operating. An Akron, Ohio, station called in and Ronne thought he would get a patch. Instead the ham wanted to put in a call to Augie's folks who live in a suburb of Akron. This made Ronne so furious that when Aug came in, he refused to get up from the second chair to let

Aug sit down at the mike. Aug stood and talked while Ronne sat with his arms across his chest and glared. Mac stood up and let Aug sit in his chair and operated the set by leaning over Aug's shoulder and turning the knobs. After about two minutes of this Ronne left and went in the radio room to talk to Forlidas. A moment later he was back in telling them to finish up because there was Navy traffic to get out. He left, whereupon Mac told Aug to talk for as long as he liked. Augie talked for 20 minutes.

Ronne did get two phone patches later tonight. Clint listened to his talk with his wife on his radio. Ronne told her that the IGY civilians were "disloyal," "disobedient," and were not doing their "duty" down here.

27 Sept., Fri. A bad day today, which started out with a bad omen. As Aug, Ed, Paul, and I started out we found that half of the developer had leaked out of our jug. I became lost trying to follow the flags out to A, visibility was so poor, and had to follow my tracks back to the first flag. There is always the danger of driving over the edge of the ice shelf when driving around blind like this. When we finally arrived at Point A and were hitching up a sled to take explosives out, the geophone cable was accidentally cut (this makes the fourth time). We had to take half the spread up and bring the cable in. I spent until 2100 splicing and checking the 50 fine wires that connect the geophones to the instruments. It's probably just as well that we didn't fire any shots today.

I talked to Ruth for a few minutes tonight.

28 Sept., Sat. Warm (about 20°F) and overcast. Mac tried to fly to Shackleton but after a half hour of circling camp and waiting for the weather to improve, the plane landed.

Aug, Ed, and Kim drove down the seismic line and fired 300 lbs at 4.5 km and 400 lbs at 6 km. When they started back a track on the Weasel broke about 5 km south of me and everyone walked home. We met Hugo, Paul, and Willie coming out to look for us when we were about a quarter mile out of camp. It was about 1830 and Hugo had become worried about our absence. They were all equipped for a crevasse rescue. As it turned out, of course, their efforts were unnecessary, but it was good to know someone thought of us out there. We missed supper. The remark in the galley was, "If you want anything to eat, get here on time."

29 Sept., Sun. I finished off *Life of Greece* and started *Caesar and Christ,* Durant's book on the Roman era. Hugo, Aug, and Larson surveyed a level line down to sea level at the unloading site, as the weather was good.

This gave us an accurate elevation of Ellsworth Station of 138 ft (42 m).

> Shackleton called in several times today. They are getting anxious about their people. Their Otter is ready to go and they planned to fly, but weather didn't permit it. They contacted Halley Bay who had talked with the downed Auster. The two men are all right.

> *30 Sept., Mon.* Ronne, Mac, Con, and Larson left for Shackleton in the Otter about 1030. In the afternoon Ed, Hugo, and I took two one-ton sleds over to the magazine and loaded them with explosive. We also drove down to the old unloading site and salvaged about 20 trail flags from the area. The sun was shining and the Captain was out of camp. This made for a festive atmosphere around the station. Everyone was relaxed; there was a lot more friendly talk than usual. Clint and Willie (who were invited) ate with the crew this noon and tonight.

> We listened to Halley Bay, Shackleton, our Otter, Shackleton's Otter, and the downed Auster on the radio at various times and combinations throughout the afternoon. The Auster (on CW) announced that they need food and "kero" [kerosene for their cook stove]. Fuchs and his crew left in their Otter about 1600 for Halley Bay, but were forced to turn back about 1800 because of bad weather. Our plane returned here at approximately 1830. They left the clutch plate and springs to be retempered—if possible.

> It seems that the fellow at Shackleton who has been doing the aurora work for Kim expressed a desire to see and talk to Kim. This was in front of Ronne, Fuchs, and Con. Fuchs thought it a good idea but Ronne hedged.

> *1 Oct., Tues.* Kim told Ronne that he had heard that the aurora man at Shackleton wanted to talk and asked if he could go over on the next flight. Ronne's "No!" was quite emphatic. He told Kim that what he had heard "was not true" and in the same breath asked who had told him. Kim answered that it was "one of the people on the flight." Ronne called Con in then and chewed him out for 15 minutes for telling Kim of this. He admitted it was true, but told Con that it caused "bitching and trouble."

> The Shackleton people flew their Otter up to Halley Bay, refueled, and found their Auster 70 miles further north up the coast. They refueled it and both planes flew to Halley Bay. Everyone, including the injured man at Halley Bay, is in good shape.

It may appear that we treated the case of the downed Auster casually, but this was not so. We had met some of the people onboard and felt real concern for them during this period. We were, however, aware that they were not injured, had food, and knew how to take care of themselves. Over the years since, I and people in my field parties have had to camp in "survival" circumstances. When there are no injuries due to a plane or helicopter crash, there is not great concern, because we always have tents, food, stoves, sleeping bags, and other emergency equipment, for just such circumstances.

I had a short phone patch home; it's Mother's birthday. Dave is disengaged. The traverse group had a meeting tonight and discussed the remaining preparations necessary. We divided the list up and each took responsibility for several items. Other than the garage work, there isn't too much left to do. Of course, there are many odds and ends of little stuff.

This confidence was not misplaced, despite Ronne's concern through the winter that we wouldn't be ready. Although we had plenty of difficulties on the traverse, the routine scientific work, camping, etc. were matters we always took for granted. We all had years of fieldwork behind us even though it was our first Antarctic expedition. Besides, by this time, we had already worked in Antarctica for seven months. We were psychologically prepared and quite impatient to get under way.

7
Final Traverse Preparations

The worldwide Asian flu epidemic was on. We received a message from the Bureau of Medicine, ordering the vaccination of all wintering personnel and civilians as soon as possible. After a year of isolation from all diseases, those of us wintering in Antarctica were possibly particularly susceptible. The rest of the U.S. Antarctic Program was preparing for contact with the outside world. In the meantime, we at Ellsworth continued in our isolation.

2 Oct., Wed. It was pretty windy today and, as we didn't want to take any chances with our large 1000-lb explosive charge of noise obscuring the seismic record, we worked in camp. I split bamboo poles and attached trail flags.

Kim took a message in to Ronne this afternoon to send to the British giving them the alidade they used for his aurora work. When Ronne saw him come in with a piece of paper in his hand he protested, "I won't take another memo. Life is too short to take any more of your memos." Kim assured him it wasn't a memo.

3 Oct., Thurs. Ronne brought the following message in to Jack:

FROM: IGY WASH DC
TO: ELLSWORTH STA
INFO: COMNAVUNITS ANT COMNAVSUPFOR ANT–
REP COMNAVSUPFOR WASH DC 021648 Z NO. 24 FOR
JACK BROWN FROM SHAPLEY [Allen H. Shapley, U.S.
National Committee for IGY, and Bureau of Standards]

ADVISE WHETHER YOU HAVE DONE ANY ACTIVE
COORDINATION OF VERTICAL SOUNDINGS PRO-
GRAM WITH BELGRANO STATION. IF NOT PLEASE
TAKE ALL PRACTICAL STEPS TO CONTACT LT.
BARICCO ON MATTER WE HAVE COORDINATED
WITH CAPT. GRUNWALDT, HIS SUPERIOR, AND

UNITED STATES AND ARGENTINE IGY COMMITTEE. RECOMMEND COORDINATION OF EXPERIMENTS AS FOLLOWS.... [TECHNICAL DETAILS] REQUEST YOU ADVISE POSSIBILITIES OF STARTING AND PROGRESS.

Jack was as surprised as Ronne, as we have not had any contact with the Argentines since last February. Jack did not even know they had an ionosphere sounder. Of course Ronne's big argument to keep Hugo from contacting his glaciologist friend there has been that they are not an IGY station and "besides, no one speaks any English." This message scared Ronne, I think. Jack immediately drafted up a message to Lieutenant Baricco and a reply to Shapley. In the latter he stated that we have had no contact with the people at Belgrano.

It was clear and sunny today, so at noon Ronne dashed in and asked Jack if he would go over to Belgrano "right now." Of course, Jack would. This however nullified the message Jack had prepared. We found out that he was planning to take a Navy man as an interpreter. As Hugo knows more Spanish and is a friend of one of them, we all thought that he should go. Jack told this to Ronne, who asked Jack in a pleading tone not to "cause any trouble" now. Jack was persistent and Ronne adamant in his refusal to let Hugo go. Finally, Ronne said he would cancel the flight. Jack said that was OK and handed him his two messages. Ronne refused to take them and became quite conciliatory. He finally put it to Jack that as they would go over anyway, perhaps he could get some good out of it without Hugo. This, of course, forced Jack to agree.

Jack, Ronne, Jackson, Mac, and Con flew over and spent an hour at Belgrano. Ronne never left Jack's side. He met everyone including Hugo's friend Lisignoli and Baricco. Both of these Argentines speak adequate English.

In 1959 I met Caesar Lisignoli at the Instituto Antartida Argentina in Buenos Aires. He was very hospitable and gave me a map of his strain-rate measurements on the Filchner Ice Shelf south of Belgrano Station. These data together with our traverse results provided the first evidence of a high rate of bottom melting at the base of the Filchner Ice Shelf, which I published in 1970, while living in Liberia, West Africa.

Jack told us that their ionosphere sounder is on the blink. They haven't the parts to repair it, but perhaps Jack can fix them up with some items. There are 18 people there, probably all military.

Although Belgrano was an IGY station, I'm sure it was placed on the Filchner Ice Shelf to partly substantiate Argentina's territorial claim. For a similar reason the British Halley Bay Station, a couple of hundred miles to the east on the coast, was also placed in British claimed territory. The British, Argentine, and Chilean claims overlap in Antarctica. There was a lot of politics involved in the IGY Antarctic Program, and not only involving the cold war competition between the U.S. and U.S.S.R.

> Ronne's visit to Belgrano was quite unannounced and unexpected. A couple of men saw the plane land and came up to meet them. One of the men (in a jumble of English, Spanish, and sign language) told Con about an accident they had, apparently recently. A Weasel broke through the sea or bay ice. A second one broke in and tipped trying to pull the first out. Both were pulled out with the help of a third.
>
> They have no plane but do have dogs. They served our people wine and gave us a big piece of meat for camp. We had nothing for them. When they were boarding the plane, Lisignoli came up to Jack and asked about Hugo. Jack told him that Hugo wanted to contact him. Ronne came up at this point, and that ended the conversation. They say they have been unable to contact us by radio, but some arrangements were made today for future contacts.

Despite the fact that the Argentines at Belgrano were unable to contact us at Ellsworth, my friend Mario Giovinetto, who was an Argentine glaciologist wintering over at Byrd Station, had been in regular radio contact with Belgrano.

> Con had to spend the time at Belgrano in the plane, as they kept the engine running because of the cold conditions.

The U.S. Hercules (LC-130) ski-equipped planes that deliver fuel and other cargo to the South Pole and other remote sites usually keep their engines running during the time that the aircraft are on the snow surface. For the same reason a diesel D-4 Caterpillar tractor, which was used at Ellsworth, was kept running essentially continuously throughout the entire winter.

> I showed Augie how to ascend up a rope which we had hanging beneath Kim's tower using "prussic knots."

237

This is a method of extricating oneself from a crevasse by ascending a rope while dangling from one end tied around the waist.

After coffee Kim, Don, Paul, and I drove down to the old ramp and walked down to the tide crack. There were some rather interesting little parallel concentrically curved ridges an inch or so high somewhat parallel to the crack but 20 ft or so inland. We saw two peculiar holes about 4 ft in diameter lightly frozen over. Presumably, they are killer whale blow holes; seal holes would have been smaller. We observed no sign of life. We skied south a bit, on the sea ice along the foot of the ice front cliff, and took some pictures. Kim and I went north a quarter mile or so by ourselves and observed some very beautiful overhanging cornices on the cliff. We climbed a little ridge beneath them and took some pictures. This was somewhat dangerous as a falling cornice would have obliterated us. We escaped, however, and returned to camp in time for supper.

Ronne had a talk with Jack after supper in which he aired his usual troubles. He referred to Hugo as a "Nazi." Unfortunately Jack

J. Malville beneath cornice at edge of Bahia Chica.

told Hugo this at the movie and it really hurt him. Hugo's folks came from Germany and Hugo spent several years there as a child before the war. One of his brothers was killed fighting Germany in

WWII. After the movie Hugo accosted Ronne in the mess hall, and had words with him in front of several of the men. (Ronne has a mortal dread of having scenes in front of witnesses.) I don't know the details, but Hugo finished by telling Ronne that there is someone else here who acts "like a Nazi!"

Implying that a Norwegian like Ronne was a Nazi was also quite an insult. A few days later, Ronne told Jack that he did not say Hugo was a Nazi; "I only said he acted like a Nazi."

The Milwaukee Braves defeated the Yankees 4–2 in the second game of the World Series.

Aug took advantage of Ronne's grudging permission of a few weeks back and inveigled Mac into giving him a plane ride to get pictures of the ice trough. Mac flew south for about 50 miles, and Augie took 12 pictures of the very heavy crevasse fields and the large rifts that block our possible (or impossible) traverse route. It looks pretty bad, but perhaps it will "go" if we swing out of camp southeast and swing back west about 30 miles out, passing the large rifts on the north side. Ronne didn't know Mac would fly out that far, as he never would have let Augie go that far. (He called Aug "insane" to Kim yesterday.)

Hugo developed Augie's films tonight and they came out pretty good. It is a shame we have to sneak our recon flights and pictures this way.

Paul and I whipped out 30 8-by-10-inch prints of Augie's flight pictures right after supper. They are quite good and the terrain looks pretty bad.

4 Oct., Fri. Ronne and Mac with [Atles] Lewis took a secret flight out to the big rift and landed on the other side. It was kept secret until takeoff, and Con and Will were not permitted to go. Ronne skied over, took a look, and decided it was impossible for us to cross a very shaky snow bridge which we hadn't considered. Ronne has been telling everyone around camp that it is absolutely impossible for our traverse to go south.

Ronne sent the following message on 6 October about this flight:

FROM: ELLSWORTH STA
TO: IGY WASH DC
INFO: COMNAVSUPFOR ANTARCTICA/COMNAV-

UNITS ANTARCTICA/LITTLE AMERICA STA. 061523 Z
IGY NO. 145.

RECON FLIGHT FROM EASTERN CAPE GOULD BAY
AND SOUTHWARD FOR 50 MILES TO HUGE RIFT RE-
VEALS SURFACE TRAVEL IMPASSABLE. FOLLOWING
RIFT EASTWARD REVEALED NO POSSIBLE CROSSING.
HOWEVER, POSSIBLE ROUTE TRAVELING SOUTH-
EAST FROM STATION AND INTERSECT WITH BRITISH
TRANSANTARCTIC ROUTE FROM SHACKLETON AP-
PEARS POSSIBLE TO ATTAIN INLAND AREAS SOUTH
OF RIFT.

Ed, Paul, and I shot our 1000-lb charge off. Even with that much
explosive (at 7.5 km) there was insufficient energy for best results.

These were amazingly large charges for the relatively short
distances we were recording at. We knew that a lot of energy was
being absorbed in the snow in which we were burying the charges,
but I think now that a lot of the explosive was not detonating. This
may have been because the porous, air-filled firn was allowing the
mass of the charge to be disbursed before it all ignited.

Don has rigged up an Angry 9 radio in his lab and was talking to us
out in the field today. His call letters are SH1. He made up a QSL
card for Paul and me.

Ham radio operators exchange QSL cards identifying their
station by mail with other hams with whom they communicate.
We had QSL cards at Ellsworth showing a penguin with headphones on, and the call letters of our "official" ham station
KC4USW. The "W" stood for "Weddell," which was the name the
Navy originally intended to call our station. The hams in the U.S.
and elsewhere) were quite interested in receiving QSL cards from
the Antarctic stations.

5 Oct., Sat. Ronne had two phone patches early in the morning
which Paul and Hugo listened to from their beds. He asked his wife
to contact [Hugh] Odishaw (executive secretary, USNC-IGY) and
ask him to send a dispatch giving Ronne full authority in planning
traverse routing and operation. He attacked Hugo and Ed, accusing them of being "prima donnas" and wanting to plan their own

route (Crary's written instructions to Ed and Hugo give them the responsibility and authority to plan the traverse route). He plans on having a phone patch with Odishaw. This is going over Crary's head. It looks like Ronne is building his case up against Crary, too. Crary is the only one (so far as we know) who has an understanding of the situation, and he is staying down for another year.

Ed, Ronne, Walt Davis, Mac, Willie, Lewis, and May flew over to Shackleton. Ed wouldn't be going but for a message from Crary requesting that he make a gravity tie. At that base everything was confusion and turmoil. Their Otter was preparing to fly up to Halley Bay for a gravity tie, and they have an advance party leaving on traverse today to mark a route to South Ice. Ed took a gravity observation and then talked with Ronne and Fuchs a bit. Fuchs has flown over this rift which they call the "Chasm" [later we all called it the "Grand Chasm"] and doesn't think we can get around the west end. Fuchs' group plans to cut around the east end of the [Grand Chasm] between it and the heavily crevassed area nearer the mountains. This involves going over a less crevassed, but still dangerous area. Ronne suggested that our traverse follow the British route around the east end of the rift. Fuchs stated that the route would be marked. [David] Pratt didn't have time to retemper the springs for the Sno-Cat clutch so Walt Davis brought them back. Hugo is going to try to retemper the springs, but our other alternative is to take two Weasels and drive the other Sno-Cat out when Lassiter gets here about 1 November. Walt Davis advises us not to waste any time trying to temper the springs for the clutch, but to work on getting two Weasels ready. Most of us think he is probably right, but Hugo plans to spend two days trying before he gives up the idea.

Ed and Hugo met with Ronne to discuss the traverse plans. Ronne got quite loud and excited and said that *he* would be giving the orders and would determine where the traverse would go. When they mentioned that Crary was still in charge, Ronne blustered a bit but refused to acknowledge that statement. He had told several people that Crary knew nothing about the Antarctic and that he made a mistake in interfering with Ronne's running of the station in the voice radio contact on 17 May.

Paul had been talking for five minutes on a phone patch when Ronne burst in saying, "Get out! I've got a schedule!" Paul didn't even have time to say good-bye but was bustled out. Hannah (who has become an operator since Don's "cancellation") made contact with

241

Jules [Madey, a teenager in Clark, New Jersey] (K2KGJ). It just so happened that we all wanted to hear what Odishaw said to Ronne. The receiver in Jack's lab doesn't have a good enough antenna to hear the stateside part of the conversation so Don ran a tap off the ham receiver this afternoon and into a tape recorder in Paul's room so Odishaw's statement could be heard.

When Jules called Odishaw, he refused to accept the call saying he was too busy right now but to call back. Jules arranged a schedule with Ronne for 0800 Z Monday (0500 Ellsworth time). Odishaw knows what Ronne wants to discuss, because Ronne's wife called him up this morning.

6 Oct., Sun. The following message was received this morning:

FROM: IGY WASH DC
ACTION: ELLSWORTH STA
INFO: LITTLE AMERICA STA–BYRD STA–WILKES STA–POLE STA–HALLETT STA– COMNAVSUPFOR ANTARCTICA–COMNAVUNITS ANT REP COMNAVSUPFOR WASH DC 052010 Z

USSR EARTH SATELLITE NOW IN ORBIT WITH APEX ABOUT 65 DEGREES SOUTH. TWENTY PLUS AND FORTY PLUS MEGACYCLES CW SIGNALS TRANSMITTED ALTERNATELY AT INTERVALS OF ABOUT ONE SECOND. MOST IMPORTANT THAT YOU ATTEMPT TO RECORD SIGNALS USING COMMUNICATION RECEIVERS AND WHISTLER TWIN-TRACK TAPE RECORDER, RECORD BOTH SIGNALS. TRY TO GET ACCURATE TIME OF ONSET OF SIGNAL. INFORMATION ON SIGNAL STRENGTH ALSO DESIRABLE. TRY TO GET ESTIMATE OF PASSAGE OF MERIDIAN OR SOME OTHER KNOWN DIRECTION. WILL TRY TO SUPPLY MORE DETAILED ORBITAL INFORMATION AS IT BECOMES AVAILABLE. NOTIFY ODISHAW IMMEDIATELY OF ANY OBSERVATION.

This message was sent specifically to Ellsworth because of Jack's whistler recorders, which were particularly well suited to record Sputnik's signals. Although we were not aware of it, the launch of Sputnik had the U.S. IGY community—and everyone else in the U.S.—in an uproar that the Soviets had put up a satellite before the U.S. had. I suppose the excellent funding available to me and all of my fellow grad students and scientists when we returned to the States, and in the coming decades, was partially related to the U.S. reaction to the Sputnik launch.

Perhaps this explains why Odishaw was too busy to talk to Ronne. Radio Moscow is blaring forth with descriptions and boasting about how Russia got their satellite up before the U.S.

Ed and Hugo met with Ronne at 1000. Nothing of any note happened. He sidetracked all their suggestions but behaved so calmly and spoke so carefully that they wondered if he was recording the conversation.

I made up a simple code to describe in my journal how one of the officers had put a microphone close to Ronne's room connected to a tape recorder so he could record Ronne's conversations. I felt that this subject was too sensitive to openly write about at the time. We were only three years out of the McCarthy era, and those of us who had come through universities during this period, particularly us physics majors, were quite paranoid by 1990s–or, for that matter, late 1960s–standards.

7 Oct., Mon. Everyone was awake bright and early at 0445 today for Ronne's talk with Odishaw. Don was up in Paul's room operating the tape recorder, and Ed and Jack and Kim were clustered around the radio in the ionolab. I stayed in bed but managed to hear because the speaker was on.

Ronne called Hugh Odishaw through K2KGJ. Ronne was frustrated in his inability to control us scientists as he saw fit, particularly as regards to the coming traverse. He had not received any support from Crary in Little America in May and now wanted to go directly to the IGY administration in Washington, D.C., as represented by Odishaw.

Time: 0515 (0815 Z; 0315 in Washington D.C.)

ODISHAW: Finn, I'm going to sound awfully guileless, but I haven't had much sleep the last few nights; I think you understand why. [He was referring to the Sputnik satellite]. . . . First of all how are you, and how is the group? And second, have you got some equipment–have you been listening to the satellite? Over.

243

RONNE: Yes, I realize that you haven't had much sleep lately. Yes, I realize that. But, I was anxious to get this message off to you, and I wonder if you have time to listen, and I will tell it to you. OK? Over to you.

ODISHAW: Fire away, Finn. Over.

RONNE: Yes, I will. I have wanted to speak to you on this for quite some time. You are familiar with my instructions outlined in Larry's [Gould] letter. But the discipline leaders [i.e., specifically seismology, glaciology and ionosphere physics] will not have recognized them. They consider Crary their only leader. This has resulted in direct refusal to obey orders. Defying my authority, causing hatred and discord among the men by their constant bickering and flows of memorandums, requesting me to arrange radio schedules to have Crary's opinion on running of the station, and many small matters have placed me in an attenuating position. And I can tell you, Hugh, that of the four winterings, the one now was the toughest. I am now tired and worn out thin by the constant bickering, questioning my every move in even matters not pertaining to them. Chances of a successful traverse, I feel, is of the utmost importance. My suggestions are brushed aside, even when it comes to the safety of personnel.

I have outlined a safe route for them to follow. This they will not listen to. Instead they demand airplane rides on a continuing scale. Three of the five traverse men have covered the area by air south, taking pictures indicating an impossible route to go in over the surface. The terrain there is dangerous. The discipline leaders lack one thing–namely being able to take orders, and their surplus demands to bother Crary on every matter. I have taken enough.

Hoping to get the traverse party off within the end of the month, I need a word from you to clarify to them three important points; first, that I am the station scientific leader; two, that my decisions are final without any further bickering; third, they must take my recommendations to reach inland areas with safety. Now, I wonder if you got that, and then I will continue a bit shorter on. Here's KC4USW turning it over to K2KGJ.

ODISHAW: It makes me very sorry to hear what I've heard. But as you know, I've had some messages from Mrs. Ronne that perhaps prepared me for this conversation. I'm a bit perplexed about this situation, and I don't know quite how to respond. One of the things about it is that I can't evaluate a situation of that kind; I can't evaluate the discipline [not scientific disciplines here] from station to station. But, one of the factors that I can't understand is this kind of a problem to the best of my knowledge, has not come up anywhere else. There has been no word of difficulty anywhere with people. But, as to this business, I don't know what to say, and I don't know if conditions have just been more rigorous up in this Weddell Sea area or not; but as to the statement of a word from me, I think what I had better do is talk this over carefully with Larry Gould. As I understand the three points that you have raised–first of all some statement about your position as station leader. On this they can have no doubts, as far as I'm concerned. They had none when they left, and I think that the documentation was adequate. Now as to the question as to these decisions being final, I would feel that in the general area of administration that they understood this, too, but in short I'm confused at this point, and I would like to have a chance to talk with Larry. But it might be well for you to repeat those three things, at least two and three. The first one, I think I got clear–in terms of your request of being station scientific leader. So why don't you repeat two and three. Over.

RONNE: Hugh, the thing is, they are bickering about every decision. You see, they are bickering about every decision, and I just won't have any more bickering. I have it running well as far as it goes, but there is just too much bickering, and the last one with regard to the traverse route, I have covered that very well. They won't take that. They want to go over it again in airplanes–continuously going over it, and I'm tired of it now. They have it–everything is outlined for them in a safe, [sic] and in the best interests of IGY.

Alright. Here is the next point, a message to cover these three points. That will help me considerably and relieve my mind, as I am much concerned about the men's safety. I cannot have a clear conscience before I put safety measures in the forefront. The experience of our traverse men is extremely limited; that I know. My proposed route through the crevasses I discussed with Dr. Fuchs at Shackleton. He agrees with me 100%, as does Commander McCarthy, in charge of the aviation unit here, who has scanned the terrain closely with me. There can be no split authority on these matters; otherwise I should be relieved of responsibility. Yes, for the safety of the IGY traverse personnel, I know the land too well to say otherwise, Hugh.

Now for the benefit, for the station leaders coming down here in the future, I will make these suggestions, which should be included in their contract when signing in Washington. First, the IGY men should have a clear understanding that the final decision rests with the station scientific leader on IGY matters. Second, they should be made aware of the clause of the Uniform Code of Military Justice. A number of the men now, this time, would not have signed the contract if they had known about that. That was also brought up here once, and I discussed it with Crary at Little America on the radio telephone. And the third one is they have a complete understanding of what is expected of them with regard to household duties. Men here flatly refuse to participate. They would not even volunteer in an emergency! I think a thorough indoctrination should be given wintering-over personnel so as to prevent my relief experiencing the embarrassment to which I was subjected. This indoctrination should be given prior to setting foot on the continent, and in a manner that all parties concerned will know exactly where they stand. . . . That is about the gist and the core of the whole thing, Hugh. I wonder if you received that. This is KC4USW turning it over to K2KGJ.

ODISHAW: Well, Finn, I don't know quite what to say about this situation. I've taken some notes, and I'm thinking about it. But first of all, let me ask you another question. Have you discussed this, both the conduct you have described of these people, with Crary, and second, have you discussed the decisions, your decisions, on the traverse route with Crary? Over.

RONNE: I didn't get exactly clear what they were. I discussed with Crary only last May, when we had trouble with the generators in order to have them not interfere with the whistler program. I needed some help then, and Crary said, "Yes, I leave it to you." But it is my responsibility if the IGY program should be curtailed in any way. And in order for them not to have come back upon, [sic] I relieved them of all household duties. See what I mean? That I—the burden was on me. I didn't want to take the responsibility, because they may lay down the tools and say the heck with it. So, I discussed that part with him only. That they should take my decision on that. That was the only discussion I had with him. But they are asking for radio contact with Crary continuously, and I have not done that; and so they have discussed it with him time and again on ham gear, and Crary has not given them satisfaction. He says that the matter is with the station scientific leader. They have to take his orders. But now I am tired of it, Hugh, to have this continuously. The only thing that you could consider sending me is that they shall recognize me as station scientific leader and my decisions are not to bickering with [sic], and that they should take my recommendations on the traverse route to reach the inland area safely. I can only give recommendations on the traverse route. I cannot direct. That is specifically in the orders. . . .

ODISHAW: As far as the traverse is, Crary is in charge of the overall program anywhere in the Antarctic, and my question is, have you discussed your traverse plans with Crary? This is something he is specifically interested in and charged with. Over.

RONNE: It has been discussed with him, but they still demand more airplane rides continuously. They feel that they control the airplanes, for example, they control the airplanes. And they will have asked for airplane rides and continuous bickering, continuously, so that is the only point. Crary–has been discussed with him. And the thing– they must take my recommendations when it comes to safety. These men do not have the experience in the field here. Over to you.

ODISHAW: When did you discuss the traverse decisions with Crary? When? Over.

RONNE: About two or three weeks ago. About two or three weeks ago. Over.

ODISHAW: Well, is, was Crary in complete agreement with your plans on the traverse? Over.

RONNE: At that time we had not completed the aerial reconnaissance immediately south of us. That time we had not completed the aerial reconnaissance of the area immediately south of us. Now I am going to cover the area again on the first opportunity with high-altitude mapping to show all of the crevasses. That we are isolated on a tip of a peninsula, where the only entrance to the interior is southeasterly to tie in to Shackleton's route, the one that Dr. Fuchs is going to follow and that is outlined in my message to you. Now this I will cover again in high altitude aerial pictures to show it. The thing is that I am against their bickering about everything. That is what I am up against. I can handle the situation, but I am just tired of the constant bickering! So, just a word to that effect, I believe, would help me considerably. Over to you.

ODISHAW: I will bear this in mind, and I will read this message you are sending us. . . . I would like to suggest that you talk to Crary in any case and review the whole matter that you have discussed with me tonight with him completely, in this fashion, if you can get him on a voice. Can you get him on a voice circuit, and talk to him personally? Over.

RONNE: I can have him on a voice circuit, but what these other people do every conversation I have, they are taking it down on tape recording, for example. Oh they are on the lookout morning, noon, and night, and out of those men here, I have six or seven eggs that the yolk is not exactly fresh. Over.

ODISHAW: I didn't get that last sentence, Finn. Can you repeat the last sentence?

RONNE: That out of the nine eggs, the yolk in six or seven of the nine eggs are not exactly 100%. You understand what I mean? Over to you.

ODISHAW: Yes, I understand. Well, Finn, I don't know what we can do at this present time. I will meditate on what you've said and try to get a message to you after I've read your cable. But, I would be interested in terms of the health of yourself and everybody else, and thinking of all. And whether or not you have tuned on 20 and 40 megacycles for the satellite. Over.

RONNE: We have been listening, and we've heard something at times on the 20, at 20 minutes after and 40 after. I haven't got the complete picture on that yet. But, anything we hear we will notify you immediately.

Coming back to the other matter again, I can handle the situation well here. I can handle it. You don't need to worry about that. I have that much ability. I can handle it 100%, but it will make it easier for me only. That's the only thing. My shoulders are broad, and my head is strong. I can handle it, but it [sic] will make it easier, and I discussed it with Jackie here some time ago. I told her that I am having some difficulties on that score. She suggested that I speak to you, and that's what I'm doing now. It is not exactly urgent. You see what I mean? It would help me only. All right this is KC4USW.

ODISHAW: I think I understand what you're after, Finn, and as I say, I'm concerned about the situation, and I want to do everything I can to help. I will get in touch with you very soon, but I think I will wait until I get your cable responding, and I may want to talk to Crary, too. But, I will answer you as soon as I can. Is that all right? Over.

RONNE: I understand that, Hugh. I received that. Even if I don't get it, it will be alright just the same. But it will only help me. It will assist me considerably and relieve my mind. That is the only thing. Otherwise I will handle the situation 100%.

Otherwise everything goes very well here. The IGY men have done a good job. They finished the 100-ft pit during the winter. That was the only work they did, by the way. They concentrated on that. The ionosphere work was going excellently, also the aurora work. And the met work has been carried on very well. We are in a very bad area as regard to weather and also radio communication. It has not been 100% due to weather, but they have done a wonderful job. Don't misunderstand me. I can give them the best recommendation, a wonderful job done. It is their personal attitude toward authority that I really resent. They cannot take orders and authority. I have to bitch and argue with them in order to shovel snow out of even their doorway into the main tunnel. Everything is a big bickering, and that is what I am tired of.

Alright Hugh, I know that you have a busy day ahead of you tomorrow. We received with great excitement the news that a satellite is there now, and we are hoping and looking for more news about it. The men, all hands, spent a nice winter. It was a long one. And sure appreciated the sun when it came back. The camp is in excellent shape; we are all set to receive the ship now. The military crew now are readying tractors and sledges to unload the ship, and I think that Captain McDonald would want to get out of here as soon as possible—not to get stuck in the ice for nine days when he went out last year.

I wonder if you received this, Hugh, and then over to you for a final. I know this is a heck of a time in the morning to be called, but then it is the only time that we have good contact here. Here's KC4USW.

ODISHAW: Finn, I got it all, and I'm very glad we had this chance, and it's good hearing from you. I don't know if you want to talk to the gang there at all about this conversation, but if you do, I want you to give them all my best wishes and to you yourself, and I hope things will work out. I'm sure that things will work out. I'm sure they will. Probably everyone has been a bit on edge as a result of a long winter and factors of that kind. I'm pleased you say they are doing their scientific work well, because after all, that is what we've got them for. First and last it was to get a certain scientific program done in the field, and you say they are doing this and they are doing it well, and this is very encouraging. Now in the area beyond that, it gets to be an extremely difficult one, and I can't comment at all on it. I'm not there. But, I will bear in mind everything you said, and I will communicate with you as soon as I can. Take care of yourself and relax. Perhaps you want to say another word before we sign off. Over.

RONNE: I got that. Thank you very much. Everything will go well. Then this would be a small matter. I know that when we look back on it later on, it's a small matter. I will handle it 100% just the same, but getting a wire on those three points to remind them, that would help some. Otherwise minimize the thing. Not to enlarge upon it, because more dust comes up from the bottom. All right, you go back to sleep again now, and I will keep you informed by the regular official channel on our progress getting into the field. We went over to Shackleton the other day to temper the springs to get the clutch going again. If that should fail, then I am giving them two Weasels so they can go out into the field until Lassiter gets here with a new clutch. Then, I will fly then. Then I will get the Sno-Cat here going to join them in the field later on, so we will work out with the problem 100% to the best of our ability. All right, Hugh, good luck to you, and don't work too hard, and call Jackie and give her my regards, and you will be hearing from us soon again. Good night and good luck.

Hugh Odishaw was very impartial and responded admirably considering the difficult position this put him in. I'm sure our problems seemed very petty and irritating to Odishaw in the light of the consternation in official Washington at the surprise launch of the Soviet satellite. Although the symbol of the IGY was the earth with a satellite circling it, no one in the U.S. seriously doubted that the U.S. would put up the first satellite. Because the Soviets had told the world that they were going to launch a satellite during IGY, we were not particularly surprised at Ellsworth. We were, however, very interested in it and managed to record signals as it passed within range of Ellsworth.

Don had a patch with his wife this morning also, and dictated a letter to Odishaw explaining a little of our side of the story. She said she would mail it this noon.

After all of the clandestine excitement of listening to Ronne's phone patch, we finally went to work. Ed, Kim, Aug, and I drove out and picked up the seismic spread this morning. It was a beautiful sunny day, about –22°F with a brisk wind.

I stopped recording the temperatures as it was warming up. It was generally still below zero during this period, but it seemed warm enough so that I didn't notice it.

After completing this task we roped up, Kim with Ed, and Aug with me. Ice axes in hand and snow shoes on feet we "explored" the steep and deep trough which was down to the ice front in this area. We saw many hummocks but no crevasses. It was very difficult coming back because our sunglasses (and my regular glasses plus sunglasses) became all frosted up facing into the wind. This is extremely aggravating and tends to make one go without sunglasses.

After lunch Ed and I drove out in a D-4 with [Carl] Crouse to Point A to bring the Sno-Cat in. Unfortunately one of the tracks was frozen such that it wouldn't turn, so we had to go back for a Hermann-Nelson heater. This is the farthest Crouse has been from camp since the ships landed, and it took 22 minutes in third gear.

He tells everyone "I drove 39 miles out and then turned around and drove 39 miles back to camp."

I don't know the actual distance, but we could walk it in about half an hour.

It was too late to complete the job, so Ed and I went out behind the met tower to probe for some boxes containing a crevasse detector buried beneath the drifted snow. The Navy sent this instrument down. It is rather new and has many defects. As it is very cumbersome and heavy, we had originally not planned on taking it. Ronne and Hugo agreed on this point. Crary, however, in order to protect himself in case we were to lose a vehicle in a crevasse, recommended that we take it. Ronne for the same reason advised Hugo and Ed to take it. They, therefore, for the reason that prompted Crary and Ronne to pass the buck, have decided to take it. Kent, in whose charge it is, piled the boxes up behind the met-communications building. We found what we think is a box about five feet below the surface. Tomorrow we'll go to work at it because there are no Navy men to dig it out—so we are assured.

I spent the next three weeks off and on digging out the boxes with various Navy men, assembling and installing the crevasse detector, which was ultimately completed on 25 October.

It is a very cumbersome apparatus involving a 20-ft structure of four redwood four by fours projecting in front of the vehicle which push three-foot circular dish-shaped electrodes and two similar electrodes dragging behind. I wonder how much faith the manufacturers have in the device, as they advise having a hundred-foot rope along at all times.

Ed and Hugo argued with Ronne and exchanged memos for the next two weeks about recon flights to examine the west end of Grand Chasm. Ed and Hugo were up on one flight and finally on 18 Oct. Ed had a good look with Ronne at the specific area we wanted to get through.

Hugo hasn't had any success with his tempering of the clutch springs yet. He tried several methods of heating the springs uniformly without success. A fire brick oven couldn't be heated hot enough with a blow torch; heating a pipe with a blow torch didn't work.

8 Oct., Tues. Another cold, clear, beautiful day. Since his talk with Odishaw, Ronne has been behaving distinctly more friendly with the civilians.

Hugo and Paul have done the impossible! They successfully retempered two springs this morning. Today they tried using the oil range in the galley with great success. Hugo holds the spring on a wire right in the flames of the fire box and then when it gets a cherry red, quenches it in a bucket of kerosene. The annealing is accomplished in the regular oven which gets up to 500°F. (We found later that the intense heat damaged the metal in the stove.) The proper amount is judged by eye comparing the color of the metal with that of the one good spring the Shackleton people lent us. The finished springs are then tested in an arrangement using a drill press, spring scale, and a small block of measured thickness. The spring is compressed to this thickness by the drill press, and the force required to do this is measured by the scale attached to the lever arm. The actual force on the spring can then be calculated. By suppertime they had ten of the sixteen springs completed and tested. This is the most encouraging and morale-raising event that has occurred in traverse preparation and planning so far. All of the credit goes to Hugo for persisting against so much discouraging advice.

I think that this was Hugo's proudest accomplishment during the entire year and possibly in his life. He is legendary among Antarcticans who know him in describing this feat. We probably never could have made the traverse had not this significant repair been made, because the Weasels wouldn't have made it through the crevasses, and Lassiter did not bring the new clutch until early December.

9 Oct., Wed. Ed repaired seismic cable. Paul and Hugo finished the springs last night and installed the repaired clutch in the Sno-Cat.

10 Oct., Thurs. Spear has manufactured a 40-ft flag pole out of 3-inch pipe stock. Al Spear, [James] Ray, Davis, ["Doc"] Mathis, Cox, and I put up the flag pole and raised the U.S. flag this morning. The Captain wasn't notified, and I doubt if he knows it is flying.

The flag had only 48 stars then, as Alaska and Hawaii had not been admitted yet.

There was a "rainbow" centered about the zenith. About 60° of arc was visible against the blue sky. The bow was 70° above the horizon and was convex to the north; there were stratocumulus clouds beneath the sun to the north.

A message came in from Crary after supper telling Ronne to get on a voice contact with him. Apparently Odishaw has talked to Crary. They tried to make contact tonight but were unable to get through.

Augie had a phone patch with his folks. His mother knows the mother of one of Lassiter's pilots who is from Augie's folks' town. They sent letters with him for Augie; Ronne of course didn't send Augie's name and address to his wife for Lassiter to bring a letter. His mother said they are in South America now waiting for good weather to fly in. She had heard that this air group was for "Ronne's expedition into the interior."

11 Oct., Fri. I helped Augie survey in our seismic shot points. Ronne asked Jack if he wanted to go to Belgrano in the afternoon. Jack said he would wait until they had their recorder fixed. Ronne, Mac, Con, Lewis, [Thomas] Ackerman and [William] Butler went on the flight. Of course they couldn't take Hugo.

About suppertime we received the word from Shackleton that they were flying a man with an injured hand over to see Clint. Their doctor is in the field. Their Otter landed about 1850 and there were three men in it, John Lewis, pilot whom we met last fall, John Stephenson, geologist, and Ralph Lenton, who had been responsible for the construction of Shackleton. Stephenson had caught his hand in a sharp snap hook on a dog harness. The dog ran, and he received a nasty gash along one finger exposing the tendon. It required 14 stitches to close the wound.

Ronne made a brief appearance to greet the visitors, but as Fuchs wasn't along he didn't hang around. It was really great to see some new faces and talk to some different people. John Lewis talked to some of us in the science building for a while about what they have found out as far as regards their route. They have one party in the field with two Sno-Cats and dogs about 50 miles out on their route to South Ice, a small three-man advance base about 280 miles south southeast of Shackleton. They took another group in today with dogs and landed them on a frozen melt "lake" at the base of the Shackleton (Onaway) Mountains. Lewis told us a little about the country west of their route but didn't know much, as they have confined their activities to the area between Shackleton and South Ice. They had not flown near the western end of the rift.

Ralph Lenton was cornered by Don and some of the others and they started to explain the situation we have here. He laughed and said that he knows all about Ronne. He came into Stonington Island (at Marguerite Bay) in 1948, just after the Ronne's Antarctic Research Expedition (RARE) had pulled out, and he heard a lot about Ronne from the fellows that had spent the previous season there. He has spent seven winters in the Antarctic in the past 10 years. He says he is going to get married when he gets back—shotgun wedding.

As John Stephenson was still being treated at 1900, Ralph Lenton and John Lewis stayed for the movie. They haven't any movies over at Shackleton. It took John Lewis quite by surprise when Ronne walked in to the movie and the master-at-arms (Beiszer at present) shouted, "'tenshun on deck!" He didn't know what to do for a few seconds and then snapped smartly to attention. It was embarrassing to me to have this sort of thing go on in front of our guests.

By the middle of the movie John Stephenson was through being treated and was available for talk. "Doc" Mathis (the medical "corpsman") knew that Augie has been wanting to talk geology with these people since we landed, so he fetched him. Aug had a good chat, and later Hugo, Paul, Ed, and I joined them. Stephenson spent the winter at South Ice with two other fellows in one small hut. I asked him how things went. He admitted that things were a little rough at times particularly when their oil stove would go out. They had a wind generator and a gasoline [or oil] generator. He told me that three was a pretty small group and implied that they got on each other's nerves at times.

Stephenson gave us a few bits of information on the geology of their area: Whichaway Nunataks—30 miles north of South Ice, Shackleton Mountains (Onaway), 60 miles north of the Whichaway Nunataks, and the Theron Mountains. Flat-lying sedimentary rock (Permian) similar to the Transantarctic Mountains across all of Antarctica. He found dark igneous rock (dolerite sills) intruded into the sedimentary rock. Fossils that look like corals and ammonites. Possible fault scarps similar to Queen Maud Range in the Transantarctic Mountains.

I recorded these brief geologic descriptions because Stephenson's work was the first to show the similarities of the rocks in this area of Antarctica to those in the Transantarctic Mountains in the Ross Sea area. These sedimentary rocks also correlate with similar sedimentary rocks of the same age in mountains in South Africa. Geologists now know that Africa was attached to Antarctica as part of Gondwana Land. Africa broke away at the time the dolerite sills Stephenson found were intruded into the sedimentary rocks about 175 million years ago. The Dufek intrusion, which we soon discovered about 300 miles south of Ellsworth, was also emplaced 175 million years ago and is associated with the same rifting event that separated Africa from Antarctica.

This visit by the three men from Shackleton was the first we had since the winter began. These were the first new faces we had seen in that time, and I realize from the extensive entry in my journal how important this was to us. It was also very exciting to talk geology with John Stephenson. Even though geology was not an official discipline of the IGY, the work that those of us did on the geophysical traverses, including that by the British at Shackleton and our party, helped lead to the acceptance a few years later of the concept of continental drift and plate tectonics.

> *12 Oct., Sat.* I worked on the seismic Sno-Cat. If only the clutch holds up, we will be all set. The tops of the Sno-Cats are painted with orange Day-Glo to make for good visibility when the planes are looking for us.

Painting the Sno-Cats that orange color never helped particularly. By 1960 we had painted all the Sno-Cats used on the traverses black, which kept them appreciably warmer.

> Dick Grob gave me some of his gear that he doesn't want, which I may be able to use. Among other things, I received a jackknife, padlock, a sweater, sunglasses, goggles, a pair of wind pants, and a good parka.

As mentioned throughout my journal, we civilians got closer to the Navy men throughout the year. Ronne greatly facilitated this when he kicked us out of the officers' mess. This closeness with the Navy officers and enlisted men was quite important when we needed their support in various things while on the traverse. There were a number of occasions when their friendship made our lives a bit nicer.

> Crary sent a follow-up on his message requesting to talk to Ronne. He now wants to try on the ham gear from 1500 to 2000 Ellsworth time. Ronne's wife, in a patch last night, told him that Crary is going in the field on 15 or16 of Oct. Perhaps Ronne is trying to stall it

out. He has been very nice to everyone lately. He told me this afternoon what a great job the boys did in fixing the clutch.

13 Oct., Sun. I spent the morning writing and the afternoon working on Will Durant's *Caesar and Christ.* We heard Dufek and Sir Hubert Wilkins arrived at McMurdo [Williams Air Facility] from New Zealand via R5D aircraft yesterday.

Wilkins was the pioneer in using aircraft in Antarctica in the 1920s. I had the privilege of meeting him briefly at the Antarctic orientation in Davisville, Rhode Island, in September 1956.

Wonder of wonders! Ronne came in to Hugo this morning and asked him if he and Paul wanted to fly over to Belgrano and talk to the glaciologists there. They with McCarthy, Beiszer, and Lewis flew over about 1200. Hugo carried on his conversations in English, Spanish, German, and French. Paul only managed to follow a little of the German. The Argentine glaciologists are leaving tomorrow by Weasel to survey a line to the nunataks near Shackleton.

As usual the Argentines served much vino and other intoxicating beverages. Mac's flying was quite wild and erratic on the way home. After Ronne, Hugo, and Paul got out, the other three went back up. Mac started buzzing buildings and antennas and came so close one time that everyone watching was sure he would hit the whistler antenna. He pulled it up, but had to bank to avoid it. I went out after supper to see a dog they brought back, which Ronne is making them keep in the aviation building. It was a pretty scared and worried-looking pup.

The glaciologist at the Pole, Remington, asked to talk to Kim on the ham radio. He wanted to know about his micrometeorite program. Kim came up and described to him how he is collecting surface snow samples each day and melting [them] down. He siphons the water out with an electromagnet under a glass plate in the jar, which pulls the magnetic meteorites down to the glass. He then evaporates the remaining water and scans the plate with Clint's microscope. He found about 50 irregular fragments and about 6 perfectly spherical metallic particles with pitted surfaces ranging from 5–50 microns in size. He has also analyzed cores from our 14-m shot holes and is planning on taking cores from the walls of the deep pit. Remington is going to try a similar experiment at the Pole.

These are the first attempts to find meteorites in Antarctica as far as I know. In 1961–62 we returned snow cores from an oversnow traverse in Antarctica for micrometeorite studies. Since the 1980s meteorites have been routinely collected from "blue ice" areas in abundance.

> Hugo was down in the galley (he putters around until 0200 or 0300 every night) taking pictures and also copying some of the 16 by 12 enlargements Cox has placed on the wall there. Ronne saw him and started to chew him out for copying official Navy photographs for his own use. Hugo stood it for a bit, and then told Ronne that he was a fine one to talk of such things, because Ronne has had Cox make copies of many pictures which Ronne is planning to use for his private purposes. Ronne told him, "That's none of your business!" Hugo told him to "stop acting like a kindergarten child with a tin star." After a few more minutes Hugo told him he could "prosecute—to the full extent of the law" if he desired, and then walked out.
>
> In the evening Mac came in to the radio room and tried to get Forlidas to get through to Little America to answer Crary's request for a talk. Ronne of course was there and (as he had done several times) let Chuck Forlidas know that he didn't care if he couldn't get through. At any rate they didn't make contact.
>
> *14 Oct., Mon.* I talked to the folks this morning. Now that the antenna is finally repaired, the radio is working very well—when there is an operator. It was windy with lots of snow in the air so we worked indoors.

This was the last strong wind we had that spring, and it was not much. We never had the equinoxial storms that Ronne had been concerned about. Although we had plenty of whiteout and weather during the traverse, which was not safe to travel in, we never had any real storms. In contrast, we had many bad storms on the Antarctic Peninsula Traverse that I led in Ellsworth Land and Palmer Land in 1961–62.

> Clint had the traverse people in right after lunch and went through the "first-aid kit" he and Mathis are preparing for us.[1]

Nowadays, neither the Navy nor the National Science Foundation would supply an Antarctic field party with some of the medications we took along, particularly the morphine, Demerol, codeine, Dexedrine, and phenobarbitol because of concern about drug abuse or lawsuits. Life was a bit simpler in those days.

Ronne came in after supper and again told Ed that the only possible route is southeast to the Transantarctic Expedition route. He offered to go ahead in a Weasel and mark the route, building a new cairn every five miles.

This is just a grandstand play for his press releases and political maneuvers. It would be ridiculous for him to go a couple of days ahead in a lone Weasel while we follow with a crevasse detector later. Hugo is violently opposed to this plan. Ed is weighing the politics involved plus the possibility that we might have the opportunity to pull the Captain out of a crevasse.

Ronne was called up to the radio room, because Forlidas had Little America. Ronne sent Camp to check Hugo and Paul's room to see if they were asleep. Hugo wasn't in bed which disturbed Ronne. However, the band dropped out before Ronne could talk. [Later] Ronne told Forlidas not to try to contact Little America any more.

15 Oct., Tues. We took the Sno-Cat out this afternoon. The clutch seems to be working fine. We hooked up one of our traverse sleds (loaded with food and fuel) and pulled it with no trouble in third gear.

Fortunately the clutch worked well for the entire traverse. Ronne's comments in his phone patch to Odishaw on 7 October, about driving the repaired Sno-Cat out or us taking two Weasels out on the traverse, showed how little he or the rest of us really knew about the crevasse problems we were soon to face. Although they weighed less than the Sno-Cats, the Weasels had a significantly greater ground pressure and would have broken through snow bridges over crevasses more easily than the Sno-Cats. It never would have been possible to safely drive a single Sno-Cat out to join the field party even if our tracks in the snow had not been drifted over.

Kim started mess duty yesterday. We essentially have daylight 24 hours per day and there are no aurora to observe. Kim has been telling us about the meals of the "silent five." Willie, Clint, Con, and Mac don't say a word at meals. [As was the mess cook's job, Kim had to bring the officers' food to their table because they did not stand in a chow line at Ellsworth.] As Clint put it, "It's like eating at the Automat with four strangers." Willie and Clint leave early. Con waits and smokes his pipe. Finally, when he leaves, Ronne and Mac start conversing.

I made some ski bindings tonight out of some GI crampons. When they were complete I took a ski tour around the base. Very enjoyable. I think I will ski along with the Sno-Cat on traverse occasionally.

I never did ski along with the Sno-Cat, but I constantly used the skis in crevassed areas and in laying out the seismic cables.

The following came in 15 Oct.:

FM: BYRD STA
ACTION: ELLSWORTH STA
INFO: LITTLE AMERICA 141800 Z

NR 1 NGD FOR THIEL. RECOMMEND YOU SUGGEST TIME FOR WEEKLY RADIO SCHEDULE CW OR VOICE WHILE OUR TRAVERSES IN FIELD. REQUEST YOUR ETD [ESTIMATED TIME OF DEPARTURE]. BYRD TRAVERSE IN NOV ONE. BENTLEY

We have only our 7.5 watt Angry 9. We have made a weekly schedule with Byrd Station traverse, but I don't know how soon we will be able to reach them. We will start about 800 miles apart. They tried to contact Shackleton on the Angry 9 in the radio room but were unable to do so. South Ice, however, 250 miles south, heard them fine with a good signal strength.

Picking up South Ice was possible because the station was at a high elevation on grounded ice.

16 Oct., Wed. Little America tried to contact us this morning about 0730 for Crary to talk to Ronne, they said. Don and Jack heard them loud and clear on their receiver, but [Ken] Kent (on the ham gear) couldn't seem to hear them at all. Don says Ronne gave the radio people the word not to make the contact.

Augie, Ed, and I took our resurrected Sno-Cat out to Point A and shot a reversed profile reflection determination of ice-shelf thickness and depth to sea bottom. We are all set to start our reflection profile on traverse. Hugo was upset that we worked on our program rather than on traverse preparation, but this was essentially our first station of the traverse.

We determined that the ice shelf was about 750 ft (230 m) thick and that the seafloor was about 2600 ft (790 m) deep. Ellsworth station was located over a trough in the seafloor (Thiel Trough), which we had first observed from the water-depth measurements made from the *Staten Island* on the voyage in the previous January.

> *17 Oct., Thurs.* The new Otter, which had been in its original crate all winter, made its trial run, and then Ronne took Jack over to Belgrano to help work on their ionosphere recorder. They dropped Jack off just in time for dinner. Jack reported to us that they had quite a meal. They served pizza, steak [Argentine beef is some of the finest in the world, and definitely superior to U.S. beef], a soup course, and finally the main course of two stews. Canned fruit for desert. Wine was the only beverage during the meal but coffee after the meal. This is the usual noon meal.

I think this meal must have been a bit special because Jack was there. I, too, had a fine meal at Belgrano in February 1959, while stopping by for a gravity tie.

> Jack told us of some Weasel accidents that the Argentines had last week. They dropped two into crevasses within two minutes but no one was hurt and the vehicles were pulled out. They have a group in the field which arrived at Shackleton a couple of days ago. They had a big party there; we heard the Shackleton operator, Taffy, telling the folks at South Ice about it.

Apparently British-Argentine relations were not too bad then, even before the Antarctic Treaty dealt with the competing claims issue—sort of.

> One of our fellows visiting Belgrano suggested taking a couple of the Argentines over here for a visit. Jack thought it a pretty good idea, but one of the Argentines explained that Captain Ronne had told them they couldn't visit Ellsworth Station without a permit from Washington. (The Brits just drop in when they want to, which I am sure annoys Ronne.)

This supposed "official" U.S. negative attitude doesn't seem very neighborly or likely. It is ironic that Ronne was so reserved with the Argentines during this year, in contrast to his efforts to work with the Instituto Antartida Argentina following the IGY. He went back to Ellsworth and Belgrano on the Argentine icebreaker in the 1958–59 season.

> *18 Oct., Fri.* I was awakened at 0230 today to talk to my brother, Dave, in Decatur, Ill, which I really enjoyed.

This was the only conversation Dave and I had that year.

> Ronne took Ed on a flight this afternoon over the key area at the west end of the rift [Grand Chasm] in question. There are crevasses, but the route doesn't look absolutely impossible. However, Ed thinks it would be pretty risky so we are all agreed now to go over to the Shackleton (Transantarctic Expedition) route. Ronne, Ed and Hugo had a meeting tonight at which the Captain was very genial and friendly.

I realize why we too must have appeared pretty stubborn to Ronne.

About two months later during the traverse, I was on a flight over this crevassed area and took pictures. I did not then, nor do I now, upon reexamination of the photographs, think we could have driven safely through that area. However, by the time I took those pictures, I had gained a lot more experience operating Sno-Cats in crevassed terrain.

> Finally Crary got through from Little America. It was a rather anticlimactical talk, as Crary seemed to be waiting for Ronne to talk about our "lack of cooperation," as he did with Odishaw, and Ronne didn't mention it. Ronne told him that there have been six recon flights so far and that he would take another one to convince Thiel that we can't get through the crevassed area except towards the Shackleton route. Ronne closed the talk rather soon. Ed went up and wanted to talk to Crary, but Ronne wouldn't let him. He never even told Crary that the clutch was repaired.

> *19 Oct., Fri.* The Seis Sno-Cat, which Ed and Aug were using, developed symptoms as if it were running out of gas. It coughed and wheezed such that they left it about a quarter mile out and walked in. I went to bed right after supper but got up at 2100 to help Ed and Aug lower a 300-lb box of ice cores down to the first shelf of the pit to keep them cold while we are on traverse.

> The past two or three days have been very clear and sunny. Although it was –10° to –15°F, I was able to work in comfort in only a

Area at west end of Grand Chasm from air looking east. The en echelon segment in the foreground is estimated at about one-half mile wide and several miles long.

sweater today. Of course I had a cap on over my ears, and mittens on. In a couple of days the sun will remain above the horizon 24 hours/day. It has ceased to get dark at night for some time now. Everyone wears goggles or sunglasses all the time when outdoors. Spear and his crew have been digging out all the sled loads of supplies that Ronne had him pack up against the tunnels last fall. Many things (e.g., 10-ton sleds, pipe, iron stock) are being damaged by the scoops of the D-4s.

Ronne and Jack had a meeting. Ronne wants to put Don on mess duty, and Jack won't let him. He told the Captain that we still have the tape of Crary's talk of 17 May and that he doesn't consider this an emergency. He refused to allow this unless Ronne contacts Jack's boss at the National Bureau of Standards.

20 Oct., Sun. In the afternoon I started packing my bags for traverse and going home. We will be all set to go aboard ship when we leave on traverse. What a discouraging job it is to pack.

21 Oct., Mon. Mac, Ed, Ronne, and Willie left camp about 1030 this morning in the Otter on a significant reconnaissance-exploration flight.[2] They flew south on a bearing of 190°. Somewhere about 100 miles out the snow surface rose up to 3000 ft but no rock showed. [They were over Berkner Island.] Whether or not Ronne saw any land in 1947, he can legitimately claim Edith Ronne Land exists at this point. Mountains were seen in the distance to the east [probably the Shackleton Mountains]. About 300 miles out they noticed the surface dropped to about 1700 ft, but a range of mountains trending east-west roughly for 20 miles rose up to about 9000 ft giving a local relief of around 7000 ft. These are pretty big mountains.

These mountains are the Dufek Massif and the Cordiner Peaks, all in the Pensacola Range. The highest peaks in the Dufek Massif are about 7200 ft (2200 m). It is difficult to accurately estimate elevations from planes like this considering that the barometric altimeter had been set at Ellsworth and barometric pressure changes couldn't be corrected for. Elevations of many peaks observed on early aircraft flights in Antarctica were erroneously estimated this way. It is only human nature that these estimations always erred on the high side.

The Dufek Massif and Pensacola Mountains were photographed and named from a U.S. Navy P2V aircraft flight from McMurdo in early 1956. However, that flight mislocated the Dufek Massif about 100 miles to the east, because the only method of air navigation in Antarctica until inertial navigation became available in the 1970s was dead reckoning supplemented by crude sextant observations of the sun.

They flew around the range and Ed took pictures. This was at approx 82°28.5'S, 49°40'W.

Ronne is reported to have dropped a claim marker on this flight, which was the last made by the U.S. in Antarctica and is also significant because it was made after the beginning of the IGY on 1 July 1957. This is probably why he did not want to take Hugo. Ronne apparently also made a claim for the U.S. on a VX-6 flight in January 1957. These claims were likely classified in 1957, but Deborah Shapley found the actual record. It gives the date of this flight as 23 October, as reported by Ronne, and the position of the claim as 85°30'S, 49°W (about 208 miles south of the Dufek Massif).[3] This position seems impossibly far from Ellsworth for the range of the Otter. What is more, Ronne was at Ellsworth on Wednesday, 23 October, so the flight could not have taken place that day.

Ronne, in his book, *Antarctic Command,* reports flying "80 to 90 miles south-southwest" of the Dufek Massif, so that is probably where he reported this claim drop. He indicated seeing more mountains in the distance, which must have been the Schmidt Hills in the Neptune Range of the Pensacola Mountains. If this is correct, Ed did not report any of it to us.

There was no crevassing in the snow surface and very little for the whole distance which they flew. By this time over half their gas was gone, so they turned back and needed the tailwind, which was fortunately present, to get them home. The weather closed in about 1530, but the plane landed safely at 1730. They had 20 gallons of fuel left (the Otter uses about 35 gal/hr).

Ed wants to head for this range as soon as we get around the east end of the rift. Ronne agrees with him, but Hugo favors heading directly towards the rendezvous point with the Byrd traverse at 81°S, 75°W. At present there is more enthusiasm in the group than there has been since we left the States. Hugo is understandably bitter because Ronne wouldn't let him go on the flight. If we can reach these mountains, then swing over to meet the Byrd group and get on to Mt. Hassage at 77°30'S, 71°40'W, we could have the best of the three U.S. traverses. In spite of what Ronne says, Ed and Hugo think it will be fairly difficult and dangerous getting around the east end of the rift.

Jack posted the following on our board:

> THE POLAR NIGHT IS OVER
> Oh I have passed a miserable night,
> So full of fearful dreams and ugly sights,
> That as I am a Christian faithful man,
> I would not spend another such night,
> Though 'twere to buy a world of happy days,
> So full of dismal terror was the time.
>
> > −W. Shakespeare
> > *Richard III,* Act I, Sc 4

22 Oct., Tues. Overcast most of the day but clearing around 1900 with the temperature dropping down in the low −20s°F. I spent the day doing odd jobs such as getting the climbing ropes recoiled and into a box in the staging area and getting the paper, hypo, and developer we will need ready for the seismic work. Jack went into continuous operation at 2100 (0000 Z) to record any effects of the solar eclipse that is due here tomorrow morning early.

Ronne had Cox develop Ed's black-and-white pictures of the flight. He wants prints to submit to the Board of Geographic Names. As I write this, Kim is remarking about the various expressions that cross my face as I furiously scribble away. He has compared me to a monk in his little cell with a single candle burning, copying ancient documents. He sits cross-legged on his bed typing with his portable typewriter and most disconcertingly looking anybody who happens to be addressing him right in the eye as he does so.

23 Oct., Wed. We all went out about 0140 to watch the eclipse of the sun. It was really quite spectacular and the only solar eclipse I have observed. It was about –30°F and only a few people were out. I climbed up in Kim's tower and watched through the theodolite in the dome. Gary Camp also came up. The rest shivered and stamped outdoors and froze their cameras. It was not quite total, but the colors were quite beautiful, particularly at the darkest point when an eerie purple light covered everything.

I went back to bed only to be reawakened at 0600 for a phone patch with Ruth. Augie and Hugo worked in the pit until 0630 and slept in. Ed's exertion in watching the eclipse kept him in bed most of the morning. Jerry and I were the only civilians at breakfast. I spent the morning carrying things out to the sleds and packed a supply of food for several days in a box Paul had prepared. I drove out in the afternoon and loaded the explosives we will use on traverse.

Paul and I mounted the gyrocompass in the #1 Sno-Cat after coffee this afternoon.

The three traverses were supplied with fragile, expensive gyrocompasses, mainly because of the generally false impression that magnetic compasses do not work in Antarctica. Despite this myth to the contrary–particularly among pilots–magnetic compasses work well in Antarctica except very close to the south magnetic pole, more than 2000 miles away from Ellsworth. The mistaken impression comes from the very high magnetic declination due to the geometric effect of the convergence of longitude at the poles. For example, if one were to walk around the geographic south pole (the location of South Pole Station) holding a magnetic compass, the needle would point in the same direction all of the time, but the magnetic declination would have changed 360°.

Actually the magnetic field is lower in the area of our traverse than in much of the northern conterminous U.S. The magnetic pole is on the other side of the continent from Ellsworth about at the coast, hundreds of miles from the geographic south pole. By the time of the Antarctic Peninsula Traverse, which I led in 1960–

61, we had changed to Army surplus tank magnetic compasses. These worked very well and were rugged enough to withstand the rough ride of the vehicle.

In early 1961, I was flying aeromagnetic profiles out of Byrd Station (80°S, 120°W) in a Navy R4D8 (a DC 3) aircraft, when the gyrocompass failed. The magnetic compass worked fine, but as the navigator had no tables of magnetic declination, which was known from the oversnow traverses, he had to resort to rather heroic measures to get us back to the base.

> The five Wisconsin men, McCarthy, [Dick] Grob, Cox, Ed Thiel, and I had our picture taken with the Wisconsin flag after lunch. Cox and Ronne then took individual stills and movies of the traverse people.

This is the day Ronne reported that he, Ed, and McCarthy made the long flight to the Dufek Massif and Pensacola Mountains. As I noted in my journal, these three men were at Ellsworth, so, again, Ronne must have had his date wrong.

> Don really gave it to the Captain at the movie tonight in the form of remarks and disturbances distinctly aimed to upset Ronne. It did. This sort of thing seems childish to me.

The next day, there was a note on the bulletin board announcing that Don Skidmore was going on mess duty the following Monday. It was widely assumed that Ronne was retaliating.

> Ed is doing very little towards the general traverse preparation. He is working on the seismic preparation, but on nothing else. This morning when he got up he just packed his gear and wrote in his log. I defend him to the rest, but I feel Hugo is somewhat justified in his resentment of Ed's attitude.

It sounds like the stress of final preparations for the traverse was getting to me also.

> After the movie Paul, Hugo, and I worked on shelves in the Sno-Cat.
>
> *24 Oct., Thurs.* Clear, sunny, and about –30°F. Ronne, Beiszer, Mac, Willie, Gary Camp, and Larson flew over to the penguin rookery

just west of Gould Bay. They landed and walked right amongst the emperor penguins which showed no fear. There were many young birds, as this species hatches its eggs in the winter. They saw many frozen chicks. Apparently any youngster that wanders too far from its parents freezes pretty quickly. They brought six of the frozen birds back. Willie and Mac each plan on having one stuffed. Beiszer wrestled with one of the larger ones and found it very strong. Ronne plans on going back tomorrow.

This, and pretty much everything else I describe in the following pages about the penguins and the seals, is now illegal under the Antarctic Treaty Agreed Measures for the Protection of Antarctic Flora and Fauna. Those provisions, however, were not established for a number of years to come (1964).

The helicopter boys spotted a seal with a newborn pup down at the tide crack. Con landed, and they brought the pup back to camp. We all took pictures and then Beiszer, Brown, Jackson, Greaney, and Ed lugged it back to mama in the Weasel.

The Captain talked with Fuchs 300 miles out of Shackleton tonight. We all listened. They are having a difficult time finding a route up the icefall to the inland ice. Ronne told him about the gentle crevasse-free slope to the southwest that he found on 21 Oct. Fuchs was glad to hear of this but hopes to find a way where they are, as it would delay them quite a bit if they had to shift their advance base from South Ice to somewhere else.

Fuchs and his party could have probably traveled a much easier route south along the Filchner Ice Shelf to the south of Berkner Island and climbed to the polar plateau passing to the west of the Dufek Massif and Cordiner Peaks in the Pensacola Mountains. However, none of us knew of this unexplored territory in 1957.

[Sir Edmund Hillary] has reached the inland ice and is well on his way with the support party from McMurdo.

Sir Edmund Hillary, who with the Nepalese sherpa, Tenzing, had made the first ascent of Everest, was leading the New Zealand support party for Fuchs' Transantarctic Expedition. His mission was to find a safe route from Scott Base at McMurdo Sound to the 10,000-ft-high ice sheet of East Antarctica, so the Fuchs party would have a known route down to the Ross Ice Shelf for the final part of their crossing of Antarctica. He also was scheduled to lay fuel caches at 80°S and 83°S.

Fuchs wished our traverse the best of luck. They must have quite a powerful transmitter, as we heard them clear as a bell on Jack's radio.

25 Oct., Fri. Ronne, Con, Cox, Brownie, Lewis, Jackson, and Greaney flew over to the penguin rookery. They ran around taking pictures and picking up eggs and dead chicks. Ronne brought two of the birds back alive. He intends to kill them and present them to the Smithsonian Institution. They had quite a struggle getting them into the plane, but once in the air [the penguins] stood quietly looking around at the people and out the window. They obtained their revenge when one kicked an egg and broke it. This released such an awful stench that everyone came very close to vomiting. . . . Most had no appetite for supper.

There are only seven known emperor rookeries in the world (other than this one). Only one rookery has been studied so far as we know, and that was only for a short time. It seems a real shame that someone with some scientific training wasn't allowed to get over there and make some observations.

Eventually, while we were in the field on the traverse, Kim was allowed to fly over to the emperor penguin rookery and make the only scientific observations ever made at this site to my knowledge. As of about 1990, Robert Hofman, a marine biologist, told me there is no record or knowledge of this rookery, located at the coast near Berkner Island, so perhaps it has been vacated by the birds.

Hugo, Augie, Kim, and I drove #1 Sno-Cat down to the old seismic ramp tonight after supper and walked out to see the Weddell seal cow and her pup. They were doing fine and we all took lots of pictures. The beast just lay there with the youngster, suckling all the while. The mother hardly bothered to raise her head to look at us. She was about eight or nine feet long and very fat with a light grey coat. It was –30°F with a wind, so we froze our noses a bit. The seals were across the tide crack on the bay ice, which we reached with no difficulty. The sun was low and the colors were quite striking.

I walked over behind the airdale buildings and looked at the penguins. They were imprisoned in a box and looked quite pathetic with blood all over them and inside of the box.

Emperor penguin with chick in rookery west of Gould Bay (Official U.S. Navy photo by W. Cox).

In examining my old color slides during the writing of this book, I found several pictures of these beautiful emperor penguins in the blood-spattered crate in which they were imprisoned while waiting to be butchered.

When he came in from the penguin rookery, Ronne jumped in his private Weasel (there is only one other still running) and tried to drive under a low antenna lead-in wire. Of course it broke, and most of the work that Don accomplished in his days in the ham

269

shack was for naught. One lead came down all the way out to the antenna farm. There is no ham gear tonight.

Ronne was reported as saying that someone deliberately lowered the antenna wires where he drove his Weasel in an attempt on his life.

26 Oct., Sat. Kent and I finished checking out the crevasse detector. We read the detector from a dial on the dash. After lunch Ken, Al Spear, and I drove down to the unloading site for the ship. The device showed a few anomalies where there were some visible cracks and a few in other places. I'm not sure that we can depend on this apparatus too much.

Ronne and Mac killed the two penguins today in the most brutal manner imaginable. First they had to catch them again because someone let them go. Unfortunately, the injured one was not very ambitious, because they didn't get very far. First the Great Antarctic Explorers jabbed the birds in the eye with an ice pick hoping they would die when the brain was pierced—they didn't. Then they kicked them down and stood on their heads. Next they tied ropes around their necks and dragged them back and forth across the snow in an effort to strangle them and clean the blood off their breasts.

After they dragged them around camp from the airdale building to the garage, the one with the injured wing died. The other got up, and with blood streaming from its eyes tried to walk away. Finally Ronne kicked it down and stood on its neck until it died. The whole operation took over an hour. Everyone here is pretty disgusted at the whole affair. I've heard that some rotten penguin eggs are being saved for Ronne's room for Halloween. Clint took some movies of the slaughter, and Hugo wants to show them to the Explorers Club. Ronne chuckled (perhaps embarrassed) and joked during the proceedings about the penguin's ghosts coming back to haunt him. It seems they could have found a more humane way to kill them.

I did not actually observe the killing of the penguins, only partly because I was too busy on traverse preparations. There were many witnesses taking pictures including several of the scientific group. Everyone was pretty upset at the manner of the penguins' deaths, but in 1957 we were not particularly bothered by the thought of taking them back as "specimens." As we were not biologists and had no scientific need to take samples, however, there was really

F. Ronne in process of killing emperor penguin (Photo by J. Malville).

no justification for this needless killing. It was this sort of "collecting" that ultimately led to prohibitions against killing Antarctic penguins, other birds, and seals. Now there are serious criminal penalties under U.S. law and the Antarctic Treaty against disturbing penguins and other wildlife. Any person who travels to Antarctica is given very specific instructions on the legal prohibitions regarding interference with penguins.

Paul and I split a 25-roll pack of 36-exposure Kodachrome at $3.25/roll (including processing).

This was Kodachrome 12 (ASA 12), all that was available in 1956. We bought it from Ship Stores, the Navy base exchange. Actually we wanted fresh film that had been kept cold all winter, so had to go search it out in storage in the unheated Jamesway huts. We feared that film kept at room temperature for the past year would have deteriorated. Ship Stores items were kept away from the station to prevent pilferage, I assume.

27 Oct., Sun. Busy, busy, busy! We all spent the day on various odd jobs that needed doing. I tried to start the Sno-Cat #2 and found the engine raced. After a little trouble I fixed that only to find gas spraying out underneath the vehicle. The gyro compass wasn't working properly, and the receiver in one of the radios was dead.

271

With Dave and Kent helping we repaired both. I finished my packing and loaded all my gear on the sled.

Ronne wants Hugo to take more gas on the sleds, but Hugo does not want to load them over 2.5 tons each and burn the clutch out. Ronne is worried about avgas. He had Haskill tell Lassiter, while he was at the rookery, that he had 9000 gallons for him. We threw off as much stuff from the sleds as we could. Ronne is now screaming about overloading. The way it is now, if anything goes wrong on traverse he will blame us, and anything accomplished he will take credit for.

That's exactly what he did in his book, *Antarctic Command.*

Captain Ronne, Mac, Con, and a large group of men (no civilians) flew over to Shackleton in an Otter and the helicopter. One of their geologists showed Lewis some rocks and tried to tell him about them but he couldn't remember much when he got back. It's too bad Augie couldn't have gone over.

While they were gone someone stole the dead penguins. Ronne is in a rage; he doesn't know what to do. I understand that he walked out of the movie tonight because everyone was making noises imitating penguins. They clapped when he left–Skidmore the loudest. Don is wearing a big knife and remarked in the movie that there have been "two murders" lately and "you never can tell who is next." Ronne saw him in the galley after the movie and asked him to come up to his room for a talk. Don told him that he is too busy, but to come over to the science building and see him if he likes. Ronne called Ed in and told him he is convinced that Don stole the penguins and stuck the knife in the door. He has no evidence, but he told Ed he was going to restrict Don from movies, rec hall, and ham shack. Ed told him that Don could sue possibly for any such action.

Some of the airdales were down by the tide crack tonight and found some emperor penguins. They captured five and brought them back. Don got one and had it walking around in our traverse supplies staging area in the tunnel, so we all could see it. They plan on taking the birds back to be stuffed. They killed the five in a box with carbon monoxide using a hose from a Weasel exhaust. The execution took 10 minutes. . . . [?! or so I rationalized at the time]. Ronne will really be furious now that Don has a penguin to take back.

Don (with Ed Davis' help) baked us a batch of cherry turnovers to take on traverse tomorrow. It's supposed to be a surprise, and as head of the commissary department I'm the only one who knows.

We came to the end of the second phase of this expedition and were about to enter the third and most crucial part, an oversnow traverse south of the Weddell Sea coast. The previous pages have described the life and happenings at Ellsworth Station. Although there was a lot of trouble and strife, we did have a lot of fun.

Among the many positive things implicit in my preceding journal entries was the strong camaraderie developed among us as we coped with our arduous winter work and indoor troubles. I was only 24 when I left the States, and despite the various stresses found I could live comfortably among an isolated group of men (I would have preferred some women around) and quite enjoy myself. I did some growing up.

I really appreciated the opportunity to observe the changing Antarctic seasons, the wildlife, the wind, aurora, sea smoke backlit at midwinter by the sun below the horizon, and the Southern Cross as we observed it directly overhead in the night sky at noon. I may have more trips to Antarctica, but I doubt I will ever spend another winter there.

Notes

1. A partial list of first-aid kit supplies includes: Donnatal (inhibits secretion in the digestive tract); Geluselor (reduces acid stomach); paregoric (relieves diarrhea and intestinal pain); eugenol (for toothache); ZnO (for mixing fillings); procaine 2% (local anesthetic); epinephrine (adrenaline); Pyribenzamine (antihistamine); oxytetracycline (antibiotic); penicillin (antibiotic); streptomycin (antibiotic); morphine; syrettes (for pain); Demerol (for pain); foot powder; fungicidal ointment; Auralgan (for earache); codeine (for pain); procaine hydrochloride; boric acid (antiseptic); phenobarbitol (sedative); Seconal (sedative); Tetracaine ointment; tetanus toxoid (immunization); Bacitracin ointment (antibiotic); Vaseline sterile petrolatum gauze dressing (for serious burns); caffeine and sodium benzoate (for overdose of morphine); APC (aspirin and caffeine); Cortone acetate (cortisone); sodium sulfacetamide; Tetracaine ophthalmic ointment; Dexedrine (amphetamine); moleskin; dextran (IV food); *Cascara sagrada* (laxative); brandy; surgical soap; absorbent cotton; gauze; battle dressings; eye pads; eye cup; tourniquet; hemostats; 4-0 nylon suture with needle; syringes and needles; thermometer; traction splint; wire ladder splint; *Merck Manual;* Excavator.

2. I am sure of the 21 October date of this reconnaissance flight because of this narrative taken directly from my journal. I checked with Kim Malville in 1996, and his diary agrees on the date. However, our first geographic paper published in 1959, by the five traverse people with Hugo as senior author, gives the date as 24 October. Ronne, in his book *Antarctic Command*, gives the date as 23 October. The 23 and 24 October dates are incorrect because there is no uncertainty that our traverse party departed 28 October, and my journal tracks consecutively to that date.

3. Deborah Shapley, *The Seventh Continent, Antarctica in a Resource Age* (Washington, D.C.: Resources for the Future Inc., 1985), p. 315. Shapley attributes finding the record to Henry Dater in the Records of the Office of the Secretary of Defense, Records of the United States Antarctic Projects Officer.

8
Ellsworth Station to Berkner Island

Finally after three months at sea, the Antarctic winter at Ellsworth, and an intense few weeks of preparation, we left on an oversnow geophysical-glaciological traverse across the essentially unexplored area south of the Weddell Sea coast. Now we would find out whether the establishment of Ellsworth on the sloping ice front of the Filchner Ice Shelf the previous February had left us a reasonable route into the interior of Antarctica or isolated us north of the Grand Chasm.

Our primary scientific objective was the measurement of the snow-surface configuration, the ice thickness, and the depth to underlying bedrock, using the seismic reflection and gravity methods. We would measure snow accumulation, average annual temperature, and other glaciological characteristics of the ice sheet, make observations of the earth's magnetic and gravity fields, study the geology of any mountains we encountered, and make other scientific observations.

As we approached the Weddell Sea in late December 1956, all that was known of the area we were now entering was the approximate edge of the ice shelf to the base of the Antarctic (then called the Palmer) Peninsula based on the flights of Ronne and his pilots, James Lassiter and Charles Adams, in 1946–48.

On the *Wyandot* and *Staten Island* we had determined that a 4000-ft-deep (1200-meter) trough, of unknown trend, existed beneath the Filchner Ice Shelf east of Gould Bay and that the water depth was only about 1000 ft (300 m) west of Gould Bay, deepening to about 2000 ft (600 m) towards the base of the Antarctic Peninsula. Finn Ronne, Ed Thiel, Hugo Neuberg, Chuck McCarthy, and Willie Sumrall had made a flight south over the ice shelf on 16 March, where they rediscovered a large rift (the Grand Chasm, which Dr. Vivian Fuchs had seen the east end of the previous year) of unknown length, apparently blocking any direct route to the interior.

On 21 October, Finn Ronne, Ed Thiel, Chuck McCarthy, and Willie Sumrall had made a flight due south of Ellsworth over the high-grounded ice of what is now named Berkner Island, to the Dufek Massif. These mountains had been first seen, but mislocated, on a flight by William M. Hawkes of Navy squadron VX-6 from McMurdo in January 1956. All else was unknown and unexplored.

We did not know if the high ice area was extensive or not. Ronne had named this general area Edith Ronne Land, based on his flight from the west on the 1946–48 Ronne Antarctic Research Expedition (RARE). It was on this flight that Ronne had discovered and named Gould Bay. We did not know how extensive the Filchner Ice Shelf was nor what the sub-ice bedrock configuration was. The only information we had on mountains to the west was the reported existence of Mt. Hassage seen by Ronne at 77°30'S, 71°40'W, where we hoped to meet or at least intersect the track of the Byrd Station Traverse.

The Filchner Ice Shelf Traverse, as our traverse came to be known, was one of three major field parties working in the U.S. Antarctic Program during the 1957–58 austral summer. The other two were the Ross Ice Shelf Traverse (led by Albert P. Crary) out of Little America Station, and the Sentinel Traverse (co-led by Charles R. Bentley and Verne Anderson) out of Byrd Station at 80°S, 120°W.

Although there was some local fieldwork in the areas around Little America, McMurdo, and Wilkes Stations, the major logistics efforts in the U.S. IGY Program, other than station resupply, were in support of these three geophysical-glaciological traverses. Together, we were continuing the major effort started by Charlie Bentley's Little America–Byrd Traverse and the Soviet traverse of the previous summer, led by Andrei Kapitsa, to map the configuration and thickness of the Antarctic ice sheet. The French also started similar geophysical traverses during the IGY. By 1966, we had accomplished this objective to a first approximation, entirely from seismic reflection and gravity methods. Although Goeffrey Pratt on the Transantarctic Expedition made seismic measurements, this was a secondary objective of traversing the continent, and he managed to obtain only sparse ice soundings, due to their need to move fast. The radar ice-sounding method used from airplanes revolutionized the ease of ice-thickness determination over grounded ice, but did not become routine in Antarctica until the late 1960s.

Because at the time of the IGY most of Antarctica had not been seen from the air, and even the coastline was not completely mapped, all of us on the oversnow traverse program had, by necessity, to be explorers as well as geophysicists and glaciologists.

We left Ellsworth with two Sno-Cats each pulling a 2.5-ton sled filled with fuel, food, explosives, and all of our scientific and other equipment. I had made a small flag with the emblem of the Wisconsin Hoofers (University of Wisconsin outing club), which I flew for the entire traverse from the antenna of our seismic Sno-Cat, but we did not fly an American flag as we did on the Antarctic Peninsula Traverse in 1961. The vehicles were not running as well as we would have wished, but we were psychologically ready to head out no matter what was in front of us. We were also very glad to leave Ellsworth Station behind!

28 Oct., Mon. 0–30.6 mi. This morning when we got up there were two dead penguins sans heads propped up in the main tunnel. They were Ronne's. He told Kim, whom he chanced upon in the tunnel, that no Navy man would dare do a thing like that. It would mean five years in jail. He found a penguin head in the seat of his Weasel.

By this time we were really ready to get out of town! Our mental attitude had already shifted to the traverse despite this dramatic event, so I spent little ink discussing it or speculating on the identity of the perpetrator. None of us in the traverse party ever made any attempt to find out who might have stolen or decapitated the penguins after we eventually rejoined the group, and to this day I never have found out more.

Ed Davis fixed us a lunch and gave us a gallon of coffee. With all the last-minute things, it was 1030 before we were ready to leave. By the time all the photographers (almost everyone in camp) had taken their pictures and we had shaken hands all around, it was 1130. Ronne gave us a bottle of wine for Christmas. It was a beautiful sunny day, about −10°F, when we left Ellsworth Station.

It was heartwarming and encouraging to see the number of well-wishers there were. With one exception they are all a pretty good bunch of fellows. Kim was very wistful. He really wanted to go with us. Other than the traverse group, he is the only one down here who is interested in this sort of thing (of course there is Ronne, too).

Traverse party just before departure from Ellsworth (left to right): E. Thiel, J. Behrendt, P. Walker, H. Neuberg, and N. Aughenbaugh (Official U.S. Navy photo by W. Cox).

I realize now what a cheap shot this comment was. Certainly Finn Ronne would have wanted to explore Edith Ronne Land as leader of our traverse. At 58 years old, he was as physically fit as any of the rest of us. From my perspective of 65, as I write this passage in 1997, I have a better appreciation of what this might have meant to Ronne. I am still an active Antarctic field geophysicist and climb 14,000-ft peaks occasionally. Kim Malville was still climbing 20,000-ft mountains in the Himalayas at 59, in 1993. Nolan Aughenbaugh plays a couple of hours a week of racketball at 67 in 1997.

> I put in my first magnetic station at Point A and we then headed on an azimuth of 140° (southeast), taking gravity, magnetic, and altitude observations every five miles.

We used the gravity and magnetic measurements to study the variations in density and magnetic properties in the rock and therefore to make inferences about the ice-covered geology. We also used the gravity data to determine the depth to bedrock between the seismic reflection stations; this is possible because the rock is much more dense than the ice or water. The lower the gravity, the deeper the bedrock.

The "terrain" was absolutely flat most of the way and the driving was uneventful. The Sno-Cats worked fine except that the exhaust pipe in #1 kept setting the floor on fire.

Traverse at intermediate station. I'm reading magnetometer (foreground), P. Walker, standing, and N. Aughenbaugh (left background) making snow hardness measurement at lead vehicle. E. Thiel on track of #2 Sno-Cat. Gravity and elevation measurements are being made. Note bicycle wheel odometer on rear sled. Crevasse detector on lead vehicle.

The floors of the Sno-Cats were wood, and I helped put such a fire out with snow. The exhaust pipe was adjusted and caused no more problems.

Hugo, Paul, and Aug rode in the first vehicle with the crevasse detector while Ed and I took the second. We had 120-ft coiled nylon (military olive green) climbing ropes hanging at the ready from the useless headlights of each Sno-Cat.

We had a radio in each vehicle, and the drivers were in constant contact using headphones to hear over the roar of the engines and noise of the vehicle tracks on the surface.

The logistics of our IGY oversnow traverse were dictated by the fact that state-of-the-art electronics at the time depended on the vacuum tube rather than solid-state electronic microcircuits available today. The hundreds of tubes in our seismic system required large amounts of battery power. The power requirements, in turn, required two 250 amp-hour batteries weighing 175 lbs each to produce the 24 volts we operated at. The only recording system was the heavy oscillograph "camera" with its tanks of photographic solutions.

The seismic Sno-Cat carried a total load of about 1000 lbs of electronic equipment, gravimeter, magnetometer, and seismic batteries. Counting the weight of two people in our vehicle, we carried about the maximum allowable load. Each Sno-Cat used about one gallon of fuel per mile or about 420 lbs for a 30-mile day for two vehicles. This fuel—a little more than one barrel per day—would determine how frequently we needed resupply by the single-engine Otter aircraft available. These planes could only carry a few barrels of gas in one trip depending on our range out of Ellsworth.

Unlike many Antarctic field parties today, we could not have used snowmobiles (which had not yet been developed) because of our heavy loads. There were two other significant reasons for using the high fuel-consuming Sno-Cats on the traverses. The first was safety. As mentioned elsewhere, a Sno-Cat was the lightest snow-pressure vehicle available at that time, which proved very important in crossing crevasses. Also, we were not on an adventure expedition, but were a working scientific field party. Therefore any convenience in general camping greatly speeded up our progress. After a number of occasions when we had been up for 24 hours or more, it took less than a minute to crawl into a sleeping bag after stopping for the "night" or after downing a quick meal.

Although Augie usually put up a small "pop tent" for himself, putting up and taking down Scott tents, as geologists and geophysicists commonly use in semistationary Antarctic field camps today, would have been inconvenient for a field party moving every day. This was particularly true when stopping in a storm or when surrounded by invisible bridged crevasses.

Navigation over the course of a day's travel was by dead reckoning, using the gyro compass mounted in the lead Sno-Cat, #1. As the odometer was broken in that vehicle, Hugo used a bicycle wheel with an odometer he had bought in Chile, and attached it to our sled to measure the distance. This is the way Scott, Shackleton, and Amundsen had done it, so Hugo would, too. Considering that he had repaired the clutch on our Sno-Cat, and that Ed and I had a working odometer in our vehicle, we could have worked something out if Hugo had wanted to. However, Hugo, in his determination as co-leader to manage this aspect of the operation, insisted on using the bicycle wheel. At any rate the compass–bicycle odometer system worked well.

Hugo also wanted to be in the lead vehicle, because the crevasse detector mounted in it (projecting about 16 ft ahead) was necessarily in the lead at all times. This suited Ed and me just fine. Several years later, when I led a traverse with three vehicles, we traveled with one four miles ahead of the other two for leapfrog barometric altimeter corrections.

About every 30–40 miles, Hugo measured the exact position of the sun using a theodolite on a tripod. He determined the time with a chronometer checked with a time signal from the U.S. National Bureau of Standards radio station WWV, which we received well. He then calculated our position using a slide rule (pocket calculators did not exist) to better than a half-mile accuracy using a nautical almanac. It was easy to steer a Sno-Cat in a straight line despite the weaving, which averaged out. Therefore, we could correct our dead-reckoning position every day that we stopped for station work, using the accurate position obtained from the sun shots. Hugo was the only one of us who knew celestial navigation.

The Sno-Cats with compasses and odometers were amazingly accurate to steer on a planned course. In 1960–61 I navigated by dead-reckoning to poles left by an earlier traverse and in blowing snow to a field camp. Unlike ships and airplanes, Sno-Cats didn't drift sideways. Traveling at only 3–5 miles per hour, they did not get very far off course in 8–12 hours.

We had no geographic information, so we used a blank gridded chart as does a ship plotting its position at sea. In this manner we mapped the course of our traverse and any features of the snow surface that we could observe. The process somewhat resembled blind men attempting to describe an elephant, as our horizon was quite limited.

About seven miles out we came across a trough with the detector indicating crevasses. About this time the sled behind #1 broke through and sank about three feet but was pulled out by the Cat without stopping.

As described earlier, crevasses are tension or shear fractures in the ice shelf, with steep vertical sides, and extend from 50 to hundreds of feet deep. This small crevasse was probably about 70 ft deep, pinching out at the bottom, but we generally could not see the bottom when looking down. The extreme case on our traverse was the Grand Chasm, which extended entirely through the ice shelf at 1500-ft thickness there.

Although we saw open crevasses on the traverse, the ones that gave us the most trouble were bridged with snow and could not usually be seen from the surface as we drove along. Sometimes we could safely drive across snow bridges, but other times we broke through. The Sno-Cats were nearly as safe as a man on skis because of their relatively low weight and four wide tracked pontoons. We estimated about three to four pounds per square inch of snow pressure. At any rate, as noted earlier, they were much less likely to break into crevasses than the Weasels.

It is much easier to see bridged crevasses from the air, but this method is severely limited, even when a plane is flying directly over crevasses. The crevasse detector was never of much use to us. There were many false indications or indications of crevasses with bridges too thick to concern us. This detector was probably meant as a surveying instrument and, as such, during the unloading of the ship, for example, might have been useful in locating dangerous spots on the route to the camp. However, at the three to five miles per hour we were attempting, it wasn't effective. When we encountered serious problems, we realized from the start that we had to leave the Sno-Cats and search each crevasse out with long T-handled tubular aluminum probes.

Con and Brownie flew out in the helicopter and landed. They said they would fly ahead and come back if they saw anything bad. They didn't come back. About this time (1600) the weather closed in and we drove in near whiteout getting gradually worse until 2230 when we stopped to camp, as visibility was too poor to continue. We are now 30.6 miles from camp.

29 Oct., Tues. Visibility was poor when we woke up, so we put a station (seismic and glaciology) here today. It was about −10°F all day. We discussed driving tonight, as visibility wasn't too bad. . . . Most people objected. Hugo and I favored it. We camped here again.

The pair of field trousers I have been wearing since the ships landed finally went to pieces, and I had to dig my only other pair (brand new) out of my sea bag.

The observations we made at each seismic-glaciology station consisted of a seismic reflection to measure the depth to bedrock; seismic measurement of the increase in sound velocity (and thus snow density) with increasing depth; and digging a two- or three-meter snow pit to measure snow accumulation and other glaciological parameters such as density, layering, and temperature.

Although I have previously described our seismic reflection work around Ellsworth Station, some repetition here may be helpful. Ed and I would lay out our 1200-ft seismic cables in an L shape, which we unrolled from chest reels. We would hand-drill a four-inch diam-

P. Walker digging snow pit for accumulation measurements.

eter hole from 6 to perhaps 25 ft (2–8 m) deep, usually at the apex of the L. We fired a small explosive charge of one to five pounds of ammonium nitrate detonated with an electric blasting cap and a one-pound high-explosive primer charge. The sound waves penetrated to the ice-water contact (in the case of the floating ice shelf) and to the water-rock (or ice-rock) contact and reflected back to the surface where they were picked up by the geophones. Each of the 24 geophones was attached to one of the channels in the cables.

Firing seismic reflection shot. Box containing explosive charges of ammonium nitrate (Nitramon) and cable reel in foreground.

I'm operating seismic equipment in Sno-Cat. These instruments contained hundreds of vacuum tubes that required power from two 175-lb batteries.

The seismic signals were amplified and recorded on photographic paper for each of the channels. We could identify the reflection by noting the wave form on each channel at slightly longer times the farther the geophones were from the shot point at the center of the "spread" at the Sno-Cat. By knowing the velocity of the sound waves in the snow, ice, and seawater beneath the ice shelf, we then calculated the depths to the various reflectors.

There was some hazard associated with laying out the cables when we were working in crevassed areas. In these cases we skied, which offered some protection. We also used skis when we were not in areas of known crevasses, if the snow was soft.

In addition to the pit, Hugo and Paul would hand-drill a hole 30 ft (9 m) deep and place an electric-resistance temperature probe on a cable in the bottom. This would come to equilibrium "overnight," and the average annual temperature of the surrounding area was obtained. This is possible because the winter-temperature cold waves and the alternate summer-temperature warm waves damp out essentially a constant temperature by that depth after several years.

The mean annual temperature was measured this way to an accuracy of about 0.1°C at intervals of 30–40 miles on thousands of miles of oversnow traverses crossing Antarctica. If repeat measurements were made at some of these locations today, any global warming greater than about half degree during the intervening 30–40 years could be detected. In 1991, I and two others proposed to do a pilot study of this close to the South Pole, where about eight different traverse tracks converge, but it was not funded.

We lost radio voice contact with camp almost immediately and couldn't hear them this morning (on CW) [carrier wave]. Hugo tried to contact them at 1000, for we missed our first sked [schedule] at 0800 but couldn't. He sent the weather in anyway.

"Carrier wave" consists of using the dots and dashes of the Morse code, which was the method the Navy radio operators at Ellsworth used for most of the message traffic.

Hugo can send and receive about 15 words per minute. I can send about 10 and receive about 5. No one else of our group even knows the code.

Hugo did all of the communications this way, and we essentially never communicated with Ellsworth on voice at all with our Angry 9 radio.

Radio communication was very difficult throughout the traverse. This was not only because our 7.5-watt transceivers were not very powerful, but also partly because we were on the ice shelf floating on seawater—a good electrical conductor. Our traverse had the worst communications during this season of any of the three. Our best communications with the Angry 9s occurred when we were on high-grounded thick ice. Radio communication is much better for field parties in Antarctica now and has been for several decades.

Visibility improved, and about 1300 the helicopter appeared again with Con, Ronne, Cox, and Beiszer. Ronne wanted to take pictures of us working. He wanted to see a shot, but we were changing spreads at the time and he couldn't wait. The people who flew out told us that our radio had been received in camp.

These two trips on 28 and 29 October were the only times on the traverse we saw the helicopter.

We had tenderloin steak and mashed potatoes with butter for supper. I have been doing all the cooking. Oatmeal for breakfast this morning and a stew of hamburger and mashed potatoes last night. Snacks for lunches.

Ed, Augie, and Paul were soon taking turns at breakfast while I slept in. Hugo never cooked because he was the mechanic, which kept him plenty busy.

Water is our big problem, as none of our heterogeneous collection of stoves is very efficient at its production. Needless to say we don't wash to speak of.

We never washed dishes but just wiped the remains of food out of pots and the Army canteen cups or tin cans we ate from. Each of us had his own cup and utensils (usually just a spoon, as we had sheath knives or pocket knives to cut meat). I had an Army canteen cup and Hugo used an old tin can. We had no problems with this crude method and suffered no harmful health effects because it was too cold for the food remains to decay.

Cooking was always done outside at Hugo's insistence, and we all ate in the #1 Sno-Cat, which was also Hugo, Paul, and Aug's bedroom.

Augie usually slept in a tent for some privacy. Paul and Hugo slept on long shelves in their vehicle, while Ed took the empty shelf in ours (seismic gear was mounted on the other), and I had

I'm cooking at about –30°F.

the floor. We each used double Army sleeping bags with 60% feathers and 40% down, and they were always very warm and comfortable. As the summer progressed and it warmed up, we removed the outer "shell" bag and were quite warm in the inner bags only. Because we traveled with the sleeping bags on the shelves, any moisture that had condensed in or on the bags dried out each day and never caused any problem. We had air mattresses that we never deflated, which we kept on the shelves while driving and working in the Sno-Cat.

There are clothes, dishes, and miscellaneous junk tucked into every available nook and cranny of both vehicles. #1 has shelves with doors built underneath the two main shelves. We have a set of metal drawers taken from Ed's room locker mounted in our Cat.

We burned four quarts of oil and about 40 gallons of gas yesterday. Today, in running the engine to keep the heater going so we can do seismic work, we used a quart of oil and 12 gallons of gas. Of course, we don't have any heat at night in order to save fuel. [As the weather warmed up, we did not use the Sno-Cat heaters at all.]

Con brought a letter from Jack and told us that a dispatch had come in from Harry Wexler (chief scientist for Antarctica; Crary was acting as same during the winter) this morning stating something to the effect that IGY people shouldn't be doing household duties, as it interferes with their work. Jack called [H. G.] Celery [IGY ionospheric physics panel] a week ago secretly on the ham gear and explained some of our situation.

Jack's note told of another incident between Don and Ronne. Don is mess cooking now. In the galley during a meal he told Ronne to stop making accusations about him. Ronne (through Al Spear) sent a signed letter to Don similar to that given Jerry quoting a clause in the UCMJ and restricting him for an indefinite period from movies, rec hall, and use of ham gear. Don is complying and keeping the letter.

Ronne came up to Kim this morning and told him that the "emergency" situation was over and he wouldn't have to mess cook in December. He was very friendly, asking about his work and everything.

Ronne sent the following message to Washington on 29 October about the status of our traverse party, but we did not get a copy until 9 November:

TRAVERSE PARTY DEPARTED AT NOON 28 OCT ON COURSE 144 TRUE. FIRST COMPLETE STATION 30 MILES OUT REACHED SAME EVENING AND FIRST STATION FOR SEISMIC AND GLACIER STUDIES UNDERWAY. WILL FLY OUT IN HELICOPTER AFTERNOON 29 TO OBSERVE. 35 MILES FURTHER TO END OF RIFT SHOULD SEE PARTY SAFE TO CONTINUE WESTERLY. TRAVERSE PARTY INTENDS DETOUR ABOUT 120 MILES TO MAKE MOUNTAINS RECENTLY DISCOVERED AT 82°30'S, 49°W BEFORE CONTINUE WESTERLY TO RENDEZVOUS WITH BYRD PARTY. FULL SCIENTIFIC PROGRAM MAINTAINED AT STATION IN THAT FIERLE HAS TAKEN OVER GLACIER MEASUREMENTS OF NEUBURG AND MALVILLE. WITH RETURN OF DAYLIGHT CONTINUE OPERATE

MAGNETOGRAPH, COLLECT METEORITES, AND
WORK OVER COLLECTED DATA FOR REPORTS.
BROWN AND SKIDMORE MAINTAIN IONOSPHERIC
AND WHISTLER PROGRAM UNINTERRUPTED. . . .
HEAVY WORK SCHEDULE BY STATION PERSON-
NEL CAUSED MALVILLE TO ASSIST THE MESS HALL
FOR 14 DAYS AND SKIDMORE PRESENTLY ASSISTING
FOR SAME PERIOD. . . . EVERYTHING SMOOTH AND
PROCEEDING FINE IN BEST INTEREST IGY PRO-
GRAM. REGARDS

Ronne wouldn't let the discipline chiefs write their sitreps this month, as Jack mentioned that his program was curtailed by Don doing mess cooking.

After the traverse left Ellsworth, the situation between Ronne and the civilians deteriorated further. Without the five of us, he was able to put even more pressure on the remaining four.

30 Oct., Wed. 58 mi. Again we overslept for the 0800 radio sked, but Hugo got through, using CW, at 1000. He had to use our radio because the one in his Cat wouldn't receive properly. It was pretty white at 0700 when I looked out, so I went back to sleep. Hugo had some more work to do in his snow pit, so we didn't get under way until 1230. It cleared as we headed on to the southeast.

We developed engine trouble in our Sno-Cat about mile 46. It seemed to be getting insufficient gas. Hugo cleaned the filter. Our heater, which has been working poorly since our last engine trouble, just about quit today, and it became very cold inside. I nearly froze my feet driving. Hugo decided to drive this vehicle so I rode in the other one. The temperature dropped with our clearing south wind and was –28° when we finally stopped at 2230.

We crossed two large troughs about 40–45 ft deep and about a mile wide. As we started up the second side, we came upon a large crevasse crossing our route about 40 ft wide. It was bridged with snow but visible.

We got out to probe. It seemed as though we could proceed through, but as it was 2330 by this time we decided to camp and wait for the helicopter to come out tomorrow and look ahead for us.

We had 5-in-1 rations heated on the heater in #1.

We would usually thaw these canned goods by putting a case in the vehicle for several days while driving. When we were in a hurry and had none thawed, we just put frozen cans in boiling water.

It was beautiful out but cold with a low sun making long shadows. It was down in the –30s°F. We all sat around in #1 enjoying the warmth and singing songs with Hugo playing his harmonica and Paul his uke.

31 Oct., Thurs. Hugo talked to camp at 0800. The receiver in his Sno-Cat wasn't working, and the heater in ours is out so he had to use the key at –30°F. He was so cold he switched to voice and barely managed to get through. Bob Haskill [the Ellsworth radio operator] came in fine. We asked for a helicopter to scout for us. Visibility wasn't too good there, so we contacted them again at 1000. Bob said they were just taking off. They never arrived. Poor visibility must have forced them to return. It was hazy when we got up. Visibility worsened all day, and it was quite white in a few hours.

We stayed here all day, at first waiting for the 'copter and later because of bad weather. Hugo worked on our engine. He and Ed took it for a spin, and it seemed to work all right. Hugo worked on the heater without much success. The rest of us sat around and read. Paul slept. We ran one of the jet heater tubes we have over to the sick Sno-Cat from the other heater so Hugo would have a little warmth.

Paul skied ahead for a quarter mile this morning and reported a bigger crevasse, also bridged, parallel to the one right here. He saw a line of hummocks trending east-west an undetermined distance ahead [which suggests crevasses there]. We spent a very lazy day. I made a big batch of onion–chicken noodle soup for supper with baked beans, fruitcake, canned peaches, milk, cocoa, bread, and butter.

Generally we preferred the frozen meat and other food to the 5-in-1 rations. However, the canned fruit was particularly appreciated. Carefully, we would divide up the peaches or cherries, counting each portion exactly. Invariably there would be an odd number of pieces left in the bottom of the can. We used a counting game, "horsengoggle," to award the last items to the lucky winner or winners.

As I write this we are all gathered in #1 Sno-Cat, which has become our dining room/living room and bedroom (for Hugo, Aug, and Paul). Oh yes, Hugo also uses a corner as his office to do his glaciology work. We have the radio on and are listening to music on the BBC. Outside at present it has cleared somewhat (2230). There are rainbow sun dogs visible around the sun on the southern sky. It warmed up to –10°F but cooled down again as night approached and is now –19°F and dropping. I just mixed myself up a pint of McKee's Instant Orange Juice Crystals. (Sample, Not for Sale.) This is very good stuff. It contains 96% of original ascorbic acid and needs no refrigeration. Delicious.

1 Nov., Fri. Cloudy again in the morning, so we decided to go back to our last gravity station (about a mile) and put our second seismic-glaciology station in. By the time we were back, it was 1230. I melted up a big pot of water for photographic solutions. We laid out our seismic reflection spread and drilled our 8-m shot hole at a 300-m offset. We fired a one-half pound TNT block and got reflections from the bottom of the ice shelf and the bottom of the ocean. We then set a short spread with two-meter spacing and pounded on the wall of Hugo and Paul's snow pit to measure the velocity of the near-surface compressional and shear waves. We finished our work by 1800, but Hugo and Paul worked after supper on theirs.

After supper Augie, Ed, and I ran a gravity and level line across this large trough. I was rod man.

It cleared off again tonight and turned cold. I got cold. I went to bed at 2345 and slept like a log. It was down in the –20s°F.

2 Nov., Sat. 74.8 mi. Ed got up at 0700 and fixed breakfast. Hugo was on the radio at 0800 and told camp that we needed air support. We were all packed and ready to go. It was a beautiful, clear sunny day. Hugo took some sun shots to get an accurate position determination. We waited and waited and waited until at 1400 we decided to go east without the planes. Just then an Otter appeared and landed behind us. Mac, Lewis, and Kent jumped out. They had been looking for us for some time. Kent fixed up a poor receiver we had, and we unloaded the three barrels of fuel and a small assortment of other items they brought. These latter included a pineapple upside-down cake and a case of beer.

It seems they have been looking for us for the past three days. Two days ago, Con tried in the helicopter. He ran low on fuel and returned for more. When he landed he found he had an oil leak and had lost five gallons of oil. If he had found us and landed, he would have gone down on the return to camp. Willie tried yesterday in an Otter with no success. They left their lunches in the plane and we ate them this afternoon.

Mac gave us his copies of some dispatches that came in this morning. One [from Hugh Odishaw] read: "WITH DEEP SORROW I FORWARD TO YOU INFORMATION RECD FROM MC-CALL GLACIER EXPEDITION [AN IGY STATION IN THE BROOKS RANGE, ALASKA] THE DEATH OF DR HUBLEY. AERO MEDI-

Otter bringing supplies. One Otter flight could carry only two to six barrels of fuel (depending on range), or 1.5 to 10 days' supply.

CAL LABORATORY FAIRBANKS ANNOUNCED THAT DEATH WAS CAUSED BY PROLONGED EXPOSURE. REQUEST CRARY FORWARD MESSAGE TO OTHER FRIENDS OF HUBLEY IN ANTARCTICA."

Dick Hubley used to be head of the Juneau Ice Field Research Project (JIRP). I met him there and spent a couple of days with him when he hiked up to the Lemon Glacier and worked with Ed and me in summer 1956.

In one of our initial scientific reports, we named the large island separating what is now the Ronne Ice Shelf from the Filchner Ice Shelf as Hubley Island. When Lassiter flew in he brought a *Time* magazine, and it contained the startling note in its "Milestones" column that Dick Hubley died "by his own hand." This came as quite a surprise to us. He stripped to the waist and walked away from camp (on McCall Glacier in the Brooks Range) and lay down in the snow to "die–Eskimo fashion." We later learned he had also taken a dose of sleeping pills.

The island was officially named Berkner Island after the chairman of the IGY. To my knowledge nothing was ever named after Hubley, who really was a casualty of the IGY winter that drove him to suicide.

Another message [sent 1 Nov.] from Radm. Dufek to Ronne ["slapped his wrist" about the long flight to the Dufek Massif]:

FROM: COMNAVSUPFOR ANTARCTICA
ACTION: ELLSWORTH STA
INFO: NAF MCMURDO COMNAVUNITS ANTARCTICA. AIRDEVRON SIX [VX-6] IGY WASH DC. CHINFO. REP COMNAVSUPFOR WASH DC.
012331 Z NO. 11

CONSIDER YOUR RECENT FLIGHT TO THE SOUTH HIGHLY COMMENDABLE AND OF REAL SIGNIFI-CANCE TO IGY PROGRAM. AM OF OPINION, HOW-EVER, THAT FLIGHTS TO DATE PROVIDE SUFFICIENT TERRAIN INFORMATION FOR EARLY PHASE OF IGY PROGRAM AND THAT U.S. AIRCRAFT SHOULD BE EM-PLOYED IN LOCAL SUPPORT OF TRAVERSE PARTY AS PLANNED. PROTRACTED FLIGHTS IN SINGLE-ENGINE AIRCRAFT SUCH AS NOTED IN YOUR 251347 Z OCT. NECESSARILY ASSOCIATED WITH CONSIDER-ABLE HAZARD DUE LACK ADEQUATE SAR AIRCRAFT WEDDELL SEA AREA. POSSIBLE NEED TO DIVERT US-ABLE AIRCRAFT FROM MCMURDO OR LITTLE AMERICA IN EVENT POSSIBILITY WOULD UNDOUBT-EDLY NECESSITATE RETRENCHMENT OR ABANDON-MENT ASSOCIATED IGY PROGRAM AT ROSS SEA.

REFERENCE TO NEW DISCOVERY VIEWED WITH INTEREST SINCE AREA INVOLVED SUPPOSEDLY IS INCLUDED IN TRIMET PHOTO COVERAGE OB-TAINED BY P2V [A LONG-RANGE ANTISUBMARINE AIRCRAFT USED FOR HIGH-ALTITUDE PHOTOGRAPHY] DURING DEEP FREEZE I, AND SELECTED PHOTOS WERE PROVIDED BRITISH TO ASSIST CONTINENTAL PARTY IN PENETRATION RANGE CURRENTLY REFERRED TO ON HYDRO-GRAPHIC OFFICE AND NATIONAL GEOGRAPHIC CHARTS AS PENSACOLA MOUNTAINS.

They say Ronne is "all shook up" by this dispatch.

This message "damned with faint praise." Dufek obviously considered that the risk of such a long flight by the single-engine Otter was not justified by the geographic "discovery" of mountains that had actually been photographed and named by the Navy nearly two years previously. I wonder if Dufek was unaware that Ronne dropped a claim marker. There was no mention of a U.S. claim in any message I saw. Was Ronne making claims independently of Dufek and Operation Deep Freeze? The particular range in the Pensacola Mountains that Ronne reported "discovered" had been named the Dufek Massif, so I suppose George Dufek had his eye on it even if it was not accurately located. The flight referred to is the one of 21 October with Ed, Mac, and Willie. It is interesting that a copy of this message was sent to the chief of information (CHINFO), where Ronne sent his press releases. Obviously Dufek wanted to alert CHINFO that these mountains were not new discoveries and to hold or revise any press release that Ronne had sent.

> Ronne was not in the plane, so Mac took all five of us up for a spin to check the terrain ahead. In the direction we had been heading (about south) there are many crevasses and also to the east. We saw several bridged crevasses we have crossed already. In fact our camp spans one such. Our Sno-Cat was on it all night, while I had the best sleep I've had in months. There were lots of crevasses all around, but we thought we could make it by heading at 50° [northeast] for a while.

I noticed how difficult it was to see our vehicles from the air. The single-engine Otters were not equipped with radar, which could easily locate the aluminum-sided Sno-Cats and did with the aircraft supporting the other two U.S. traverses.

> Mac left and we loaded the gas on our sleds. We found that by hooking the edge of a drum on the side of a sled, two of us can load the 365-lb barrel without too much trouble.
>
> We headed northeast for six miles and put in a gravity station. Con flew in just then with three more drums of gas. He was accompanied by Lewis and Jackson. It seems that just as they were about to leave, Jack Brown with Clint Smith drove a Weasel into a cre-

vasse near the edge of the barrier. They climbed out all right, but now Dave is mad as hell and trying to get the Weasel out. Jackson told Augie of an accident they just heard of. The way I understand it, the aurora observer at Little America fell into a 60-ft-deep crevasse and is in pretty bad shape. He was going to go on their traverse and they're supposedly in the field now, so perhaps it happened on traverse.

The accident occurred on the Ross Ice Shelf Traverse (Crary's party), and the man was Peter Schoek. Hugh Bennett, the assistant seismologist, went down into the crevasse and pulled Schoek out. With difficulty, an Otter landed in the crevassed area and the injured man was evacuated. He was flown to New Zealand, where he made a successful recovery. Schoek had been a mountaineering guide in the Austrian Alps. He probably had more experiences in crevasse work than any of us.

Con looked around for us and headed us on a safe course (he thought) by buzzing us in that direction. We started out at 142° but three miles along we turned right (to 170) to avoid a disturbed area we could see, with open crevasses. We crossed a large trough and several bridged crevasses. Two miles further we turned left to 115°. Another five miles along we changed again to 135°. From this point on, we found ourselves in a field of bridged crevasses, some up to 40 ft wide, which we crossed the way porcupines make love (very, very carefully). None that we crossed looked as bad as the one we didn't cross two days ago. At 2200 we stopped. Hugo plotted our position from the sun shots he took. This took about three hours. We tried to contact base and ask for air recon to no avail.

3 Nov., Sun. 85.1 mi. At 0200 we started up again with Augie and Ed driving #1 and #2, respectively. (Paul and I had driven up to this time.) There was quite a discussion prior to pushing on whether it was advisable or not. I put my air mattress down on the floor and went to sleep.

I recall this discussion clearly today. I was very sleepy (having been up 19 hours) and figured that we were either going to break into the crevasse or not. At any rate, I wasn't going to do anything about it since I stopped driving. It was safer in the Sno-Cat than walking. Perhaps it was all denial!

295

We crept out of the crevasses in a few more miles. Pursuing a course changing back and forth from east to south as terrain dictated, we arrived at 0415 (81.5 mi.) at the edge of the big rift, or Grand Chasm, as the British call it. We took a few pictures and headed east along the edge looking for a place to cross. We saw a snow petrel while driving along the north edge of the Grand Chasm. We decided to stop at 0730 and get some sleep.

When I woke up at 1400 it was clouding up. I let the rest sleep for a while and wrote. . . . I made some mashed potatoes and fried some steak for a belated breakfast at 1600. We packed up and started on, but drove a few miles when it became so white we had to stop.

Hugo probed into a crevasse at this point. We (i.e., Ed and Hugo) decided that rather than waste a day, we would put in a station. We drove back to our last gravity station where we had slept, and went to work. We started our seismic work about 1830 and finished by 2300 and I cooked supper. I heard on radio Moscow tonight that the Russians have launched their second earth satellite.

4 Nov., Mon. The poor glaciologists are still working now at 0135. I'm glad I'm a seismologist.

Sno-Cat approaching Grand Chasm.

Still whiteout when I got up at 1130. Ed and I spent the afternoon reading, as it was too white to travel and there was nothing else to do. I fried up some hamburgers and cooked some rice about 1730. I woke the three in #1 and we had supper (or breakfast?). We sat around reading in the other vehicle. The temperature was about

0°F, as warm as we have had it since we left Ellsworth. We kept our vehicles warm by running the Coleman stoves.

I suppose there may have been some carbon monoxide risk from the stoves but in the drafty Sno-Cats this never became a problem. We used the Colemans from then on as well as on other traverses.

The regular heaters burn too much gas and necessitate the engine operating to keep the battery charged. We put out a long wire antenna tonight, which improved reception quite a bit.

Because of the low conductivity of the snow, a transmitting antenna can be placed on the snow surface with no problem. A greater problem on the Antarctic ice sheet is finding an electrical ground.

On the BBC news tonight we heard that Hillary has managed to get up the Skelton Glacier and onto the inland ice. No news about the main party of the expedition.

Aug and I played bridge with Ed and Paul. As the game dragged on, it began to clear.

5 Nov., Tues. Finally about 0300 we decided we would try to push on. I cooked some cereal and we were ready to go when we found to our dismay that the thermostats in the gravity meter had gone haywire; it was overheating. We put in a new thermostat and waited several hours for the instrument to come to equilibrium. It was 1210 when we finally started on the road. When it cleared off this morning we could see the escarpment of Coats Land [east of Shackleton and the Filchner Ice Shelf] along the eastern horizon. As we progressed, we kept it in view for many miles. This is the first "land" (i.e., grounded ice) I've seen since the ships landed.

We had just started when an Otter whizzed in; Willie and Fred Drydal climbed out. They had three barrels of fuel for which we gave them two empties (the Navy wants all the empty drums back).

By 1960–61 we were using rolling fuel transporters on the oversnow traverses, consisting of 500-gallon tires filled with fuel and air. At present fuel is delivered to remote geophysical parties on the ice sheet from wing tanks in the Hercules ski LC-130s.

Willie told us of a big row between Ronne and McCarthy. Mac resigned as executive officer. He refused to let Ronne come along on the flight today. As far as he is concerned the aircraft are only going to be used to support the traverse. Willie brought five copies of *The Daily Sandcrab,* that Jack typed up, giving us the lowdown on what is happening at Ellsworth these days.

Willie took the five of us up and we looked around. We found that we were not far from the east end of the Grand Chasm. There were many open crevasses in the area between which we had to make our route. We saw that the trail we had made Sunday (3 November) during the whiteout ran parallel to and about 20 ft away from a long bridged crevasse. This is what Hugo had probed into. We are lucky we didn't try to continue on that day.

I have a picture from that flight which shows our tracks alongside and only a few feet away from a bridged crevasse as wide as our vehicles. We had turned away from this crevasse and retraced our exact tracks to our present position.

Willie stayed with us as we drove through this area. This was really wonderful for us. He kept in close radio contact and flew back and forth directing us to the right or left as required. We never saw any of the trail flags from the Transantarctic Expedition. It began to cloud up, just as we entered the dangerous area, but Willie stayed with us even though he must have been worried about the flight home. For 10 miles and over two hours he helped us around the rift and into the clear area on the south side. After the way we stumbled around not knowing what direction to go Saturday night, we really appreciated this. Willie finally left us about 1530 and went home. It is so easy to see a good route from the air and so hard from the ground. Crevasses just are not visible even in clear weather until one is nearly on top of them.

It turned out to be a blessing in disguise that we had trouble with the gravity meter. Otherwise we might have been blundering around in the crevasses yet. After Willie left we headed south (at 185°) for five miles to avoid the end of the rift and then swung onto a course of 225 which we pursued for 25 miles.

6 Nov., Wed. 121.1 mi. Our engine started acting up again, but not as badly as before. We kept on going until 0140 when we stopped. Directly in front of us is a high escarpment of ice or land. This took us by surprise because we knew of no land here. We will have to see about this.

Crevasses near east end of Grand Chasm. Traverse party was guided from air by Otter (Official U.S. Navy photo by W. Cox).

It is now 0235. I have been up for 40 hours. We just finished a couple of cans of 5-in-1 kidney beans heated on the heater. I think I will go to bed now.

Although I described our progress around the east end of the Grand Chasm rather matter-of-factly, I realize that the adrenaline must have been flowing to keep me awake that long.

We woke up about 1600 and put in a seismic station. The bottom of the ocean is deeper here than at Ellsworth, indicating something resembling a fjord running south paralleling the escarpment to the east.

We named this the Crary Trough in a paper published in 1958. However, the official name, Thiel Trough, after Ed, is a major feature, as we discovered in the days to come.

7 Nov., Thurs. We ate breakfast about 1500. Aug and I skied down and looked over this feature which rises up to the southwest of us. It is much smaller and closer than we first thought, and consists of several crevasse-like tears in the surface of the shelf. The major one runs east-northeast–west-southwest and is about 50 ft deep. The "high land" seen from the end of our reflection spread is at the

299

same level as the ice shelf. We had driven down into a trough, and there was some sort of rift at the end.

8 Nov., Fri. 168.1 mi. We drove until 0800. Our engine gave us troubles again but Hugo thought we should try to coax it along, which we did. It cleared off and dropped down to the −20s°F. A 15-knot south wind blew. We continued at 225° after a slight jog east around our "midget rift," as Augie called it. We can see the high land toward which we have been heading to the west of us. It is about 25 miles distant and covers about 120 of horizon. Looking with the binoculars, I could find nothing to mar the regularity of its white expanse. Ronne and Ed say that it rises to 3000 ft. Our engine will have to run better than it does for us to pull up that. [We were approaching Berkner Island.]

We sacked in all day until about 2100. Mac flew out about 1100, but I didn't see him. He brought three drums of fuel and gave the news of camp. It seems that all the ham operators got sick of being pushed to get Ronne's phone patches so they quit en masse. Ronne threw up his hands in disgust and opened the ham gear to everyone who wants to operate it. Now he can go back to Washington and tell them that everyone on the base was allowed to operate the ham gear.

Willie, Brownie, and Bill Butler flew in at 1600 with more gas. Ed and I got up and helped them off-load. Ed cooked breakfast at 2100, and we started our seismic work.

9 Nov., Sat. We finished around 0400. The ocean bottom is deeper here than at the previous station. This is contrary to our expectations, considering that land is only 25 miles away.

I cooked dinner as usual. This time, however, I tried one of my famous (infamous?) stews. First I threw some frozen hamburger patties into some water (at −25°F with a wind, I decided it was too cold for frying). I had planned to use the broth for mixing up powdered potatoes, but I decided to experiment a little. I added some dehydrated cabbage, then a little celery salt. Two packages of dehydrated onion soup mix went next, followed by a small amount of curry powder (unfortunately these people aren't too fond of curry). Finally a box of Minute Rice and a half pound of butter. Reactions were generally favorable. Augie: "This is the best meal yet! You should patent the recipe." Paul: "Pretty good under the circumstances(?)" They all took seconds. Their compliments will, I hope, spur me on to new heights of culinary achievement.

It's sunny and clear right now (0700) and very beautiful out. This backward schedule we are now on has us sleeping during the warmest part of the day, and working during the coldest. Oh well, it will work its way around to normal in a week or so. We seem to be living a 30-hour day. Consequently everything we do regularly comes at a later hour each day.

I just crawled into my sleeping bag when a plane buzzed us. It repeated the maneuver about five times by which sign I knew that Ronne must be up there taking movies. They landed and Con, Ronne, Lewis, Mac, Camp, Cox, and Jackson climbed out. Ronne was all set to shoot movies of us working and was quite disgusted that we were finished already. He tentatively suggested that we shoot a shot for him, but received a cold reception to the idea. It is a holiday in camp. Exactly one year ago we sailed from Davisville.

While Ronne was here he began politicking with Hugo and Ed. He wants to give Lassiter gas to fly caches for us beyond the 250-mile limit of the Otter. I don't think we have the chance of a snow-ball in hell of finding a cache. Of course we all know what ax he is grinding by this maneuver. He wants to give Lassiter VX-6 gas and is using this as an excuse. If Lassiter would fly stuff to us directly we would be more enthusiastic over the idea. He also tried to talk Ed and Hugo out of heading for the mountains.

I went to bed when they left. About 1400 Mac flew in. Walt Davis examined the carburetor and took it back to camp to fix. About that time the heater in the other vehicle quit so there are no heaters in either Sno-Cat operating.

Jack sent us another letter, and Don sent a note offering to relay any messages via phone patch to our folks that we may have.

10 Nov., Sun. I awoke at 0100 and found it overcast and whiteout. I was so hungry I couldn't stay in the sack any longer. I lit up the Coleman stove, and Ed and I heated up some canned chicken and the rest of the cold fried bacon Ed Davis sent out. He also sent a delicious apple pie, some cookies, and a loaf of gingerbread, which we rapidly finished off. I also finished off Durant's *Caesar and Christ* and started another book. I wrote in my log and answered Jack's letter. Hugo, not to be outdone, wrote another letter (two page) re-stating everything I had said in his own words.

Some minor tension between Hugo and me, and within the group in general, existed. Had we not had Ronne on which to focus our anger, we probably would have had more dissension among the several strong personalities in our small party.

We started a bridge game after supper (I had finished the new book) and played until about 0100. Aug and I won by 500 points. When I went to bed, I had been up for 24 hours and didn't feel particularly tired.

11 Nov., Mon. I slept in until 1800. About 17 hours. Overcast most of the day, I understand . . . but it cleared with a south wind tonight. No regular meals. We opened a can of pre-fried bacon and found it quite good. Much better than that in 5-in-1 rations. The little buttons of ice which form on rivet heads in the ceiling when we use the Coleman stoves for heating are constantly melting and dripping down one's neck and on the paper one is writing upon. Most annoying!

12 Nov., Tues. 188.6 mi. More bridge; Aug and I won tonight. It is now 0440. I am going to start *Adventures in Ideas* by Alfred North Whitehead presently.

I slept from about 0700 to 0800 and then got up for breakfast. About 1030 a plane carrying Willie, Lewis, Jackson, Cox, and two carburetors landed. Willie took the five of us up to take a look at the terrain around the escarpment to the west. What we saw didn't look too good. A sort of point juts out slightly north of our direct route. A gentle, apparently crevasse-free slope goes up from there. Southward the slope steepens and there are many crevasses. Some of them are slightly arcuate while others are straight and run parallel to the strike of the slope. Another pattern observed ran perpendicular to the general trend.

The main objection to the gentle slope near the point was the existence of a number of small lenticular-shaped crevasses (some bridged) in the level shelf adjacent to this end. Some were broken through, while others were hardly visible. This struck us as being a particularly treacherous area. Four possibilities suggested themselves: (1) We could head for the point and hope to navigate the crevassed area adjacent to it; (2) we could try and find a route up a ramp Augie thought he saw to the south a bit; (3) we could try and approach the steep slope south of the point and then drive up the apparently crevasse-free alley at the foot of the slope to the point; (4) we could head south and look for a good route elsewhere.

We decided against heading south and to head on a bearing of 225° for five miles and then at 250°. Hugo put the engine back together and it wasn't until 1800 that we were underway. I drove the first 20 miles. Wally Cox is staying with us a while and is riding with Ed and me. He shot numerous pictures of our various activities. When we started driving, Wally left his Omega camera sitting on the shelf. This was a mistake, as it bounced off, knocked the lid off our big water pan, and fell into the water.

13 Nov., Wed. 200 mi. Ed took over driving and I caught a little sleep between stations. We had come a little over 30 miles and were getting close to the escarpment. We were quite a bit south of the point and could see vertical ice walls at the base of the slope. We came within 20 ft of an open crevasse. Then Ed remarked that he saw a crack in the smooth snow surface where it crossed by their trail. Suddenly about 100 yards ahead of us the #1 Sno-Cat and sled broke through a five-foot-thick bridge of a crevasse.

Fortunately it was a little narrower than the vehicle and sled. Unfortunately they happened to be driving right on the long axis of the bridge. The Sno-Cat passed the weak point but the sled broke in, pulled the Cat back in. The front tracks of the Sno-Cat held on solid "ground," but the rear two broke through. It scared the boys, and when they decided it had fallen as far as it was going to, Hugo and Paul practically pushed Aug out the front door as all three made a precipitous exit.

Ed, Wally, and I left our vehicle and with skis, ice axes, and a rope cautiously approached. After surveying the situation and probing a bit, we tried to extricate the Sno-Cat. Hugo unhitched the sled and Paul tried to drive the Cat out. The tracks spun. Ed unhitched our Sno-Cat from its sled and cautiously drove it down in front of the other. Using one of the 70-ft-long steel cables Ronne tried to get us to leave behind, we pulled the #1 Cat up on solid snow with ease.

Hugo and I then roped up, and belayed by Augie and Ed we climbed out into the sled suspended above the crevasse and unloaded all the boxes and equipment. I took a moment to look down into the depths from my point of vantage. The crevasse is about 100 ft deep with sharp jagged pinnacles and ridges of ice projecting upward from the bottom giving it a quite formidable appearance.

We unloaded the five drums of fuel from the uphill side using the sling and #2 Cat to pull each barrel out. We had a hurried supper of ham and kidney beans. Poor Wally was so tired that he couldn't eat. He hasn't become used to our unorthodox schedule. We hitched up a Sno-Cat each to the front and rear runners. Then as easy as you please we pulled the sled up and out of the hole onto the solid snow. By this time it was 0800 and quite clouded up so we all went to bed. Wally shared a tent with Augie.

Hugo made radio contact at 1000 with camp and told them that we were having trouble with crevasses and wanted some air recon. He did not tell them we had gone into one.

Sno-Cat and sled broken through snow bridge of crevasse.

Other than an hour sleep from 0700 to 0800 on 11 November and "a little sleep between stations" while Ed drove on 12 November, I–and essentially everyone else–had been up about 36 hours. No wonder Wally Cox couldn't eat!

4 Nov., Thurs. We slept in until 0800, about 24 hours.

I recall waking at one point and discussing with Ed whether we had been in our sleeping bags 6 hours, as he argued, or 18, as I maintained. Because we were in a total whiteout by this time, we could not tell from the sun. My kidneys forced me out to urinate, so I knew I was right although it seemed nearly impossible to have been "out" that long.

It was whiteout most of the day, so we played bridge. We don't want to move until a plane comes in. About 10 inches of snow fell covering our tracks and all the snow bridges. I fried hamburgers for supper. It began to clear around 1900 and we could see the slope [of Berkner Island] with all the crevasses quite clearly. From here we can't see any route up it. Perhaps we can run north along it and find a way. We know there are crevasses around here which are difficult or impossible to detect from the surface. The crevasse detector did not show the one the Cat and sled broke through. The bridge was about five feet thick and quite hard and difficult to probe through, so maybe we can't even check by probing.

We were in an area of "shear" crevasses resulting from the fast-moving ice shelf in contact with the much slower-moving grounded ice sheet of Berkner Island. These crevasses were bridged by snow and not visible from the surface even during clear sunny conditions.

Unloading sled stuck in crevasse (left to right): H. Neuberg, J. Behrendt, P. Walker (Official U.S. Navy photo by W. Cox).

They were about 50–100 ft long, 70–100 ft deep, lens shaped from above, about 20 ft at greatest width, and at right angles to each other. However, we did not understand this at the time. In contrast were long, linear open crevasses, visible a few miles to the west of us, on and subparallel to the steep east-facing escarpment of Berkner Island.

> It has been very warm during the past day, and up to 23°F this morning. Last night is the first time it has stayed above 0°F. With six of us eating in Hugo's Sno-Cat, it is quite crowded. The food box is more or less in the middle and generally provides a seat for two people. This unfortunate pair are continually having to get up and delve into its turbulent interior to pass the sugar or salt or milk powder etc., to the more fortunate souls who sit on the battery box and crevasse-detector control unit. It's no wonder Hugo is at his wits' end. Paul remarked that Hugo just doesn't have the right psychology for this sort of life. He is unhappy when things aren't clean, neat, and orderly. His favorite adjective describing the situation is, *"Schweinerei!"* In addition to the usual mess, Wally Cox has numerous boxes of photographic equipment stuffed into our "home." He has been shooting pictures of all our activities with black-and-white and color movies. He really strained to get to our meal tonight and our bridge game.
>
> I listened to the radio again early this morning. The only English-speaking stations I picked up were Radio Moscow (booming in on five frequencies) and several religious stations. One in Quito, Ecuador, comes in loud and clear all the time. We heard Voice of America this afternoon. All they ever have is jazz. I suppose that's what most of the world wants to hear from the U.S. BBC gives news at 2000 and 2300 each night and I try to catch that.
>
> It's now 2330 and I am sitting writing, warmed by our roaring Coleman stove. I don't feel too sleepy, but I suppose I'd better go to bed because tomorrow is apt to be another long day if it stays clear and a plane comes out. They could see perfectly now but VX-6 never operates except between the hours of 0900 and 1600 on clear sun-shining days. I shouldn't knock them though; they have been very cooperative and helpful.

The flying they had done and would do for us in the coming days of the traverse can be truly described as heroic!

> *15 Nov., Fri.* Breakfast at 0800. About 1000 we heard the approach of an Otter. It came in and attempted a landing. We marveled at the audacity of the pilot at making a high-speed landing in a crevassed area. Con Jaburg was at the stick and he thought better of the attempt, when they passed over one open crevasse. He gave it gas and took off again, just missing the slope of the rising land. The

plane landed OK on a second try, leaving a plume of loose-blowing snow behind it. Lewis was with Con.

Ed and Augie went up with Con to look over the terrain. Augie has the sharpest eyes and has the most experience in this sort of observation of the five of us. They flew north and saw that we are about three-fourths of the way through the present visible crevassed area. These bridged, lenticular, shear crevasses are slightly more visible from the air. When we clear this, they thought we could drive along a narrow, apparently crevasse-free path to the base of a crevasse-free slope that we could pull. To the south is an excellent ramp but unfortunately the way to it is blocked by a very bad crevassed area.

Cox, Lewis, and I were standing watching the plane come in and land again and taking pictures. It stopped and Lewis started towards it. I turned to do something, and when I looked back a few seconds later I didn't see Lewie. The first thought to cross my mind was, "My, he reached the plane fast." Then, just as I saw an open hole in the snow, Wally yelled, "Lewie fell into a crevasse!"

I ran to a rope nearby and tied myself in and grabbed an ice ax. Ed was out of the plane and at hand by this time. Paul was running for a rope ladder. Ed belayed me, and probing each step, I gingerly approached the hole. I felt my ax probe through the bridge I suddenly realized I was standing on. This crevasse was perpendicular to the one nearby that we had broken into, and I was walking along the thin snow bridge. Lying down on my stomach I crawled to the edge and looked down, not knowing what I would see. There about 15 or 20 ft below me was Lewis. He was wedged in between the walls of the crevasse. He was all right and was managing to hold his position, by jamming with his arms. He was mighty glad to see me as I was to see him. I had to wait a couple of minutes while the others managed to get another rope out to me. The lack of experience in rope handling was quite manifest throughout the proceedings.

While waiting, I took a picture of Lewis down in the crevasse and another of the open hole with my ice ax jammed into the snow beside it. I still carried my folding Kodak Retina IIa camera in my pocket all of the time.

I finally lowered one end of the second rope to Lewis and he tied in with a bowline. Meanwhile Augie came up with a wire rope ladder and the aluminum ladder which we bridged the crevasse with. Snapping the rope ladder onto the other ladder with carabiners, we lowered it to Lewis. I had him on belay all this time. He managed to pull and scramble his way up and out of the hole. He was pretty shaken and a little cold but otherwise OK. As he was climbing up the ladder and out, I took another shot, while belaying him.

It only took 10 minutes from the time Lewie fell until he was back on the surface. He dropped his movie camera, which he held in his hand when he fell. We looked and Hugo climbed down as far as he could, but it wasn't found. For the rest of the time until the plane left, Lewis walked around on tiptoe as if each step was about to reprecipitate him back to the depths.

He had tried to call and shout but, of course, we didn't hear him, as the walls of the crevasse absorbed all the sound. He said he was the most frightened when he heard me probing down the length of

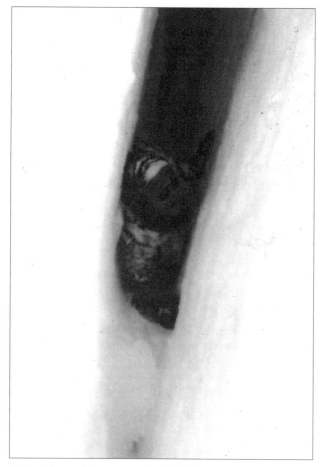

A. Lewis jammed in crevasse about 20 ft down.

308

A. Lewis climbing wire rope ladder out of crevasse. Note rope belaying him at edge of crevasse.

the snow bridge and saw my ice ax tip poking through. He tried to warn me and expected to see me break through at any minute. The place where he fell through was about 40 ft from the backdoor of Hugo's Sno-Cat and in an area we had been walking around in for the past two days. The crevasse was probably about 70 ft deep.

While Ed and Aug were up flying, Lewis had been asking us if we could lower him down in the crevasse we broke the Sno-Cat through. He said he wondered what a crevasse looks like from the inside. Now he knows. He was pretty lucky.

Not many people fall into crevasses unroped and live to tell about it. If Lewis had fallen in a couple of feet to the left, he would have gone down much farther where the crevasse widened considerably, and almost certainly would have sustained serious injuries.

I hope this mishap serves as a lesson to all of us. Familiarity breeds contempt, they say, and we have been rather careless lately. Cox decided to go in to Ellsworth.

Leaving three barrels of fuel behind to lighten our load, we started on the road again at about 1330. Con flew around to direct us, and we slowly worked our way in towards the escarpment, hoping to swing north along the base of it. About 1415 Con announced that there were 10 crevasses that he could see ahead of us. He suggested

309

we go a little faster. It was clouding up and he was low on gas. Five minutes later the lead vehicle broke through another bridged crevasse. Again there was no surface indication . . . and the crevasse detector indicated nothing. This time it wasn't as serious as two days back, because the crevasse was crossed perpendicularly. Unfortunately it was much more difficult to extricate. Hugo sent Con off just after we went through the crevasse, as there was nothing he could do to help.

The sled never reached the crevasse. The front pontoons of the Sno-Cat had crossed the crevasse, but the rear ones were on the other side of the open hole. Both pairs of pontoons were angled down into the crevasse. To get the vehicle out we attached cables to the tracks of the front pontoons, ran these over the rear pontoons, and pulled with the other Sno-Cat.

Finally after four hours we pulled it out and clear. The forward universal joint on the forward drive shaft of #1 was broken in the afternoon's activities.

I fried up steaks for supper; they were greatly enjoyed. Things don't look too good right now. Ahead of us are unknown numbers of crevasses like these which cannot be seen from the air. If we turn back from this particular area, we have to recross all the bad terrain we have already come through. Haskill told Hugo at a 2100 radio sked that Ronne is coming out tomorrow at 0800. I suppose camp is buzzing with greatly exaggerated stories tonight.

The day's events did not need any exaggeration to cause excitement at Ellsworth.

16 Nov., Sat. The plane left camp this morning, but had to turn back due to bad weather. It whited out more and snowed a bit. We read and played bridge while waiting. Aug and I won. I cooked a stew of cabbage, noodles, and ham. Garlic and pepper, to individual taste. Quite a favorable reaction. I'm reading Whitehead. I prefer this sort of stuff to fiction when I'm in the field. I wrote letters and hamgrams tonight.

The hamgram I wrote to my brother, Dave, read: "Dear Dave: At present we are stopped in a bad crevassed area at foot of rising land. Our lead Sno-Cat has gone into two crevasses, but we got it

Air view of Sno-Cat broken into crevasse (Official U.S. Navy photo by W. Cox).

out each time. A man fell into a crevasse but was rescued without injury. All this in the past mile. We are stopped by a broken drive shaft at present. Don't relay this to folks, Morale high. John."

It is interesting that the ham radio situation had improved to the extent that this was, probably surreptitiously, sent out from Ellsworth on 18 November without Ronne seeing it and stopping it. My brother is a journalist who was working for a newspaper in Decatur, Illinois, at the time, but did not write a story about it.

17 Nov., Sun. Whiteout this morning but it cleared around noon. While we waited for the plane to come out, Ed and I tried a short reflection spread to find out how deep the bottom is here. Aug and Paul rigged a rope ladder in the crevasse, so I climbed down about 55 ft and planted a charge in the wall. It was quite beautiful down there. I stood on a ledge and could see down another 20 feet or so. It seemed to die out in both directions.

When we fired the shot there was a lot of collapse and reverberation in the crevasse. We recorded no reflection. We drilled an eight-meter hole and tried again. Apparently we drilled almost through a snow bridge, because again there was a lot of collapse and another poor record. A third shot produced similar results.

311

I was wearing skis when I laid out and took up the cables and geophones. The cables were, as usual, laid out for 330 m from the Sno-Cat and crossed numerous crevasses covered by snow bridges. The seismic energy barely traveled to the end geophones.

It was calm, sunny, and consequently very warm. Paul dug a snow pit wearing a T-shirt. As I skied along the spread picking up the jugs [geophones], I realized what a good profession I've got. [Assuming I did not get killed in the process!]

Ronne, Mac, and Lewis flew out about 1800. We directed the plane to land in our tracks, as that is the only area proven to be safe. It had just cleared at camp. They brought some parts for the Sno-Cat but left one item behind. Lewis was in the plane today but stayed right with it and didn't walk over to the Sno-Cat.

They took Ed and Augie up to look around. The lighting was good, and Augie said that he could see crevasses all around us. In this light

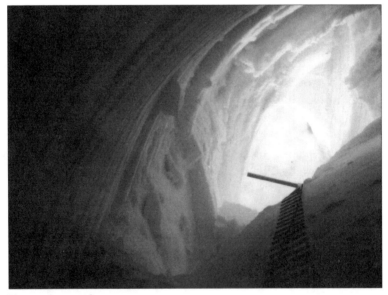

View up from inside crevasse.

we can also see several from the surface that we couldn't see before. They flew south and east and saw crevasses everywhere. We had just about decided to back track out of this area, but they could see bridged and open crevasses almost all the way back to our last seismic station. We were lucky to get this far. To the south there are masses of crevasses so I'm not sure just where we will go now.

312

This was late in the day, and a low sun angle made it somewhat easier to see a bridged crevasse from either the surface or the air.

While they were up I helped Hugo drill an 18-ft (9-m) hole. As I was drilling the last few inches, the auger dropped out of my hands and down the hole. I had drilled into a crevasse. The handle jammed and held the rods and auger about five feet down. Hugo and I managed to fish it out with the handle of a probe and a shackle. It would have been a serious blow to both programs to have lost the snow auger, as we have no replacement.

Ed went in with the plane to see the doctor, because he seems to be developing a case of hemorrhoids.

H. Neuburg explaining crevasse situation to F. Ronne (center) and C. McCarthy. Note escarpment of Berkner Island in background.

18 Nov., Mon. Bad weather at Ellsworth today, so the plane couldn't make it out. Intermittently overcast and clear throughout the day here. South wind. Temperature about 13°F. It has been getting warmer the past week. I had the unprecedented luxury of a Sno-Cat all to myself for most of the day, as the others slept in until 1900. I woke up at noon and read all day. After supper Aug, Paul, and I played sheepshead [a card game] until 0130. Aug won one game and Paul the other. And to think that I taught the game to them!

Time is marching on and we aren't getting very far. We left Ellsworth three weeks ago today. Hugo is worried Ed will shave while in camp. Beards are a touchy subject with old Hugo. When Ronne wanted everyone to shave all winter, it was the first chink in the plaster of the statue on a pedestal that Hugo thought him (Ronne) to be.

Things are getting messier and more cluttered than ever during these protracted halts. While moving, a semblance of order is imperative; otherwise, junk is bouncing and flying all over the place. Then things (theoretically at least) must be secured as in a rolling ship. I haven't been drinking any coffee up til now; I always make milk or orange juice with my meal. Today, however, I had the stove going and would fix a cup of the caffeine-loaded stuff at intervals.

Coffee is a diuretic, which can contribute to dehydration in Antarctica because of the very dry air. Because we had to melt snow for all of our water and because we didn't feel particularly thirsty in the cold, we probably were barely getting enough fluid. However, we drank very little coffee during the traverse, mainly because hot water was even more scarce than cold water.

19 Nov., Tues. Overcast, pretty white with snow off and on all day. I wrote a letter to my parents which reads in part:

Well, as I write this I am sitting in our Sno-Cat listening to some South African station on the radio. . . . Every night we catch a brief news report on BBC. Radio Moscow booms in on five frequencies with its North American Service. We get a little news here, but of course there is so much propaganda that everything one hears must be judged as to its source. I was listening the night they announced their second satellite. I suppose IGY (in U.S.) is all excited about this; they were when the first was launched while we were in camp.

Outside the wind is blowing and we are in a whiteout. We are in the bad crevassed area where we dropped one vehicle twice and one man (rescued) about which you no doubt have heard. I sent Dave a hamgram about it with instructions not to tell you. We aren't particularly worried, and I saw no reason for you to be either. I have a Coleman stove going, which is providing very adequate (albeit stratified) heat. Everyone else is asleep (it's 1:30 P.M.). We can't travel on days like this and are waiting for a plane right now before we move.

I just took my weekly wash (hands and face), and treated myself to a brunch of tuna fish, bread, coffee, and fruitcake. We are really eating wonderfully (I am the cook and commissary officer) compared to previous Antarctic field parties. No pemmican (although we have something similar in our 30-day emergency rations) but lots of fresh-frozen meat. . . . Last night we had a fresh cherry pie sent out from camp. The cooks at camp are really swell that way; hardly a flight comes out that doesn't have some fresh pastry and bread. . . .

These people are woefully inexperienced in mountaineering techniques particularly rope handling. They have read how to do it and seen it demonstrated, but they waste a tremendous amount of time when it comes to tying in, coiling and uncoiling ropes, etc. This delay could have been quite serious the other day when we had to extricate a man from a crevasse. I find that I am the most experienced of our group in this sort of thing, and you know how little experience I've had. They're swell fellows, but I wish we had the background of our bunch on the Lemon Glacier back in '56. . . .

Our seismic work has been going OK. I could get a thesis out of this if I choose to return to school. I really haven't decided what to do. I know I'd feel like a quitter if I stopped before I finished my Ph.D. . . . I don't know how much I've written in my log but it is over 100,000 words. That and my exposed film are my most precious possessions.

The first opportunity I had to mail this letter was not until we arrived in South America in February 1958.

Bad weather at Ellsworth. Ed talked to Hugo by voice. It seems that Davis is forced to manufacture the U-fitting for the universal joint. Ed wanted us to try and probe and mark a route up to the apron of the escarpment. Unfortunately visibility was too poor. #2 Sno-Cat is now the living and dining room of the traverse since Ed is away. It seems that wherever I live, mobs of people always drop in. Oh well, I enjoy people.

Cards this afternoon and philosophy reading tonight. Stimulated by my reading Whitehead, Aug, Paul, and I started a discussion of whether there is a God. We didn't resolve the question. We heard some good music on BBC this afternoon. I also listened to Australia, Switzerland, Japan, and Radio Peking—all in English. Radio Peking isn't as subtle and sophisticated in its propaganda as Radio Moscow.

The wind blew hard all night. It is quite warm (about 23°F) and, although it is overcast, there is melting taking place due to sky radiation.

Melting on the Sno-Cats and other dark surfaces, that is. The snow surface of the ice shelf never melted, so we didn't see the snow even get "sticky." We never needed any wax for our skis, as the snow was always cold enough to be dry.

At 1845 we were all sitting in the Sno-Cat when we heard a low rumble . . . to the southeast of us. We figured that it must be a snow bridge collapsing under its own weight. Not too pleasant a thought. I slept on the empty shelf in our vehicle for a change tonight; Ed usually sleeps there. I didn't like it and will return to the deck tonight.

I'll bet this is one of the few Antarctic field parties to have beer with it. We didn't bring any originally but they flew some out. Very little is drunk, however–then only by Paul, Ed, and Aug during bridge games.

I imagine the Ross Ice Shelf Traverse party had plenty of beer.

20 Nov., Wed. Whiteout overcast and 20-knot north wind. Read and played sheepshead. About 2330 it cleared, and we went out to probe a route to the escarpment.

21 Nov., Thurs. It was dead calm and quite warm (about 26°F) when we started about midnight. We found crevasses. The four of us were roped up with Paul probing. Augie didn't approve of Paul's course and soon Augie was probing. Progress was slow, and by 0300 we had only gone about 100 yards. Much time was wasted in roping up and deciding how to proceed. Hugo and I had a slight altercation. We were all a little edgy due to being cooped up so long.

The probe handle broke, and we returned to fix that. As we started probing we saw a snow petrel (or similar bird). Hugo made the repairs so I grabbed an hour's sleep.

About 0600 we started again with Hugo probing. Progress was infinitely slow. We took 30 minutes to move 20 ft at one stretch. At 0800 we returned for a radio schedule. With the weather OK at 0900 and another sked at 1000, I slept two more hours. Paul had sacked out at 0300 and stayed there. Hugo, Aug, and I started again at 1030. They were a little mad at Paul, but I didn't blame him a bit.

This time Hugo planned a cursory job, only a trail to ski over to the escarpment. By noon we had progressed a half mile when we saw a plane approaching. We could tell by the actions of the plane that Willie was at the controls. That boy loves to fly! The plane indicated a new course we should change our trail to which we did. We skied back and the plane landed. Willie, [Earl] Herring, and Ed were aboard; the first two stayed in the plane. They had the part for the Sno-Cat. There was quite a wind from the south by this time, and they had trouble turning so as to take off, but finally made it.

By this time I had been up since 1130 yesterday while the rest of the boys didn't get up until supper. Hugo and I went to bed at 1400 while Ed, Paul, and Aug probed down the rest of the way to the escarpment. Hugo worked on the Sno-Cat.

After five hours' sleep and a supper of 5-in-1 rations, Aug and I (he wouldn't go to bed) reprobed the questionable spots, and Paul and Ed dug through the snow bridges we found and looked at the crevasses. There are over a dozen fairly bad ones in the mile and a half or two miles down to the hill. (We actually go down hill a bit before reaching the escarpment.) There was a 20-knot wind with lots of blowing snow, and we didn't get down there until almost midnight. Aug and I skied up the slope of "Hubley Land" [Berkner Island] and waved a red trail flag (we marked the crevasses with these). It was quite beautiful and I really enjoyed this last ski trek of the day.

The latest news from camp is that Don received another court martial from Ronne. Don had, with Ed's permission, moved into Ed's vacated room. Ronne, who hadn't been in the science building for weeks didn't know this. He came in the other night to see Ed and found Don there. He grabbed Don's arm and started chewing him out. Don knocked his hand away saying, "Take your hands off me!" Ronne ordered him to move out by the following noon. Don, of course did not move. Ronne had Spear move all Don's things back into the room with Jack. He then handed out various memos to Spear, Don, and Jack, specifying that Don was restricted from all buildings except the head, science building, and galley at meal time (no coffee break). Jack was ordered to see that Don works during the daytime. Don added the order to his collection and decided to obey. He thinks he can get Ronne later. Ronne also made copies for Crary, Dufek, and the Bureau of Standards. He had Chief May write a dispatch for him on Don, which he sent out today stating that Don was bad for morale, etc., etc. The reason given for this punishment is that Don illegally moved into Dr. Thiel's room.

Of course Ronne really couldn't hold a court martial on his own authority. However, he did use the "Nonjudicial Punishment" clause of the Uniform Code of Military Justice to restrict Don.

Listening to the tales of troubles in camp, I decided I prefer crevasses to Ronne. Ed picked up a bit of news on the Byrd traverse

Aughenbaugh on marked route to Berkner Island in background. Flags mark bridged crevasses.

from a surreptitiously copied dispatch: "DEPARTED 19 NOV, PERSONNEL: ANDERSON, GIOVINETTO, BENTLEY, OSTENSO, HALE [THE AURORA MAN] HELFRET (TO BE RELIEVED BY WM. LONG), JACK LONG, MECH. THREE SNOCATS, THREE 2.5 TON SLEDS, 1 MESS WANAGON. 30 MILE STOPS PLANNED. . . . RADAR DISCOVERED MOUNTAIN ABOUT 75°20'S, 109°45'W SENTINEL MTS."

Bill Long had worked with Ed and me in Alaska on the Juneau Ice Field during the summer of 1956. The original plans had anticipated that the aurora men at Little America, Byrd, and Ellsworth would possibly go on the oversnow traverses. This turned out to be the case at Little America and Byrd, but not Ellsworth. Kim had wanted to go, but Ronne would not let him.

Ed heard that the Little America traverse is at Roosevelt Island. That is only 40 miles from Little America so they are apparently having other troubles also. Of course they have had it far worse than we have, losing a man in a crevasse accident.

In general, I think we had worse crevasse problems on this, the Filchner Ice Shelf Traverse, than the other two that season. It was just luck that we had not lost someone in what we had traversed so far. The Byrd Station Traverse (Sentinel Mountain Traverse) was on grounded ice the entire time and had little crevasse difficulty.

The Brits flew over to Ellsworth. They took five weeks to cover 250 miles to South Ice. They, too, had much difficulty with crevasses. Ed tells of Ronne's growing concern at the amount of avgas Mac is using in the traverse support. The present attitude is, "Is this trip really necessary?"

22 Nov., Fri. Hugo did not want to move on until we obtained some lumber from camp to try to bridge the worst of the crevasses. Therefore, we all went to bed abut 0200. Breakfast at 1100. Still clear with the wind down a bit. Hugo went back to fixing the Sno-Cat. Ed, Aug, and Paul looked for alternative routes around the worst crevasses; I loaded sleds, made water, etc., around camp.

Mac flew in late in the afternoon and unloaded six 12-ft, 4-by-8-inch, and six 8-ft pieces of the same. They had to saw them this way to get them in the plane. I hope they are of some good.

The boards were of no use because they were too short.

Just when the U-joint was nearing completion, Hugo found that both the front pontoons had been ripped open by our exertions in pulling the Cat out of the crevasse. These, if repairable at all, will require welding and, consequently, the proper tools will have to be flown out from camp. Just about this time a cloud bank moved in from the north. Probably more days of waiting for it to clear just when we thought we were going to break out.

The crevasse crew came in ravenous for supper about 2300. I cooked up a stew of rice, beans, and canned ham with various spices. In opening the can of ham, my hand slipped and I slashed cuts across three fingers and the thumb of my right hand. The middle fingers were cut quite deeply while the others are superficial.

319

Normally, it would require some stitches, but I will see how it heals during the next few days. I'm afraid I won't be good for much work requiring heavy use of the right hand. Right now (2250) it is throbbing rather painfully. A bad day!

23 Nov., Sat. I woke up at 0400 with my hand hurting and slept little thereafter until we had breakfast at 1000. It was intermittently cloudy throughout the day, becoming a solid overcast by evening. Hugo worked on the track; Ed, Paul, and Aug donned skis and took a jaunt down to the escarpment, much to the envy of Hugo and me. They skied north up the "apron" for about 1.5 miles and found no evidence of any crevasses.

There are 18 crevasses that we have probed into and opened between us and the escarpment, a distance of about 1.5 miles. The largest is about 40 ft wide. All are bridged over with arched bridges ranging in thickness from a few inches near the center to several about 10 feet near the walls. Our hope is that we can pick the thickest parts of each to drive over. I wonder how many exist that we haven't found.

Mac told us [yesterday] that the two USAF C-47s had flown down the Palmer [Antarctic] Peninsula as far south as Mt. Tricorn (73°58'S, 61°45'W) before bad weather forced them to turn back. They landed somewhere on the Palmer Peninsula. Ellsworth informed Hugo this morning that one of Lassiter's planes was 60 miles out and that Mac was flying out. . . . Later Ellsworth told Hugo that one of Lassiter's planes arrived. It carried no mail.

24 Nov., Sun. Overcast all day again. We slept in and played bridge in the afternoon. Today is our twenty-eighth day in the field. We are over a third done (time wise) and haven't accomplished too much. We listened to BBC most of the afternoon and evening. I wish we could hear Voice of America a bit better. We heard news from Radio Brazzaville in Central Africa. BBC announced yesterday that the main party of the Commonwealth Transantarctic Expedition will leave Shackleton today if weather permits. I wonder if they left.

As I sit writing this to the strains of a Schumann string quartet, I look around in #1 Sno-Cat at the three other occupants. Supper is just over (2115) and Ed has gone over to our vehicle. It is about 26°F outside, so we are quite comfortable inside without any stove or heater. I am seated next to the rear door reading *Scott's Last Expedition.* Paul is lying in his sleeping bag on the shelf at my left. He has an old wool Navy watch cap on and is propped up against a box of 5-in-1 rations. Augie is sitting on the control unit of the crevasse detector studying a report on geology. He has his red ear jock holding his long hair out of his eyes. He and Don are the last two at the station not to have had a hair cut since leaving *Wyandot.* He has bunny boots [white felt boots–not the rubber thermal boots I wore, which are now called bunny boots] on his feet and has his feet propped against another empty 5-in-1 case. Hugo is occupying the other chair and is reading Bemelman's *I Love You, I Love You, I Love You.* He, too, is wearing bunny boots and every so often chuckles happily to himself as he reaches a humorous part. He has his old red plaid shirt on with a wool undershirt on the outside. (It scratches next to his skin, he says.)

All around is a clutter of food, pots, water jugs, sleeping bags, air mattresses, and other impediments. A wire from a blasting cap runs the circuit of the vehicle where the ceiling meets the walls, held in place by the screws which hold the wall board on. From this I can see miscellaneous dirty socks, mittens, head phones, clothespins, and a pair of sunglasses.

25 Nov., Mon. Cloudy and overcast, but very warm in the morning. The thermometer read above freezing but was influenced by direct radiation. We ate breakfast outdoors, much to Hugo's delight. It began to clear about noon and was intermittently cloudy and blue the rest of the day. Paul and Ed won their first bridge game this evening. About 2200 it cleared off for good. At 2400 we heard a plane approaching–after we had gone to bed.

26 Nov., Tues. Con and Jackson landed and brought out some silver solder and a brazing torch to repair the Sno-Cat pontoon. I flew back with them to see Clint about my hand. It was ideal weather for pictures to be taken, with the sun at a very low angle. The surface features stood out strikingly clearly. At least 10 miles north we passed the "point" with the gentle slope up to the higher land. The escarpment [of Berkner Island] stretched on to west and continued north almost as far as Gould Bay.

We crossed right over the west end of the rift, and I got a good look and several pictures of the area we tried so hard to get Ronne to let us see. It's clear enough except in the space between the two sections of the rift where we had wondered about going through. This is pretty badly crevassed, but the crevasses are open and linear so I think it might have been possible to get through. We aren't in too good a place right now!

We circled Ellsworth, and I had a good view (and pictures) of the drifted up camp. When I arrived at 0300 I dropped in at the ham shack. Ed Davis was operating. I ordered a phone patch to the folks and within three hours I was wakened to talk to them. Times have certainly changed.

Radio reception was definitely better to the U.S. during the austral summer.

Right after breakfast I dropped in on Clint. After soaking the cut fingers in hydrogen peroxide for a bit, Clint managed to get the bandage off. The dead flesh had begun to smell a bit, so it was too late to suture it. He put a Vaseline bandage on. It's probably just as well I came in, as I'd have had some troubles with it in the field. If I could have come in right away he would have sewn it up.

Camp has changed a bit. There is a lot of melting and many of the roofs are leaking.

This melting, and ever deeper drifting of the snow in the winter, is what eventually dooms the stations built on the Antarctic ice sheet, in contrast to those built on rock, such as McMurdo. The high cold stations such as South Pole and Vostok last longer but eventually have to be rebuilt.

The snow has all been shoveled off the roofs, but some water remains, due to absorbed radiation by the black tarpaulins covering the buildings. There is much ice in the tunnels and all the doorsteps are quite slippery. I'm surprised no one has hurt himself yet.

The boys were all quite glad to see me, and we had a good talk about recent happenings. Don is now restricted to within 50 feet of the base without special permission from Ronne. He and Kim went exploring Sunday. [Last] Saturday Kim and Spear blew the snow bridge open on a crevasse down by the new site planned for the *Wyandot* off-loading. The next day Don and Kim climbed down into it and took pictures. Captain Ronne got the word that Don had fallen in "head down with his hands behind his back."

Ronne had used this expression in his book, *Antarctic Conquest,* in describing an accident on his last expedition. Kim told Ronne that Don did not fall in, but Ronne did not believe this. Ronne even put this same description in his book about our expedition, not realizing the phrase had been used by Kim and Don sarcastically.

Jack has called Don's wife and explained that Don can't talk to her anymore. He had her call Dufek's office in Washington about it. She called on Saturday last and couldn't talk to anyone high, but was told that they are having a special meeting about Don's case. Jack is going to try and contact her again tonight.

Haskill couldn't contact Hugo this morning. He heard him sending but could not read him. This now is the second or third day in a row without contact. I wonder if the track is repaired.

27 Nov., Wed. Lassiter's crew brought a *Time* magazine which contained the note about Hubley's suicide.

I spent several hours reading this copy of *Time,* starting at the beginning and reading everything.

It was really a treat to read a magazine only a few weeks old–even if it is *Time.*

I remember being snobbish about *Time* in those days. There was a common expression that "*Life* magazine is for people who can't read and *Time* is for those who can't think!" There was nothing like being cut off from the world for a year to change my perspective.

After supper I wandered over to the old Jamesway galley which the Air Force people are using and spent a very pleasant and enjoyable evening with them culminating in a bridge game in which "Rod" Roderick and I were edged out by Jim Lassiter and one of his other pilots. I had a good long talk with Rod about dogs compared with Sno-Cats, and with Bill Chapman about working for USGS. It was the best bridge game I have played since we left the *Wyandot.*

The boys [on the traverse] drove along our flagged and probed route with no trouble at all. They crossed the crevasse area, drove north along the apron and climbed the escarpment [of Berkner Island].

For the next couple of days they worked on Berkner Island without me. There were no crevasses on the grounded ice, and the going was excellent. They drove about 70 miles.

28 Nov., Thurs. Thanksgiving. I didn't think I'd be in camp for Thanksgiving turkey dinner but it turned out differently. Still overcast so the Gooney Bird [Lassiter's USAF C-47] didn't fly. I slept in until noon.

Kim has reconsidered some of his more rash doings with Ronne over the past year and thinks that he and the rest of us made some mistakes in our dealings with the Captain. Don, of course, is locked in a fight to the finish (maybe Don's finish) with Ronne and resents Kim's attitude. He has been riding him a lot about it. Tonight it finally got under Kim's skin and they came to verbal blows. Jack and I went over for coffee.

The following came in the morning:

FROM: COMNAVSUPFOR ANTARCTICA PRIORITY
ACTION: ELLSWORTH STATION
INFO: COMNAVSUPFOR ANTARCTICA–ANTARCTIC
PROJECT–ADMIN O COMNAVSUPFOR ANTARCTIC-
REPCOMNAVSUPFOR ANTARCTICA WASHINGTON,
DC–IGY WASH DC
NO. 2P 280648 Z (NOV)

ALL PERSONNEL AT ELLSWORTH STATION ARE FREE
TO USE HAM RADIO AND SAY WHAT THEY WISH.
RADM DUFEK

Jerry brought a copy over about noon, Forlidas brought one at about 1300, and Ronne saw it about 1500. It looks like Don's wife talked to someone. Ronne has no idea what this is about (he did not notify anyone as to how he had restricted Don).

Ronne answered with a dispatch which I saw but could not copy, stating that there are no restrictions on the use of the ham radio, that he censored hamgrams to take out statements detrimental to the Navy for the first few months only, and that the nine operators were at present, sending all hamgrams given to them. He did not rescind his written order that Don is restricted from use of ham facilities and restricted from the radio building. Ronne, of course, has no idea that anyone has seen either of these messages. Actually everyone in camp either has seen or knows the contents of each.

The Air Force people came over for Thanksgiving dinner (officers' setting). Walt May made up a menu, and Wally Cox made enough photo reproductions so that everyone had one.

29 Nov., Fri. It began to clear about 2100, and the Air Force people planned to fly out. I had a brief phone patch with the folks (the boys put it through without knowing I had one two days ago) of very poor quality.

30 Nov., Sat. Still more or less cloudy this morning so the Gooney Bird stayed in camp. Mac thought we could take off about 1400, but the weather which almost cleared changed its mind and socked in. Hugo got through on the radio. They were at mile 247 and had put in one station. I really feel left out to read such a message and be back here.

The greatest thing of new interest at Ellsworth was the arrival of the Lassiter Air Force party in the C-47. I spent a lot of time with this group while I was in camp and had many interesting conversations in these few days.

For whatever reason, the rest of the people at Ellsworth had relatively little contact with the newcomers and as Kim described it to me in 1997, they felt a bit xenophobic. I later noticed this feeling when the *Wyandot* arrived in January, but during this brief visit to Ellsworth, I craved new faces and conversation. I suppose after a month on the traverse I was getting a bit tired of all of the bickering with Finn Ronne that still preoccupied everyone else at Ellsworth.

James Lassiter, major USAF, with three other pilots (all captains), a sergeant, and a civilian topographic engineer (William Chapman of the U.S. Geological Survey), had arrived at Ellsworth. They, with the two C-47s and four more people, had been trying to fly in several days ago when they hit bad weather at Mt. Tricorn and flew back up the Palmer Peninsula to Dolleman Island (about 500 miles from Ellsworth). There they found themselves nearly out of fuel (there hadn't been an expected cache at another place), so they loaded up everyone and a lot of stuff and attempted a flight in. They couldn't take off whereupon they unloaded everything (including all cooking equipment) and with six men, flew towards Ellsworth.

They arrived in the area Friday, 22 November, by flying along the Filchner Ice Shelf, but found camp closed in by clouds. Lassiter found a clear spot to the south and landed immediately. They were about 75 miles south of the base, about 25 miles from us. They couldn't hear the beacon at Ellsworth nor contact it via radio, but they contacted the other plane at Dolleman Island and had them relay a message to Ellsworth. The next morning, Saturday, 23 November, Mac, Ronne, and Willie flew out to them, brought them some gas, and guided them in to Ellsworth. They did not have a very good idea of their position but could see the escarpment (of Berkner Island) about five miles away. When the plane landed, about 25 of the station crew were out to greet the new arrivals, who, upon disembarking, were met with the general question, "Where is our mail?" There was some disappointment when it was found that the mail for us—if any—had been left behind with the other plane.

Lassiter's plane, the Douglas DC-3, was designated C-47 by the U.S. Air Force, R4D by the Navy, Dakota by the British, and by the slang expression of Gooney Bird by many. The last of these aircraft was built in about 1944, but I saw some operational ones at the airport in Bangkok in 1994. The Navy version, R4D, on skis was one of the several types of aircraft called "workhorse of the Antarctic" by the press over the years. Three and four years later in Antarctica, I flew many hours in Navy R4D-8s operating mostly out of Byrd Station making aeromagnetic measurements. On one of these flights, we dented a wing tip on a mountain in a whiteout but didn't crash.

Mac told me about 0300 [the morning I flew in] that Lassiter brought an order from Dufek to give him 15,000 gallons of avgas after 15 December. This came as an order from the Security Council, to the Defense Department, to Dufek to VX-6, to Mac. Someone has friends in high places. [The Lassiter mission was a CIA operation, as noted above.] Lassiter has borrowed 2000 gallons of avgas from Mac to be paid back on 15 December to use to get his other plane back. They planned on flying up to Dolleman Is. with a load of fuel for the other plane and then bring both in here.

The night they arrived and were fueling the C-47, the electric pump they were using arced and started a fire. The fuel on the wing and engine nacelle began to burn. The two fire extinguishers in the plane refused to operate, and by the time the fire was put out with our fire-fighting apparatus, damage was done to the wing, flaps, etc. Fred Drydal did the repair job. He had put in 27 straight hours when he quit work for some sleep. The next morning he was right back at it with Willie's help; they finished late that evening. Lassiter took off about 0000 [27 November] and flew as far as the area of Bowman Peninsula where he hit bad weather. He landed, left a fuel cache, and came back about 0700.

Immediately after Lassiter's arrival, Ronne closeted himself with "Jimmy" and told him about how the sand crabs have been causing so much trouble all winter. Shortly thereafter, one of the Navy men started sounding off to Lassiter about all the troubles Ronne has caused. Lassiter remarked something to the effect that they couldn't tell him anything about Ronne because they only spent a year with him while he (Lassiter) had spent 18 months with him. At any rate, his statements made quite an effect on the men here; they all think he is a swell fellow. Lassiter placed camp practically off limits to his men. They do their own cooking and live in the Jamesway village. They do come over and use the showers. No drinking is allowed, but the other pilots have been consuming beer with Con in his room.

On the night of 26 November on his radio program, Lowell Thomas announced that Lassiter and six men had arrived at Ellsworth and that the other plane was out of fuel at Dolleman Island (Ronne had a phone patch with Thomas on 25 November). He and Ronne, Clint Smith, and Hannah were in the radio room listening to the program together. Lassiter is reported to have turned red in the face, slapped his head, and said, "You've done it now, Finn; we are all in trouble! Ronne protested, "Oh no, Jimmy!" "Oh yes, we are all in trouble now. Now you've screwed everything up! If I had wanted anybody to know about that second plane I would have told them myself!" and stalked out of the room leaving Ronne visibly shaken.

Lassiter had talked with his wife in a phone patch a few days ago and told her to tell his commanding officer in the Air Force of his safe arrival and further that four people in the second plane were out doing "fieldwork."

Thomas also embarrassed Ronne in his phone patch by asking about the troubles down here. Apparently, there was something in the *New York Times* about it. On his program Thomas mentioned asking Ronne if he had a "mutiny on his hands down there."

Walter Sullivan of the *New York Times* told me in 1989 of a conversation with Larry Gould about the secret messages Ronne sent to IGY referring to us scientists by code designations as various fruits; perhaps he had written something of the dissension at Ellsworth.

While I was in the infirmary getting my hand treated, the morning I arrived in camp, Ronne came through with Jim Lassiter and introduced me to him. I also met one of Lassiter's pilots, Captain

327

Roderick, from Augie's hometown. Lassiter is a tall (over 6 ft) man with a very pleasant personality. He offered to airlift all our loads from where we are now to the top of the escarpment.

This would have been impractical; Lassiter obviously didn't realize the amount of stuff we had.

I told him of the crevasses but he said he could land in our old track; anywhere we could drive he could land. He asked me about our elevation control. He wondered if he could put the USGS topographic engineer in with us at our main stations to get an accurate position determination. I told him I thought this would be fine with us. It would save Hugo the trouble of sun shots and would give us a much more accurate fix.

We didn't discuss it further at this time. I soon met the U.S. Geological Survey topographic engineer with the Lassiter party, Bill Chapman. Chapman, and other USGS topographic engineers, later became regular members of the oversnow traverse field parties.

I had an hour chat with Chapman on the morning of 27 November. They spent a month in Punta Arenas before heading south. His job is to accurately determine the position of a number of points that they will use for control in their program by measuring three sun line positions each hour for 24 hours with a theodolite. Their Radist method involves a master-slave radar at two control points. The plane with trimetragon cameras will fly 40-mile-wide strips for a distance of 200 miles on each side of this line, and will accurately determine its position electronically from the signals sent out from these stations.

The mapping program plans to cover 200,000 square miles, to an accuracy of 1 mile. They plan to put stations at 30-mile intervals in a line. Their object is ambitious: to map, by the Radist method, this quadrant of Antarctica. Lassiter is talking about using South Ice as a base when the Brits depart.

The mapping plans were completely impractical considering both the time and fuel available.

It seems that when the Navy was asked how much it would cost to map Antarctica, they answered $34 million. Lassiter [told the CIA] he could do it for $4 million, and thus this project developed. It is sponsored by the Defense Department and the planes and some men are on loan from the USAF.

The Lassiter photos were used to make maps of the Dufek Massif. However, the CIA probably used them for control of satellite images collected in 1963. These data were declassified and released in 1995.

As USGS can't pay men working on mapping areas outside the continental U.S., Chapman is on the payroll of the Central Intelligence Agency.

This policy was changed by a law passed in 1958 allowing the USGS and other federal agencies to work in Antarctica.

Chapman told me that, whereas we at Ellsworth have a dictatorship, they have a sort of anarchy with Major Lassiter and the three captains [Air Force captains have the same rank as Navy lieutenant, e.g., Jaburg; major the same as lieutenant commander, e.g., McCarthy] changing their minds and unable to come to any quick decisions. As his theodolite is not in camp, Chapman is now cooking for his crew. He is somewhat disillusioned about their project and seems to think that their fly boys don't know exactly what they are doing. He said that he didn't think Ronne has anything to do with their program. This may be; he may be just trying to butt in on the basis of his old "friendship" with "Jimmy."

I still do not know exactly where Finn Ronne came into the picture. I wonder if he also had a CIA connection.

Jim (unlike Ronne, it's first names with them) and I had a long and very interesting talk about Ronne, the situation here, how the traverse program and his can integrate, and the Ronne Antarctic Research Expedition (RARE). He told me that he knows Ronne far better than any of us and stated that he was just an old man full of idiosyncrasies. He is quite aware of how difficult he is and mentioned that we had an easy time compared with the RARE (personality wise). He mentioned something about the way one had to deal with these "Queeg types," as he put it.

Lassiter thinks we have a lot of immature men among the Navy personnel and that this contributed a lot to the trouble (referring to the way they talk to Ronne and the other officers). Ronne has him convinced of Don's guilt in trouble making, and regards Don as one of the immature people. He got the impression from Ronne that the rest of the IGY people are pretty level-headed. Perhaps this is because the Captain is particularly down on Don at present. He paid me the compliment of discussing these things with me because he thought I was a rather "solid (as he put it) sort of fellow."

I realize now that Lassiter had the charm and talent (as did Ronne) to easily snow people. Obviously he used his talent to set up this mission.

Lassiter made several offers and suggestions to me as to how he might assist the traverse. He hopes that we can work together so he can use our avgas. The fact that we would be operating in the same area gives both our groups an additional safety factor. The C-47s . . . are quite a bit more efficient than the Otter in hauling capacity vs. gas consumption. The Otter can carry 3 drums of fuel and gets 35 gallons/hour. The C-47 can lift about 20 barrels and burns 100 gallons/hour. We can carry a maximum of 16 drums of fuel with the Sno-Cats at one time (on level, crevasse-free terrain). I told Jim that we traverse people don't really care what happens to the avgas as long as we get supported in the field. He said that was the way Hugh Odishaw looked at it. Lassiter won't have both planes ready to go for another couple of weeks, by which time, I hope, we are beyond the 250-mile range of the Otter so any such transition could be accomplished without any hard feelings (with VX-6). The situation is a bit delicate.

Lassiter could give us a 100-watt transmitter with an auxiliary generator. They have Angry 9s only for emergency use. This would be a great help, as we are having trouble communicating at 100 miles' distance. I think it might be a good thing for us that one of us was in camp to talk with Jim Lassiter. I'm sure we couldn't have gone as smoothly as this may now go if we had to work with Ronne.

In *Antarctic Command,* Ronne mentions that Lassiter volunteered to fly fuel out to the traverse party, so perhaps these conversations I had with Lassiter helped.

One rather amusing thing Lassiter told me about was one of the methods used on the last expedition to irritate Ronne. The fellows (knowing how much Ronne detested yellow spots in the snow) used to write his initials, "FR," around camp in the snow with their urine. He asked me not to repeat this or undoubtedly the same thing would happen here and would only serve to stir up more "hate and discontent," particularly between Lassiter and Ronne.

Of course, I did tell the traverse party as soon as I rejoined them, and "FR" was soon being inscribed across the Antarctic ice sheet.

Lassiter has done a lot of flying in the Himalayas including support for climbing expeditions. He said he landed on Everest, Kachenjunga, Makalu, and others. He told me that Ronne's '46–'48 expedition came down with two of the icebreakers of Operation Highjump and that they spent some time with Edisto and Burton Island. This phase of the expedition did not get into Ronne's and Darlington's books.

Jim Lassiter also talked about his dislike of admirals . . . particularly George Dufek. He apparently had a lot of trouble with him in Washington over whether Lassiter would be under his command down here (whether he would get VX-6 gas, I imagine). I gather that Dufek can get quite rough in the notes he throws at people.

Clint, Mac, and a few others from camp plus myself were over in the old chow hall in the Jamesway camp shooting the breeze with Lassiter's crew on Thanksgiving afternoon. Lassiter told us an item which struck us sand crabs as very interesting. Odishaw tried to get him to bring Dr. M. J. Brennan, next year's station scientific leader, down with him. Lassiter refused because they could not carry the extra weight. Ronne has already made the arrangements for next year's living quarters. Brennan will be put in Ed's room and the base commander, a lieutenant, will get Ronne's much larger, private room.

I suppose I could have stayed with the traverse and not had Clint treat my hand, but it healed well after that with only a big scar on one finger. On the other hand, so to speak, it was interesting to be in camp and talk to the new people.

9
Dufek Massif to Korff Island

1 Dec., Sun. I got up at Ellsworth about 1000 and we flew out to the traverse [on Berkner Island] about 1130. Mac, Walt May, and I were in one plane and Willie and Herring in the other. We carried five drums of gas between us. It was good to get back (at about 1400). They were putting in a station about 12 miles south of their location reported at the last radio contact. We exchanged news and I gave them all the latest camp scuttlebutt.

After getting through the crevasses, the Sno-Cats climbed Berkner Island, which we called Hubley Land at the time.

On 29 November they put in a station and recorded a very good reflection from about sea level or a little above; their elevation was about 2100 ft. Continuing on a bearing of 190°, another station was put in on 30 November–1 December, where I rejoined them. We started about 2100 and drove all night.

2 Dec., Mon. 309 mi. After 50 miles we stopped, had supper, and went to bed about 1000. We got up about 2300 and started a station.

My journal entry for 2 December consisted of only the two previous sentences. The more routinely we worked, the less time and inclination I had to write about it.

3 Dec., Tues. 335 mi. We decided to put in a seismic station in the bottom of the bay that we could see this morning coming in from the east.

What we saw was not actually a bay, but the ice shelf south of Berkner Island. Today there is a nice satellite map of all of Antarctica showing our traverse area quite well, but in 1957 we could not quite comprehend what we were exploring, even with the recon flights. Everything looks white down there!

About 0700 we left Paul and Hugo and drove another five miles and down to the ice shelf level. The weather was very warm and sunny today, although it was –10°F last night. I sat in the sun with only a T-shirt on for a while this morning and was quite comfortable. We put in our shots and took up the spread before Hugo and Paul arrived about 1700. After supper we drove another 20 miles and stopped for another station, as the gravity seemed to indicate that we were across this deep trough. Our seismic reflection showed bedrock about 3000 ft below sea level. We measured the floating ice to be about 2000 ft thick here.

In 1978 I flew in a U.S. Hercules ski LC-130 operating from McMurdo on the other side of the continent with David Drewry (Scott Polar Research Institute, Cambridge University) and Charles Swithinbank (British Antarctic Survey) over this same area of Berkner Island. We measured the ice thickness (using a radar ice sounder) and the magnetic field. The radar method does not penetrate seawater beneath the ice shelf, however, and the seismic soundings to bedrock that we made on this traverse, which defined Thiel Trough, are still the only ones on this part of the ice shelf.

We found no crevasses in this area where the Filchner Ice Shelf flows up against Berkner Island. The ice is in compression here, approximately where what is now called the Ronne Ice Shelf separates from the Filchner Ice Shelf.

4 Dec., Wed. We went to bed about 0100 and slept until 2200. We had been up 26 hours. I managed to get the two lines out and the jugs in before breakfast. It was a bad "morning" for poor Augie. It was his turn to fix breakfast and for hours he procrastinated getting up. When he finally did get going and had the stove started, it ran out of gas in five minutes. This made him mad at me because he had filled it last time, and I used it to melt water and cook supper in between. By the time he started it again, I was up and I asked him to keep an eye on the unwinding reel of cable I left behind as I walked out with the end to lay it out. He had to interrupt his work twice to adjust this. He experimented with some dehydrated fruit mix in the cereal and no one (including him) liked it. After all his troubles most of his breakfast was dumped out in the snow.

5 Dec., Thurs. 375 mi. We recorded four reflections, all quite deep. This deep trough may be a major geologic feature. . . . I wonder if it runs through to the Ross Sea? [It does not.] The glaciologists beat us through their work today. If they can do it once they can keep up with us every time. I guess they tried to make up for last station. Aug mentioned yesterday that he preferred to work with Ed and me because we work straight through until the job is done while Paul and Hugo are always taking time off for one thing or another.

I cooked a dinner of pork-rice, etc., and we were on the road about 0900. We couldn't make radio contact again when we stopped at 1000. We haven't had a contact since the one I heard in Ellsworth.

The Sno-Cats were over 2000 ft high at that last contact and on grounded ice. I believe we could have used the poor radio transmission to indicate when we were above seawater beneath the ice shelf as an approximate indication of floating ice. The only good radio transmission we ever did have with the Angry 9 radios was on high grounded ice.

Another beautiful sunny warm day of the type that will make Antarctica seem so fine a place when I remember it in the future (forgetting all the windy cloudy days). Mac and Ronne flew out and landed about 1500. They brought three barrels of fuel. We were nearly down to our last drum.

We were 116 miles south of our position where I had been dropped off, on 1 December. Mac had found us only by following our tracks; the sun reflected off the churned-up snow. On even the slightest overcast day, tracks are not visible in the snow.

Mac and Ronne were surprised at the progress we have been making. We are 250 miles out from camp and at the limit of allowable VX-6 range, even though they had made that long recon flight to the Dufek Massif, just before the traverse left Ellsworth.

Ronne and Mac told us that the mountains are visible ahead, and another range can be seen to the west of us. Another range is to the southeast of us that looks like the Pensacola Range (as photographed in Deep Freeze I).

As noted previously, Dufek Massif, Forrestal Range, Cordiner Peaks, Neptune Range, etc., make up the Pensacola Mountains. All of these ranges are named after men who served in the Navy or have U.S Navy and VX-6 air squadron antecedents. (Forrestal was secretary of the Navy; Neptune is a P2V airplane; Pensacola is a Navy base in Florida.)

It is possible that what they reported to the west were the high peaks (over 16,000 ft) of the Sentinel Range in the Ellsworth Mountains, now known to be about 400 miles away, especially if they were flying at 10,000 ft or higher, as they sometimes did. This may have been the first sighting of those peaks. Because the main range was obscured by clouds, Lincoln Ellsworth only saw the northern foothills of these majestic mountains that now bear his name, on his historic flight across West Antarctica in 1935.

At the time of our traverse in 1957 the great extent of the Ellsworth Mountains was not known. As we crossed the ice shelf, Charlie Bentley, Ned Ostenso, Mario Giovinetto, and Verne Anderson were approaching the Sentinel Mountains, which they first saw on 7 January 1958, on the Sentinel Mountains Traverse from Byrd Station. Ronne, in his book *Antarctic Command*, does not mention seeing any mountains to the west on the flight this day.

> Ronne was in a very genial mood; he even shook hands with Augie. Perhaps the reason for this lies in the fact that they talked to George Dufek on a plane headed for the Pole, while flying out. Mac heard his plane talking to McMurdo and broke in. So Ronne had a friendly chat with George. They told us that Lassiter had finally flown out yesterday to get his other plane and that Ellsworth had informed them that both planes were presently on the way in.

Radio communication is much better flying at 10,000 ft than on the ice shelf, but all the aircraft radios were far superior to those we had on the traverse.

> All in all, things look pretty good right now. If we can keep moving this fast and can spend some time doing geology (with perhaps a little mountaineering on the side), we will all be happy.
> While Paul drove back to get part of their glaciology equipment left at the last five-mile stop, I started frying steak. On Thanksgiving the boys had drunk most of the wine Ronne had given us for Christ-

mas, but a little was left, which was finished off with the meal. I managed to get one sip out of the whole bottle. This is from some wine that the Brits at Shackleton gave Ronne. All we ate was steak, mostly by hand, as the "eatin' tools" were in Paul's Sno-Cat. Paul returned in plenty of time to get his share. Scores were Ed: 3, Paul: 3, Augie: 4, Hugo: 4, and myself: 4.

We weren't vegetarians! Every time we had steak, I sawed up a seven-pound beef tenderloin—or two. Despite eating this way, we were losing weight. I fried outside on a griddle because Hugo Neuburg allowed no cooking in his Sno-Cat, and we couldn't cook in the seismic Sno-Cat because of the electronic equipment.

After wiping the grease from our beards, we pushed on for another 10 miles, making a total of 40 miles today. We got to bed about 2200.

Although morale was not particularly low during our earlier crevasse difficulties, it definitely was higher now that we were making such good time and getting interesting results. Naturally Ed Thiel and I found a bit of excitement immediately after we fired an explosive charge and I developed the record to see how deep the bedrock was. We seismologists received a sense of the changing bedrock elevation directly from the raw gravity observations on the flat ice shelf as well. Unfortunately, there was no similar excitement for the glaciologists in measuring the slowly varying snow accumulation and temperature.

From now on to nearly the end of the traverse, we were completely dependent on Lassiter for air support—fuel only. Of course, in an emergency the VX-6 could have rescued us by relaying fuel for the Otters—that is, if there had been any radio communication.

6 Dec., Fri. The clouds ahead cleared. When we awoke about 1700, we could see the range of mountains for which we have aimed so long, directly on course to the south.

Although they were still 70 miles away, we thought they were much closer. The highest peaks are about 7200 ft, but we were on the Filchner Ice Shelf, near sea level, so they looked about as high as the Teton Range from the floor of Jackson Hole, Wyoming. However, the jagged peaks and spires of the Dufek Massif are even more spectacular than the Tetons!

The mountains trend roughly east-west with the more rugged and spectacular peaks towards the western end, while the lower ones at the eastern extremity appear rounded. No doubt these were over-ridden by ice. East of the range, a rising escarpment of ice- and/or snow-covered rock was visible. Several cirques with small glaciers could also be seen. Of course, this long-awaited sight raised our presently high morale still higher. I looked at their rugged appear-ance and stated categorically that I thought they were probably ig-neous in composition.

Most ranges that I have seen, which are as rough, are igneous (rocks that have solidified from molten magma). I reasoned that

Approaching Dufek Massif.

they must be very hard ("competent" is the geologic term) for these sharp peaks and spires to withstand erosion by the ice.

Augie, affronted by my gall in diagnosing the geology at this dis-tance, bet me three dollars that they were sedimentary rocks.

7 Dec., Sat. 425 mi. We completed our station about 0100; the glaci-ologists didn't finish until 0400. After a dinner of hamburgers, we hit the road again at 0430. All day we drove towards the moun-tains, which didn't seem to come close very rapidly. It was clear and sunny with a few scattered clouds. At about 2000, after 50 miles with the mountains still ahead, we stopped for another station. The wind was blowing quite hard from the east and it began to cloud over.

We observed very prominent sun dogs at 2100, which formed a complete ring around the sun, accompanied by a rainbow (not complete) above and convex towards the sun and centered at the zenith. The old Greeks or Romans would take this as some sign, probably of good fortune. Lets hope it brings us some good luck.

We heard on BBC tonight that Fuchs is having a lot of trouble with crevasses. Apparently they have done a fair amount of damage because we heard John Lewis say in a recorded statement that he had to fly some pontoons and other repair stuff out. We gathered that Fuchs' Sno-Cat has broken through three times.

We found it interesting and frustrating that although we had no communications with Ellsworth, we could hear these BBC broadcasts from England, about Fuchs' party only 200–300 miles to the east of us.

We went to bed about 2330.

8 Dec., Sun. 440 mi. Ed got us up for breakfast at 1030, which brought forth much protest from everyone. We thought that a 28-hour working day deserved at least 12 hours in bed!

It is interesting that Ed, the leader, woke us. Four years later, when I led the Antarctic Peninsula Traverse in the Ellsworth Land–Palmer Land area, we lost a lot of time because of wind and storms. Inevitably, it was I who noticed that the wind had died and that we should wake up and get going.

It was very hot and occasionally sunny as we worked. We all were stripped down to our undershirts. We thought we would drive down to within a couple of miles of the base of the mountains and shoot again, while Hugo finished his work. We didn't get off until 1630. Augie has been getting quite anxious to get into the hills and start doing geology, and so came with us. He was going to leave us and go to the rocks by himself, but at Hugo's request, Paul (he didn't protest very much) came along to accompany Augie for safety sake.

The spot we aimed for on the range caused our course to trend about 45° to the strike (trend) of the range so we approached very slowly. Gradually we went up about 600 ft (about 200 m). As we

339

drove closer, we saw that the mountains appear to be of sedimentary rock with nearly flat-lying beds. I was forced to admit that I probably had guessed wrong about the Dufek Massif being igneous. The rock is very dark in color with several prominent black beds near the higher summits, which can be traced through the range. Very little structure is obvious and that is only at the extreme east end. There are numerous valley glaciers with several quite striking icefalls.

At this distance we could see the entire range; when we were actually in the mountains we obviously could not. Four years later when I led the Antarctic Peninsula Traverse we had a Polaroid camera and used it very effectively in exploring previously unseen mountains. We then used pictures taken from the air or from the surface at a distance as maps. As we approached the Dufek Massif in December 1957, we were not much better off than Lewis and Clark approaching mountains rising from the plains, a century and a half earlier, despite the fact that we had undeveloped pictures in our cameras.

We stopped at 2300, when we had come 20 miles, to put our seismic station in here and wait for Hugo. It was pretty overcast, and the tops of the peaks were covered.

9 Dec., Mon. 452 mi. After supper, Aug and Paul borrowed the outer halves of our sleeping bags and with a tent, some trail rations, their geology tools, ice ax, crampons, skis, and an akio, set out at 0145 to get to rock. Ed and I have just finished our seismic station now at 0300. Augie and Paul are visible with binoculars, climbing the snow slope up to the rock spur they headed for. I'm going to bed. . . .

We were awakened briefly by Hugo's arrival at 0800, but slept through until 1200. We were roused by the noise of Lassiter's C-47 taxiing up right next to us. Jim Lassiter, Bill Chapman, Ronne and two other crew were aboard with 12 drums of fuel and letters for Ed, Paul, and me from home.

As mentioned earlier, Jackie Ronne had contacted our parents and told them where to mail a single letter each that Jim Lassiter would carry down. Despite all of our griping about Finn Ronne, this was greatly appreciated. Augie and Hugo apparently didn't receive any mail on this flight.

View to south at west end of Dufek Massif from air (photograph taken in 1978). Left to right: Aughenbaugh, Neuburg, and Walker Peaks; Hannah Peak in foreground. Rock comprises layered gabbro 175 million years old. Dark layers are pyroxinite.

J. Lassiter USAF C-47 resupplies Sno-Cats at Dufek Massif.

341

Lassiter had also brought the Sno-Cat clutch we had so desperately needed all winter. This, however, was left at Ellsworth, because the repaired clutch was working fine.

The Air Force group plans to spend 24 hours and put a station in for their geodetic control. Bill Chapman was up all last night getting sun shots at Ellsworth and now commenced 24 hours of the same here.

In 1994, Bill commented to me how hard Lassiter would work him on many of these occasions. The second plane of Lassiter's operation had only arrived at Ellsworth early on 6 December.

They brought the 100-watt transmitter for us but apparently just before leaving, Ronne decided that we couldn't have it, as mentioned in the first chapter.

Ronne had said on Thursday, 5 December, that Lassiter would bring 6 drums of fuel out to us on Sunday, weather permitting. In his book, Ronne reported that we contacted Ellsworth on 8 December and requested this resupply flight, but this is not correct. We had managed to get only one radio contact with Ellsworth Station in the past three weeks. I believe he wrote it to protect himself regarding our radio situation on the traverse.

It was agreed that we will head for Mt. Hassage upon leaving these mountains. Lassiter will bring us probably two loads of gas after which time Ronne wants us back within the 250-mile Otter range. This is extremely doubtful to us. We have managed to get only one radio contact with Ellsworth in the past three weeks and in all probability this condition will continue or get worse if we have to rely on the Angry 9.

Ed and I loaded eight drums of fuel (with Air Force help) on our sled, giving us nine drums total. Hugo has more bulky gear on his and more food so we left the other four drums for him. When Lassiter arrived we had full tanks and one half drum (about 25 gallons) of fuel left. Hugo planned on waiting in case we could get the radio, so Ed and I accompanied by Ronne and his cameras drove off on the track left by Paul and Augie. It was very warm and again I was running around in my undershirt.

As we drove towards the base of the peaks, the sun was at a good angle for pictures and we all shot up a lot of film. Augie and Paul had pitched their tent near a rock spur of the lower "front" range [now named Cairn Ridge because Augie built several cairns on its crest] that runs parallel and to the west of the main massif.

I had been convinced by Augie that we would find sedimentary rock. Thus the surprise I felt when I picked up the first piece and saw that it was not.

> This part of the range, at least, is composed of gabbro, an igneous rock, which was unexpected, because we can see bands that look like stratigraphy of sedimentary rocks high upon the big peaks.
>
> No one was around the tent when we arrived, but Paul soon came across a snow field, separating our spur from the next one to the east. He had been working that ridge and had found nothing but gabbro also. He found some algae growing in a little pool of melted water in the rocks, and had a small sample in a vitamin pill bottle.[1]

Paul and later I took samples of this algae back to the U.S. I gave my samples to botanists at the University of Wisconsin. We also found a few examples of yellow lichens growing sparsely in protected places. The climate in the Dufek Massif is apparently so harsh that lichens cannot grow on most rock exposures. Later we found some bird tracks, larger than a snow petrel's, on a ridge.

> When they reached the rock at 0600 this morning, Paul had gone to bed, but the indefatigable Augie had tramped right up this ridge and has been at it ever since. I cooked some supper by just heating up some cans of Army 5-in-1 rations, and after eating, Ronne loaded up a little sled he had with his photographic equipment and skied off towards the plane. It was six miles but downhill all the way, so he probably made it in an hour.
>
> After supper, Paul, Ed, and I prepared to ascend the main ridge and see what was on the other side. Just as we were getting ready to leave, Aug came back. This ridge is completely separate from the main group. He suggested we drive around the spur to the east and go up that way. After grabbing a bite to eat, he decided to join us.
>
> We left the tent and our sled about 2145 and cautiously drove around the next spur and up the valley between the two parts of the range. This was one of the most beautiful and scenic mountain drives I have ever taken.

Several years later, Art Ford and a United States Geological Survey (USGS) field party named this Enchanted Valley, which is quite apt.

On each side towered the peaks. We finally arrived at a spur running up to the left (about east), which looked as though it might eventually connect to the main ridge. We set out about 2240 and worked our way up the edge of the ridge. We were on to this low summit by midnight.

Sno-Cat in Enchanted Valley below Aughenbaugh Peak. Left to right: N. Aughenbaugh, H. Neuberg, and E. Thiel (standing by crevasse detector).

10 Dec., Tues. We saw that this was not a good route to the main ridge—in fact it was no route at all. Thus far it was mostly between

344

Class 3 and Class 4 climbing (requiring a rope to belay), but from here on it became more difficult and we would have had to descend a long way also.

We had also forgotten to bring a rope from the Sno-Cat, which I did not mention in my journal.

Aug had stayed behind a short way up the slope, when he found that this rock was still the same old gabbro. From a rock-climbing standpoint it was excellent, with a very rough surface and handholds and footholds everywhere. Ed descended while Paul and I sat up there for a while, waiting for the sun to get a better angle for pictures. We finally came down, met the others at the Sno-Cat, and drove back to camp. After some soup and canned pineapple we hit the sack about 0500. Augie had been up 42 hours.

Hugo pulled in about 1300 (while we were all asleep). He had an enjoyable time with the Air Force people, much to Ronne's chagrin. When the Captain had skied into their camp last night and found Hugo there, he asked him why he hadn't shown up for the conference on a future route that was supposed to have taken place with Ed and him. Hugo answered that he had been waiting to see if we could get the radio. Apparently Ronne had forgotten this or had hoped Hugo had.

Ronne and Hugo sat down in the Sno-Cat and planned a route between here and Mt. Hassage (i.e., they drew a straight line on our blank plotting chart between the two points). We will get a load of fuel at a point more than 200 miles along on 26 Dec. When Hugo brought up the point of our not being able to communicate, Ronne brushed it aside with remarks such as some risks being necessary, and trail parties years ago didn't have radios.

I realize now that Ronne did not want us to communicate with other Antarctic bases and field parties.

[Ronne] told Hugo that we had better be there or it would necessitate a search-and-rescue operation. Hugo pointed out that this would burn more avgas than regular resupply, but Ronne ignored it. Ronne then drew up a memorandum concerning these plans, which he had Hugo sign. Hugo has a copy:
At 82°30'S, 52°W 9 Dec. 1957 Memorandum for the record:
Lassiter will deposit fuel for the Sno-Cats and other required supplies as follows: On Dec. 26th or as soon thereafter as weather

permits, a cache of material will be flown to a position in latitude 79°30S, longitude 65°W. The traverse party is urged to make daily position determinations to be certain the party is at the right place at the right time. Unless terrain and other features are such that it would not be advisable to land, it is agreed and fully understood that the plane will land and deposit the cache in the aforementioned location.

Finn Ronne St Sc Ldr
(Hugo A C Neuburg)

What we did not pay much attention to at the time was the phrase that Lassiter would leave the fuel cache whether we were there or not. My subsequent Antarctic experience makes me doubt whether we would have been able to see the cache at any distance, and aircraft navigation at that time was notoriously inaccurate, relying on a sextant in a moving plane.

Ronne's memo was prepared without even consulting with, or asking, Lassiter. Ronne had drawn Hugo away from Lassiter to make these plans with him and then called Jim aside to confer with him immediately after.

Hugo stayed up puttering, as usual, and finally Ronne went to bed. Jim and Hugo started talking and Hugo found out that Jim hadn't been told any of these new plans. Lassiter has told Hugo that he would come out several times with fuel if needed, but Ronne's plan calls for just one more flight.

I got up about 1800. No one else was up yet, so I climbed up the ridge where we were parked to get some pictures of the peaks in back. I came down in time for breakfast. Augie is suffering from chafing in the groin from all his activities of the past couple of days, and it is very painful for him to walk fast. We dug out the first-aid kit and I dug up the *Merck Manual* and looked for a treatment. As we don't have the medicines they recommend, Augie had to be content with soap and water and foot powder.

In addition to the medical briefing Clint Smith had given us, I was the only member of the traverse party who had taken the Red Cross Advanced First-Aid Course. At 25, I felt prepared and willing to deal with any medical emergency! Now in my mid-60s, after helping raise two sons I'm more humble.

J. Behrendt in front of ridge in Dufek Massif.

When we finally had both Sno-Cats (less sleds) moving it was 2200. We drove down a couple of spurs east of our camp and climbed up a small peak, still looking for sedimentary rock.

11 Dec., Wed. Augie and Paul (who stayed low) found some samples that looked like certain radioactive ore minerals. Unfortunately we have no counter with us so could not check them.

The samples we found were not radioactive ore. The uranium boom was on in the Colorado Plateau area in the U.S. when we left in 1956, and the search for radioactive ore for nuclear weapons was an important national objective of the USGS there.

We drove still further east, and Ed, Hugo, and I climbed another of the lower peaks. We started up at 0415 and Hugo and I reached the summit at 0615. Ed got there sooner by a roundabout route, but Hugo and I enjoyed ourselves coming up the direct ridge, which involved some rock climbing. There was no sedimentary rock here either, just gabbro. The dark bands that look like stratigraphy in sedimentary rocks, are just different mineralogy in the gabbro.

It is now known that some of these are bands of a dark rock called pyroxinite that crystallized out in layers from the originally molten rock.

It was clear, sunny, and quite warm. I was a little sunburned.

Although we were in the sun all day every day, we normally never got sunburned at the essentially sea-level elevation. We always wore sunglasses or plastic goggles but didn't have any sun screen. The sun is always at a low angle in Antarctica, and there was no ozone hole in 1957. During my last several trips to Antarctica in the 1990s, I did get sunburned mildly a few times on the snow near McMurdo at sea level. Most people working outside there regularly these days do use sunscreen and are concerned about sunburn.

We relaxed on the summit for quite a while. Another slightly higher peak was separated from this by a snow arete [a narrow snow ridge]. Ed didn't want to go over, and started down. I crossed it, but Hugo didn't like the looks of it halfway across and turned back to wait for me on the first peak. I built a small cairn on the second summit and returned to Hugo. We built another cairn in which we left a note with the date and names, etc.

We left only one or two cairns (conical piles of rocks) with notes in the Dufek Massif because we scorned what "old Antarctic explorers" had done, and therefore did not want to clutter up the place. Now, as an old Antarctic explorer myself in the 1990s, I wish we had left a few more. For instance, it would have been quite appropriate and useful to future visitors had we left some cairns with records of our visit at outcrops we reached with the Sno-Cats along the north side of the Dufek Massif.

> We called the two peaks Mutt and Jeff. The south face of Jeff is nearly vertical, and directly across the way is a very jagged peak which I named Stevens Point after my hometown in Wisconsin. Augie named the small peaks in the ridge he traversed the first day [Cairn Ridge] after various members of his family. I suppose Ronne named all these peaks from his pictures anyway so our names won't count, but that doesn't mean I can't name them anyway.

Almost all of the men at Ellsworth that winter have peaks named after them by the U.S. Board of Geographic Names in the Dufek Massif and Forrestal Range to the east, except Finn Ronne, Ed Thiel, Walt Davis, and me. These names are now shown on USGS 1:250,000-scale topographic maps. The elevation and position control for these maps were established in 1965–66 by a large USGS field party (I led the geophysical group) working all over the Pensacola Mountains, using helicopters and fuel airlifted from McMurdo, about 1300 miles away. Brass benchmarks were set in the peaks at this time, which similar to benchmarks in the U.S., are embossed "United States Geological Survey." They do not, however, say "$250 fine for removal," as do USGS benchmarks in the continental U.S.

The Thiel Mountains, the next range, about 300 miles to the west along the Transantarctic Mountains, were named after Ed because he later led an airlifted party to this area in 1958–59. The Behrendt Mountains in Ellsworth Land were named because I led the Antarctic Peninsula Traverse in this area in 1961–62. Walt Davis has a peak in the Thiel Mountains named for him because he participated in a D-8 tractor train party from Byrd Station to the South Pole in 1960–61. "Smith" was also omitted from the names in these mountains because there are so many other features with this name. Instead, the name "Clinton Spur" was attached to a ridge in the Dufek Massif.

> Hugo and I met Augie about two thirds of the way down. I told him about the layer of gabbro banded with a white rock directly beneath the summit, which looks just like sandstone from a little way back. We descended leisurely with him. I found a nice specimen of malachite with a little azurite mixed in with it. We also found a bunch of nice cavity deposit crystals which we haven't identified yet.
>
> Augie thinks we have really hit it. He cheerfully conceded that he lost his bet with me and showed us some dark mineral which he thinks is of commercial concentration. He is sure that this would be an economic ore if it were in the States. This is most significant, if true, because no other commercial deposits of minerals have been reported in Antarctica so far.

As of the 1990s, no mineral deposits have been found in Antarctica that would be economic to mine. Nonetheless, our finds in the Dufek Massif–part of a vast-layered body slowly solidified from molten rock about 175 million years ago–have stimulated additional geologic fieldwork by Americans, Soviets, and Argentines and much speculation about the potential for economic exploitation of platinum group metals here.

Considering the difficulties we had in reaching the Dufek Massif by ship and Sno-Cat, it is unrealistic to think that *economic* development could take place here even if significant deposits were found. The cost of the required energy alone means that even with late twentieth-century technology, mineral development of the Dufek intrusion would be impractical. Consider building and maintaining a railroad across the rapidly moving, crevassed Filchner Ice Shelf ! Perhaps 50 years in the future, as suggested in the Environmental Protocol to the Antarctic Treaty adopted in 1991, the question of mineral resource development in Antarctica will need to be reconsidered.

We had lunch about noon in the Sno-Cats parked at the bottom of this ridge. There was a moraine blocking our way further eastward right here, so we had to drive back away and around a little hump of a nunatak, to continue. The snow slopes around here are all underlain by ice, which makes glissading (sliding downhill on our feet) somewhat treacherous. We had to drive on a few gentle ice slopes, and the sharp points on the Sno-Cat tracks worked just like crampons.

> Hugo put up his Explorers Club flag on the side of the Sno-Cat and we all posed for a group picture. After this foolishness was complete we proceeded to the northeastern part of the range where the peaks are low. Hugo hiked down the other side to a little lake where he discovered some pinkish-looking water plants of which he collected a sample [more algae].
>
> We had some canned chicken for supper, cooked in the can directly on the small Coleman stove, which burned it slightly. The regular equipment is back with the sleds. This was a hard day, and we slept well when we finally crawled in at 2000.

I had been up for 26 hours, which I did not think to mention in my journal.

12 Dec., Thurs. We didn't get up until afternoon. Aug went off by himself. I went to the top of the ridge and then down the other side

Traverse party with Explorers Club flag on Sno-Cat. Left to right: H. Neuburg, E. Thiel, P. Walker, J. Behrendt, and N. Aughenbaugh.

351

to the little lake that lies in the large (several miles in each dimension) snow-free area. There is actually dirt and much patterned ground in this spot. The lake itself is about a hundred yards across and roughly circular. Ice covers about 70% of it, but there is water under the ice and along the border. The bottom slopes very gently, and the lake can't be but a few feet deep at most. Perhaps this is the southernmost unfrozen lake in the world. The bottom is covered with a strange pinkish plant, which is somewhat leafy but has no stems or roots that I could discern. A pale green ooze-like substance forms the base and lies directly on the rock bottom.

There was a large area of dried leaves around the lake which indicated that it is larger (or was larger) at certain times. The plants were giving off bubbles of some gas which, if oxygen, would indicate that they were photosynthesizing. I took specimens of the dried leaves, wet plants, and "soil."

Forlidas Ponds Specially Protected Area.

I gave this sample to soil scientists at the University of Wisconsin when I returned to Madison. I was later informed that there was no evidence of chemical weathering of the particles, only mechanical weathering by freezing and thawing and wind.

Based on this work and other geologic fieldwork in the area by USGS geologists Drs. Arthur Ford, Richard Reynolds, and Steven

Boyer, environmental concern developed amongst us. In 1990 we proposed that these ponds–which had been named "Forlidas Ponds" after Chuck Forlidas, a radio operator at Ellsworth–be considered a "Special Protected Area" under the Antarctic Treaty, because of their biological sensitivity. In addition to the algae samples that Paul, Hugo, and I collected, there could be other forms of life present that we were not competent to recognize. Biologists in the U.S. concurred, despite the fact that these ponds have only been visited by geophysicists and geologists.

Our suggested management plan was put forward by the U.S. delegation to the Scientific Committee for Antarctic Research, which approved it in 1990 as a proposed recommendation to the Antarctic Treaty Consultative Meeting in 1991. I had the privilege of negotiating the recommendation for the U.S. delegation at the Antarctic Treaty Consultative Meeting in Bonn, Germany, in 1991, where the Forlidas Ponds Specially Protected Area was adopted in the form of a Recommendation of the Consultative Meeting.

> When all of us had returned, we proceeded around this peak and continued east. We drove on a lot of bare ice and over some very rough sastrugi. As Ed drove slowly along the front of the range for an hour or two, I read about Amundsen's trek to the South Pole in 1911–12. I occasionally gazed out the window at the spectacular unexplored scenery. As we rounded the point of the ridge we camped at, we could see into the ice-free area. There are several more ice-free areas between the subsequent ridges to the east. The main ice sheet stops short of these areas and has the appearance of the tongue (terminus) of a glacier, as it is at a higher elevation than the bottom of the basin.

This large ice-free area, termed a "dry valley" in Antarctic parlance, was subsequently named Davis Valley (after Ed Davis at Ellsworth). In 1990 when we proposed the Forlidas Ponds Special Protected Area (SPA), we also proposed the Davis Valley as part of a special reserved area (SRA), which went through the same process at the same time as the Forlidas Ponds SPA. It was approved as the Dufek Special Reserved Area #1 in 1991 at the Bonn Antarctic Treaty Consultative Meeting. I also negotiated this agreement there, as a member of the U.S. delegation. I include the discussion about the SRA here, as it stems directly from the

Davis Valley from ridge on east side.

excitement we felt at being the first people to view and enter this magnificently scenic, pristine area.

In the Management Plan that was approved, we proposed that, in the SRA, only those activities that would not have a permanent effect on the environment could take place. Therefore, no roads, permanent buildings and other structures, or tracked vehicles and wheeled trucks would be permitted; tents, helicopters, and foot travel on trails are allowed, but sewage and garbage must be removed. Scientific drilling is also permitted as long as the site is restored as near as possible to its original condition. (Drilling was authorized because we earth scientists who proposed the SRA hope that someday drilling to the base of the Dufek intrusion takes place.)

We felt that the tour groups operating with increasing frequency in Antarctica, rather than mining companies, which have no interest in the continent, be required to use care if they ever visit the Dufek Massif. This pristine area is particularly beautiful and has spectacular scenery. The north side of the range, where protected from the prevailing south wind, has a very benign climate for Antarctica, which is in sharp contrast to the south side of the Dufek Massif.

We defined the boundaries of the SRA to be the entire north side of the Dufek Massif including some of the "blue ice" area south to the crest of the range. Enchanted Valley, all of the peaks, and

354

dry valleys we had visited in December 1957 are included within this boundary.

Under the prohibitions of the adopted Management Plan, no hotels or airstrips for large aircraft can be built within the SRA boundary. However, there is nothing to prohibit aircraft operations or lodging facilities for tourists on the ice sheet outside the SRA, assuming that the provisions of the Environmental Protocol to the Antarctic Treaty are complied with. The hard, blue ice area immediately to the north of the SRA boundary probably could be used as a landing strip by wheeled aircraft and, no doubt, will be in the not-too-distant future.

After approval of the draft management plan for the Dufek SRA by the Scientific Committee for Antarctic Research (SCAR), the matter next came to the attention of the U.S. Antarctic Policy Group, which sets the negotiating instructions for the U.S. delegation to the Antarctic Treaty meetings. Because the name "Dufek" triggers thoughts of commercial mineral deposits, the Department of the Interior (DOI) representative at the Antarctic Policy Group meeting objected on the grounds that this would restrict mineral development in this area.

This time period was during the Bush administration, when the DOI was very supportive of mineral development in Antarctica in the interests of the U.S. mining industry. The Dufek SRA, however, includes only a small part of the Dufek intrusion, which consists of the entire Dufek Massif and the much larger Forrestal Range, about 50 miles to the east.

The State Department chairman of the meeting (F. Tucker Scully) pointed out to the DOI representative that the proposal had been initiated by one of his people (me) from the USGS. The proposal was ultimately approved by the U.S. Antarctic Policy Group. Later, I was informally asked (and eventually reminded when I ignored the request) by the DOI to provide the paper trail in the U.S. government on this proposal.

The only record I discovered was a letter I submitted with the draft management plan to Sherburne Abbott, director of the National Academy of Sciences–National Research Council Polar Research Board in response to a form letter from her to all U.S. Antarctic researchers, requesting nominations of areas. As I learned from my winter with Finn Ronne and subsequent Antarctic seasons with the U.S. Navy, it is always easier to be forgiven than to receive permission. I submitted these two letters with our draft management plan to the DOI and heard nothing further.

> We stopped at one of the eastern-most ridges and drove up the east side to several hundred feet above the bottoms of the snow-free basins. From here we could see a half dozen rock outcrops protruding from the ice escarpment trending further northeast. Possibly this escarpment runs continuously to the Shackleton Range.

The Transantarctic Mountains, of which the Dufek Massif and the Pensacola Mountains are a part, are now known to extend continuously across Antarctica from the Ross Sea to the Weddell Sea coast. Beyond the Dufek (highest elevation about 7200 ft) are the Shackleton Range (about 5000 ft) and the Theron Mountains (about 2000 ft), named by Fuchs' Transantarctic Expedition.

> Augie has the geology roughly under control—in a sketchy way of course. He thinks that probably the whole range was originally sandstone but was replaced by the intruded gabbro.

The "granitization" hypothesis, which influenced Augie and Paul in early reports on the Dufek Massif, has been generally superseded. Geologists later concluded that the Dufek intrusion was formed from a magma body.

The Dufek Massif consists of igneous-layered gabbro formed from crystallization of a vast body of molten rock (magma) about 175 million years ago, associated with the failed Transantarctic Rift at about the same time that Africa separated from Antarctica. Uplift and erosion since that time have exposed these spectacular mountains.

This large gabbro body is called the Dufek-layered intrusion, and is now known to extend to the Forrestal Range about 50 miles to the east of the Dufek Massif. It is possibly the second largest such geologic body in the world. I and other colleagues in the USGS (Art Ford, Dwight Schmidt, Richard Reynolds, and others) have been studying the Dufek intrusion geophysically and geologically at widely spaced intervals of time up to the 1980s. Soviet and Argentine geologists and geophysicists have also worked in the Dufek intrusion.

It really is somewhat thrilling when one stops to think of it (which we usually don't) to be seeing beautiful mountains and climbing on rocks where no one has ever set foot. The same feeling is absent when driving around on the flat ice shelf. Augie could happily spend weeks or months doing detailed work here. It was sunny and warm all day, but when we were near the east end of the range, a very strong wind came up, making it difficult to work barehanded. Augie found a place where we could get down to one of the black (pyroxinite) bands we have observed continuing across the range. I belayed him while he climbed down (using crampons) a 60° icy slope of a sort of crevasse separating the cliff face from the ice.

We headed back towards camp about 2230 and the wind continued to blow. We stopped at one outcrop, several miles north of the peaks. The wind must have been in excess of 40 knots, with much blowing snow. There we found some nice samples of atacamite (a copper mineral). The wind abated as we got in close to the range again, but we could see that it was still strong by the beautiful white streamers of snow blowing off the high peaks.

The north side of the Dufek Massif is essentially protected from the strong katabatic winds (chinooks) flowing by gravity down from the polar plateau to the south.

13 Dec., Fri. We arrived back to the sleds about 0500. I fried up all the steak everyone could eat and we went to bed about 0700. . . . We slept in until 2300 when Paul finally got up and burned some oatmeal for breakfast.

14 Dec., Sat. 459 mi. We had a conference as to our future course of action. Ed and Hugo have differing viewpoints as to what we shall do. Hugo thinks that, as we have no radio and as Ronne expects us to do, we should try and get to the rendezvous point by 26 December, even if some of the program is sacrificed. Ed thinks, on the other hand, that we should not make the program second to anything. Better that Lassiter should burn more of his precious avgas looking for us than we omit anything such as the range that Ronne and Mac saw to the northwest of our present location. While no definite decision was reached, the consensus of opinion seemed to favor Ed's viewpoint. There are strong arguments on each side. At any rate it was agreed to spend one more day at this range and then push on for Mt. Hassage, with a detour to these new mountains when and if sighted.

After Sno-Cat maintenance, we finally started moving at 0400. We worked our way up the aforementioned beautiful valley [Enchanted Valley] we entered last Monday night, which separates [Cairn Ridge] from Dufek Massif.

Three particularly spectacular peaks along this valley are now named Mt. Neuburg, Mt. Aughenbaugh, and Walker Peak.

I took magnetometer readings at 2.5 mile intervals, but Ed forgot the tripod for the gravity meter so unfortunately we obtained no gravity observations.

These were the first measurements of the spectacularly high magnetic anomalies (i.e., a difference from the regional magnetic field) caused by very high concentrations of magnetite (a magnetic mineral) in the Dufek intrusion that we were traversing. Because I only had a few measurements in this valley, I did not report these extreme anomalies until I acquired two airborne profiles over the Dufek Massif in 1963–64.

We stopped at every little spur to do some geology. It was clear, warm, and calm at our campsite and through the valley to the southwest end. As we rounded the corner and started southeast along the back (south) side of the range, we were struck by a blast of wind and lots of blowing snow. Ed and I were about a mile ahead of the others at the time. The snow surface, while not the glare ice we found at the northeast end of the range, was so hard that the vehicle made an almost indiscernible track. To the south (from 15 to 30 miles away) we could see another range not quite as rugged in appearance and somewhat parallel.

These mountains are the Cordiner Peaks and are now known to be composed of sedimentary rocks.

We started to head for this range, but found ourselves in an area of small crevasses and turned back, reasoning that now was no time to take any chances with the vehicles.

This was the southernmost point we reached on the traverse. I have often thought, regretfully, that had we better cooperation with Finn Ronne, we could have continued from here on to the South

Pole, only about 450 miles away. This would have been the sort of adventure that would have excited Ronne. I am sure George Dufek would have been supportive, and we probably would have beaten Fuchs and the Transantarctic Expedition to the Pole. This probably would not have been viewed favorably by Hugh Odishaw and Bert Crary but still would have been scientifically very worthwhile. No scientific oversnow traverse has ever been made through this area. Having flown over the area between the South Pole and the Dufek Massif several times since, I don't think the crevasses are any worse than those we had already managed. Adventure tourist parties routinely use this route today to ski to the South Pole or across Antarctica.

We drove up the back slope of a very jagged-topped peak [Walker Peak, named after Paul] which is the southwestern most one of the main massif. By this time #1 had caught up with us and the geology work began. The wind was a howling gale, making working conditions very unpleasant. Ed and I considered climbing this peak but with the wind blowing so hard, I couldn't quite talk him into it. Everyone else was most emphatically not interested. From what we could see, the snow comes up higher on the south side of the range and the peaks may not be quite as rugged.

It was a relief to get back into our little valley again out of the katabatic wind. At one place we stopped, and we all took naps in the sun on the warm flat slabs of rock that were so conveniently placed for loafers. We finally drove back to the sleds and our little wind-free camp around the east end of [Cairn Ridge].

At one point while Hugo was driving, the Sno-Cat came out of gear and went free-wheeling down a steep slope. He couldn't get it back in gear for a bit, and as I heard the story, there was much turmoil and confusion until he finally got things under control. I was driving along behind at the usual 2 or 3 mph pace Hugo sets, when all of a sudden I saw him speed up to 8 or 10 mph. I stepped on the gas and went roaring along behind. I understand that they were quite startled to see me so close behind when they were finally back in gear.

Hugo had another incident today. He took a long slide down a snow slope without an ice ax. He was glissading on his fanny, controlling himself with his feet, when he hit an icy patch. Completely out of control, movie cameras bouncing along behind, he slid several hundred feet down until the slope leveled out. Fortunately the only injury was to his pride, and not much there.

We were all pretty nonchalant about these rather minor risks, compared to the crevasses, after a year in Antarctica. Fortunately no one was hurt in these incidents.

> I took four pratfalls in succession trying to get out of a little icy patch to a rock outcrop. Ed came along and walked right up, much to my chagrin.
>
> We were back in camp about 2000, ate supper, and moved back out to the spot Lassiter surveyed in as his control point. To bed finally at 2300.
>
> *15 Dec., Sun.* 474 mi. Clear and sunny all day. We ate breakfast at 1400, but due to delays it was about 1830 before we finally got underway on a course of 319°. We had troubles with the gyrocompass for the full 40 miles that we drove.

We were now proceeding into the totally unexplored area, of what is now called the Ronne Ice Shelf, heading for the rendezvous point that Ronne and Hugo had agreed upon.

> *16 Dec., Mon.* 500 mi. We stopped at the site of seismic station #16 at 0450, but it was 0700 before we had dinner and got to bed. Aug cooked breakfast at 2000 and we put in our station. Our reflection came in at about 1.7 seconds, which is quite deep (5500 ft, or 1700 m).

The Thiel Trough, which we had been mapping geophysically beneath the ice shelf since we left Ellsworth, continued at least this far from what we could tell. In 1965–66 I led a geophysical party using helicopters in the Pensacola Mountains. Working with a Stanford graduate student, Laurent Meister, temporarily with me at the USGS, we determined from seismic reflection measurements that the 6000-ft-deep trough continues about 300 miles to the southwest beneath the 4000-ft-thick floating ice shelf.

> Another sunny clear day. Temperature about 15°F. We reached mile 500 of the traverse, but put in 68 miles driving in the mountains.
>
> *17 Dec., Tues.* 541 mi. Finished the station and drove on to the next, arriving there about 1615. Steak for supper. Hugo wants to finish off all the fresh meat, as he thinks it will spoil. I don't. Paul and I drilled a nine-meter hole before retiring at 1830. We could see the moun-

tains behind us when we stopped, but the view was obscured by clouds by morning.

The altimeter shows that we have been going down gradually ever since we left the mountains, and at present we are traveling on about the level of the ice shelf.

We were, of course, traveling *across* the ice shelf but were only beginning to determine this.

18 Dec., Wed. 584 mi. Our reflection at 1.2 seconds shows that the bottom is coming up beneath us.

We were crossing the Thiel Trough. Although the reflection time was 0.4 seconds earlier than observed at the previous station, the bedrock was only about 450 ft (about 140 m) shallower. This was because the ice shelf was thicker here and the higher velocity of sound in ice partially compensated for the shorter reflection time.

It was clear all day, but started clouding up in the late evening.

My journal is exceedingly terse as we proceeded uneventfully across the heavily crevassed ice shelf. The snow bridges covered the crevasses, and we could not see them from the surface, partly because of overcast during these days.

19 Dec., Thurs. 584 mi. By 0315 when we stopped for our station it was completely overcast. There was a 10-knot breeze which felt so cool that we turned the heater on in the #1 Sno-Cat, although it was about 20°F outside. The warm weather we had at the mountains really spoiled us. I cooked chicken rice curry without curry (except on my own serving) due to popular request.

Up for breakfast at about 1830. The bedrock is more than 3000 ft (1130 m) below sea level. We have seen no trace of the range of mountains that we think should be in this area. Just before the visibility completely disappeared, we thought we could see a rise ahead of us on course.

We never did see any mountains to the west from the surface.

20 Dec., Fri. 620 mi. We started driving about 0300; it cleared and warmed up during the day. About 0500 the gyrocompass went berserk and began precessing about six cycles per minute. This made it somewhat difficult to steer by, so after trying for an hour to repair it, the boys shut it off.

From here on we used magnetic compasses to steer by. The fragile gyrocompasses gave so much trouble to all of the oversnow traverses that eventually these were replaced by rugged Army surplus tank magnetic compasses.

About 0730 we reached a rising slope to the northwest with some crevasses. We detoured around to the left of it and passed by several gentle rises and valleys. Finally we drove northwest up a gently sloping valley, climbing about 50 m. We contoured a slope which increased in elevation gradually to the right (northeast).

Trying to figure out the terrain we were traveling through was like the blind men describing an elephant—a simile I used before but bears repeating. In 1992 the USGS published a composite satellite photograph of Antarctica in the form of a map that shows the area we traveled through on this traverse very clearly. We certainly didn't understand it at the time. We were leaving the Filchner Ice Shelf and climbing up what is now named the Henry Ice Rise.

We stopped for the next station after traveling 36 miles at 1730. Hugo and I drilled the nine-meter hole which they use for measuring mean annual temperature, and we use the next day as a shot hole. It was 2100 when I went to bed.

21 Dec., Sat. 645 mi. Up at 0300 and done with the station by early afternoon. We did not get any reflections, however.

We were on Henry Ice Rise, a grounded area in the middle of the ice shelf, about 300 ft higher than the area of the ice shelf we had crossed to the south. The bottom is probably a slurry of morainal material and ice being moved along fairly rapidly by the barely grounded ice shelf. It is not surprising that we could not get a reflection.

On the maps we published from this traverse, we show Henry Ice Rise as a peninsula connected to Berkner Island to the northeast. We thought this was a peninsula because we could see an appearance of a rising snow surface and a disturbed crevassed area from here to Berkner Island. We later saw this area twice from the air and used these observations to supplement the traverse measurements in the making of this map.

I speculate that the rapidly moving ice has changed its configuration in the years since our traverse and the satellite images acquired in the 1970s and 1980s. There may actually have been a low-elevation peninsula ("ice rumples") connecting Henry Ice Rise to Berkner Island in 1957. If the ice has thinned in this period (by global warming?), this barely grounded zone in 1957 might now be a floating ice shelf.

It is now known, from our traverse results, that this disturbed area is where the very thick ice shelf (greater than 4000 ft, or 1300 m), where we had crossed it to the southeast, is just equal to the depth below the surface to bedrock (about 3000 ft, or 1000 m) at this point. Henry Ice Rise exists as a 700-ft-high area to the northwest because the ice is grounded and the snow accumulation has formed a dome-shaped island surrounded by the floating ice shelf. Berkner Island is similar but much higher and greater in area.

Overcast but very warm. It cleared toward the end of the day as we drove along. About 2100 and mile 637 we began going down into a large east-west-trending trough. The altimeter showed a decrease of over 200 ft (70 m). At mile 640 we began crossing east-west-trending cracks, about two to four inches wide, with indications of recent movement. We crossed over a dozen of these in the mile or so around the bottom of the trough. Looking west down the trough we could see that it abutted against a higher, gently rolling snow surface.

These cracks were probably tidal in origin. We were crossing from the grounded to the floating ice of the thinner Ronne Ice Shelf. Had we thought of it, we should have measured sea tide on the innermost ice shelf, with the gravity meter during the "night" or during other extended periods when we were stopped. We did do this in the winter, at Ellsworth, and had planned to do so on bedrock on the nunataks at the east edge of the Filchner Ice Shelf, so we could not use ignorance as an excuse. If we had made the gravity measurements, we would have found that the tides were possibly as great as 15 ft (5 m). Tidal ranges this great were measured with a gravity meter on the inner Ronne Ice Shelf in the

1990s by Dr. Edward King of the British Antarctic Survey. These measurements are significantly higher than the 6-ft (2-m) tides we measured at Ellsworth at the ice front.

> *22 Dec., Sun.* 661 mi. We stopped at 0250 and I cooked steak for supper. Paul and I drilled the nine-meter hole and I got to bed at 0530. It began to cloud up just about this time. It was completely overcast when we woke up at 2300, and snow was falling.

> *23 Dec., Mon.* 692 mi. Everything went wrong in the seismic work. We couldn't get a reflection here either, and the voltage regulator in the dynamotor power supply is giving intermittent trouble. One bit of good news: Hugo calculated that we are only 45 miles from the rendezvous point. It looks like we may have a holiday (enforced) on Christmas, as Lassiter isn't due until the 26th. Since leaving the mountains, we have been driving in fourth gear for the first time on the traverse. Heretofore the tracks were so tight that it was impossible to shift gears while moving, so we drove in third gear continuously.

This is how we had burned out the clutch originally. Obviously the tracks were not that tight on the traverse.

> We were underway again at 1330 and drove all the next 50 miles in complete whiteout. The lead Sno-Cat was steered with the aid of a geologist's Brunton (magnetic) compass taped to the windshield. The snow surface today was the smoothest we have had anywhere on traverse, and we roared along in fifth gear at about eight miles per hour with little of the usual bucking and pitching of the vehicle.

An old friend and colleague, Charles Swithinbank, of the British Antarctic Survey, commented to me that he had flown over this part of our traverse many years later, and was amazed at the crevasses bridged by snow that were visible from the air.

> At 1800 we stopped for three hours and put in seismic station #21 at mile 681, where we obtained a good reflection at .48 seconds.

The bedrock was about 2000 ft below sea level, much shallower than over the Thiel Trough. However, the floating ice was about 1800 ft thick, so there was not much seawater beneath the ice. To the northeast towards the front of the ice shelf, the bottom is still shallower at about 1000 ft below sea level.

24 Dec., Tues. 712 mi. (Christmas Eve) We drove on 30 more miles where we stopped at 0400. Hugo's calculations show us to be approximately at the rendezvous point for Lassiter on 26 Dec. After fueling we had 2.5 barrels (about 125 gallons) of gas left. We went to bed about 0700.

Up again at 1900, we completed our seismic work before midnight. A poor reflection at .42 sec. was the result. Still whiteout. I listened to Christmas music on BBC while I worked in the Sno-Cat.

Although we could receive stations all over the world, we had no radio contact with Ellsworth since Ronne and Lassiter had left in Lassiter's plane on 10 December at the Dufek Massif.

25 Dec., Wed. (Christmas) After rolling up the spread I proceeded to fix Christmas dinner. Our menu included: shrimp cocktail (with Behrendt's special cocktail sauce), onion and potato soup, tenderloin steak, mashed potatoes and butter, whole kernel corn, applesauce, bread, butter, cheese, raspberry jam, peanut butter, canned apricots and pears, steamed fruitcake, coffee, brandy, and milk. I was complimented on the meal, which was generally conceded to be the best of the traverse.

Probably because we had no sexual outlet, we were preoccupied with food. This is not unusual for Antarctic field parties, but cannot be explained in our case by any shortage of food. We were consuming 4000–5000 calories per day and still losing weight.

We were finished eating by 0300, which I'm sure is the earliest that Christmas dinner has been completed anywhere. After dinner we sat around and discussed future plans. We would like to recommend putting in a small station (consisting of just a Jamesway) at the mountains, to be manned for a few months by traverse people.

Geologists started doing this in about 1960. In 1965 I led the geophysical part of a combined USGS team of geologists, topographic engineers, and geophysicists operating from a Jamesway field camp in the Pensacola Mountains south of the Dufek Massif. We used helicopters and snowmobiles for transportation and worked in the Dufek Massif and surrounding ice sheet and throughout the Pensacola Mountains.

We discussed coming down for Deep Freeze IV and running a traverse from the mountains to the Pole. Ed and Paul defeated Augie and me in a bridge game, which lasted until 1400 when we quit and went to bed.

26 Dec., Thurs. We waited all day for the weather to break and the plane to come. It cleared in the late afternoon, but no plane. Augie and I soundly trounced Ed and Paul in the bridge game today.

We were losing good working days, which would cut us short in January.

27 Dec., Fri. 717 mi. Overcast again today. Hugo figured that we were five miles west of exactly 79°30'S, 65°W (where Ronne's memo of 9 Dec. specified that we rendezvous with the resupply aircraft), although it is impossible to navigate from an airplane that precisely. Hugo insisted on driving east and a little south to be nearer that spot. So we did.

This quirk of Hugo's created an anomalous jog on our traverse track as published and republished on many maps. No one understands what obstacle caused our apparent detour, but all map compilers faithfully reproduce it, sometimes exaggerating the distance.

When we aren't playing bridge we listen to the radio and speculate as to when Lassiter will get here. We jokingly discuss the possibilities of wintering over here (impossible with the amount of food and fuel we have) and not so jokingly the possibility of Ronne ordering us to head for Ellsworth rather than continuing on to Mt. Hassage.

We heard (on BBC) that Fuchs and party have reached South Ice and are now proceeding on to the Pole. We are really glad that they made it up their escarpment. Hillary is only 300 miles from the Pole coming from Scott Base at McMurdo Sound.

We had come 258 miles from our farthest south point on 14 December where we were only 450 miles from the Pole; we could have beaten both Hillary and Fuchs there.

28 Dec., Sat. Clear, sunny, and cold (4°F) but no plane.

My, how my perception of "cold" had changed in the past month or so.

This afternoon, as we were about to start our bridge game, we heard Byrd Station trying to call Little America. . . . As usual we tried to make contact, and much to our surprise were successful at 1520 in getting through. Hugo conversed with them. He asked them to relay our position to Ellsworth and tell them we are waiting. Informed Byrd that we only have an Angry 9. It is interesting to speculate on the reactions of various people (viz. Dufek and Ronne) to this contact. I'll bet we get a plane pretty quickly. It cheered us up (not that we have been at all downcast) to know that there really are other people in the world.

29 Dec., Sun. 758 mi. We were awakened at 0300 by the beautiful sound of a C-47 buzzing us. Roderick was pilot. Willie was also aboard with the Air Force people. They have tried on three previous occasions to fly out, but weather and other things turned them back. On Christmas Day both planes headed out in the evening with some hot Christmas dinner for us, but the weather was bad. Yesterday . . . both planes again started but Jim's developed flap trouble so they had to turn back. Rod took off alone and finally got here. Because both planes were coming, they only brought seven drums of gas and Category C of our food in this load.

They brought the 125-watt transmitter with them; Dufek OK'd Ronne's query on it. Rod told us that they have been a little concerned about us with no radio contact, etc. Ronne especially was worrying. He should have been, what with refusing to give us the transmitter before!

As it happened, we had had no radio contact with Ellsworth for the 24 days since the last resupply and for more than 400 miles and many crevasses along our complex traverse route.

Ronne sent the following note out to Ed and Hugo:

Ellsworth station 28 December 1957
From: Station Scientific Leader
To: Leaders of the Traverse Party (Thiel and Neuburg)

As I already told you on 9 December, permission has been granted for you to terminate your traverse at the West Cape of Gould Bay. Reconnaissance on 15 December revealed a safe route to the Cape as indicated on map accompanying this letter. The route is drawn in light red pencil. This is only a suggestion based on what I saw from the air. There are large areas of crevasses, and I believe the only possible route would be along my proposed track, from your location at 79°30'S, 65°00'W.

The ship is on its way from Capetown and is expected to be here around the 8th or 10th of January. I do not believe the ship will stay here more than 10 or 14 days before heading back north. In view of that, I suggest and strongly recommend that you commence your return journey to Gould Bay within the next few days. You must also remember that the new men taking over next year where you finished this year will have to be flown out into the field to the West Cape–Gould Bay, Sno-Cat site. It all will take time, and the ship, when departure date is set, will not wait for anyone. That is a direct order from the Commander, Naval Support Force, Antarctica.

As a reasonable date for reaching West Cape of Gould Bay, I would set it for no later than 15 January.

I think you have done a wonderful job in covering the distances and investigated [sic] such a large portion of the Ice Shelf. Happy New Year to all of you.

Sincerely,
Finn Ronne, St . Sc. Ldr
Ellsworth station

Hugo and Ed told Rod to inform Ronne we are proceeding to Mt. Hassage. The next plane won't come out until we request it to. Rod told us that all the avgas troubles are over. There is plenty, he said. I wonder if Ronne is of this opinion.

Jerry sent a note to us, the main points: Skidmore off restriction 24 December. Ronne found out around early December that the cooks were sending us bread, etc., and ordered them to stop. Ronne takes any leftover pastry, bread, etc., over to Lassiter's crew. When Jim went out to the Airdale building the other day, the subject came up. Lassiter told them that he didn't know we were not getting these items, and was under the impression that they were leftovers.

Ronne gave Ed Davis the following memo on 24 December:

To: Chief Commissary, E. H. Davis
From: Commanding Officer, Ellsworth Station
Subject: Christmas Holidays

1. As you know the IGY traverse party has been away from Ellsworth station for almost two months, thus not been able to enjoy the good food and other niceties the rest of us have had, and hope to enjoy during the next few days.
2. Major Lassiter will contact the party for the first time since December the 10th on 26th of this month (the day after Christ-

mas), and I think it would be very nice if you could possibly make up some special food for the five traverse men in the form of possible turkey, Christmas cakes, and other baked products. 3. This gesture will be highly appreciated by me and well deserving to the men in the field who is [sic] doing a splendid job for the IGY program. Thank you.

Captain Finn Ronne USNR, Commanding Sta. Scientific Ldr.

Ed Davis sent some bread (smuggled in with the other food) and some other pastry. Openly he sent some ice cream and some rolls.

I suppose the two-week stint in the galley that Paul and I did, working for Ed, was paying off.

Ronne and Cox are at outs again. Ronne is threatening court martial because Cox made copies of pictures for people. Consequently a nice set of traverse pictures he made for us had to be given back.

Later Jerry got all those pictures back for us in spite of Ronne. During his short stay with us, when coincidentally we had those accidents in crevasses, Cox made a number of fine photographs. Ronne and others used Navy photographs taken by Cox on this expedition. Most of the pictures in Ronne's book *Antarctic Command* were taken by Wally Cox with no acknowledgment to him personally. As these are official U.S. government photographs in the public domain, there is nothing improper about this. However, Wally Cox's outstanding Navy photographs taken during this year were published in many places with never an acknowledgment except "Official U.S. Navy photo." One spectacular picture by Cox (page 269), of an emperor penguin holding a chick on its feet for warmth, was published as a full page in *Life* magazine.

Roderick told us that they took seven drums of mogas out to Fuchs. They are pulling two sleds with each Sno-Cat and are running short of gas. The BBC announced tonight that they made only 15 miles on their last day's haul (yesterday?) and are having mechanical trouble with four vehicles. They have had nothing but trouble right from the beginning. Hillary, on the other hand, made 44 miles in his latest day's trek and is only five days short of the Pole.

Ronne sent out the following IGY message to us, on the back of which he sent his New Year's greeting, "My regards and Best."

ANTARCTIC NOTES . . . RADIO MOSCOW ANNOUNCES 3 DEC SOVIET ANTARCTIC EXPEDITION HAS REACHED FINAL STAGE IN CONSTRUCTION OF IN-LAND STATION VOSTOK. . . . SEVERAL VEHICLES FROM INTERMEDIATE BASE VOSTOK ONE 734 KM SOUTH OF MIRNY LEFT FOR MAGNETIC POLE ON 1 DEC WITH SCIENTIFIC PERSONNEL, FUEL, AND FOOD. . . . REMAINDER OF FIRST SOVIET SATELLITE ROCKET . . . FELL ON 30 NOV . . . IN ALASKA AND U.S. WEST COAST. . . .

FIRST SUCCESSFUL MEASUREMENTS OF GRAVITY FROM A SURFACE VESSEL ON OPEN SEA WERE MADE 22 NOV. BY J. LAMAR WORZEL OF LAMONT GEOLOGI-CAL OBSERVATORY USING GRAVIMETER DEVEL-OPED BY ANTON GRAF OF MUNICH, GERMANY.

The U.S.S.R. traverse was led by Andrei Kapitsa, whom I later came to know. I most recently met him in Rome in 1994, where he was showing seismic records from that IGY traverse, which show a 1500-ft-deep subglacial "lake" at Vostok Station beneath about 12,000 ft of ice. The marine gravity measurements appeared truly revolutionary to Ed and me, because a gravity meter measures acceleration and to do this on a moving ship was quite an accomplishment.

In his message, Ronne also included a list of the IGY wintering-over party for 1956–57 and the names of the summer personnel.[2] Among the names of the ordinary IGY folks, like us, were those of other very prominent and future-prominent scientists.

We started driving at 0830 and stopped about 0930 to set up and try our new radio. We used a doublet antenna array and put in a strong signal for our first contact with Ellsworth in weeks. As the plane had just left, we didn't have anything to say.

This was the first direct radio contact we had with Ellsworth since 30 November, at mile 247 on Berkner Island, 29 days and 573 miles back. From this time on, radio communication with Ellsworth was routine.

We drove 40 more miles across the smooth, featureless ice shelf today, stopping about 1800. It was cold (4°F).

30 Dec., Mon. 773 mi. We put in station #23 today and recorded a good reflection from a depth of about 1800 ft (550 m). It was brightly overcast with very little wind, and so warm that I worked stripped to the waist. We have been using skis in laying out the spreads, since we left the sastrugi behind. This is not only faster, but is much more enjoyable. The snow is just right. I have been reading *Human Destiny* by LeComte de Nouilly and find it quite interesting, even if his biochemistry is better than his physics.

We started on our way again at 2015. As we progressed, we saw that we were approaching a rising snow surface, which extended in a north-south direction to both sides of us, as far as we could see.

This grounded ice island is now known as Korff Ice Rise.

31 Dec., Tues. 794 mi. About 20 miles along we found that as we approached the rise, we began encountering our old nemesis–crevasses. These were long linear ones pretty heavily bridged, about 20–30 ft wide and parallel to the strike of the rise. We stopped at 0230 and decided to radio for a recon flight–if we could get one. We camped for the meanwhile.

As mentioned previously, we had never really left the crevasses. We just hadn't seen them because of the snow bridges and poor visibility.

When Hugo talked to Ellsworth this morning, he was told that we couldn't get a flight today, as they were busy elsewhere. We got on the road again about 2010. We decided not to try to cross the bad area where we were, but to try elsewhere. We backtracked four miles to our last gravity station and then headed south, parallel to the hill. Five miles further, we tried again–and again turned back because of the crevasses. Another five miles to the south and a third try to cross the crevassed area.

During this backtracking, Hugo and I had different ideas about the safest way to cross crevasses with partly broken snow bridges crossed by our tracks. We did agree that we would exactly retrace our tracks in the snow. Hugo thought the best way was to go very carefully and slowly as possible. I favored driving as fast as possible and keeping up momentum. The other three decided to be outside the Sno-Cats watching. We got our vehicles across without incident, but I now realize Hugo was probably right. I was a pretty impatient 25-year-old!

> The weather was still clear but we figured that if we waited until a plane came out, so much time might elapse that we would have to turn back before reaching Mt. Hassage. This time we carefully turned and twisted our way across dozens of bridged crevasses. Some of the worst ones we probed but found the bridges quite thick. At about 2350 Paul called us from the lead Sno-Cat and said something to the effect that, "There is an open crevasse directly in front of us. Why don't you and Ed come up to our vehicle and join us in welcoming in the New Year?" We immediately accepted this cordial invitation.

> *1 Jan. 1958, Wed.* 809 mi. Toasted the coming of 1958 with some of the Aughenbaugh designed "Antarctic Whiteout." (This concoction of medicinal brandy and grapefruit juice was first tried and christened in the middle of a whiteout at Christmas.) Even Hugo and I took a little on this festive occasion. After the New Year was properly inaugurated, Hugo and Augie probed around the open hole and we drove by with no trouble at all.

I'm sure the Antarctic Whiteout gave us "attitude" for crevasse travel.

> From here on it was clear sailing. We crossed a few more bridges, and then started up the gentle slope. We climbed about 1300 ft before we stopped for a seismic station at 0615. There was a 25-knot wind and it was 9°F, which made it fairly unpleasant. We had chicken and rice for our New Year's dinner.

> When we got up at 2200 it was overcast and foggy, which made us quite glad we crossed the crevasses last night. We received a very good reflection from the bottom of the ice and two reflections a few tenths of a second later. We also tried firing a TNT block on a pole 7 ft high and obtained a reflection of higher amplitude than that from the usual method of firing at the bottom of a 28-ft (9-m) hole. The snow surface is 1300 ft high here [on Korff Island], but the bedrock is still about 600 ft below sea level.

> *2 Jan., Thurs.* Hugo calculated our position. It appears that we came quite a bit more west than desired, so we were still about 90 miles from the position of Mt. Hassage shown on the map. [This was incorrect as it turned out.] It was after 0900 when we finally started.

We decided not to set up for the radio sked, but only listen with the whip antenna. Wonders of wonders! Not only could we hear them, they could receive us, perhaps because we are so high.

We were also on grounded ice again like the communication with Ellsworth from Berkner Island. As it turned out, this was an unfortunate accident, as we received a message from Ronne:

> Attention Thiel and Neuburg: Lassiter doubtful of next resupply flight. Priority his own operational requirements; aircraft maintenance troubles and adverse weather negate probability of further support by him. Therefore, return within operational range of Otter aircraft, which is 250 miles from Ellsworth, with fuel presently in your possession. Unfortunately there is no other alternative but for you to comply. Suggest you retrace track to last supply cache, then follow my proposed route on map in your possession to West Cape, Gould Bay, where air evacuation will be effected. West Cape, Gould Bay, should be achieved no later than 15 Jan. Ships' departure, next traverse party familiarization makes imperative you comply this schedule. You have all done a wonderful job covering distances and investigated such large portion of ice shelf. Happy New Year to all of you.

Needless to say the reaction to this was violently unfavorable. Many unprintable comments were made in loud voices. A meeting was held in #1 Sno-Cat. The basic question seems to me to be, "Is Ronne our boss?" There is no room for doubt or misinterpretation of his wishes as expressed in this message. All sorts of violent, revolutionary suggestions were made and everyone got quite excited and righteously indignant.

The facts stated in the message are fairly accurate from our end. We do have just enough gas (six barrels plus full tanks) to get us to within the 250-mile range by backtracking our old trail–if we turn back now! We do not have enough to proceed to Mt. Hassage and then backtrack. If we went to Mt. Hassage and returned to the 250-mile range by the shortest straight distance, we could make it provided that there are no obstacles such as crevasses or topographic features, which would block our way or cause detour in crossing the unexplored area en route. This latter was the course of action decided upon by Ed and Hugo. It was also decided not to keep the radio schedule tomorrow. We reached this decision and proceeded on our present course.

Hugo did not acknowledge receipt of this message, so it was sent again on the next contact. Technically, no one at Ellsworth knew we had received it at this time, which is why we decided not to make radio contact the next day. This was somewhat foolhardy and certainly insubordinate, but we felt we were so close to Mt. Hassage that we had to keep trying.

About an hour later (1230), while Ed was driving, we heard a snapping sort of noise and immediately stopped. To our dismay, we found that our left forward pontoon had been damaged. Hugo and Paul jacked up the front end of our Sno-Cat, removed the track, and fixed the pontoon. By the time we had finished, it was 2100 and becoming quite a whiteout. Before the visibility became too bad, we could see that we had to go down quite a way (perhaps to ice-shelf level) and then up on the other side of a trough or estuary which crossed our projected route. We decided to go to bed and wait for the weather to improve, as there is a good likelihood of crevasses ahead.

3 Jan., Fri. A lazy day. The wind blew hard all day and it was impossible to see very far due to whiteout and blowing snow. We stayed in bed all day. I read *The Wall* by John Hersey. Paul got up for a few hours and tried to stir up interest in a bridge game, but I was more interested in reading. I finished the book about midnight and went back to sleep.

We heard that Hillary and party reached the Pole yesterday, traveling the last 70 miles in one spurt. They are using farm tractors [Ferguson rubber-tired tractors with improvised tracks]. Fuchs is still more than 200 miles away, making steady progress.

4 Jan., Sat. 826 mi. Still whiteout. Hugo contacted camp again this morning using the whip antenna. He told them that we haven't progressed since the last contact due to weather and track troubles, mentioning nothing about our future plans. We "officially" received the message from Ronne sent 2 Jan.

We had a brief radio contact with Charlie Bentley and the Byrd traverse party and discussed our plans. We agreed to make regular contact every day but never talked to them again.

We finally started on our way again about 1300. It was quite white by this time, and we had to go slowly because of very hard sastrugi. After a delay for resetting the gravity meter, we descended to the level of the shelf ice again. We began crossing crevasses, which the vehicle in front had broken open in passing. We gingerly passed over six of these; one was only slightly narrower than the sled runners. When we came up behind them, they were probing another crevasse in front of the useless crevasse detector.

We discovered a leak in our gas tank caused by the tank bouncing against the brace that supports it. While Hugo and Ed removed the tank, the rest of us roped up and on our skis probed ahead for a mile or so, finding many crevasses. This area is quite similar to that where the Sno-Cat dropped through twice. Upon returning, we recommended not going any further in this direction. The gas tank was finally repaired with Duco Cement. I wonder how long that will hold.

5 Jan., Sun. 838 mi. We crawled into bed about 0100. . . . Hugo received the following message from Ellsworth:

> Realize your disappointment not able to continue but wish to let you know that Lassy is not a completely free man as four flights already made in your support. Two failed due weather. He has his own program too besides aid to British. Please let us know when inside 250-mile limit. Should Lassy be able to, he will bring out sufficient fuel to cover your needs to reach Gould Bay. If not, VX-6 aircraft will make piecemeal delivery to you. Washington and other parties concerned informed of this arrangement for you to meet the January 15 date at West Cape Gould Bay. Ships are expected here in two or three days. Good luck to all of you.
>
> Capt. Finn Ronne

We worked our way back along our trail across the crevasses and stopped at our last gravity station to discuss future plans.

At this point we were back on the grounded ice of Korff Island.

> Ed and Hugo agreed that the sensible thing to do was start back along our old trail as weather, gas, Ronne, and vehicle breakdowns all seem to be conspiring against us. Then we continued on our way towards Mt. Hassage anyway, by trying to find whether we are on an island or peninsula and headed roughly northeast along the trend of the slope. It began to snow and became foggy. As we had no idea where we were heading, we stopped after five miles.
>
> We played bridge while we waited for the weather to clear. BBC told us that Hillary's party were flying from the Pole back to Scott Base while Fuchs is still about 350 miles out and having difficulties.

375

We went to bed about 2100, but around 2300 it cleared somewhat and we tried to push on. The slope curved around to the right (northeast) which indicated that we are actually on an island, as we had thought. The clouds moved in again and we were forced to stop after five more miles.

6 Jan., Mon. 848 mi. We went to bed at 0100. It was decided that if clear in the morning we would still try for Hassage and if cloudy we would start back.

At 0800 when Ed got up to cook breakfast it was so white we couldn't even see the tracks. Consequently we didn't eat but sacked in most of the day. About 1830 it began to clear a bit, and with Ed's 30-power telescope on a tripod we could see a nunatak at an azimuth of 320° at least 20 miles away.

Charles Swithinbank and I have tried to figure what nunatak we actually saw. The only possibility, from what is now known of the geography, is that it was Mt. Haag. Swithinbank calculated that at the elevation we were at on Korff Island, Mt. Haag could just be seen, although it is 320 miles distant. As viewed in the telescope, this nunatak looked like a sharp narrow pinnacle, which is how Mt. Haag would appear when viewed from our location. Mt. Hassage was really about 200 miles away, as I checked in 1997, from its correctly mapped position.

Interestingly, about 30 miles northwest of Mt. Hassage lie the Behrendt Mountains. The existence of this range was unknown to us while on the Filchner Ice Shelf Traverse. While leading the Antarctic Peninsula Traverse around the Behrendt Mountains (which we may have discovered then) in February 1962, I dropped our Sno-Cat partly into a crevasse. But that is another story!

Between us and the nunatak was a broad expanse of shelf ice which looked disturbed, indicating probable crevasses. Again a long discussion was held and a straw vote of opinion was taken. Paul and I thought it unwise to try to go ahead as time, etc., were too much against us. Aug was definitely in favor of going on with Hugo and Ed, reluctantly so. Of course we all wanted to get to Mt. Hassage, but we can't have everything, I suppose. At 2030 we started driving around the northeast end of the island in hopes of finding an outcrop. No success.

At this point, we turned back. We had pushed about as hard, considering the crevasses, the imminent arrival of the ships, and Ronne's unequivocal orders, as we could have.

> We crossed the island and after 10 miles, when we were descending the southeast slope [of Korff Island] that we had come up, we turned right.

> *7 Jan., Tues.* 988 mi. We intersected our old trail 10 miles further on, and followed this across the crevasse field we traversed New Year's Eve. We then struck off southeast again leaving the trail and rejoined it 15 miles further on. This saved us all the meandering around we did, trying to find a route across the crevasses the first time. We then followed our old course to the seismic station about 20 miles north of [Henry Ice Rise]. Here we cut off more to the east, and Ed and I stopped after 20 miles to put in a seismic station.
>
> By 2025 we had come 140 miles in one day, which I suppose is a record for Antarctic surface travel.

Traveling 140 miles in one day still may be a record, at least for a tracked vehicle in Antarctica. Hovercraft operating from Mc-Murdo have made long distances at high speed, but I doubt if any have traveled this far in one push.

> Hugo et al. continued on for another 20 miles, as he didn't want to put his station there. The total distance of this spurt (counting the 20 miles #1 drove on tonight) is 168 miles.

Edith Ronne Land was the name Finn Ronne gave to the ice-shelf area we had been traveling for several weeks. Berkner Island is the name of the large island in the center of the ice shelf that Ronne had probably flown partly over in 1947. We were west of Berkner Island but thought that Henry Ice Rise was connected to it. The two are not connected now. As mentioned previously, the Ronne name is now attached to the greater area of the combined ice shelf west of Berkner Island. The eastern part of the ice shelf is the Filchner Ice Shelf.

> Ellsworth informed Hugo this morning that the *Wyandot* is through the pack and somewhere between Halley Bay and Cape Norvegia. It is expected to arrive sometime tomorrow afternoon.

8 Jan., Wed. 1006 mi. We were in bed about 0100 and up at 0930. I listened on the radio at 1000 and heard Hugo conversing with Ellsworth. We put in a station using air blasts but could not get a reflection. This is, of course, the same area where we had so much trouble before. Our gas tank leak reappeared, and during the night while we slept, and drained our nearly empty tank. We had to put in two gallons with a tin can to get enough in the tank to back up to the sled. We then put in 15 gallons which we hoped would enable us to rejoin the rest with none left over.

Meanwhile the two Otters had left Ellsworth and were trying to find us with gas. Hugo talked to them on the radio (by voice) but they could not find us and had to turn back. It was clear and sunny.

All of the previous flights to us by VX-6 in the Otters had been made either by following our trail or in reference to some geographic feature, such as the escarpment of Berkner Island. The pilots were not equipped with radar, so could not locate us other than visually. I knew from the flying I had done there, and realize even more today from looking at the photographs I took of our traverse vehicles from the air, how difficult it was to see the Sno-Cats from any distance. In 1960–61, I flew a lot in R4D8s (the Navy equivalent to the C-47 or DC-3) out of Byrd Station, and we were able to locate Sno-Cats on the snow surface quite easily by using radar. This was how Roderick had found us in the Air Force C-47 on 29 December.

We started driving about 1430 and after six miles began climbing up the very gentle slope of the north edge of the island [Henry Ice Rise]. We arrived at the #1 Sno-Cat about 1730 and found them all in bed. They had drilled a hole so we decided to shoot in it. We laid out the spread and recorded a good reflection. We are about 600 ft (160 m) above sea level, and the rock surface is 1900 ft (600 m) below sea level. Augie cooked breakfast (for them) and we ate it as supper.

Aug made a remark to the effect that Ed skied the seismic lines faster than I did. I challenged this, and one thing led to another until a race was set up. Ed and I raced to one end of our line and back, a distance of 660 m. I won by two or three lengths, but really had to push to do it. We have an entirely different style and I think mine best for sprinting. Ed now says he can beat me over a longer distance.

9 Jan., Thurs. 1015 mi. Shortly after midnight, just after Ed and I got in our sleeping bags, we heard Hugo talking to an Otter, so I turned our receiver on. Con and Willie were in the plane and they couldn't find us. Paul tried to describe our position relative to the cloud banks nearby but to no avail. They tried until 0230 whereupon they landed, took a sun shot, and pumped another drum of avgas, which they had carried in the plane into their tanks. Half an hour later they again took off, and sometime around 0330 they spotted us.

Willie buzzed us so low he nearly took our whip antenna off. It was good to see the boys again. They brought four drums of avgas for us. This is about 600 lbs overload and at that they stripped the plane of some of the survival gear. They had been flying for eight hours. They left Ellsworth and flew along the ice shelf (front) to the gas cache Lassiter left about 200 miles out when he was trying to get his other plane in. They refueled there and then came looking for us.

They had been able to find the gas cache because they had the ice front to fly along.

They gave us all the camp gossip. Kim shaved and Don has a haircut. Don took a ride in an Otter and now Ronne wants Willie to draw up some charges against Don, because he didn't have the Captain's permission.

When an Otter had come out to resupply the traverse, we all had routinely made short reconnaissance flights looking at crevasses and had thought nothing of it. Therefore, it was strange to hear Ronne fuss about a flight by one of the scientific group at Ellsworth.

Wyandot is due in this afternoon at 1500. Ronne sent a bottle of vermouth that the Argentines gave him, and a can of fruitcake. [Ronne was concerned that we apparently never thanked him for this gift.] Ed Davis sent some baked stuff.

Despite Ronne's instructions otherwise, Ed Davis always seemed to send us baked things on the resupply flights.

Fred Dyrdal sent some material to patch our gas tank. Greaney and Lewis had the first fight of the year, over some trivial item after a recent party. Two of Lassiter's pilots came to blows over a question of some cooked beans.

Con and Willie took off shortly after 0400 and got back to camp after 0600. We went to bed and slept until about 1430. The rest of the day was spent in, greasing the vehicles, repairing the gas tank, etc. We started driving again at 2145. About eight miles further on (at 2330) we stopped. Ahead of us was another escarpment.

It was this apparent escarpment that convinced us there was a peninsula connecting Berkner Island to Henry Ice Rise.

We had descended almost to ice-shelf level again. Between us and the hill ahead we could see a line of crevasses quite hummocked. While we were discussing the situation a low cloud bank suddenly formed, completely blanking out visibility. We started a bridge game while waiting for it to clear.

10 Jan., Fri. 1027 mi. We listened to CBC [Canadian Broadcasting Corporation] and heard a very interesting news roundup concerning the president's [Eisenhower's] State of the Union address today. We even heard parts of the speech itself. How strange it seems to sit down here and listen to a talk made in the U.S. the same day.

We had been listening to news of the Transantarctic Expedition throughout our traverse, but that seemed local, even though it was broadcast from London.

We ate the delicious fruitcake Ronne sent out and opened the wine. The latter tasted pretty terrible to me but Aug and Paul thought it OK. About 0430 we went to bed.

It cleared off during the day and we had breakfast about 1500. We started driving cautiously off towards the crevassed area, but a few minutes later (about 1645) we stopped and got out to investigate the area on skis. Hugo, Augie, and I roped up and moved out. We found a large, long, open crevasse about 100 yards ahead. There was a bridged crevasse directly beneath the crevasse-detector sleds. These ran parallel, and it looked as if we might get through between them, as all the crevasses we could see ran in the same direction (i.e., east-west). We skied and probed our way down the center of this area for about five miles and it seemed that the crevassing diminished. Back to the Sno-Cats and on our way east again.

Everything went well until we were about a mile along. We could not see any of the big open crevasses anywhere nearby. Suddenly a bridge collapsed slightly ahead and to the left of the lead vehicle. Ed, Hugo, and Aug roped up to probe. Soon it became evident to

Augie that we were in an area of small, crisscross crevasses of the type that have bothered us on the other side of Berkner Island. He made quite a fuss about wanting to get back out of here and go around another way. Ed and Hugo and Paul probed ahead a ways and found it advisable to follow Aug's suggestion.

About 2130 we turned around and retraced our track to the previous gravity station and then turned south, for about 30 miles, keeping the crevassed slope on our left just in sight.

Although I do not mention it, we measured gravity, magnetic field, and elevation every four miles whether in crevasses or not.

11 Jan., Sat. 1047 mi. We continued this route until 0400 when we decided that we wanted some air recon before proceeding further south. . . . We decided to camp in the meantime. I cooked some chicken and rice for supper and got to bed about 0700. Hugo sent a message to camp this morning explaining our situation and requesting a recon flight.

About 1700 the plane contacted us by voice on the way out. We also talked to McCarthy back at Ellsworth by voice. Con and Willie flew straight out and brought four barrels of mogas, and one barrel of avgas. They proceeded to load the latter into their tanks. Also brought out were five of the little Red Cross Christmas packages and a box full of mail for us.

Sno-Cat among crevasses on Ronne Ice Shelf near end of traverse.

381

We all climbed into the plane and flew south. As far as we went and could see, there were crevasses–some open, some closed. We found our old trail coming from the mountains and were shocked and surprised to see how many bridged crevasses we crossed over and how many open ones we passed nearby.

We were very fortunate to cross the 250 miles of ice shelf from the Dufek Massif to our 26 December rendezvous point with no radio communication with Ellsworth and no crevasse accidents. Nowadays if a U.S. Antarctic field party misses a radio schedule for a day or so, an evacuation plane for the party is sent out as soon as possible. On our traverse, though, this wouldn't have been easily possible because no one knew where we were.

Back at our camp after the planes had left, we spent several wonderful hours reading letters from friends and families, some of which had been mailed in 1956. I received several 1956 and 1957 Christmas cards from the same people.

Camp news, *Wyandot* is in! The new CO (commanding officer) of Ellsworth Station is an airdale lieutenant. According to Con everyone (including CO) will stand mess duty, only one serving in the galley, no segregation of head facilities. Ronne moved Skidmore out of camp and onto the *Wyandot.* New station scientific leader moved into science building. Two psychiatrists and one psychologist are running around. One is a four striper [a captain like Ronne].

We loaded on the fuel and were ready to go. Just as Paul started #1 Sno-Cat one of the wood beams for the crevasse detector broke. After some deliberation, we dismantled it for easy air transport if needed, and piled the pieces up in the snow. The shorter beams we jammed upright into the snow. The effect created resembled some weird primitive religious symbols.

This was the end of the crevasse detector as far as Ellsworth Station was concerned. The crevasse detectors on the other traverses quietly went away also. This instrument, while possibly useful in some circumstances, was totally impractical for our needs.

12 Jan., Sun. We finally started after midnight. Ed drove while I finished reading my mail. At 0525 we intersected our old trail and continued along it southeast for six miles whereupon we turned east. At this point Hugo et al. decided that those were crevasses ahead and didn't want to probe. Hugo suggested we go first. Heretofore, Hugo has always insisted that his be the lead vehicle.

Hugo's vehicle had the crevasse detector, so it would have seemed strange to have that on the following Sno-Cat. Of course Hugo, Paul, and Aug had long before stopped using the instrument.

I was driving by this time, and using my wrist compass I tried (more or less successfully) to steer a straight course.

I recall using the shadow of the antenna on the snow in front to guide me.

We continued on the new course for 15 miles and then headed northeast for two miles when our right front track slipped over the rail. We had to stop to repair this and everyone felt like going to bed—so we did (about 1730).

13 Jan., Mon. When we woke up at 0300 it was overcast and white so we stayed in bed until 1000. We spent the day reading news clippings mailed to us and writing letters. It began to clear off about 1700, so Hugo fixed the track. I tightened it, and after supper we started driving. Our gas tank is leaking worse than ever.

14 Jan., Tues. We drove north northeast until the poor visibility forced us to stop about 0400. We went to bed then. Hugo had a radio contact today in which he was asked whether he would recommend continuing use of these two Sno-Cats. Apparently they have more in camp. He replied in the affirmative particularly because these are through the crevasse area immediately around camp.

By this time the #2 Sno-Cat was getting in bad shape. When our replacements eventually tried to continue with our vehicles, they had a good mechanic. He welded eight breaks in the frame of this vehicle, but still did not get it very far before it was abandoned. I suppose I could blame this on the weight of the seismic gear, but the way I drove the Sno-Cat was probably a part of the cause of its demise. Rather than carefully driving over the sastrugi, I would set the throttle and take the bumps and bangs as they came.

We upped about 1900 and put in a station, finishing by midnight. We recorded a reflection from bedrock at about 3600 ft (1100 m) below sea level, indicating that we are well away from land.

We were starting to cross the Thiel Trough again.

15 Jan., Wed. It was still too white to drive so we played off the final round in the Antarctic Championship Bridge Tournament. Of course Augie and I emerged victorious. About 0430 it began to clear enough to drive. At 0830 we came to a long open crevasse, about 30 ft wide and very deep. Ed belayed me and I skied out on a snow bridge crossing at one point and took some pictures. It was quite beautiful with sheer vertical walls and a bottom (or false bottom) covered with rubble from fallen cornices. There were icicles hanging from the corniced north edge.

A radio message at 1000 told us that they would relieve us with two Otters as soon as weather permitted. We drove another five miles and ate and camped about 1500. The weather remained uncertain, although the sun was shining and there were large patches of blue sky.

16 Jan., Thurs. I'm writing at 0350. It is overcast and almost whiteout. At this rate we probably won't be relieved today. I'm reclining on the deck of our Sno-Cat in my sleeping bag. There is nothing to do so I thought I'd write. Well, we have just about come to the end of what five of us devoted a year and a half of our lives to. Our traverse certainly had the cards stacked against it and yet as I look back upon the past 81 days, I'm not too dissatisfied.

I shouldn't have been dissatisfied, because I eventually got a Ph.D. out of it in 1961.

We have come about 1200 miles. If anyone had told me we would get this far even two months ago, I'd have thought him a wishful thinker. We don't have as much seismic data as we should have for the distance traveled (only 27 stations), but it looked (back in early Dec.) as if we would have to stretch our station interval to 40 miles in order to get anywhere in the time left. At any rate it's still too early to discuss how much we accomplished in the scientific sense; that will await the reduction of the data.

Actually we did quite well scientifically, as did the other two IGY scientific oversnow traverses. We, the Soviets, and the French made a good start in mapping the ice thickness of Antarctica, following up on the short pioneering geophysical traverse work of Gordon Robin on the Norwegian-British-Swedish Expedition in 1951–53. The glaciology and geophysical work on the Filchner-Ronne Ice Shelf system, its vast extent, the discovery of the Thiel Trough, the tidal measurements, the evidence of a high rate of bottom melting beneath the Filchner Ice Shelf, and the preliminary geologic reconnaissance of the Dufek intrusion were significant contributions, of which we could all be proud.

> We aren't the best crew that could be assembled nor the most compatible, but we don't have to be ashamed of our accomplishments and can hold our own with the other traverses, I believe. We wrangle amongst ourselves quite a bit, but only as does a family, and quite strong bonds have developed amongst the five of us that won't be easily broken by outside forces.
>
> I feel that I have been fortunate in having a scientific discipline that is my chosen profession. Yesterday, as I worked on the last seismic station, I enjoyed my work even more than at the beginning. There is a fascination about it which has kept me from developing a dislike for the routine tasks required. The glaciology team on the other hand has come to loath its work and will look back on the supposed reason for their volunteering as one of the least pleasant parts of the traverse. Paul remarked yesterday that he would enjoy coming down in a year for another traverse, if they would not have this type of a glaciology program. The fact that Ed and I like our work and Hugo doesn't his has embittered him somewhat towards his program, I believe, but he has striven (for the most part successfully) to conceal this feeling.
>
> 0800–McDonald (CTG 43-7) sent a dispatch ordering us to head for Gould Bay as rapidly as possible. I wonder what he thinks we've been trying to do the past two weeks.

I think most of the Navy men, like Captain McDonald and Admiral Dufek, expected us to be able to go from point A to point B in the area where we were working (just blank on Antarctic plotting charts with only a latitude and longitude grid away from the coasts), similar to a ship on the ocean, or a plane across Antarctica.

> 1000–Weather clearing. Ellsworth reports clearing there. Planes ready to go. Listening sked at 1300.

385

It cleared off nicely and camp reported at 1300 that the planes were on the way and would arrive about 1530 or 1600. About 1500 it clouded up. We tried to drive but it became so difficult to see that we stopped and played bridge. About 2200 it began to clear again and we started driving.

17 Jan., Fri. We got about 45 miles in a northeast direction before our gas gave out. To the left we could see the escarpment [connecting Berkner Island to Henry Ice Rise] in the distance. A ground fog came up and made it difficult to see very far ahead, but the sun came through and we could see the snow surface easily. I cooked chicken and rice and we went to bed at 0800.

Thus, our traverse ended. We had no more fuel and the seismic gear had been prepared to remove it to Ellsworth, so we did not put in a station.

At 1300 two Otters came in and landed. Capt. McDonald and Willie were the only familiar people; the rest were the new support personnel. The ships were planning to pull out as soon as we got back. This shook Hugo and Augie up as Hugo had to get cores out of the deep pit, and Aug wanted to resurvey the trough. After some discussion McDonald agreed to hold the ships until Hugo pulled the cores out.

It was fogging up pretty badly when we took off.

With no nostalgic comment we abandoned our Sno-Cats and most equipment. Our replacements continued our work for about a month. At the end of January they made a few reconnaissance flights and then worked to the west from our final location, until they were evacuated back to Ellsworth on 10 March. The lateness of their season was the result of some harrowing aircraft incidents. The following season the Ellsworth traverse party used four new Sno-Cats and followed our route out of Ellsworth. Their story is told by John Pirrit, chief glaciologist, in his 1967 book, *Across West Antarctica,* published posthumously.

We flew across [Berkner Island] and across Gould Bay. This latter was quite interesting. We saw several newborn icebergs. This was the first I had seen of the badly crevassed area directly west of Ellsworth, the area Finn Ronne wouldn't let Ed and Hugo get a look at for so many months prior to the traverse. We probably couldn't have driven around the west end, as Ronne told us. Unfortunately, by that time relations were so bad that we did not feel confident in anything he said. In retrospect it worked out well that we had to zigzag around the Grand Chasm, because we got two geophysical profiles across the Thiel Trough. Although airborne radar ice-sounding flights made measurements over the Filchner Ice Shelf, no one has made any additional seismic measurements of depth to bedrock, in this area, in the 40 years since our traverse.

Notes

1. This alga was identified as *Phormidium incrustatum* (Naeg.) *Damong* with possibly some *retzii* by George Llano and George Prescott.
2. Edward A. Alf, Anthony Morency, Paul A. Siple, Edward C. Flowers, Virgil W. Barden, John A. Alvanez, William F. Johnson, William S. Sough, Wesley R. Morris, A.V. Landolt, Robert F. Benson, Herbert L. Hansen, Robert H. Johns, William Moreland, Joseph Krank, Bruce J. Lieske, Hans J. Bengaard, Carl O. Wyman, Benjamin F. Remington Jr., Samuel A. Wilson, William C. Larvis, Norbert F. Helfert, Gene L. Jarter, Walter C. Sutton. The following summer personnel have also returned: J. B. Campbell, John R. Reed, Lawrence M. Gould, W. Gortlein, William O. Field, Ernest A. Wood, Athelstan F. Spilhaus.

10
Heading for Home

After nearly three months on the traverse, we began our slow return to civilization. Fortunately it was slow because there was plenty of cultural shock (displacement anxiety) awaiting us, which was quite unexpected. As mentioned in the previous chapter we quickly disconnected our heads from the traverse.

> *17 Jan., Fri.* (continued) Our pilot circled the *Wyandot* and the *West Wind* so we could take pictures.

The *West Wind* was an Arctic veteran Coast Guard icebreaker, essentially the same as the Navy *Staten Island,* which had

Wyandot and Coast Guard icebreaker *West Wind* (outboard) moored to front of Filchner Ice Shelf. Note break in slope probably resulting from high melt rate at ice front. This results in low elevation of ice front permitting ship unloading, and enabled Ellsworth Station (two miles inland) to be constructed on Filchner Ice Shelf.

accompanied the *Wyandot* the previous season. This season the *Wyandot* was commanded by Capt. F. M. Smith (USN) and the *Staten Island* by Capt. W. J. Conley Jr. (USCG).

> Kim, Jerry, and our replacements were standing waiting for us as we landed. Dr. Matthew Brennan (the new station scientific leader) was standing there with a scraggly gray beard and red and blue wool cap with a tassel.

I meant this comment about Brennan as a compliment, in contrast to Ronne's always trim, clean-shaven Navy appearance.

> We met Tom Turcotte and Father Bradley, the two seismologists, and Bob Goodwin the assistant glaciologist.

Father Bradley was a Jesuit seismologist, which was not at all uncommon in the 1950s. A few weeks earlier, Father Daniel Linehan attempted to make the first seismic reflection ice-thickness measurement at the South Pole shortly before Fuchs' party got there on 19 January. Neither he nor Goeff Pratt, of the Transantarctic Expedition, managed to accomplish this measurement successfully. A few years later, a Soviet traverse to the South Pole, led by Andrei Kapitsa, made the first successful ice-thickness determination there.

> McDonald made noises about getting underway pretty soon, and Augie blew his stack in his usual Captain-hating fashion. He started telling all and sundry about how two years work was down the drain because he couldn't resurvey the trough east of Ellsworth a half mile. At this outburst McDonald said, "OK Hothead, do your surveying!" Augie got his own way.

It's tough to hold up a U.S. Navy ship movement; I know, I did it in a similar situation departing for Antarctica 10 months later.

> It was rush-rush-rush for the next few hours. Ed and I tried to explain a year's work while Bradley took notes. Unfortunately there was not enough time to provide them much information. Our traverse replacements were ready to come out to us the day after the ship landed, but McDonald wouldn't let them. Their traverse plans are grandiose.

Actually, they did get all the way to Byrd Station. They also learned some valuable lessons from our experience. They used a powerful "Angry 19" radio and had good communications throughout. On the following season they used four new Sno-Cats and had a full-time cook and mechanic which Pirrit (in his book) reported to be very important. Despite John Pirrit and Bob Goodwin's far greater experience in crevasses than we had when we arrived in Antarctica, they had great difficulties in the same areas we did.

Pirrit reported they broke into a crevasse two and a half hours out of Ellsworth. After great difficulty and close air support, they got around Grand Chasm. (There was, of course, no evidence in the snow of our tracks after the next winter.) They tried to follow our route to Berkner Island but got stopped in the same crevasse field that gave us so much trouble as we approached the escarpment in November 1957. Finally, they were forced back by the crevasses before getting very far in, and headed south. They drove up Berkner Island farther to the south and crossed our route on Berkner Island. Continuing west, they descended onto the ice shelf again, and after more crevasse problems got up on the grounded ice and eventually to Byrd Station.

We got everything aboard the ship (I hope) and pulled out about 2200. All of our people were onboard the ship and were out to greet us. It was heartwarming to see the sincere welcome they gave us. They had all but given us up, as McDonald had planned on sailing last night, with the icebreaker planning to come back for us later. Fortunately for our peace of mind, we knew none of this.

It was quite moving to me to see us pull slowly away while the ship's whistle blew and our new friends waved from the shore. I envy them in a way, and I'm almost sorry not to be staying on. It looks like they will have a good winter. I was so overtired I didn't sleep when I finally got to bed about 0030 on 18 January.

In 45 hours, I had gotten only about five hours' sleep.

We knew we were back on a Navy ship when we heard the squawk box blaring out with the bosun's whistle and the familiar, "Now Sweepers, man your brooms! Sweep down for and aft! Empty all trash over the fantail!"

391

Traverse party at end of traverse on *Wyandot*. Left to right: P. Walker, E. Thiel, H. Neuburg, N. Aughenbaugh, and J. Behrendt.

Because emptying trash over the fantail is no longer legal in Antarctic seas, or elsewhere in the world, I assume this announcement is no longer made on U.S. Navy ships.

A few days later I had the first real eggs in over a year, and fresh onions, oranges, and grapefruit. It sure was a sudden change from cooking on traverse to being served in the wardroom.

> I've heard that the reason for the rush to get the ships out was that the Russians are sending a ship (presumably an icebreaker) into the Bellinghausen Sea area and Dufek wants *West Wind* to beat them there.

Throughout the cold war and for decades to come, a great deal of the driving force in the U.S. and Soviet Antarctic programs was the awareness of each other's massive presence in the Antarctic. I have discussed this occasionally over the years with Soviet and Russian colleagues, and they agreed that they could obtain better Antarctic research budgets because the Americans were there.

In 1994, Andrei Kapitsa told me of a plan he and Bert Crary half seriously made at a meeting in California that we all attended in 1963. Crary had so far been unsuccessful in convincing U.S. funding sources to support some ambitious work in Antarctica. According to Kapitsa, Crary gave an interview to a U.S. newspaper describing the planned work. He then sent a clipping to Kapitsa, who gave the story to Tass, and it was published in the U.S.S.R. Kapitsa then convinced the Soviets that they had to conduct a complementary program in Antarctica. When this was reported in the Russian press, he sent a clipping to Crary who then succeeded in getting funds for the U.S. program.

Fortunately, the Antarctic Treaty, which was adopted in 1959, prohibits any military activities in the area south of 60°S, and U.S. military have been only used as support for science, as in the IGY. To my knowledge, the Soviets have never sent military planes, support ships, or people to Antarctica.

18 Jan., Sat. 0000 Z 75°26'S, 26°38'W. The Weddell Sea is wide open "as far as the eye can see."

This quote is but one of the optimistic messages sent from our ships in December 1956 and January 1957 when we were making our difficult passage through the Weddell Sea to establish Ellsworth.

We made good time all day. Many icebergs were passed. There was even a slight roll and whitecaps were visible—inside the pack. Normally pack ice damps out the waves, but we are obviously close to the open sea here. Not like last year! We passed Halley Bay about 2030.

We traverse people took Asian flu shots this afternoon. I also got a smallpox vaccination.

As mentioned previously, there was concern that the Asian influenza epidemic that had swept the world during 1957 might have a serious effect on those of us isolated in Antarctica. I and others developed some reactions to the vaccine—a sore throat, in my case. Paul and Ed, who did not, got quite ill, possibly with the Asian influenza, when we returned to the States.

I had to pay my Ship Store debts, so the ship cashed a $500 check for me. I lent Ed $100 and Kim $30 so they could meet their current expenses. After lunch I went down to Ship Stores and bought

393

a $75 Omega watch for $42 and an $80 slide projector for $38. The money is burning a hole in my pocket. I now have $150 cash.

I had just finished more than a year without any cash, checkbook, or driver's license on my person.

The boys have been filling me in on all the camp gossip. Apparently things got worse the past two months. The head of the Ionospheric Physics panel, Dr. Millett Morgan, came down on the ship and is quite appalled at the situation. He thinks Ronne did damage to the IGY program and wants us to tell our story to IGY in Washington, D.C., on the way home.

There are two psychiatrists and a psychologist that the Navy sent down in an effort to find out what makes Antarcticans tick. Ellsworth was chosen at random, but they are getting an earful.

I doubt that Ellsworth was chosen at random. The reason given by the Navy that Ellsworth was picked for the psychiatric study was that it was the most isolated U.S. IGY station. Perhaps. However, there was enough gossip and semiofficial communication back to the U.S. about our personnel difficulties that I suspect that this was also part of the justification in selecting Ellsworth. What follows are my initial impressions of being interviewed by a Navy psychologist.

There are Capt. Charles Mullin, Lt. Fred Wouters, Lt. Mike Connery (the latter being a psychologist). The two lieutenants live in with us sand crabs. I had my first interview with Mike this afternoon. He tape-recorded it. The questions were quite interesting and I enjoyed answering them. Personal reactions, group relations, apparent physiologic reactions to light-dark, heat-cold. They expected to find that there were different effects in winter (and dark) and summer. There weren't, aside from a slight raising of morale when the sun came back. I'll bet that the Ronne situation interests them.

During the interview, I refused to discuss masturbation but Mike did not press me. We also took a battery of written psychological examinations.

Charles Mullin and Mike Connery published a paper on the results of their psychological study.[1] This report mentioned no names, including the name of our station. The authors noted that this was the most isolated of the seven American IGY stations in Antarctica. One of the authors flew in to Ellsworth by helicopter several hours before the ships arrived, and the team spent the days at the station interviewing people in the conditions as they were there. Contrary to expectations, no one refused to be interviewed, and as expected, "There was a mild evanescent xenophobia." They reported that "no psychosis, disabling depressive states, obvious psychological illness, or clear-cut neurosis developed at this station."

The report noted that "two or three individuals might well have been eliminated as unsuitable, not because they developed any emotional illness that was a source of distress to them or prevented them from carrying out the physical requirements of their duties, but because of personality characteristics that were a frequent source of annoyance, irritation, and tension within the group."

The report went on:

A crucial factor in understanding the dynamics of this particular group was the existence of an antithetical attitude between the leader of the station and the remainder of the group. This attitude arose partly because the leader, a highly able explorer in civilian life, who had been ordered to active duty [in Ronne's book he states he was "offered the assignment" and "accepted gladly"], had little experience in military leadership and was somewhat inflexible in his interpersonal dealings; and partly because the leader provided a convenient and plausible focus for the hostilities that are inevitably generated in a group of men whose interests and background are disparate, and who are thrown together under conditions of enforced close personnel associations for a long period of time. Paradoxically, there was good evidence that this group leader tension had a salutary influence on the group as a whole.

Further on the report states, "Despite the general critical attitude toward the policies and practices of the leader, among civilians, and officers and enlisted personnel, there was general, albeit often reluctant, agreement that the basic objectives of the mission of the station were realized and in some ways exceeded."

I am sure that this last statement by the naval officers was meant as complimentary to Ronne, but I also take it as a compliment to the carrying out of the scientific program, which after all was the reason we all were there. I think one of the basic problems between Ronne and the civilian scientific group was that the planning of our program was done by our scientific superiors who were not present and to whom we felt our scientific obligation and loyalty.

The report mentions elsewhere, "One curious source of disappointment and disillusionment, that affected an appreciable number of the younger or romantically inclined members was the relative luxury of the living conditions and the comparative absence of excitement, danger and real hardship. This spoiled the whole adventure for them."

I do not believe that the authors were referring to the traverse party here. In fact, in the extensive interviews that we traverse people had with the authors after we were on the ship, I do not recall that the subject of what it was like on the traverse came up. In contrast, they were mostly interested in interpersonal relationships, etc.

The authors found:

Insomnia was quite widespread during the early weeks of the winter season of 24-hour darkness, the so called "big eye" [a term that was never heard at Ellsworth, but was common in the McMurdo–Little America area that winter, and I understand widely used in newspaper stories]. As might be expected "oral needs" were enhanced because of the absence of other basic gratifications. Appetite and consumption were enormous. Weight gains of 20–30 pounds were not unusual and slight pot bellies on otherwise slender young men were notable. Fortunately, the cook was competent, imaginative, and very anxious to please. His prestige was enormous. [Although we traverse people gained weight in the winter, we lost it during the traverse.]

Psychosomatic complaints were infrequent, with headaches being the most common. Of the 9 civilians and 4 officers, 6 complained of fairly frequent headaches, while of 21 enlisted men whose records were available for review, only 3 complained of this symptom. . . . It is possible that the more sophisticated headache group felt the need for more complete repression of their hostilities.

So, we gave each other headaches! Regarding sex they reported: "To us the amount of and interest in pin-up activities seemed almost extreme. There was no evidence of any overt homosexual practice, scandal, or gossip, although as might be expected, there seemed to be some indications of mild covert manifestations throughout the group." I find this interesting but not surprising. I imagine that of the 39 of us there were several gay men who did not dare come out of the closet in 1956–58.

There is more to the report, and a few individuals in addition to Finn Ronne are recognizable to those of us who were there.

The day after my interview, I wrote in my journal that it was a good idea from the psychiatrists' viewpoint to put their men in with us. This was noted in the Mullin and Connery report. I wonder who affected whom? I suppose the first impressions and interviews were the least subjective and carried the most weight in the analysis and interpretation of their data.

We've gotten quite friendly with Mike and Fred. A couple of days ago Mike walked in and, as automatically as used to happen in the science building, conversation ceased for a moment and a new topic was begun. We had been talking over "old times." Tonight amidst a similar discussion, he entered and conversation kept on. Mike remarked that apparently he is now a member of the club. After listening a while to our wild tales, he even volunteered a tidbit. It seems that Ronne didn't come down to the movie last night because he didn't know there was one. No one had come to get him when the movie was due to start. Captain Smith (the *Wyandot* captain) informed him that the movie schedule was printed in the plan of the day and that on this ship no one came to get anyone.

I shot the breeze in our room with Ike Schlossbach (who rode the ship down again this year), Don, and Chuck Forlidas who dropped in. We are fortunate in the location of our room. Our officer friends and our people on the 02 level can come down to see us and also the boys from the lower decks can come up and visit without feeling ill at ease, as the Chief's quarters are on the same level as ours.

Well, I got shaved. I talked about it and Don offered to take a scissors to my beard. I left the moustache but it's coming off tomorrow. Augie got his first haircut and shave in over a year today. He didn't look out of place on traverse with his long hair but with a shirt and tie in the wardroom he presented quite an incongruous appearance.

21 Jan., Tues. 0000 Z 67°24'S, 15°36'W. We spent the day banging ice floes around as we finally hit the pack just about on the

Antarctic Circle. On the way in one of the prop blades got bent, and today the damage was increased slightly. This means that the ship vibrates when above about 80 turns/minute.

The contrast in ice conditions with the previous season in the Weddell Sea was striking. In 1958–59 I returned to the Weddell Sea and Ellsworth Station on the Navy icebreaker *Edisto* and we were beset for a total of 21 days.

The U.S. Navy managed to get ships in to Ellsworth in February 1957, January 1958, and February 1959. I was present on all of these cruises and only in 1957–58 was little damage sustained by the ships in the ice. Partly because of this inaccessibility, the U.S. turned Ellsworth Station over to Argentina in February 1959. The Argentines managed to get the *San Martin* into Ellsworth in January 1959, at which time they evacuated most of the U.S. personnel who had been brought down by the *Wyandot* the prior year.

The *San Martin* was stopped by ice during the resupply attempt in 1960 and the personnel, including one U.S. scientist, were forced to spent a second winter with no mail or food resupply. After evacuating these people in 1961, Argentina abandoned Ellsworth Station. Argentina closed Belgrano Station on the Filchner Ice Shelf (about 35 miles east of Ellsworth) after the IGY, and now operates a station, also named Belgrano (or Belgrano II), on a bedrock exposure east of the Filchner Ice Shelf.

Shackleton Station was abandoned after Fuchs' Transantarctic Expedition. I made a gravity measurement there in February 1959 by helicopter from Ellsworth, which may have been the last time it was visited. The British Halley Bay Station about 250 miles east of Ellsworth has been occupied since 1956. Continuous observations there first documented the development of the ozone hole over Antarctica between the 1950s and the 1980s.

Norway, the U.S.S.R., and Germany carried out a number of marine geophysical and oceanographic cruises in the southern Weddell Sea during the late 1970s and 1980s. Only the Germans and the Soviets have ever taken ships along the front of the Filchner-Ronne Ice Shelf as far west as the *Wyandot* and *Staten Island* did, while seeking a site for Ellsworth in 1956–57.

Since the IGY, the U.S. Antarctic Program has never operated ship-supported programs on the Filchner-Ronne Ice Shelf and sur-

rounding inland area, although the U.S. has had several oceanographic cruises to the Weddell Sea.

22 Jan., Wed. 0000 Z 66°35S, 16°21W. Out of the pack and into the
open sea. *West Wind* left us today. It is getting dark now. Stars were
visible last night.

This was the first night we had seen since early October. I have
to say that I've really gotten to enjoy 24-hour daylight during my
Antarctic trips, particularly when I do not have to experience the
24-hour dark of the following winter.

25 Jan., Sat. Still rough sea today but diminishing towards evening.
I spent an hour on the fantail trying to get pictures of an albatross
which was following the ship. I hope some come out because it was
quite interesting watching this huge bird soaring on the wind and
skimming the water in a trough between two breaking waves. Occasionally a wave would break right under the bird and send spray
flying upwards; the bird was always quick enough to rise the foot or
two necessary to keep dry.

26 Jan., Sun. We must have crossed the Antarctic convergence last
night because the air is balmy and the water is 10° warmer today.
Paul and Jerry have shaved their beards leaving Hugo the only civilian left with a beard.

27 Jan., Mon. The wind blew up to 55 knots tonight and the ship
had to change course to head into it. We rolled pretty heavily, and
Hugo is seasick again.

29 Jan., Wed. Started mailing my journal, pictures, maps, etc. Clear
and warm. Very hot in our stateroom. Holiday Routine in the afternoon. Beard-growing contest judged on #4 hatch; Walt Davis won.
A bunch of us observers and scientists spent part of the afternoon
sunning on the signal bridge. We played bridge, and I got sunburned.
Boxing was held on #4 hatch at 2000; Crouse won his match.

A dinner for all the wintering-over officers and civilians, ship's
officers from last year, Captain Ronne, and Captain Smith was held
in the wardroom this evening. Filet mignon was delicious. Ronne
said a few words about "Our trouble" and mentioned that "Time
heals all things." He wished us luck. He is leaving the ship in BA.

While in Buenos Aires, I kept running into Ronne and his interesting wife, Jackie, whom I met there for the first time.

30 Jan., Thurs. We had a severe rain squall this morning with 60 knot winds but it only lasted 30 minutes or so. It's unbearably hot in our room.

We were, of course, acclimated to the cold and there was no air-conditioning on the *Wyandot.*

We entered the mouth of the Rio Plata around noon. About 1400 we passed Montevideo and took our pilot aboard. We will land at BA tomorrow morning.

My journal ends abruptly there.

We spent a great several days in Buenos Aires. Paul and I met a couple of English-speaking college "girls" who showed us the sights of this fascinating city. We then took the ship to Santos, Brazil.

Upon arriving in Santos, we took a train to São Paulo, which is about 3000 ft high. We also enjoyed São Paulo a lot. In 1958 it was still a small city of only two to three million and had no air pollution. What I particularly recall was the cooler climate contrasted to Buenos Aires and Santos. Carnival was approaching, and samba bands were playing everywhere. I saw my first new movie in two years, *Giant*, with Rock Hudson, James Dean, and Elizabeth Taylor. I recall encountering the Ronnes in our hotel. Finn seemed surprised to see us there.

That was the last I ever saw of Finn Ronne. I was quite angered to read his book about our winter, *Antarctic Command*, when it came out in 1961. Finn Ronne died in 1980 at the age of 80. I still see Jackie Ronne occasionally, at dinners of the Antarctican Society in Washington.

After a few days in São Paulo we winter-over people (except Ronne) flew back to the States on a U.S. Air Force transport plane. We arrived on a cold winter morning on 12 February at Andrews Air Force Base in Washington, D.C., and went our separate ways for the most part. The Ellsworth scientific party was met and debriefed all day at the National Academy of Sciences building by members of the U.S. National Committee for IGY, including geophysicist Merle Tuve. They were particularly concerned and interested in the troubles we had with Ronne. I think it was quite important that we had people with the stature and credibility of Ed Thiel, Jack Brown, and Hugo Neuburg to tell most of the story. We were received very cordially and told of the events at Ellsworth including the scientific results of our traverse.

I have often wondered what action was ever taken as a result of our account, and where the records of the debriefing are at present. Finn Ronne never went to Antarctica again with the U.S. Navy or with the U.S. Antarctic Program.

I worked with Ed, Augie, Paul, and Hugo on the first paper on our traverse results during the summer of 1958.[2] Later, Ed and I shared an apartment for a few months in Madison.

I returned to Ellsworth in the 1958–59 season (summer only) on the icebreaker *Edisto.* Ronne came to Ellsworth the same season on the Argentine icebreaker *San Martin,* which got in and out before *Edisto,* so we did not cross paths. Ed Thiel went to McMurdo and Byrd Stations in 1958–59 doing airlifted geophysical work. Hugo Neuburg wintered over as station scientific leader at McMurdo in 1960–61 and made a few other trips to Antarctica. Nolan Aughenbaugh went back to Antarctica in 1958 to work with James Zumberge on the Ross Ice Shelf.

Of the Navy men, Walt Davis wintered at Byrd in 1959–60 and really ran that station, as I saw it, for the Navy under the hands-off direction of the Navy physician. I met John Beiszer on a Hercules LC-130 supporting our field party in 1961. Jim Hannah wintered again. No other of our IGY scientific people ever returned.

A month earlier I wrote in my journal that the five of us on the traverse had developed bonds that wouldn't easily be broken. But, unfortunately, death has a way of doing just that.

Paul Walker died of a brain tumor in December 1959 at the age of 25. He needed an emergency evacuation from a summer glaciology field camp in the Arctic. Ed Thiel was killed in November 1961 in a plane crash at Wilkes Station, Antarctica, doing geophysical survey work; he was 33. Jerry Fierle died of a heart attack in 1959. Nolan Aughenbaugh is a professor at the University of Mississippi and lives in University, Mississippi. Hugo Neuburg worked for some years for Virginia Polytechnic Institute, is retired, and lives in Blacksburg, Virginia.

Don Skidmore is retired and lives in Brewster, New York. Jack Brown continued his career at DuPont until retirement and lives in

Delaware. Kim Malville is a professor of astrophysics at the University of Colorado. Kim is also an archeoastronomer and makes frequent trips to India to study ancient temples. He lives in Boulder, a few blocks from my home, and I see him frequently. By 1995, Con Jaburg had retired as a Navy captain. In 1995 he was teaching English literature at a junior college in Florida. Clint Smith is retired in Arizona after a civilian career as a physician. Al Spear is retired in Florida. I lost track of the others.

Notes

1. Charles S. Mullin and H.J.M. Connery, "Psychological Study of an Antarctic IGY Station," *U.S. Armed Forces Medical Journal* (March 1959): 290–96.
2. H.A.C. Neuburg, E. Thiel, P. T. Walker, J. C. Behrendt, and N. B. Aughenbaugh, "The Filchner Ice Shelf," *Annals of the Association of American Geographers* (1959): 110–19.

Epilogue

Over the course of my scientific career since the International Geophysical Year 40 years ago, I have come to realize how much the research methods I learned back then established the pattern I have followed ever since. What we geophysicists and glaciologists set out to do in IGY had only the very general objective of determining the three-dimensional configuration of the Antarctic ice sheet and, ultimately, of discovering whether it was increasing or decreasing. As broad as our research seems by today's standards, we found many scientifically significant and interesting results through inductive reasoning. That is, we looked around Antarctica in a general way to see what we could find. This method resulted in the establishment of the U.S. Geological Survey in 1879. George Woollard used inductive reasoning in making a gravity map of the U.S. in the 1950s and 1960s and so did Maurice Ewing when he set out to study the ocean floor.

The inductive method has probably resulted in the greatest geological and geophysical discoveries, but it is no longer in fashion. Now the deductive method begins with a specific hypothesis or problem and then searches, not broadly, but narrowly, for evidence to support or reject the hypothesis. At the close of the twentieth century, the deductive method is necessary for writing scientific proposals to funding agencies for very expensive research programs with shrinking funds.

Sadly, the inductive approach to research planning appears to be viable no longer. Because of the large number of excellent scientists competing for limited resources in Antarctica and elsewhere, careful attention must be paid to the specific problem being investigated and its importance relative to other competing, and more or less equally significant, proposals. Perhaps there is no other way, but much of the excitement of heading into the unknown, which

we experienced in the IGY, is missing today. I am not just referring to the fact that Antarctica was still largely unexplored then,
but to the attitude of seeing and sampling and mapping *everything*.

Although we scientists who went to Antarctica in the IGY were
certainly "innocents," as I have suggested, I admit to being somewhat disingenuous when I also used that term to apply to the scientific planners of the oversnow traverse program. Yes, they had no
Antarctic experience, but these seasoned researchers who had recently come through the applied research programs of World War
II, working with the military and using the inductive approach,
had, *not* serendipitously, made great scientific advances. They took
us young Ph.D.s and grad students and threw us to the wolves;
they expected us to manage without supervision for a year and
produce results. We did.

Because we innocents who headed south in 1956 were born
during the Great Depression and were part of a generation few in
number, in contrast to the baby boomers who followed, we had a
tremendous advantage in starting our careers just as large increases
in research funding were made after World War II, particularly as
a result of Sputnik and the cold war. We rapidly advanced in our
careers in the 1960s, not because we were better than today's young
scientists but because there were fewer of us and more dollars to
spend. Nevertheless, what I miss now as an Antarctic scientist is
not primarily the money but the sense of excitement that can only
come when a scientist is among the first to investigate a vast unknown area without restriction or inhibition.

Glossary

akios: fiberglass sleds pulled by a man; banana sleds

balaclava: wool knit hat

bay ice: fast ice floating on the sea but not attached to land or ice shelf

bergy bits: small pieces of icebergs

beset: stuck in pack ice

brash: loose pieces of sea ice

Byrd cloth: windproof clothing material

casrep: casualty report

Clements huts: permanent base buildings

cornice: a curved edge of a vertical ice cliff, built out by wind blown snow

crevasse: a fissure in a moving glacier

CTF: Commander Task Force

CTG: Commander Task Group

fast ice: several-year-old sea ice attached to land or ice shelf

firn: compacted snow

growlers: small pieces of icebergs, smaller than bergy bits

HO4S: a large helicopter referred to as a "horse"

hummock: a ridge or hill of ice

ice front: vertical cliff forming seaward face of ice shelf

ice sheet: a floating or grounded mass of ice and snow of considerable thickness (over 4000 m in some places)

ice shelf: a floating ice sheet of considerable thickness (up to 1300 m)

LCVP: landing craft vehicle/personnel

lead: a linear path of open water in pack ice through which a ship can pass

Nitromon: ammonium nitrate explosive

pack ice: large area of floating sea ice

Petrogel: 60% nitroglycerine dynamite

polliwogs: those who had not crossed the equator on a ship

polynya: a lakelike, clear area in the ice pack

sastrugi: windblown linear ridges on the snow surface

sea ice: floating ice frozen from seawater

sea smoke: water vapor from the relatively warm open sea, condensing in the frigid air as fog

Seabee: Construction Battalion, CB

seismic waves: sound waves traveling through ice, water, or rock

shellbacks: those who had crossed the equator previously

shield: a very old crystalline part of a continent

sitrep: situation report

UC: single-engine Otter aircraft

whiteout: condition in which daylight is diffused by multiple reflections between overcast cloud cover and snow surface

Bibliography

Alberts, Fred G., comp. *Geographic Names of the Antarctic: Names Approved by the United States Board on Geographic Names*, 2d ed. (Washington, D.C.: Dept. of Interior), 1995.

Beebe, M. P., ed. *Operation Deep Freeze III*. Paoli, Pa.: Dorville Corp., 1958.

Behrendt, J. C. "Geophysical Studies in the Filchner Ice Shelf Area of Antarctica" (Ph.D. diss., University of Wisconsin, Madison, 1961).

Behrendt, J. C. "Geophysical and Glaciological Studies in the Filchner Ice Shelf Area of Antarctica." *Journal of Geophysical Research* 67, no. 1 (1962): 221–34.

Behrendt, J. C. "Structure of Filchner Ice Shelf and Its Relation to Bottom Melting." ISAGE Symposium, International Association of Science Hydrology, publication no. 86 (1970): 488–96.

Bull, C., and P. F. Wright, eds. *Silas: The Antarctic Diaries and Memoir of Charles S. Wright*. Columbus: Ohio State University Press, 1993.

Darlington, J. *My Antarctic Honeymoon*. Garden City, N.J.: Doubleday, 1956.

Dufek, G. J. *Operation Deep Freeze*. New York: Harcourt Brace, 1957.

Filchner, W. Zum Ersten Erdtum. *Die Zweite Deutsche Sudpolar Expedition im Verlag Ullstein*. Berlin, 1922.

Fuchs, V., and E. Hillary. *The Crossing of Antarctica*. Boston: Little, Brown, 1958.

Giaever, J. *The White Desert*. New York: E. P. Dutton, 1955.

Gould, L. J. *Cold*. Northfield, Minn: Carleton College, 1931, 1984.

Lewis, R. S. *A Continent for Science*. New York: Viking, 1965.

MacDonald, E. A. *Polar Operations*. Annapolis, Md.: United States Naval Institute, 1969.

Morgan, J.J.B. *Psychology of Abnormal People*. New York: Longmans, Green, 1953.

Morrison, S. E. *The European Discovery of North America: The Southern Voyages*. New York: Oxford University Press, 1974.

Mullin, Charles S., and H.J.M. Connery. "Psychological Study of an Antarctic IGY Station." *U.S. Armed Forces Medical Journal* 10 (March 1959): 290–96.

Neuburg, H.A.C., E. Thiel, P. T. Walker, J. C. Behrendt, and N. B. Aughenbaugh. "The Filchner Ice Shelf." *Annals of the Association of American Geographers* 49, no. 2 (1959): 110–19.

Oglesby, J. E., ed. *Operation Deep Freeze II.* Paoli, Pa.: Dorville Corp., 1957.

Pirrit, J. *Across West Antarctica.* Glasgow, Scotland: John Smith and Son, 1967.

Robertson, R. B. *Of Whales and Men.* New York: Knopf, 1954.

Ronne, F. *Antarctic Conquest: The Story of the Ronne Expedition, 1946–48.* New York: G. P. Putnam's Sons, 1949.

Ronne, F. *Antarctic Command.* New York: Bobbs-Merrill, Inc., 1961.

Ronne, F. *Antarctica, My Destiny.* New York: Hastings House, 1979.

Shackleton, E. *South.* New York: Macmillan, 1920.

Shapley, D. *The Seventh Continent, Antarctica in a Resource Age.* Washington, D.C.: Resources for the Future, 1985.

Siple, P. *90° South.* New York: G. P. Putnam's Sons, 1959.

Sullivan, W. *Quest for a Continent.* London: Secker and Warburg, 1957.

Sullivan, W. *Assault on the Unknown.* New York: McGraw-Hill, 1961.

U.S. Navy Department. *Sailing Directions for Antarctica.* Hydrographic Office, H.O. No. 138, 1943.

Walton, Kevin. *Two Years in Antarctica.* London: Lutterworth, 1955.

Wouk, Herman. *The Caine Mutiny.* New York: Doubleday, 1951.

Index

Italicized page numbers refer to pictures; n. after a number refers to a note.

A